Humans Are Not From Earth

Humans Are Not From Earth

a scientific evaluation of the evidence

Second Edition

Ellis Silver, PhD

ideas4writers

Published in Great Britain in 2017

by

ideas4writers
2a New Street
Cullompton
Devon
EX15 1HA

www.ideas4writers.co.uk

ISBN 978-0955011696

Cover design and internal layout by Dave Haslett

Contents

1

Introduction

You've no doubt heard of the book *Men are from Mars, Women are from Venus* by John Gray. But have you ever considered the wider implication of that title: that neither men nor women are from Earth?

The evidence against us having evolved on Earth is overwhelming. I'll prove this throughout the book, using examples that are in the public domain.

We'll discuss other issues too. For example, where did we really come from? Who brought us here? And why did they choose the Earth as our new home?

We certainly didn't come from anywhere in this solar system, so in Chapter 10 we'll look at the most likely stars our real home planet might orbit. We'll also consider the physical and environmental conditions that might exist there. The aim is that we'll be able to recognize our true home planet if we ever find it.

In the first edition, I asked for your comments on the things I'd missed, got wrong or failed to make clear. I also appreciated that there were a few areas where the evidence lacked credibility. You left thousands of comments on the many websites that reviewed or discussed the book. You also sent in dozens of emails. My publisher thinks he found most of the comments (thanks to Google Alerts), and he passed them all on to me. If you were one of those who responded, thank you. Your contributions played a huge part in shaping this new edition.

You'll find lots of new and credible evidence this time around. I've also tried to dispel some of the most common fallacies that people kept mentioning. For example, countless people said black people can't get skin cancer. The worrying thing is that not only can they suffer from it, but many of them die from it.

This fallacy is widespread, and means that most black people don't take any precautions when they're out in the sun. They also don't bother checking themselves for the signs of skin cancer. The lesions are harder to spot on dark skin, so they often don't realize they have it until it's too late to treat.

Dark skin naturally affords more protection than white skin, but not enough to give full protection. Dark-skinned people still need to take precautions. So let's try to clear up this common misconception. It could save someone's life.

Several people said there was other evidence available that I didn't mention in the first book – but they didn't say what that evidence was. I've dug deeper into each topic this time around, but if you think I've missed anything important, please let me know what it is. It would help if you could provide a link to a relevant website, the title of a book, the name of a person I should contact, a photo and description of an artifact, and so on. You'll find my email address in the "About the Author" section at the end of the book.

Several respondents said I'd neglected to mention the work of other people working in this field. But the names they mentioned were people I'd either never heard of or whose work I don't consider credible. Here's a list of those whose work has at least some credibility in my opinion, and whose names came up most often during my research. I believe they're well worth checking out:

- Art Bell
- Lee Carroll
- Matthew Delooze
- Michel Desmarquet
- Graham Hancock
- Fred Hoyle
- Phil Kernow
- Marshall Klarfield
- Thomas Charles Lethbridge
- Susan B. Martinez
- Elaine Morgan
- Lobsang Rampa
- Zechariah Sitchin (some but not all)
- Erich von Däniken (some but not all)
- Chandra Wickramasinghe

There are claims that some of their work isn't credible, but that's something of an occupational hazard in this field. You need to bear in mind that those who try to discredit them may have different agendas. Use your judgment and look for similar evidence from sources that you know are reliable – there's plenty of it. In most cases, you'll find that the work that was criticized was in fact correct.

Many people recommended Lloyd Pye's presentation *Everything You Know Is Wrong*, which is available on YouTube and well worth watching. There's also a book of the same name. It illustrates many of the topics from this book, though I found some parts rather far-fetched, particularly those relating to planetary formation.

The documentary *Ancient Aliens Debunked* was also recommended. Again, it's available on YouTube. I didn't mention any of the topics it covers in the first book, so I'm not sure why so many people recommended it. I haven't mentioned them in this edition either. Even so, it was entertaining to watch.

Some people claimed I'd stolen some of the theories I mentioned in the first edition. They then listed people I'd never heard of, books I'd never read, and movies and TV shows I'd never seen. Again, this sort of thing goes with the territory when you're writing about a subject like this.

This book is my own work – as was the first one. I researched it from scratch and based it on my own ideas, observations, and – most importantly – the evidence. Other people have studied some of the same topics, of course, and I've provided links to websites and publications that feature their work. You'll find an extensive reference section at the end of the book. The links there are well worth following up if you're interested in any of the topics. They provide far more detail – and some interesting alternative theories – that I didn't have room to cover in this book.

Of course, once I had all the evidence, the fun part was seeing how everything linked together. I'm fascinated by how well it all fits – and how weak some of the mainstream theories are in comparison.

There were a few topics where the credibility of the evidence seemed a little shaky. I've either excluded those or found corroborating evidence from reputable sources. I only included something if at least one credible source gave reliable evidence. I've also added some links to a few less reputable sources, but only where they corroborate a reliable source and provide additional information.

Many of the sources I've linked to include images, so I decided not to include them in the book as well. I would only have been able to include a limited number of them anyway, they'd have taken up valuable space, and getting permission to use them would have meant delaying publication.

Several people wanted to know how much it cost to research and write a book like this. Don't worry; I didn't spend any of your tax dollars. Both this book and the first edition were self-funded, and I carried out the work during my down time.

I'd like to thank the 859 people who took part in an online poll which asked: "Are humans alien to this planet?" 59 percent of respondents agreed that we are, while a further three percent considered it was possible.

This edition is far more wide-ranging than the first one, and that's all thanks to you. You asked questions about all sorts of things, and when the same subjects kept cropping up, I took the time to research the answers. The book goes off-topic a few times because of that, but I think most of you will find it interesting.

With your help, I've expanded Chapter 2 which looks at the factors which suggest we're not from Earth. There are a lot more factors this time around. Chapter 10, which looks at our real home planet, is much more in-depth this time too. And there are brand new sections on:

- the different types of extraterrestrial
- how space travel works
- government and scientific cover-ups
- DNA
- evolution
- God and religion
- alien technology
- and a whole lot more

There's also a comprehensive revised timeline of human evolution that you won't find anywhere else.

You're about to see some extraordinary evidence that proves we couldn't possibly have evolved on Earth. Someone else brought us here, not just once but perhaps a dozen times or more over the course of millions of years.

We'll see evidence that human civilizations existed on Earth long before mainstream science says they could have done. Archaeologists already know this with absolute certainty, but they deny it and either hide or ignore the evidence. I'll explain why that is in Chapter 4.

Throughout history, many renowned scientists and philosophers thankfully ignored the mainstream constraints. They were labeled "crackpots," of course, but they were proven right in the end – even if it took centuries for their work to gain acceptance. These are the people whose work has done the most to drive science forward.

So come, fellow crackpots, let's explore the truths the mainstream scientists and governments of the world would prefer you didn't know.

2

Why Humans Could Not Have Evolved on Earth

In the first edition of this book, I outlined seventeen factors which suggested we couldn't have evolved on this planet. With your help, I thought we might be able to add a handful more. But in fact, we've now identified more than fifty, creating an *extraordinary* body of evidence.

Let's start with the sun. We depend on it to keep us alive, yet it seems to be doing its level best to injure and even kill us. That's something of a conundrum.

Scientists tell us the following things are true:

- The Sun formed at about the same time as the Earth.
- Life on Earth can't exist without the Sun.
- Life has existed on Earth for at least 4.2 billion years. [2-01]
- Humans evolved from that life.

That all seems fair enough, doesn't it? But if that last one were true, and we descended from a life form that began over four billion years ago, surely we'd be well used to the Sun by now. The fact that it causes us so much harm means we have to ask some fundamental questions. Such as: do we even come from Earth at all?

As you read this book and learn about the wealth of everyday evidence that's all around us, I'm sure you'll reach the same conclusion as me: Humans are, most definitely, *not* from Earth.

2.1 The Sun dazzles us

This is the thing that originally made me think we couldn't have evolved on this planet. I was walking along the street, turned a corner, and was hit full in the face by the Sun's powerful glare. Total whiteout. I couldn't see a thing. I had to shield my eyes with my hands and hurry to the next corner while blindly stumbling along and hoping I wouldn't hit anything. When I reached shade, and my vision returned, I looked up at the sky and saw birds flying around perfectly happily in all directions. They weren't shielding their eyes with their wings. They weren't in pain, as I had been. They weren't blindly crashing into buildings and trees. They weren't diving for shelter.

After the billions of years that life has existed on Earth, and with humans now supposedly sitting at the top of the evolutionary ladder, how can it be possible that the Sun still hurts our eyes and causes us to injure ourselves? We might expect this in species much further down the evolutionary ladder. But in fact, they're all well-adapted to it too, just as the birds are. They've been well adapted to it for millions of years. Even our reputed ancestors, the ancient hominins, had prominent brow ridges that shielded their eyes. The fact that we don't have them now makes no sense – if we came from Earth.

The only plausible explanation is that we only arrived here comparatively recently, and we haven't had time to adapt to this type of sun yet. That also means we couldn't have evolved from Earth's ancient hominins. And, sure enough, there's plenty of evidence to support that idea too.

So how do birds avoid being dazzled? It's simple enough: they have a translucent third eyelid, known as a nictitating membrane,[2-02] that moves horizontally across their eyes. Nictitating membranes would prevent us from being dazzled too, so why don't we have them? Well, it turns out that we *did* have them in the distant past. You can still see a non-functioning remnant in the corner of your eye – the plica semilunaris (or semilunar fold).

Most animals have nictitating membranes: fish; amphibians; reptiles; and lots of mammals, from aardvarks to camels, polar bears and seals. But when we reach the more advanced primates, such as ourselves, they all but disappear.

Nictitating membranes don't just protect eyes from the sun; they serve a variety of other purposes too. They protect against water, sand and other debris, and, in some cases, sharp beaks, teeth, and claws. They prevent woodpeckers from damaging their retinas when they hammer their beaks against tree trunks. In polar bears, they protect against snow blindness.

The fact that we don't have nictitating membranes, at least to any functioning degree, is extraordinary. If we had them, they'd prevent a great deal of discomfort, a significant number of injuries, and quite a few deaths.

OBJECTION!
"I doubt that not flinching at the sun
is essential for a species' survival."

True, but in that case why do so many other species have nictitating membranes, and why are they a vestigial feature in us? They may not be essential, but built-in sunglasses that flip across your eyes as and when you need them would be a highly desirable feature. We had them once, but evolution decided we didn't have a strong enough case for keeping them. That may have made perfect sense back on our home planet – and we'll see why in Chapter 10 – but it makes no sense at all here on Earth.

OBJECTION!
"The other advanced primates don't have nictitating membranes either."

True again, but that's a behavioral thing. They don't go out in the sun; they stay in the shade. They're not explorers and wanderers like we are. It makes sense that they lost theirs; they have no real need for them. But we do.

OBJECTION!
"But we had them once."

Indeed we did. But that would have been when we were back on our home planet. How we came to lose them is a bit of mystery. I suspect it's to do with some of the native hominins' DNA being spliced into our genomes. That was probably done with the best intentions: to make us more resilient and better able to withstand living on a planet that doesn't completely suit us. Unfortunately, the aliens that spliced the hominin genes into us failed to take into account our different type of behavior. We're wanderers and go out in the sun, so we need our nictitating membranes. The hominins and primates that had lost theirs always kept to the trees and shade.

The question of how many people are injured or die from being dazzled by the sun is a hard one to answer. I couldn't find any statistics, but an online search led me to plenty of cases of injury or death by car crash where the driver was dazzled by the sun. I won't mention any individual cases, but they're easy enough to find. There was also a dazzled driver who made a wrong turn into a National Security Agency facility, where he was promptly arrested and his car impounded.[2-03] And there was a particularly grisly case where a pilot blindly stumbled into his own propeller.[2-04]

The internet has plenty of guidance on how to drive safely[2-05] in sunny conditions and advice for skiers on how the right choice of goggles can prevent snow blindness.[2-06] So it's a well-known problem.

Engineers are working on a solution where car steering wheels vibrate when drivers stray out of their lane.[2-07] The development of self-driving cars should also alleviate this problem.

If the reports of alien autopsies of the Greys are to be believed, they have a dark, non-blinking membrane over their corneas, which the surgeons were able to peel off.

You might be interested in the results of a test I commissioned to see how different animals react to the sort of light that dazzles us. The following experiments were carried out by a qualified veterinarian while I watched and took notes.

First, cats: the vet exposed several domestic cats to sudden light from both natural and artificial sources. Their pupils reacted as expected, but they didn't flinch or appear the least bit concerned. The vet said this was exactly what she expected. Healthy animals rarely squint; if they do, it can be a sign of disease. Cats have a nictitating membrane, but none of the ones we tested used it.

Dogs: the vet repeated the same experiment with several dogs, with mixed results. German shepherds, retrievers, and labradors didn't react at all – apart from their pupils. But boxers, bull terriers, and pugs showed noticeable discomfort. The vet suggested this was most likely a man-made issue: those that didn't react were purer breeds, closer to the wolves they descended from, whereas those that demonstrated discomfort had been deliberately inbred for many generations. Ironically, the breeds that were deliberately inbred are now called purebred. They also suffer from other diseases and medical conditions that the more wolf-like breeds don't.[2-08] Dogs have nictitating membranes but rarely use them. If you see them, it could be a sign of an eye infection or disease.

Apes: we didn't have access to any apes, but we contacted someone who did. She told us that healthy animals rarely had any problems with the sun. She only saw that sort of issue in those that were sick. Their brows shield their eyes quite effectively, they generally live in shaded areas, and they don't put themselves in dangerous positions where the sun could harm them. If the sun shone in their faces, they'd turn away from it. She added that she would never shine a light into an ape's eye without warning, and especially not into a gorilla's, as it would annoy it and it could turn violent.

Humans: we already know that we react badly when a bright light is shone into our eyes without warning.

Birds: for this experiment, we decided to do a direct comparison between a bird and a human. We captured a seagull in a soft net, transferred it to a cage, and kept it in the dark for an hour, along with a human volunteer. The cage was then covered with a black cloth, the human volunteer was blindfolded, and they were taken outside into the bright sunshine. The cover and top of the cage were removed at the same moment as the human's blindfold, exposing both test subjects to the full glare of the sun. The human volunteer was asked to locate an orange cone placed thirty feet away, point to it, and then walk to it. In repeated runs of the test, the human subjects took an average of between 11 seconds (when the sun was directly overhead) and 22 seconds (when the cone was placed in direct line with the sun when it was lower in the sky) to complete the task, and they exhibited noticeable pain. The seagulls always flew away immediately – too quickly for us to determine whether or not they'd used their nictitating membranes. (We didn't have access to a high-speed camera, which would have shown this.) Despite the unnatural conditions of the test, the birds were clearly able to cope much better.

Deer and rabbits: in the first edition of this book, I considered the case of deer and rabbits caught in car headlights. I was uncertain whether they'd failed to react (because the light didn't bother them) or if they were frozen in shock. Experts were divided in their opinions and couldn't reach any definite conclusions. In any case, this type of light is man-made and wouldn't occur in nature, so testing it wouldn't tell us anything useful. When we examined video recordings of deer and rabbits caught in headlights, we noticed that they never blinked, and generally continued on their way after a few seconds, apparently without concern.

After conducting these tests, we can safely conclude that the other animals on Earth have built-in physical and behavioral mechanisms which prevent them from being dazzled by the sun. We don't have these things and are clearly designed for an environment with indirect or weak sunlight. Because we're now in the wrong environment, we suffer frequent discomfort, sometimes get injured, and occasionally killed.

Just as I was writing this section, a car crashed into a wall further up the street. Police, ambulance and fire crew arrived quickly, and the elderly occupants were airlifted to hospital by helicopter. Their car was wrecked. The driver said he had been dazzled by the sun.

2.2 The Sun damages our eyes

Cataracts[2-09] are a condition in which the eye's lens turns cloudy, impairing vision and eventually leading to blindness if not treated. They're generally caused by ultraviolet light, and most commonly affect older people. They affect every human population in the world. As living conditions, medical support and the availability of decent food and clean drinking water in developing countries improves, people there are living longer, and cataracts are becoming an ever-growing problem.

Cataracts are rife in the tropics, where we supposedly originated, so it's strange that the people living there now have no resistance to them. But they're also rife in more temperate regions, which suggests we have no resistance to them whatsoever.

They're the leading cause of blindness in developing countries,[2-10] mainly because of a shortage of surgeons. 400,000 Africans become blind each year because of cataracts, and two million are blind in total because of them.

A further four million Africans are blind for other reasons, including glaucoma, macular degeneration and loss of retinal sensitivity caused by diabetes.

Worldwide, nearly 50 percent of cases of blindness are caused by cataracts. Glaucoma is the leading cause outside Africa, but it's worth noting that Africans are also more susceptible to glaucoma than Caucasians.

Until about 7,700 years ago, all humans had brown eyes.[2-11] You'd expect brown eyes to offer more protection against cataracts than blue eyes, especially since brown eyes are predominant in warmer climates. But that isn't the case at all. In fact, dark brown eyes are two and a half times *more* susceptible to cataracts than blue eyes.[2-12] No one knows why this is. One suggestion is that they might absorb more ultraviolet light and cause the lens to heat up.

Since blue eyes offer more protection against cataracts, it's surprising that they didn't evolve much sooner. And it's bizarre that they're rarely found in climates where the sunlight is strongest. I wondered whether this might be because people with blue eyes are more sensitive to sunlight overall. But that turned out not to be the case. Blue eyes are more susceptible to *blinding* light,[2-13] though I was unable to find any data concerning the degree to which this occurred.

Blue eyes evolved in a temperate climate – most probably Scandinavia. Everyone with blue eyes has a single, common ancestor who lived about 7,700 years ago and had a genetic mutation – a single switch that turns off or limits the eye's ability to produce melanin. Researchers have found that if this gene is completely destroyed, it leads to albinism.

Around the same time that blue eyes first appeared, so did white skin, and again this occurred in cooler climates. Researchers theorize that this was most likely the body's attempt to get more vitamin D.

Lack of vitamin D can cause rickets. But rickets was unknown until around 5,000 years ago – which is 2,700 years after white skin had evolved. So there's obviously something else going on that has yet to be explained.

> The first known sufferer of rickets was almost certainly sickly and probably lived their entire life indoors.

Cataracts occasionally occur in other animals, though dogs are particularly susceptible. This is because they spend longer in domestic conditions than they would naturally, and also because the diet we feed them is far richer than their natural diet would be. This can lead to obesity and diabetes, which in turn causes cataracts, as we've already seen in humans. Purebred (or inbred) breeds are more susceptible to these problems than purer (more wolf-like) breeds. Or in other words, it's all our fault.

Most animals, including cattle, sheep, pigs, horses, and kangaroos, rarely get cataracts, despite being out in the sun all day. If they do get them, it tends to be a congenital condition (a weakness they were born with) rather than something that develops later in life.

Researchers are working on eye drops that can cure cataracts.[2-14] The drops dissolve the cataract but leave the lens intact, so it doesn't need to be surgically replaced. That's a development that's well worth keeping an eye on!

Intriguingly, our eyes can actually see ultraviolet[2-15] – or at least our retinas can. Our lenses block UV light, but if they're removed or replaced with synthetic ones that allow UV to pass through, we can see it.

OBJECTION!
"Our eyes are overly sensitive to sunlight because we're always cooped up indoors in front of the television."

Not true. People who spend most of their lives outdoors have an almost identical incidence of cataracts. Those living in the tropics, who rarely spend time indoors and don't even have televisions, also have a similar incidence to those in temperate countries in the developed world.

Ultraviolet light is a significant component of natural light on Earth, so once again our inability to cope with it, even after millions of years of evolution, is surprising. It's further evidence that we must have come from somewhere where the light is weaker or more indirect. For example, our home planet might have permanent cloud cover, a thicker ozone layer which blocks more UV light, or it might even orbit a red dwarf star – although, as we'll see in Chapter 10, that's less likely.

2.3 The Sun damages our skin

UV light is harmful in several other ways. As well as causing cataracts, it's also believed to be one of the leading causes of skin cancer, and it dries and shrivels up our skin, making us look old before our time.

All of the other creatures on Earth (apart from those we've modified through selective breeding) have thick body hair, thick skin or scales, or they live underground, or under water, or they only come out at night. That limits their exposure to UV, meaning that they avoid most of these problems.

Humans are the only exception. If we go outside, we have to wear clothes, not only to keep us warm but to avoid exposing ourselves to too much damaging UV light. On occasions when we don't wear many clothes, we have to slather ourselves in Factor 50 sunscreen to avoid getting sunburn or skin cancer. Most of us only bother doing when we're deliberately sunbathing – and even then, many men don't bother. In fact, researchers say we should be using sunscreen almost every day, whenever we're planning to be outside for more than a few minutes. But why do we need to do this? Surely we can't have evolved to depend on such an artificial product?

If thick body hair or thick skin or scales are essential to staying safe and avoiding premature aging – and it seems that they are – then why don't we have any? Something is clearly not right here.

Unfortunately, researchers have found that more than a quarter of a middle-aged person's skin may have already made the first steps towards cancer.[2-16] Samples taken from people aged between 55 and 73 had more than 100 DNA mutations linked to cancer in every 1 square centimeter (0.15 square inches) of their skin.

So why do we have to wear wide-brimmed hats and long-sleeved tops and sunscreen and sunglasses, or stay out of the sun altogether, if this is our natural environment? The simple answer is that the Earth can't be our natural environment.

A few animals have been known to suffer from sunburn or skin cancer, particularly on the tips of their ears where they aren't protected by fur. Some selectively bred animals, such as domesticated pigs, have much thinner hair than their wild counterparts, and they've been known to suffer too. But this is a man-made issue, not a natural one.

Even animals with thick skins, such as elephants, rhinos, and pigs, often coat themselves in mud to keep cool and further protect themselves against the sun.

OBJECTION!
"Most of us are perfectly adapted to our climate and would never get burned if we were out all day. The problem is that people are stuck indoors for months and then suddenly expose their skin on the first sunny day in May."

This is a popular misconception. We'd get burned if we were out all year round, even in temperate climates. We would – and indeed do – suffer massive amounts of UV damage, premature aging, wrinkles, and eventually skin cancer. Most UV damage only shows up under a UV light[2-17] – we can't see it under natural light until it's too late. Try shining a UV light on a regular sunbather who claims they've never suffered any ill effects from it. I guarantee you'll be horrified – and so will they if you show them. Advertisers often use this technique when promoting sunscreen products – the results can be genuinely shocking.

It's absolutely not the case that we only get skin cancer because we're stuck indoors all the time. The National Health Service (NHS) in England said those who spend much of their time outside, including farmers, builders, gardeners, sportsmen, and fishermen, were the most likely to be affected. It's launched a campaign urging them to cover themselves up.

OBJECTION!
"Only light-skinned people suffer from
sunburn and skin cancer."

Not true! This is a dangerous misconception that needs to be corrected urgently. Dark-skinned people die from skin cancer all the time. Because their skin is dark, cancerous lesions are harder to spot, so they often leave it too late before seeking treatment. Their mortality rates are significantly higher than those with light skin.

Dark skin does not prevent skin cancer.[2-18][2-19]

If you go out in the sun in a temperate climate, and the UV index is 3 or higher,[2-20] health experts say you need to use a sunscreen with an SPF of at least 15. If you're going out for a prolonged period, you should use at least SPF 30.[2-21] Even the very darkest black human skin only has a natural SPF of 13.4. So don't think you can get away without it if you have dark skin. It's true that you're twice as safe as someone with white skin (pale skin has a natural SPF of about 3.4), but twice as safe doesn't mean safe. You *can* still get skin cancer.

Very dark black human skin is comparatively rare. Dark-skinned people living in temperate regions usually have a lighter skin shade, which offers them far less protection than the SPF 13.4 of the darkest shade. For example, there are millions of Asians, African Americans and Latin Americans in the USA and the UK, and thousands of them are suffering (and sadly dying) from skin cancer right now. Thousands more have significant signs of skin damage and premature aging.

Skin cancer is most common on the parts of the body that aren't often exposed to the sun, such as the soles of the feet.[2-22]

Sunscreen with an SPF of 15 screens out 93 percent of UVB rays. SPF 30 screens out 97 percent – just 4 percent more. (Dr. Elizabeth Hale, the Skin Cancer Foundation)

Researchers from Yale have found that the sun continues to damage skin cells for up to three hours after you've been exposed to it.[2-23][2-24] So going indoors when you feel like you've had enough sun doesn't mean you're safe.

OBJECTION!
"Cancer is a modern disease caused by our unnatural lifestyles and environment."

The earliest known case of malignant cancer in hominins dates from 1.7 million years ago.[2-25] A benign growth was also found in a 2-million-year-old Australopithecus fossil. However, these were both bone tumors. We may have become susceptible to this disease when hominin DNA was spliced into our genome, or if we interbred with the native hominins.

Skin cancer (melanoma) appears to be more recent: the first documented cases arose around 2,400 years ago.[2-26] It was thought to be caused primarily by exposure to UV light, which results in malignancy of melanocytes. But there's also some evidence that a lack of vitamin D increases the risk.

Incidence of cancer cases in Africa

Let's take a look at the prevalence of cancer in Africa, as that's where we supposedly originated and where we would expect to find the most resilience. Interestingly, most African languages have no word for cancer. The common perception among Africans, both in developed countries and in developing ones, is that cancer is a disease of the wealthy. They blame it on high-fat, processed-food diets, alcohol, smoking, and sedentary lifestyles.

They might be right. Or it could be age-related. Before the current generation, Africans had shorter lifespans than most of the rest of the world. Now that they're living just as long as everyone else, their incidence of cancer is growing too.

Breast cancer and cervical cancer have suddenly become two of the leading causes of death in Africa.[2-27] There were an estimated one million new cancer cases in Sub-Saharan Africa in 2015, and that number is expected to double to two million per year within the next decade. So they just can't win: on the one hand, better access to food and health care and better living conditions has extended their lifespans, but on the other hand, they've now had to come up with a word for cancer. Education is important too, of course, because they had never been taught how to reduce their risk of getting these diseases.

Interestingly, since skin cancer is generally (though not always) age-related, it doesn't affect most people until after they've had their children.[2-28] Your susceptibility to skin cancer won't affect your ability to reproduce, because the cancer probably won't develop until you're past your reproductive years. This suggests that there's no connection between skin cancer and the development of our diverse range of skin tones.

Skin cancer (malignant melanoma) incidence by region and ethnicity

Cancer of all types generally has a lower than average incidence in Africa, India, and the Middle East. Worldwide, 1.6 percent of cancers are skin cancer.[2-29]

Skin cancer cases per 100,000 people:

White males: 13.1 – 13.6
White females: 14.7 – 15.2

Black males: 0.6 – 2.6   Asian males: 0.2 – 0.8
Black females: 1.0 – 3.6   Asian females: 0.2 – 1.1

Research shows that the different races also have different susceptibilities to other ailments too. For example, African-Americans have a higher incidence of diabetes, prostate cancer, and hypertension. Caucasians have a higher incidence of dementia and osteoporosis.

Skin thickness and lack of hair

Another aspect we should consider is skin thickness. If we look at other mammals, those that aren't protected from UV by thick body hair typically have thicker skins. And it's the same with us: darker skin is slightly thicker than light skin.

Scientists have also found structural differences between black, white and Asian skin, in terms of thickness, water content, and lipids (fat and fat-soluble vitamins).[2-30] Dark skin is thicker, and the dermis is more compact. This provides further protection against skin cancer and also explains why people with darker skin typically get fewer wrinkles than those with lighter skin.

Even so, if you compare the thickness of darker skin with that of a bare-skinned mammal such as an elephant or rhino, human skin is much thinner. And that means we're all susceptible to excess exposure to UV radiation, and all the problems which stem from it.

Interestingly, elephants are pretty much immune to cancer. Geneticists have found that they have twenty copies of the cancer-suppressing gene p53 (TP53), whereas humans and other mammals only have one.[2-31] This gene churns out copies of the p53 protein if it detects that a cell has suffered DNA damage. Or it kills the cell if the damage is too bad. So cancer never has a chance to develop.

Lizards need to bask in the sun for hours at a time to warm their bodies. In doing so, they also receive UV radiation and create vitamin D. They can do this without suffering any ill effects because their skin is perfectly suited to the task. So why isn't ours?

What about other animals?

Many animals get skin cancer,[2-32] but the highest incidence is in those that have been altered by man. These creatures are no longer the original species that evolved on Earth, and they're no longer adapted to their environments. It's no wonder they get sick.

Dogs are an obvious example, as we saw earlier. Many of them get cancer. Those with the highest incidence of it are the ones that have been repeatedly inbred to look the least like the wolves they descended from. And vice versa.

Pigs also get skin cancer. But again, you need to compare the domesticated, selectively bred pig with the wild boar it descended from. Boars have thick, coarse hair to protect them. Pigs' hair is much thinner, far less coarse, and usually light in color. It offers them little protection from UV radiation. Pig skin is similar to human skin,[2-33] so it requires protection. It's no surprise that they get skin cancer. They really ought to be wearing sunscreen.

But we haven't only altered the animals, we've also taken them out of their natural environments. We often force cattle, horses, sheep, and deer to live in open pastures where there's no shelter from the sun. In their natural environments, they'd seek shade, but our fences prevent them from doing that. Most countries legally require that pigs are given a place to shelter, but pig shelters can get stiflingly hot and they only tend to use them at night. They don't use them as shelters from the sun because the heat would probably suffocate and kill them.

Pollution is another issue, particularly in the oceans. It's not just the endless list of pollutants we dump there but what happens when those pollutants react with UV. They can become extremely toxic and hazardous to life, and have untold effects on marine life.

Whales have been found with blisters and lesions from sunburn – though no skin cancer so far.[2-34][2-35] Sunburn affects light-skinned whales more than dark-skinned ones. Would this have happened if the sea wasn't polluted? We don't know, and unfortunately it's too late to find out. As with human skin cancer, the marked increase in UV radiation over the past 200 years, caused by the damage to Earth's ozone layer, is thought to be the primary cause. But viruses and fungi – and toxins from pollution – may also play a role.

Dolphins can suffer from sunburn when kept in artificially shallow conditions such as sea cages or oceanariums. When kept in enclosures, they're also exposed to harmful chemicals such as cleaning products, which they're unable to escape from.[2-36a]

White rabbits get skin cancer, especially on their ears.

Horses can get it on their muzzles if they are light colored.

Dr. Paul Calle, chief veterinarian at the Wildlife Conservation Society in the Bronx, New York City, said[2-37] "Wild animals are marvelously adapted to their environment, so those in areas with lots of sunlight usually have scales, feathers or fur to protect them. They also retreat to burrows, shady areas or water; wallow in water or mud; or spray dust or water on themselves when the sun is at its peak. Wild animals that are sick, injured or in distress, like stranded whales or dolphins, can develop serious sunburn because they cannot protect themselves from excessive exposure to the sun."

Does more UV reach us now than in the past?

We know that the ozone layer which shields us from UV radiation has declined over the past 200 years. This has resulted in about 30 percent more UV reaching polar and temperate regions. These areas have seen a corresponding increase in skin cancer, while the tropics have been less affected.[2-38] I was unable to find any data going back further than this. Fortunately, the ozone layer is now recovering well.

2.4 We don't seek shade from the Sun

Even with their built-in protection, most animals also seek shade from the sun if they're able to. But they can stay out in it for hours if they have to. Even lizards know when they've had enough and move into the shade.

Now picture a hot, sunny beach packed with sunbathers. Most of them stay there far longer than is safe – and they absolutely know that they're doing it. Many of them, especially the men, won't have bothered using sunscreen unless their partners have made them do it. And remember what we learned earlier: the sun will continue to do its damage for hours after they move into the shade.

People used to regard peeling skin as entirely normal after a day in the sun. My parents certainly did. We went to the beach a lot when I was a child, and we never used sunscreen. The top layer of skin on my back, shoulders, and arms peeled off dozens of times. We just used to laugh about it. We didn't associate it with what it really was: radiation poisoning.

There are two problems here. The first is that we crave the sun. The second is that there's an abundance of sunlight here on Earth. Why do we crave it? And why aren't we protected against it? Once again, if we consider that the Earth isn't our natural home, the answer is clear. It makes perfect sense if the surface our original home planet received little direct sunlight. We aren't used to it, and now that we have it we can't get enough. But even though we crave it, and some of us spend more time exposed to it than is good for us, most people living in temperate regions *still* aren't getting enough vitamin D.

2.5 Our vitamin D levels are too low

While too much exposure to the sun can be a bad thing, not getting enough of it might be even worse. Skin cancer is more common in indoor workers than in outdoor workers, and, as we saw a moment ago, it occurs more commonly on areas of the body that are rarely exposed to the sun. A recent theory suggests that it might not be caused by too much exposure to the sun after all, but by a vitamin D deficiency due to *lack* of exposure.

Vitamin D is essential for bone growth, as it regulates the calcium and phosphorus content.[2-39] It also plays other vital roles, such as in cell communication.

It seems obvious that as you move out of the tropics and the sun becomes less intense, you need lighter skin to make sure you get enough vitamin D. Those with darker skin are advised to take vitamin D supplements if they live in temperate regions.

Doctors have been telling us for decades that we should avoid the midday sun. But the latest theory suggests that this might actually be terrible advice because it's the time of day when vitamin D production is at its peak. Some researchers now suggest it might be better to go outside when the sun is at its height and stay there until your skin just starts to turn pink. For light-skinned people, that takes about twenty minutes, or up to two hours for the darkest skin. Once your skin begins to turn pink, you should go inside or under shade as you've got all the vitamin D you need. Your body won't produce any more no matter how much longer you stay in the sun, and staying outside any longer will damage your skin.

You don't need to do this every day, but at least two or three days a week is a good idea. Don't use any sunscreen as it will block vitamin D production. If you're taking vitamin D supplements, you don't need to stay outside for so long.

In temperate regions, including the UK and northern Europe, northern Asia, most of the USA, and Canada, as well as southern Australasia, southern Africa, and southern South America, our bodies produce little or no vitamin D for six months of the year. The deficiency levels in these regions are shocking[2-40][2-41][2-42] – and extremely harmful. It could explain why skin cancer rates there are rising even though exposure to the sun is decreasing and sunscreens are improving.

It's important to note that this theory hasn't yet been generally accepted. Most mainstream scientists still subscribe to the more traditional – and opposite – view that you should stay out of the sun when it's at its strongest. But it wouldn't be the first time they've turned out to be wrong.

How animals with hair, fur, and feathers get their vitamin D

Animals that are covered in hair or feathers produce vitamin D in a different way. Sunlight converts a chemical in the oily secretions in their hair or feathers into vitamin D, and the animals ingest it while grooming.[2-43] In fact, the vitamin D we take in vitamin supplements is extracted from the greasy secretions in sheep's wool that has been exposed to UV light.

Reptiles produce vitamin D in much the same way as we do, by basking in the sun, or under a UV lamp if kept as pets. Most of them would die if they were unable to do this.

Inexperienced reptile keepers sometimes inadvertently kill their pets by not using UV lamps. Regular light bulbs emit very little UV radiation, so the animals can't produce enough vitamin D. Putting them near windows doesn't help either, as UV can't pass through the glass.

What about animals that never see the sun?

Deep-sea fish get little or no sunlight, but they get all of their vitamin D from their food, such as plankton. They store their vitamin D in their livers. Fish, and especially fish livers, are a particularly good source of dietary vitamin D for other animals – including us.

In the case of nocturnal creatures and those that live underground, the question is harder to answer. We assume they must get their vitamin D from their food, but they might also have evolved to need less of it.

The human conundrum

We don't have much body hair, and we don't groom ourselves by licking our hair, so we don't get vitamin D from our oily secretions, which we produce very little of anyway. We wear clothes, so most of us aren't exposed to as much sunlight as we need to be. If we do expose ourselves, we burn and get skin cancer, or cover ourselves in sunscreen that blocks UV and prevents vitamin D from being produced. Most of us don't eat much food that's rich in vitamin D, such as oily deep-sea fish. So vast numbers of us are deficient in vitamin D, and suffering from terrible diseases and medical conditions as a result, with skin cancer potentially being one of them.

The light skin conundrum

Earlier, we learned that light skinned people appeared on Earth more recently than most of us realize. Researchers believe the first white people appeared in Sweden 7,700 years ago, which is when the allele associated with light skin first originated in the SLC24A5 gene. Light-skinned people then became more widespread across Europe around 5,800 years ago.[2-44]

According to the conventional timeline of human evolution (but not mine – see Chapter 12), our dark-skinned ancestors left Africa and migrated to temperate regions about 60,000 years ago. And, apart from a single known case of rickets that probably occurred in someone who was housebound, they appear to have suffered no ill effects at all from a lack of vitamin D.

This suggests that lighter skin, like blue eyes, might simply have been a genetic anomaly rather than a necessity.

Things get more complicated at this point. Anthropologists who have studied the Neanderthals, whose range spanned Western Europe to Central Asia, believe they probably had the same distribution of skin color as us – including fair skin and freckles.

As the Neanderthals became extinct around 40,000 years ago, light-colored skin must have evolved at least twice, completely independently. Some researchers believe we may have inherited our light skin from the Neanderthals when we interbred with them,[2-45] but the 33,000-year gap between them dying out and light skin first appearing in humans rules this out.

Although dark-skinned people living in temperate climates have lower levels of vitamin D, it might not be because of their darker pigmentation. Recent research suggests it might actually be caused by the parathyroid hormone.[2-46] Large-scale studies of vitamin D insufficiency in Caucasians also found no links to skin pigmentation.

Do you have a vitamin D deficiency?

Vitamin D deficiency doesn't just cause rickets and bone problems; it's a contributory factor in numerous chronic diseases that kill up to a million people globally each year.[2-47] Increasing the general population's levels of vitamin D3 would cut the incidence of several types of cancer by 50 percent.

Vitamin D particularly reduces the risk of colorectal cancer and prostate cancer, but it also reduces the incidence of a wide range of other deadly cancers by between 30 and 50 percent. It helps reduce cardiovascular disease, hypertension, atherosclerotic heart disease, heart attacks, and strokes, as well as autoimmune diseases such as multiple sclerosis and inflammatory bowel disease. And it helps us fight infections of all kinds, including colds and flu.

The American endocrinologist Dr. Michael F. Holick estimates that 50 percent of the US population is at risk of vitamin D deficiency. This figure rises to 95 percent for senior citizens because they not only spend more time indoors, but their bodies produce less vitamin D in response to exposure to sunlight.

The key areas of concern are the use of sunscreens and clothing to block sunlight, limiting outdoor activities, people with darker skin, the overweight, and the elderly. This takes us back to our earlier conundrum, because several of these things are also said to help prevent skin cancer.

If you have dark skin, you might need up to ten times as much exposure to the sun to produce the same amount of vitamin D as a person with light skin. But remember you're still susceptible to skin cancer.

Vitamin D is fat-soluble. If you're overweight, your excess fat will soak up vitamin D and your body won't get enough. You need a lot more of it than a slim person. The same thing applies if you have a digestive condition such as Crohn's disease, gluten sensitivity or an inflamed bowel. In this case, your body might not be able to digest the fat that contains the vitamin D.

Exposure to the sun, or bright light, can help in other ways. Bright light causes a rise in serotonin, which elevates our mood and relieves depression. (See *Seasonal Affective Disorder* later in this chapter.) UV rays also penetrate our skin, where they help our bodies use vitamin D to absorb more calcium and make our bones stronger. If your bones ache or become weak, it's often a sign that you're not getting enough vitamin D.

Dietary solutions

The dark-skinned native people of the Arctic, particularly those in coastal Alaska and Canada, get high levels of UV in the summer when the sun reflects off the snow and ice, but they don't need to take vitamin D supplements in winter as they get more than enough from their seafood-rich diet.

In fact, some researchers believe we could manage perfectly well without sunscreen if we ate the right foods.[2-48] Chemical sunscreens can be toxic, not only to us but to sea life, particularly coral.[2-49] And although sunscreens block UV, they also block vitamin D. So a change of diet might be the answer – at least for those who are prepared to do it. But let's face it, that won't be very many of us.

Of course, vitamin D is readily available as a dietary supplement. Unlike other vitamins, which are generally considered unnecessary in supplementary form, vitamin D (and especially vitamin D3) will almost certainly benefit you. I take one every day.

So what does all of this mean?

It's a complicated picture, but it becomes clearer if you piece it all together. Most of us need a lot more vitamin D than we're getting, to ward off horrible diseases. But the main way we get it is to go out in the sun, which might give us skin cancer and at the very least makes us age prematurely. There are ways of mitigating this but few people know about them, and even the scientists get it wrong.

It's clear that we aren't meant to be on this planet. If we were meant to be here, and if we were meant to behave the way we've seen throughout this section, then the correct behavior would be built in and natural, just as it is in other animals. We'd do the right thing automatically. But we don't have that type of behavior – and as far as researchers can tell, we never did.

The logical conclusion is that we came from a planet with lower levels of UV radiation, which didn't give us skin cancer. The light levels there must have been relatively consistent throughout the year, which implies a lack of seasons. Most of our vitamin D – and perhaps all of it – must have come from our diet, and whatever we ate must have been rich in vitamin D and enjoyable to eat. It appears that this type of food is unavailable on planet Earth. There's probably a version of it, but it might taste horrible. The best dietary source of vitamin D here is the livers of oily fish, which most people don't (or won't) eat, even if it could save their lives.

2.6 Loss/lack of body hair

This is another example of us being poorly adapted to our environment despite millions of years of evolution. Even in Africa, where we supposedly evolved, it can get pretty cold at night. We have to wrap ourselves up to stave off hypothermia and death. So the big question is: why did we lose most of our body hair in the first place? The world's finest scientists have struggled with this issue for hundreds of years. There have been plenty of plausible-sounding theories, but almost every year another one comes along that overturns everything that's gone before.

Some of the ideas that have been proposed to explain our loss of body hair include:

- fewer body lice and other external parasites

- we're less likely to catch on fire

- it's easier to lose body heat by sweating

- we can regulate our temperatures by adding or removing layers or using different materials, allowing us to colonize parts of the world that would otherwise be inhospitable

But these can easily be refuted:

- other primates cope perfectly well with lice by mutual grooming

- we probably lost our body hair long before we learned how to make and control fire

- other primates sweat, despite having hair

In the end, it probably does come down to the issue of cooling. But there are two sides to the cooling debate, and this has presented scientists with a centuries-long conundrum.

The thing is, having hair can actually make sweating more efficient because each hair acts as a wick and carries moisture away from the skin. This increases the rate of evaporation and helps the animal cool down more quickly. The hair on our heads has also been proven to help with cooling rather than hinder it. Other mammals, such as the big cats, generate far more body heat than we do when hunting their prey. If having less hair enabled them to cool down more quickly, or stay in the hunt for longer, they'd have lost their hair as well. But they haven't, and it's clearly advantageous to them that they have it. And, of course, it also keeps them warm when it's cold.

Another once-popular theory suggested that we don't have body hair for the same reason that animals like elephants and hippos don't: because they can cool themselves down by spraying or submerging themselves in water or wallowing in mud. Swimming and bathing in cool water can certainly cool us down, but it's not a particularly common activity, especially in the tropics and the developing world; water can be scarce in Africa. And I don't think humans have ever wallowed in mud to cool down. (Mud baths at health spas don't really count.)

There's also the theory that we lost our hair during a period of glaciation when food on land became scarce and we were forced to hunt in the water. The theory suggests that those with less hair dried off (and therefore warmed up) faster than those with more hair (who were more likely to die of hypothermia). The problem here is that we also needed to keep warm on land during the glaciation period, and having hair would have been a *good* thing. What we really needed was a different type of hair, or oily secretions to make it waterproof – the same sort of thing that you'd find in ducks and seals, for example. This theory has pretty much been ruled out. And rightly so.

The aquatic ape theory
(also called the marine mammal theory)

There are a couple of other interesting theories that are worth mentioning here. The first is the suggestion that we may have been created when extraterrestrials inserted genes from a highly evolved sea mammal into one of the Earth's native hominins. That would go some way towards explaining our thick layer of subcutaneous fat, which we see in several species of marine mammal but no other land mammals.

The second interesting theory suggests that the mammals we evolved from returned to the sea around 10 million years ago – again, perhaps in search of food which had become scarce on land. By the time they came back out onto the land again, they'd become practically hairless and gained an extra layer of subcutaneous fat for insulation.

The problem with this idea is that our skin has a completely different structure from that of marine mammals. It gets waterlogged and disintegrates when exposed to water for prolonged periods. You can see the beginnings of this if you examine your fingertips after a few minutes in the bathtub. While some say this is proof that we didn't evolve from sea mammals, it does lend credence to the idea that we're a hybrid species: partly terrestrial or extraterrestrial hominins and partly sea mammals.

Another problem with the theory is that as far as we're aware, all of the Earth's hairless marine mammals evolved tens of millions of years ago. Evolutionary scientists say the hominins and the apes only split into their separate branches between five and seven million years ago, and both branches have remained firmly on land ever since. If the marine mammal theory was correct, the apes should also be hairless and have subcutaneous fat. Since that's not the case, most scientists now dispute that this temporary return to the sea could have happened.

So the hybridization version of the theory is the only one that holds water.

Interestingly, we also have several other characteristics of sea mammals. We'll look at these later in this chapter.

So what really happened to our body hair?

The latest theory suggests that as the hominins became more active and developed bigger brains, they needed to sweat more to keep cool.[2-50] They seem to have reached a point where the wicking effect that carried sweat away from their skin was less efficient than losing their hair, developing more sweat glands, and letting the sweat evaporate directly.

Anthropologists believe this happened between 1.3 and 1.4 million years ago. The hominins were then able to run faster for longer periods, move more freely, forage for more food, and become more successful hunters, without the danger of their larger brains overheating.

The theory also suggests that when they had hair, the hominins had light-colored skin. But as they lost their hair, their skin darkened to compensate for the increased exposure to UV radiation.

But why do we still have hair on our heads, armpits and pubic regions? Well, the hair on our heads is probably there mainly for UV protection, but it also helps with cooling using the wicking effect. Our pubic hair has the triple role of acting as a cushion against friction, helping to distribute pheromones, and signaling sexual maturity.[2-51] Our armpit hair also helps distribute pheromones – or at least it used to before we started washing frequently, shaving it off, and using deodorant.

Strangely, all of the great apes have thinner, shorter hair in their pubic regions than on the rest of their bodies – the opposite of what we have. Scientists aren't sure why this is.

Did we evolve during an ice age?

If we evolved on Earth, then yes. The current ice age began about 2.58 million years ago and is still in effect.[2-52] No one is sure how much longer it will last, but we seem to be well past the middle period and heading towards the end. Historical records show repeated cycles of glaciation and retreat (known as interglacials) within each ice age, with each glaciation period lasting for 12,000 to 15,000 years, followed by a 10,000-year retreat. We seem to be nearing the end of the current interglacial, which means we could be due to enter a new period of glaciation quite soon. But there's considerable debate about when – or if – this might happen. The high level of carbon dioxide in the atmosphere right now has led some scientists to suggest the current interglacial might last another 15,000 to 50,000 years.

During our time on Earth, we've survived several glaciation periods and retreats, but the most significant changes have occurred during the current retreat. That includes the evolution of lighter skin and blue eyes, the establishment of civilizations and agriculture, the world's religions, and all of our present technology.

Conclusion

If we evolved lighter skin and blue eyes when we moved out of the tropics, you have to wonder why we didn't also evolve more body hair. There was a gap of more than 50,000 years between us supposedly migrating out of Africa and getting lighter skin and blue eyes. Some say we didn't regrow our body hair because we wouldn't get enough vitamin D. But the great apes get enough, and they're covered in hair and spend most of their time in the shade.

The main problem with the story of humans on Earth is that the science and timelines are all mixed up and confused – though most mainstream scientists argue that they aren't. My hope is that this book, and the timeline in Chapter 12, will go some way to helping everyone make sense of it.

Our original home planet must be (or must have been) constantly and comfortably warm, with day and night temperatures both about the same. That might be because the thick cloud cover prevents heat loss at night; because the ground absorbs heat during the day and radiates it at night; because the planet has binary suns, so it never gets cold or dark; or maybe because the planetary crust is thin and heat from the core radiates through it.

2.7 Wearing clothes

There's some confusion about when we began wearing clothes. There's a long-standing theory that it began around 40,000 to 50,000 years ago, but recent research based on the origins of body lice (which actually prefer living in clothing) gives a different figure of between 83,000 and 170,000 years ago.[2-53] Since we began migrating out of Africa at least 60,000 years ago (and probably a lot earlier) those dates make a lot more sense. Otherwise we'd have been naked in a cool climate for 20,000 to 30,000 years, and it's doubtful that any of us would have survived.

But even if we accept the earlier dates as being correct, that still leaves an extended period when we (and our supposed ancestors) were hairless and naked. And that takes a considerable amount of explaining. Bear in mind that the humans of 200,000 to 300,000 years ago were exactly the same as us – but naked. We must have been uncomfortable, and we didn't exactly thrive. DNA evidence suggests that our numbers may have dwindled to a total global population of between 1,000 and 10,000 following the Toba super-eruption in Indonesia about 75,000 years ago.

We would have been critically endangered at that point,[2-54] and it's incredibly fortunate that we ever recovered from it. Having said that, this may have been the event that triggered the main exodus out of Africa. We'll look at that in more detail later in Chapter 9.

There's no physical evidence of clothing more than 30,000 years old. No one has even found any crude sewing needles made of bone.

There's a theory that the Neanderthals' inadequate clothing may have led to their demise.[2-55][2-56] It would have limited their hunting grounds to southern climates and restricted the amount of time each day when they could have hunted and foraged. Humans, who had warm clothing made from animal skins and other materials, could easily out-compete them. This, of course, poses a further question: why didn't the Neanderthals have body hair, when we know they were active throughout Europe during an ice age? How did they survive for so long? We don't really know.

Would we regrow our body hair if we stopped wearing clothes?

Our hair would grow back *if* it was an evolutionary advantage and *if* those with longer body hair reproduced more than those with shorter body hair or no body hair. But we obviously aren't going to stop wearing clothes. For a start, we'd all have to move back to the tropics. And if, as the latest theory suggests, we lost our hair to help keep our large brains cool, then we might have to lose some of our intelligence too. That's a heck of a price to pay.

2.8 Our response to the seasons

The Earth is not unique in having seasons. Every planet in our solar system has them to a degree, though they're almost unnoticeable on some and quite extreme on others. Seasons are caused by a planet's axis being shifted off-center, or by a planet having an elliptical (non-circular) orbit, so it's sometimes closer to and sometimes further away from the Sun (or whichever star it orbits).

We know that something big hit the Earth billions of years ago and knocked it off its axis by about 23.5 degrees, and that's what gave us our seasons. The Earth's orbit is reasonably circular, so that has minimal effect.

If we look at our closest neighbors: Venus has a tilt of just 3 degrees and the most circular orbit of all the planets, so its seasons are barely noticeable.[2-57] Mars on the other hand has a tilt of 25 degrees and a highly elliptical orbit, so its seasons are more extreme than ours. They also last longer – between four and seven months.[2-58]

But here's the thing: we don't respond to seasons in the same way that the other animals on Earth do. Seasons cause us real problems, and we don't have any kind of mechanism to cope with them.

One of the biggest problems is Seasonal Affective Disorder (SAD). This is a form of depression that some of us suffer from when we don't get enough sunlight during the winter.

In summer, millions of us suffer from allergies such as hay fever. How can we have failed to adapt to the pollen on Earth after millions of years of evolution? We'll look at these issues in more detail later in the chapter.

Another problem is that crops grow in seasons, and food can be scarce at certain times of the year. It would make sense if our reproductive cycles fitted that pattern, as other animals' do. But we can reproduce all year round, even in the middle of winter when hardly anything grows in the temperate regions.

OBJECTION!
"Babies don't eat solid food for the first few months, so it doesn't matter if they're born in winter."

That's true. And you could argue that winter is the ideal time for babies to be born. By the time they're ready to start eating solid food, it's available in abundance. But what will their mothers live on while they're breastfeeding them?

And what about the babies that were born in the summer and are ready to eat solid food in the winter?

OBJECTION!

"We evolved in Africa, which doesn't have seasons."

It's true that the tropical regions don't experience the four seasons in the same way that that the temperate regions do, or at least not to the same degree. But they do have wet and dry seasons, and these can be severe. The dry seasons can cause droughts and famines. Crops don't grow, and the livestock dies, which means the people die too unless they can get outside help. The wet seasons can be equally devastating. Farmland floods and entire communities can be swept away or buried in mud. It can be a harsh environment.

I have serious doubts that we could have evolved in Africa. It's more likely that we were dropped off there – and in several other places – when we were brought here from our home planet. I'll discuss this in more detail, and present more evidence, in Chapters 9 and 12.

We've just about managed to adapt to the Earth's seasonal changes, and most of us now survive them, but it's been a close call at times. Even today, entire communities are regularly wiped out by floods, mudslides, wildfires, hurricanes, cyclones, and other seasonal disasters. Entire civilizations were wiped out in the past – in some case several times over.

The lack of coping mechanisms

The fact that we have no mechanisms for coping with the seasons is bizarre. The Earth has probably had seasons for as long as it's had life. If this is our home planet, we would have evolved multiple mechanisms to cope with them by now.

The only real option we have is to migrate to warmer climates during the winter and cooler ones in the summer. Tens of thousands of people actually do this, but it's only a realistic option for the wealthy and retired, not those tied down by their jobs, families, health or financial restrictions.

Coping with winter

For those of us who have to remain in colder climates during the winter, things can get tough.[2-59][2-60] There are numerous winter-related ailments and issues:

- flu season strikes

- seasonal affective disorder (SAD) kicks in

- our blood pressure rises, so heart attacks become more likely

- breathing becomes more difficult, which puts those with conditions such as asthma at increased risk

- the rates of bronchitis and pneumonia rise sharply

- joints can stiffen up and become inflamed

- ice makes surfaces slippery, leading to accidents

- the hospitals are at their busiest

- and there's a significant increase in the death rate

Some animals hibernate to escape the winter, and many people say they wish they could do the same. Interestingly, humans, like all the mammals, actually possess the gene for hibernation, but our copy of it is dormant. It's dormant in most other species too; the only primate that hibernates is the dwarf lemur of Madagascar.[2-61]

But there was an intriguing incident in April 2014 when a 16-year-old boy stowed away in the unpressurized, unheated wheel compartment of a plane flying from California to Hawaii.[2-62] He somehow survived the freezing conditions (-80F, -62C) and low levels of oxygen for the five-and-a-half-hour flight, though he was unconscious for most of the journey and didn't wake up until an hour after landing. Researchers believe he must have fallen into a state of hibernation. That means our hibernation gene can be reactivated under certain circumstances. The researchers are now looking at whether it might be possible to reactivate it on command.

Coping with summer

Hot summers can be killers too. They can cause heat exhaustion, heat stroke, dehydration, sunstroke, and damage to the major organs.[2-63]

In hot climates, people used to take a siesta – a daytime nap – during the hottest part of the day. That would seem to make sense: it's dangerous to be out in the sun for very long at that time of day, and it's too hot to work, so why not sleep until things cool down?

Even in cooler climates, you'd think there would be health benefits in taking daytime naps, particularly during the summer. You feel sleepy after lunch, which makes you less productive. So why not sleep it off and wake up feeling refreshed, if it happens naturally anyway? Business executives often say one of the big secrets of their productivity is to take power naps. But the latest research suggests that it might not be such a good idea after all: waking up twice a day puts extra strain on your heart.[2-64] And in hotter countries, where the pace of living tends to be slower anyway, a long period of inactivity during the day can exacerbate things like obesity, diabetes and heart problems.

With more people now working in air-conditioned shops and offices, siestas have become less common. There's also the increasing need to deal with businesses in other time zones: you need to be awake at the same time as them to trade with them and remain competitive.

So it seems we haven't evolved physiologically to be able to cope with heat any better than we cope with the cold. But we've evolved technologically, and we're able to mitigate it, at least in the developed world.

Seasonal Affective Disorder (SAD)

Let's take a closer look at one of the main winter-related conditions that affects people in temperate climates: seasonal affective disorder or SAD.

It's a significant medical problem for many people, and it affects all of us in temperate regions in some way. How many of us miss the sun, feel depressed, experience the winter blues, and can't wait for summer to return? I'd say, with some confidence, that most people living in those regions feel this way. And it's not surprising: month after month of short days, long nights and low light levels leave us feeling depressed and lethargic. The winter weather doesn't help; we're often cooped up indoors where the light is even weaker.

Many people love the winter of course. If you live in the right place, the scenery can be spectacular, and there's a certain quality to the light that you just don't get in the summer. If you're in good health, it can be invigorating to be out in the crisp, fresh air. It's just a shame that the days are so short.

Some people argue that SAD is the equivalent evolutionary response to hibernation in other animals. That sounds reasonable enough until you realize what it does to us. It can lead to all sorts of problems: sickness, overeating and weight gain, excessive sleeping, lack of energy, difficulty concentrating, social withdrawal, loss of sex drive, clinical depression, and even suicide.

We must have come from somewhere where the light levels are consistent throughout the year. The northern half of Africa meets this condition – which the mainstream anthropologists will be happy about – but the environmental conditions there aren't right for us. We'll see plenty of evidence of this throughout this chapter.

The evidence suggests we must have evolved on a planet with consistent levels of light, probably akin to early or late summer in the temperate regions on Earth. It would have pleasant day and night temperatures, and no dangerous UV radiation. If the whole planet was shrouded in cloud, and there were no seasons, there would be little distinction between the tropical and temperate regions. Both would be highly habitable – and that fits our natural inclination to explore and colonize every part of the planet.

We can draw some additional conclusions from this:

- Since there are no seasons, our home planet doesn't tilt on its axis, or only to a slight degree.

- Its orbit must be close to circular.

- If it's shrouded in cloud, but the same amount of light reaches the surface as it does on Earth, it must either be closer to its star or the star must be a little larger or brighter than the Sun.

- In the unlikely case that it isn't shrouded in cloud, it must either be further from its star than the Earth is from the Sun, or it must orbit a different type of star – such as a red or brown dwarf – that emits softer light and less UV radiation.

Whoever brought us here probably chose Northern and Eastern Africa as two of the main dropping-off points because of their consistent light levels and warmth that were the closest match for our home planet. They didn't get it quite right, of course, but they did the best they could with what the Earth had to offer.

> There's plenty of evidence to prove that the extraterrestrials dropped us off at other locations too. These would have been much smaller groups though; the aliens appear to have been experimenting to see whether we could survive there. Most of those groups seem to have died out fairly quickly. There's also a considerable amount of evidence to suggest that they carried out these experiments over the course of millions of years, gradually refining our genomes after each failure to make us more robust.

Our natural inclination is to migrate and colonize whichever planet we're on. The evidence suggests this happened on Earth much earlier than 60,000 years ago, which is the date currently recorded in our official timeline. But the fact that we were unable to colonize a large part of the world without coming to some degree of harm – including SAD and its numerous symptoms and consequences – has serious repercussions. It's one of the strongest indicators that we're not originally from this world.

2.9 Our response to the environment

We can summarize our situation on Earth in the following way: we've spent thousands of years trying to make our environment more suitable for us when it should have suited us perfectly in the first place.

> **OBJECTION!**
> "Humans are not meant to live the way we do."
>
> It's true that our modern environment is entirely different from the one we supposedly evolved in, but it's infinitely better than what it was like when we first arrived. Very few of us would be able to survive for very long in our "natural environment" if we went back there today – especially if we had to be naked, as Mother Nature apparently intended.
>
> There are still people in the poorest developing countries who live their lives as we think our ancient ancestors once did. I guess you could say that's the way we were meant to live. They struggle to get by, and can hardly be said to be thriving. Their health is poor, food and water are scarce, education is minimal to non-existent, and their lifespans are short. I don't think many of us would want to live like that if we had any choice. People who visit these communities often feel numb and sickened when they come home, unable to even contemplate what they've seen.

You could, of course, argue that the modern world leads us to be more sedentary than is good for us. But things aren't quite as simple as that – as we'll see later in the chapter.

But it's not just us: most domesticated animals now depend on us for their food and water, and to some extent their shelter, protection, care, and breeding. They wouldn't be able to survive in their natural habitats if they returned there. They'd soon starve to death, die of exposure, or be torn apart by other creatures. Of course, the wild animals can survive there just fine.

And that leads to an intriguing thought: have *we* been domesticated too? And if so, did we do it ourselves or did someone else do it?

2.10 Chronic illnesses and medical conditions

In the first edition of this book, I made the claim that 75 to 80 percent of the human population suffers from one or more chronic conditions. I'm now going to take the bold step of revising that figure to 100 percent.

I've conducted months of exhaustive research, in multiple countries, and I haven't found a single person who is 100 percent healthy.

More than a handful of people claimed they were totally healthy in every respect. But when I interviewed them, and we drilled down into their lifestyles and backgrounds, and looked at the daily problems they face, every one of them turned out to have some sort of chronic medical condition or disorder. In a couple of cases, those conditions were actually quite severe, but they'd somehow blanked them from their minds, denying they were anything less than perfect. Interestingly, they didn't believe they were lying when they made this claim. In fact, they probably would have passed a polygraph (lie detector) test, because they were so convinced that they were telling the truth. And yet they were lying and living in denial. Our minds work in strange ways!

Anyway, the point is that if you're human and you were born on Earth, then I contend that you are *not* 100 percent healthy, and nor are you 100 percent physically perfect. It isn't possible. Because you're not meant to be living here.

> **OBJECTION!**
> "World-class athletes such as Usain Bolt must surely be physically perfect and totally free from chronic conditions."
>
> You'd think so, wouldn't you. But it's not the case. Usain Bolt was born with scoliosis (curvature of the spine) and also has hyperactive disorder.[2-65]

There are thousands of chronic, hidden (or mostly hidden) ailments, disabilities or afflictions that affect us.[2-66] Here are just a few that you might have heard of:

- Addictions
- Addison's disease
- alcoholism
- allergies
- anemia
- ankylosing spondylitis
- anorexia
- arthritis
- Asperger's and other forms of mild (and less mild) autism
- asthma
- back and spinal disorders

- binge eating or drinking
- bipolar disorder, depression and other mental illnesses
- bulimia
- bursitis
- cancer
- celiac disease, gluten intolerance, and other dietary issues
- chronic fatigue syndrome and ME
- chronic lung infections and diseases including COPD (formerly known as emphysema)
- chronic pain
- congenital disorders and weaknesses
- cystic fibrosis
- dementia and Alzheimer's disease
- diabetes
- dyspraxia
- eczema
- endometriosis
- epilepsy
- eyesight problems
- fibromyalgia
- hearing problems
- heart disease, circulatory problems, and hypertension
- hepatitis
- HIV/AIDS
- hyperactivity
- insomnia
- irritable bowel syndrome, colitis and Crohn's disease
- kidney disorders
- learning disorders and disabilities including dyslexia and dyscalculia
- lupus
- mental illness
- migraines

- muscle weakness
- narcolepsy
- nervous disorders including Tourette's and nervous tics
- neurological conditions including multiple sclerosis and Parkinson's
- obesity
- osteoporosis
- psoriasis
- psychological disorders
- scoliosis
- sleep apnea
- stress
- webbed fingers and toes ...

I'm barely scratching the surface here. There are thousands more, many of which neither you nor I have even heard of.

Take a good look at your family members, friends and co-workers. Every one of them is suffering from something or other – though they might not have told anyone, and you might not be able to tell just by looking at them. Some of them might not even know they have it.

The strange thing is, the majority of these conditions only affect humans, or are extremely rare in other species. And, of course, the big question is: why?

Planet Earth is not a happy place for us to be. In fact, as you read through that list of chronic conditions, you might begin to suspect it's hardly habitable at all.

By the way, if anyone tries to tell you they're a perfect specimen of humankind, show them the list of disorders and ask them to say how many of them they have. They don't have to name them, just say how many. In my experience, they'll be shocked when they realize the truth.

If they still insist there's nothing wrong with them, they may be hiding something embarrassing. Don't push them too hard if you want to remain friends!

I consider myself to be fit, active and reasonably healthy. I don't take any medications apart from the daily vitamin D3 pill I mentioned earlier. But I suffer from at least ten things on the list, and at some points in my life I've suffered from at least twelve. And those are the ones I know about.

No other species on Earth suffers chronic disorders like these to the massive extent that we do.

OBJECTION!

"Our ancestors would not have suffered from these ailments. These are all modern issues caused by our lifestyles, chemicals, fertilizers, pesticides, medicines and antibiotics, processed food, radiation from nuclear tests, and electromagnetic waves from phones, radio, television, satellites and wireless internet routers which overwhelm us and prevent us from tuning into the Earth's natural energies."

That's a popular fallacy, but these are *not* modern ailments, and our ancestors *did* suffer from them. The only one on the list that's considered recent is HIV/AIDS (first recognized in 1959). The others have all been known since ancient times. Many were only fully recognized when we began to understand medicine. Some weren't diagnosed or classed as ailments until this century, or they were previously known by other names. But most of them have probably existed for as long as we've been here on Earth.

Let's pick a few examples from the list and see when they were first recognized:

- Addison's disease: first recognized and named in 1849 but undoubtedly much older.

- Ankylosing spondylitis: known since the Middle Ages.

- Anorexia nervosa: first recognized in 1689 but undoubtedly older.

- Arthritis: recognized since 4500 BC.

- Asperger's: named in 1925 but it has undoubtedly existed for centuries if not longer.

- Autism: recognized in 1747 – earlier sufferers were said to be possessed by demons.

- Asthma: recognized by the Ancient Egyptians.

- Binge eating and drinking: the Romans did it at least 2,000 years ago, and probably weren't the first.

- Bipolar disorder: recognized by the Ancient Greeks but probably as old as the first humans.

- Bursitis: as old as the first humans.

- Cancer: found in human skeletons at least 120,000 years old.

- Celiac disease: known for 2,000 years.

- Chronic fatigue syndrome and ME: recognized since 1750.

- Cystic fibrosis: recognized in 1857 but undoubtedly much older.

- Depression: first described as melancholia in 2000 BC, but as old as the first humans.

- Diabetes: recognized in 1500 BC, but probably as old as humans.

- Epilepsy: recognized in 1050 BC – earlier sufferers were said to be possessed by demons.

- Eczema: recognized in 1847, but as old as the first humans.

- Fibromyalgia: recognized in 1800, it undoubtedly existed earlier but is hard to diagnose.

- Hay fever: known since at least the 10th century.

- Heart disease, circulatory problems, and hypertension: known for at least 3,500 years.

- Hepatitis: known for at least 5,000 years.

- Psoriasis: known for at least 2,000 years.

- Scoliosis: known since 3500 BC.

- Stress: known for at least 2,000 years, but probably as old as the first humans.

This is another common misconception. Look through the list of disorders again, and think about which ones only affect older people. Nearly all of them can strike at any age – even dementia.[2-66a] There are millions of children around the world who are chronically ill, disabled, or limited in some way. Arthritis is certainly more common in those over 50, but it can affect people of all ages,[2-67] including children.

It would be incredible if this were true.

The Bible says Noah lived for 950 years, Methuselah for 969 years, and other people of that time lived for several hundred years.[2-67a] Of course, we have no way of verifying this.

The most popular explanation for the significant reduction in lifespan is tied to the story of the Great Flood.[2-68][2-69] It's said that only eight people survived the flood, and of those only three couples went on to have children. There would have been a massive genetic bottleneck as their offspring repeatedly interbred.

The Earth would also have been dramatically different after the flood. There would have been significant changes to the climate, atmosphere, hydrologic cycle, geology, and the amount of radiation reaching the surface.

There would have been far less vegetation – and consequently less oxygen in the atmosphere. We may have been so desperate for food at this point that we switched from an entirely vegetarian diet (which our bodies are designed for) to supplementing it with what little meat was available. We'll take a closer look at the vegetarian versus meat-eater issue later in this chapter.

All of these factors would have reduced our lifespan from 950 – 1,000 years (Adam, Methuselah, Noah) down to 120 – 150 years (Moses) down to about 80 years today.

Interestingly, it's said that the Great Flood was God's attempt to wipe out violence in humans. We'll come back to that issue later too.

OBJECTION!
"We are ignoring our mammalian instinct to be active."

I'm not sure that *any* mammals are instinctively active. Our human instinct is to be as *inactive* as possible, except when absolutely necessary such as gathering food. That's probably because we needed to conserve our energy on our home planet. But even the most active people here on Earth are chronically ill; it has nothing to do with laziness.

I suspect that our instinct to conserve our energy stems from the fact that the food on our original home planet was much less nutritious than it is here on Earth. Even though food is now plentiful and highly nutritious – at least in the developed world – that instinct remains as one of our many vestigial traits.

I came across an interesting comment recently: "Lazy people drive progress." It's true! Most of our inventions throughout history have been all about making things easier for lazy people. For example, why chase deer with spears when you can shoot them with arrows? And why use arrows, which require you to be reasonably close to them, when you can shoot them with a rifle while sitting in your chair a mile away? You only need to go out and fetch the carcass when you've made a definite kill. And being lazy, you'd probably send someone else anyway. Lazy people always look for – and usually find – the easiest ways of doing things, and it drives our technology forward. (Well, that and war.)

OBJECTION!

"There's been a huge leap forward in medicine over the past 100 years, but we survived for thousands of years before that."

I'm not sure what you're objecting to here as this is just a statement of fact. But so many people raised this issue that I thought I'd better cover it, if only to point out that I'm aware of it.

Although we survived for thousands of years without access to modern medicine, we had much shorter lifespans, a poorer quality of life, higher death rates, and higher mortality rates in infants.

Interestingly, we've recently discovered that the Neanderthals knew at least a little about medicine. They treated pain with aspirin, which they obtained by chewing the leaves of willow trees, and they seem to have known about the antibiotic properties of certain molds such as penicillin. [2-70]

But this issue raises some important questions that we'll be looking at in more detail later in the book. For example, why were there these sudden leaps forward, not just in medicine but in technology and industry too? There was a great leap forward about 10,000 to 12,000 years ago, another one about 5,000 years ago, another one about 200 years ago and another one in the late 1940s. But before that, we spent at least 300,000 years [2-71] as simple hunter-gatherers, hardly making any progress at all. That's strange because our brains were about the same size then as they are now. Some scientists even suggest our brains might be slightly smaller now. So why didn't these great leaps forward happen 200,000 or 300,000 years earlier? And why were they sudden leaps rather than a gradual progression?

OBJECTION!

"People are chronically ill because those who have the ailments are kept alive by modern medicine and nursing. They're able to reproduce, which passes the ailment on to the next generation. Wild animals are not chronically ill to such a degree because the weak or sick ones die or get eaten before they have a chance to reproduce. No wonder we have a much higher incidence of chronic illnesses compared to other species."

That does explain the vast number of people who have chronic conditions – which is all of us. But it doesn't explain the sheer number of chronic illnesses, which seems to be a whole magnitude greater in us than in any other species. Where did these illnesses and ailments come from? It all stems from our inability to tolerate the Earth's environment. It isn't our natural home. It's close enough that it keeps us alive, but it isn't close enough to keep us fit and well.

It's worth pausing here to consider a problem of our own making. Doctors routinely overtreat their patients and fail to tell them how long they should take their medicines for. Until recently, they habitually prescribed antibiotics for viral illnesses – often just because their patients asked for them. Antibiotics have no effect on viruses.

Even in cases where antibiotics are appropriate, patients often stop taking them as soon as they feel better, rather than continuing to take them for the entire prescribed course. That means some of the bacteria may survive – and those are the ones that are most resistant to the antibiotic. As those bacteria reproduce, the resistance spreads, and we eventually reach the point where antibiotics have no effect on them. A handful of bacterial diseases have already become untreatable. It isn't a widespread problem yet, but it seems certain to become one in the future.

An unacceptable solution

One of the problems with chronic conditions is that they don't usually prevent people from reproducing. That means the "bad" genes get passed on to the next generation. The only way to eradicate them completely would be to test everyone during childhood and sterilize the sufferers and those who carry the defective genes, denying them the right to reproduce. But most of us would consider this profoundly unacceptable.

A more practical alternative might be to use the same technique but only tackle a handful of conditions at a time, completely eradicating them over several generations before moving on to tackle the next set of conditions. It would take thousands of years to work through the entire list, but it should work in theory. But of course, the public would never accept such a radical measure, and no government would pass the laws to enforce it if they wanted to stay in power. So it won't happen. And that means we'll continue to grow ever weaker as a species, and it could lead to our eventual extinction.

We'll just have to hope our scientists can find some other ways of eradicating these conditions. Individual gene therapy might be one potential solution. Just before this book went to press, researchers announced they had successfully edited a section of DNA in a human embryo. They corrected a fault that caused a heart problem that runs in families. But it was only an experiment, and the embryo was only allowed to develop for a further five days.[2-71a]

Did we get our chronic illnesses from the Neanderthals?

There's a common misconception that we evolved from the Neanderthals. We definitely didn't. But they were around at the same time as us – up until about 40,000 years ago when they died out. Many of us have a small percentage of Neanderthal DNA in our genomes, so one of two things must have happened: either we interbred with them, or some of their DNA must have been spliced into our genomes to make us more robust and better able to cope with living here. Whichever one it was, we appear to have inherited some of their genetic weaknesses along with their strengths.

Geneticists are reasonably certain that the genes for type 2 diabetes, long-term depression, lupus, biliary cirrhosis of the liver, and Crohn's disease all came from Neanderthal DNA.[2-72] We don't know if they actually suffered from these conditions or just carried them in their genes. Some Neanderthal skeletons show signs of arthritis, so that may have come from them too. And, somewhat strangely, researchers also believe we acquired an addiction to smoking from them, even though no one believes for a minute that the Neanderthals ever smoked.

So how did the Neanderthals get these conditions if they evolved on Earth and were perfectly adapted to the environment? Well, the Neanderthals might not have had those conditions at all. This is one of the interesting things about genes. They may have served a useful purpose in the Neanderthals, and only expressed themselves in the form of harmful conditions and diseases when they were passed on to us.

We might have also received some much more damaging genes from the Neanderthals, but if we did, they've long since been lost via natural selection. Those diseases would have been so severe that the people who suffered from them would have been less likely to reproduce.

According to Professor David Reich of the Harvard Medical School: "When Neanderthals and modern humans met and mixed, they were at the very edge of being biologically compatible." If the Neanderthals and humans interbred, the vast majority of their offspring would have been infertile. So we can assume that their worst genetic diseases weren't passed on to us.

On the plus side, geneticists say the DNA we received from the Neanderthals boosted our immunity and made us more robust, so we were better able to cope with the harsher climate in places like Europe.[2-73][2-74]

But it wasn't necessarily a one-way street. It's been suggested that human viruses may have wiped the Neanderthals out.[2-75] That begs the question: where did the human viruses come from and why hadn't the Neanderthal's encountered them before.[2-76] Could it be because we brought them with us from another planet?

It might not have been our fault though. There's another theory that the Neanderthals may have died from a disease similar to BSE (bovine spongiform encephalopathy – commonly known as "mad cow disease"). This theory suggests they may have become cannibals who ate each other's infected brains.

Of course, there are plenty of other theories about why the Neanderthals became extinct.[2-77] It might not have been due to genetics or disease at all. Most theories suggest that we probably had something to do with it though. We'll return to this issue again in Chapter 8.

Chronic illnesses in other animals

> **OBJECTION!**
> "My dog gets sick all the time, and he's not from another planet."

As we noted earlier, all domesticated breeds, including our beloved pet dogs, are far-removed from their wild ancestors. Dogs were created by man. They're basically grossly inbred wolves, and all that inbreeding has weakened them quite severely. Wolves don't have anything like as many chronic illnesses and ailments as dogs do.

Other creatures, particularly mammals, tend to develop age-related ailments towards the end of their lives, including things like arthritis and blindness – and occasionally cancer, though it's pretty rare in the wild.

We keep numerous domesticated species in densely populated conditions where they're much more vulnerable to disease. They'd never live in such conditions in the wild. Chickens and turkeys are a particularly notable case. Tens of thousands of them can be crammed into a shed, where they barely have room to turn around and never see daylight.

Some of the more significant illnesses that affect other animals include:

- AIDS, which originated in apes

- Bird flu and swine flu

- BSE in cattle – though it's believed to have been caused by humans putting infected meat in their feed – even though they're herbivores

Interestingly, something that's been found to help animals suffering from chronic ailments is to feed them their natural diet. That means the things they would have eaten in the wild, not the processed stuff that comes in tins and packets and is full of additives and who knows what else.

In humans, this is called the paleo diet, referring to what people ate during the paleolithic era – or Stone Age.

It's worth noting that the people who lived in the paleolithic era rarely reached the age of 30. Though to be fair, that probably had little to do with their diet.

2.11 We eat meat (but we shouldn't)

The issue of humans eating meat is an interesting one, because if you look at our physiology – which we will in a moment – it's clear that we were never meant to do it. Our ancient ancestors' diet was almost entirely plant-based.[2-78]

Many people believe that most of our chronic ailments stem from the fact that our modern diet is so heavily meat-based, especially as we lack the capacity to process it. Although we can eat meat, we can't safely eat it raw, as carnivores and omnivores can, because our stomach acid isn't strong enough to destroy the pathogens it contains.

OBJECTION!
"Vegetarianism is a modern thing. It would have been impossible – and fatal – in the days before farming."

There's a common misconception that we're naturally omnivores, and we're supposed to eat a balanced diet of meat and plants. But as the American Dietetic Association notes: most of mankind, for most of human history, has lived on vegetarian or near-vegetarian diets.

Even though many of us eat meat, we don't really have the capacity to do so. You can check this for yourself by comparing our teeth, jaws and digestive systems with other species. We're anatomically designed to be herbivores, living on a mainly meat-free diet.

Take a look at this chart from *Fit Food for Men* by A. D. Andrews, published by the American Hygiene Society in 1970.

Meat-eaters: have claws
Herbivores: no claws
Humans: no claws

Meat-eaters: have no skin pores and perspire through the tongue
Herbivores: perspire through skin pores
Humans: perspire through skin pores

Meat-eaters: have sharp front teeth for tearing, with no flat molar teeth for grinding
Herbivores: no sharp front teeth, but flat rear molars for grinding
Humans: no sharp front teeth, but flat rear molars for grinding

Meat-eaters: have an intestinal tract that is only three times their body length so that rapidly decaying meat can pass through quickly
Herbivores: have an intestinal tract 10 to 12 times their body length
Humans: have an intestinal tract 10 to 12 times their body length

Meat-eaters: have strong hydrochloric acid in their stomach to digest meat
Herbivores: have stomach acid that is 20 times weaker than that of a meat-eater
Humans: have stomach acid that is 20 times weaker than that of a meat-eater

Meat-eaters: few salivary glands in their mouth
Herbivores: well-developed salivary glands, which are necessary to pre-digest grains and fruits
Humans: well-developed salivary glands

Meat-eaters: have acidic saliva with no ptyalin (an enzyme)

Herbivores: have alkaline saliva with ptyalin to pre-digest grains

Humans: have alkaline saliva with ptyalin

Although we can eat meat, and our bodies have adapted (somewhat) to be able to digest it, we still have to cook it or process it some other way (by curing it, for example) to consume it safely. The fact that meat contains so much protein and fat, and that we eat ever-increasing amounts of it, is thought to be one of the main reasons why obesity levels are increasing. It gives us much more energy (in terms of proteins, carbohydrates, and fats) than we were designed to handle, and the excess is stored in our bodies as fat.

Even though we're naturally herbivores, we've been eating meat for an awfully long time. Stone tools for butchering meat – and animal bones with corresponding cut marks on them – first appear in the fossil record about 2.5 million years ago.[2-79]

The big question is who was eating meat back then? Mainstream anthropologists and archaeologists say modern humans didn't appear until 300,000 years ago. However, as we'll see in Chapter 3, there's evidence that we were around – at least in small groups – millions of years before that.

But it looks as if the ancient hominins were eating meat long before we first appeared. And we probably started eating it too from the day we arrived.

What we don't know is whether that was out of necessity – because the plants on Earth aren't as nutritious as the ones on our home planet; or because we saw other hominins eating meat and copied them – and found it very much to our liking; or for some other reason.

As I said earlier, I think the plants on Earth must be *much more* nutritious than the ones on our home planet, but we find them less appealing. We'll return to this point later.

There are other differences between meat-eaters and herbivores apart from the food-related issues. For example, meat-eaters don't have seminal vesicles, whereas herbivores do. We have them too, so once again we're very much in the herbivore camp.

When I say we're herbivores, I do of course mean we're *meat-eating* herbivores. Most people, including biologists, say we're omnivores because we eat plants and meat, but that's taking a rather blinkered view of things. We didn't evolve to be able to eat meat, as the omnivores did, and we don't have the digestive systems to process it. But we eat it anyway. So, anatomically speaking, we're herbivores ... that eat meat. And that makes us unique.[2-80]

Food research

One of the most bizarre things is how frequently our scientists revise their idea of which foods are good or bad for us. After millions of years of supposed evolution on Earth, how can they still not know?

As I write this, the latest scare story is that brown toast causes cancer. But if you read the fine details, you'll see that this has only been tested on mice, which are tiny in comparison with us and don't have the same physiologies. I wouldn't be surprised if this announcement is reversed within a year or two, on the grounds that you'd have to eat something like 150 slices of toast per day for it to cause any harm.

And here's another one: we've been told for years that we must eat more fruit. Yet the latest advice is to limit our fruit intake because the sugar in it rots our teeth.

How can we possibly have evolved on Earth when natural, healthy food rots our teeth, the oxygen damages our lungs, and practically every bacteria and virus is out to get us?

OBJECTION!
"You're talking about modern fruits that have been selectively bred to be high in sugar."

That's a reasonable thought. But, like the other chronic ailments we looked at earlier, this isn't a modern phenomenon. A recent study identified widespread tooth decay in early hunter-gatherer societies dating back to around 15,000 years ago.[2-81] Many of them would have been in agony. The problem was caused by their high-carbohydrate diet of fruit, vegetables, nuts, and berries. Or in other words, the exact diet that modern health professionals tell us we should be eating now. (Until they changed their minds.)

It's clear that what nutritionists regard as our natural diet is far too rich and sugary for us. But what's the alternative? There isn't one on Earth, so we have to make do with what we can find. But don't let anyone tell you it's our natural diet. The plants on our home planet would have had a much lower sugar content and far fewer carbohydrates. Interestingly, another recent piece of research has found that there's an evolutionary advantage to us eating meat – even though we aren't supposed to do it. People on strict vegetarian diets had lazier sperm and lower fertility rates, and this was even more evident in their children.[2-82] The researchers believe it's connected to the amount of protein we get from eating meat. It seems that a high-protein diet is essential for ensuring our reproductive success – and our children's too.

2.12 We can't drink the water

Just as we can't safely eat raw meat, we also can't drink from impure water sources, even though they present no problems to any other species.

Dogs, for example, come to no harm whatsoever if they drink from puddles, ponds, lakes, rivers, muddy streams and rivulets, gutters in the street, or even toilets. We'd be hospitalized within hours if we tried it.

We have to boil, filter or chemically treat our drinking water to make it safe. The consequences of not doing so are dire: the infections and diseases we can get from drinking impure water are horrendous.

As we saw in the previous section, dogs have the physiology of meat-eaters, and one of the main benefits of that is having stomach acid twenty times stronger than ours. At first glance, that explains why they can drink impure water. But, as you may have noticed, all of Earth's native herbivores can safely drink it too, and their stomach acid is just about the same strength as ours. So there's obviously something else going on.

There are three possibilities as far as I can tell:

- Our original home planet has an ample supply of drinking water that's naturally pure.

- Or it's basically sterile and contains no organisms that can harm us.

- Or we developed a resistance to those organisms. Once we arrived on Earth, that resistance was useless. We don't seem to have been here long enough to have evolved any resistance to Earth's waterborne organisms. And since we now sterilize our drinking water, it's doubtful that we ever will.

Interestingly, dog owners mistakenly apply human standards to their pets. If their dog tries to drink from a puddle, for example, they'll pull it away, telling it to leave it alone or it'll get sick. We don't find such behavior attractive, and we wouldn't dare try it ourselves, but it's very unlikely that the dog will get sick. The more worrying issue is that our children might see dogs doing it and copy them.

But we shouldn't have to worry about that sort of thing. If impure water harms us, we should all be pre-programmed to leave it alone. But our children are pre-programmed to assume it's safe. We have to override their programming by teaching them that the opposite is true. This is a clear pointer to the fact that we don't belong here. We come from a place where the water is safe for us to drink.

2.13 We dislike natural foods

Although the food on Earth is edible and highly nutritious, I'm convinced that it's pretty horrible compared to what we were used to on our home planet. When we arrived on Earth, we found that we didn't like the taste, color or texture of most of what was on offer – with a few notable exceptions, of course. We had to live with it for thousands of years, getting by as best we could, as we didn't have the knowledge to do anything about it. But over the last few centuries, we've carried out extensive selective breeding programs and turned many of the natural offerings into something more suited to our taste.

The plants we've cultivated are radically different from the wild species we developed them from. Carrots, for example, are naturally small, purple and taste of wood – disgusting to eat and virtually devoid of nutrition. So we "made them better" by selectively breeding them to be bigger, bright orange and more nutritious. And of course, we gave them their distinctive carroty flavor – which is a lot nicer than chewing wood.

We've done the same sort of thing with countless other species. Almost none of the plant-based foods we eat today were growing wild when we first arrived. We've bred them to be bigger, more attractive to our eyes, and packed with carbohydrates and sugars. They're many times more nutritious than their naturally occurring ancestors. Many people would argue that they're now *overly* nutritious, which is causing its own problems. They're generally lower in fiber and protein too.

Interestingly, some zoos have stopped feeding their monkeys bananas. They reported that the cultivated varieties were giving them gastrointestinal problems, and the excessive amount of sugar they contain was making them badly behaved.[2-83]

That makes me wonder whether they're having the same effect on us. How different would things be if *we* reduced the amount of sugar in our diet? Would it calm our violent nature? Almost certainly.

> Doctors and nutritionists have traditionally blamed the fat in our diets for causing the alarming rise in obesity and diabetes we see today. But they've recently changed their minds(!) They now say sugar is the primary cause. In fact, a small amount of fat – even the saturated variety – might actually be good for us because, as we saw earlier, it helps us absorb vitamins.

> There's more than enough food on Earth to feed our ever-growing population. The problem is that it isn't evenly or fairly distributed. Selective breeding hasn't only changed the size, color, flavor and nutritional content of the food, it's also increased yields and increased resistance to pests and disease. As a result, we can feed far more people than the Earth's other natural resources can cope with. In fact, we passed that point years ago, and our population is still rising.

But despite our efforts to make vegetables more palatable, many of us still don't like them, especially in their raw state. Most of us cook them because we don't like the flavor or texture. But there's a significant number of people who won't eat them at all. And, as we'll see later, children seem to have a natural aversion to them.

We've already noted that our herbivore-like bodies have a hard time processing raw meat, so we cook that too to make it more easily digestible. But that leads to another problem: cooking meat makes it taste sweeter, and as a result, most of us *absolutely love* the flavor. So, of course, we're eating it in ever-increasing amounts.

Our bodies aren't meant to do this. They can just about cope with tiny portions of meat, but not the tremendous amount most of us eat today. If we'd been left alone on our home planet, with our natural diet of plants that were delicious but not particularly nutritious, we'd have been absolutely fine. We wouldn't be obese, we wouldn't have diabetes, we might not be so violent, we wouldn't have so many chronic illnesses, and our population would be smaller and less of a drain on the planet's resources.

And there's another problem with the food here: many of us can't eat it at all. Despite millions of years of supposed evolution on Earth, millions of people have potentially lethal intolerances to things like wheat, gluten, cow's milk (or more specifically the lactose it contains), eggs, yeast, nuts, and more. If we evolved here, that doesn't make any kind of sense.

I can accept that we were never meant to drink the milk of other species, or eat their eggs, but the others intolerances are harder to explain. The obvious conclusion is that we *haven't* been here for millions of years, and we evolved to eat something else.

OBJECTION!

"Many people love natural food, and go fishing and hunting and foraging for berries and other wild species."

It's true that there are some lovely wild foods here on Earth, including a few naturally occurring fruits and berries that we haven't (yet) modified. Many people consider these to be our original diet; the things we must have eaten when we first appeared on Earth. Perhaps if we'd stuck with that diet – as every other creature on Earth would have done – there wouldn't be a problem. But we didn't do that. As soon as we discovered other food sources, most of us turned away from that diet.

Lots of people do, as you say, go foraging for fruits and berries today, but the proportion of the population that does this is tiny, particularly in the developed world. Most of us wouldn't even think of doing it.

You also need to remember the issue we looked at earlier: our so-called natural diet damages our health, and especially our teeth.

We also saw that modern humans were hunters from the moment we first arrived – as were some of the earlier hominins. So we can't call fruits and berries our original natural diet at all. They might have been more of an accompaniment or side dish.

And, of course, the people who go hunting and fishing today don't eat the things they catch raw. They (almost always) cook it first – and that's not a "natural" thing to do.

2.14 Food cravings

You've probably noticed that the foods we like best here are the ones that are worst for our health. Surely we can't have evolved that way? Logic says we should love the things that are best for us and shun those that aren't. That's the way it works in every other species, so why is it the opposite way around for us? Once again, the obvious answer is that we're from somewhere else, where the things we like *are* good for us.

The foods that are best for us:
raw fruit and vegetables, nuts, berries, fish, white meat.

The foods we eat least of:
raw fruit and vegetables, nuts, berries, fish, white meat.

The foods that are worst for us:
chocolate, sugar, salt, red meat, saturated fat, alcoholic drinks.

The foods we like most:
chocolate, sugar, salt, red meat, saturated fat, alcoholic drinks.

That says it all, doesn't it? Either evolution has screwed us over (and we're the *only* species that's been screwed over), or we can't be from this planet.

It's worth pausing here to take a quick look at the thrifty gene hypothesis. This suggests that our brains drive us to seek out high-calorie foods and put down a layer of fat so we can survive periods of famine. Our brains also reward us for eating those foods by releasing chemicals that make us feel happy. You'd need incredible willpower to resist that kind of double-whammy.

But there's a huge problem with this hypothesis, and it's been bothering scientists for years. The thing is, famines are rare in most parts of the world, so the instinct to store fat is rather strange. Another problem is that not everyone has the thrifty genes. Scientists are now beginning to realize there's something more complicated going on, and the thrifty gene hypothesis might not be right after all.[2-84]

> I would suggest the opposite: that the theory is correct but it applies to our home planet. Famines must be a regular problem there.

Whatever is going on, it doesn't change the underlying fact that most of us have an incredible urge to store fat, whether times are hard or not.

To me, this provides further evidence that the plants on our home planet aren't particularly nutritious. When we lived there, we'd have needed to consume significant amounts of plant material to get all the nutrients we needed. And even though we're now on Earth, our natural drive to keep on eating hasn't gone away.

We also have many other cravings which suggest that the plants on Earth contain lower levels of minerals than we're used to.[2-85] We'll look at calcium as a specific example in the next section.

Food cravings can be a useful indication of what might be wrong with us:[2-86][2-87]

- Rice or beans: indicates a need for more protein.

- Spice: indicates that we're too hot – hot spices induce sweating.

- Licorice: indicates that we're not getting enough salt or we're excreting too much of it. This can also be a sign of Addison's disease. Licorice makes our bodies retain salt.

- Ginger: may indicate heart disease. It reduces clotting and cholesterol and strengthens the heart muscles.

- Chocolate: induces feelings of peace, euphoria, and comfort. When we crave chocolate, it's often because we're feeling stressed or upset about something.

Interestingly, we're the only creatures on Earth that enjoy eating spicy food. No one knows why.

2.15 We lack sufficient calcium in our diet

Food cravings are particularly common in pregnant women. They're thought to be caused by the developing fetus demanding nutrients that its mother's body lacks. A craving for soil is surprisingly common, and it's considered to be an indication that the woman isn't getting enough calcium in her diet: the fetus needs more calcium to help its bones develop. This workaround seems to be instinctive. Soil can also detoxify the woman's digestive system, making her body a safer environment for the developing child.

But it isn't just pregnant women who need more calcium in their diet – we all do. And as I suggested in the previous section, that could be another important indicator that we didn't originate here.

In the West, our go-to workaround for getting more calcium is to drink cow's milk and eat dairy products such as cheese and yogurt. This isn't a natural thing to do, and it doesn't suit our digestive systems. But it's the best solution we've been able to come up with, and most of us regard it as being better than the alternatives.

Since cow's milk isn't part of our natural diet, there was a time when none of us could even tolerate it. We were all lactose intolerant, and drinking more than a small amount of it would have given us stomach cramps and made us feel ill. Even so, our ancestors persevered – the pain and nausea were still somehow better than the alternatives!

Thanks to them, we evolved the ability to tolerate lactose, and most of us can now consume it without any problems. Of course, there's still a significant number who can't. We tend to call them "lactose intolerant" as if there was something wrong with them, but really, they're just normal. We were never meant to eat or drink that stuff in the first place. So it's the rest of us who are strange.

Dairy products don't form any part of the Eastern diet, so they haven't developed any tolerance for it at all. Again, you might say they're all lactose intolerant, but that wouldn't be fair. There's nothing wrong with them.

But having said all of that, even those of us who can tolerate it can't drink it straight from the cow. It has to be pasteurized to eliminate or reduce the pathogenic microbes it contains. They can cause tuberculosis, diphtheria, typhoid, and streptococcal infections.[2-88]

Back when our ancestors first began drinking milk – and suffered nausea and stomach cramps – they also risked serious illness or even death from these pathogens. They still drank it anyway, such was their craving for calcium. And to be fair, they probably didn't know about the pathogens then.

The need to pasteurize dairy products, and the horrific consequences of not doing so, are further reminders that it was never meant to be part of our diet.

Some scientists, including the American liver and pancreatic cancer specialist Dr. Dmitri Alden, believe that dairy products cause tremendous biochemical changes and stresses in our bodies. This can lead to cancer, particularly of the breast and pancreas, as well as other diseases.

The problem is that cow's milk is loaded with growth factors, including estrogen and casein. These are ideal for developing calves – for whom the milk was intended – but they're not so great for us.

Casein and similar proteins are also found in meat, including the supposedly healthy ones such as salmon, chicken, and turkey. The safest option seems to be to get all of our proteins from plant-based sources such as almonds, lentils, broccoli, and brown rice.

There are other ways of getting calcium, but most people in the West won't have these on their lists of food they like. They include calcium-fortified soy milk and juice; calcium-set tofu; soybean products; several brassicas including bok choy, broccoli, collard greens, Chinese cabbage, kale, mustard greens and okra; and small fish – as long as you also eat the bones.[2-89][2-90]

Let's take a quick look at Japan as an example of an Eastern culture. The Japanese don't eat dairy products and have no tolerance for it. They have access to all of the other calcium-rich foods we looked at above, but they still don't get enough calcium from them.[2-91] As a result, their bone mineral density is lower than that of Western cultures, and as a consequence, many of them suffer hip fractures or become bedridden. Out of necessity, their elderly population is less active than their Western counterparts, and they have to adopt a different sitting position.

So we're in the dubious position of having to consume dairy products that can potentially kill us in multiple ways, or non-dairy foods that most of us don't like and which don't contain enough calcium anyway. It's no wonder so many pregnant women have a craving for soil.

This leads us to another conclusion about our home planet: the edible plants must be naturally rich in calcium. That's probably because the soil is calcium rich.

2.16 We don't have a fixed diet

Every other creature eats a narrow range of food, and they stick to that diet. Many species only eat one thing, such as grass, which is difficult to digest and contains little in the way of nutrients. Yet they thrive on it and need nothing to supplement it. Their digestive systems are of course quite different from ours, and they're able to get the most from what they eat. Some species only eat nuts. Some only eat berries. Some only eat earthworms. Koalas only eat eucalyptus leaves. Giant pandas only eat bamboo shoots.

But we eat an extraordinarily wide range of foods, and what one person eats might be entirely different from what the next one eats. We might decide to start eating something completely different tomorrow, and it would be considered perfectly rational and reasonable.

That doesn't mean we come from another planet, of course, but so many people raised the point that it was worth including here. At the very least, it confirms that we're different from every other creature on Earth.

> The people with the most limited diet on Earth are the Inuits who live in the Arctic. They survive almost exclusively on raw meat, typically from whales, walruses, caribou, seals, polar bears, muskoxen, birds, and fish. They supplement this with the small amount of plant material they can find during the short summers. Nothing grows there at all during the long winters, and cultivating plants for food is impossible. Approximately 75 percent of their diet is fat, and the rest is mainly protein. Although they generally enjoy good health, their life expectancy is 12 to 15 years lower than their nearest neighbors, the Canadians.[2-92]

Unlike almost every other creature on the planet, if there's a better-tasting alternative available, most of us will choose that rather than the healthy option. We do this even if it's been highly processed and most of the nutrients have been replaced with artificial colors, flavor enhancers, and sugar. Dogs will eat this appalling stuff too, but only because they've grown up sharing our food. It makes them just as sick as it does us. Some other species, such as cats, might take a quick sniff out of curiosity, then leave it well alone. But most species won't go anywhere near it.

2.17 Excessive growth of internal parasites

Parasitic worms and other parasites inhabit the guts of most creatures – probably all of them, in fact. In native species, they remain small, harmless and virtually undetected. But when they get into the human gut they find themselves in such an alien and nutritious environment that they grow many times larger than normal and can multiply out of control. They can sometimes fill the entire gut, killing their unfortunate hosts – and themselves.

The pork tapeworm (*Taenia solium*), for example, usually grows to 2 to 3 meters in length (6.5 to 10 feet), but in humans it can grow to 8 meters (26 feet). Some tapeworms can grow up to 25 meters (82 feet) in humans.[2-93][2-94]

Other problems resulting from a worm infestation can include malnutrition, anemia, mental retardation, bloating, diarrhea, and the slowing down of digestion which leads to the release of potentially fatal toxins.[2-95][2-96] Again, if their human host dies, the worms die too – a consequence that was surely never intended.

Most of the toxins come from decomposing meat, of course. That takes us back to the earlier section where we noted that carnivores and omnivores have much shorter digestive tracts so they can avoid this sort of problem.

That sounds plausible at first glance. But oversized parasitic worms are especially common in parts of Africa and Asia where food is scarce and nutrition rates are low compared with the rest of the world. The people there still forage for food in its natural, wild state – it hasn't been selectively bred to be more nutritious. The simple truth is that when a parasitic worm finds itself inside a human host – well-nourished or not – it grows to giant size or multiplies out of control, depending on the species. They don't do this in any other animal.

2.18 Back problems

Approximately 90 percent of adults experience back pain at some point in their life. 50 percent of working adults suffer back pain every year. It's the second most common cause of lost days at work (behind upper respiratory conditions) and the single leading cause of disability worldwide. Most back pain is caused by inflammation.

The most common back problems are:

• Herniated or degenerated discs

- Muscle tears and inflammation

- Joint degeneration (osteoarthritis)

- Narrowing of the spinal canal caused by the bones thickening as we age

149 million working days are lost in the USA each year because of back problems,[2-97] and around 31 million in the UK.[2-98] So there's no doubt that it's damaging the world's economies.

Most anthropologists will tell you that these problems all stem from us being bipeds that walk upright. They claim this strains our backs. Many of them suggest that twisting of the spine is the main problem. But that doesn't fit with the list of the most common back problems we saw a moment ago. And even if it did, surely evolution would have sorted the issue out after all this time?

There's a common misconception that our bipedalism is a recent phenomenon, and that evolution hasn't yet had time to iron out the problems. This isn't the case at all – or at least it isn't if we evolved on Earth.

Modern humans have walked upright ever since we first appeared on Earth. The current accepted date for our first appearance is around 300,000 years ago, but in reality, we've been here at least 400,000 years and probably longer. If we'd been the first hominins to walk upright, everything would make perfect sense. 400,000 years wouldn't have been long enough for evolution to sort out the problems. But we weren't the first. The earlier hominins were walking upright millions of years before we turned up.

The British paleoanthropologist Mary Leakey discovered footprints of bipedal hominins (known as the Laetoli) in Tanzania and dated them to around 3.6 – 3.8 million years ago. There's also evidence that an earlier species, Australopithecus, was walking upright as much as 4.2 million years ago.[2-99]

An even earlier species, Sahelanthropus, discovered in 2001, may have walked upright as long as 7 million years ago,[2-100] although the scientific community has yet to reach a consensus on this.

Chimpanzees and gorillas can walk upright just as well as we can if they choose to,[2-101] despite their different body shape. (They often do this in captivity, but it's rarely been seen in the wild). They belong to the ape branch of evolution that split from the hominin branch about 7.2 million years ago.

> Interestingly, one the first members of the *Homo* genus, *H. naledi*, which appeared around 3 million years ago, was probably better at walking than we are.[2-102] It had an outward-flared pelvis that shifted its hip muscles away from its joints, giving it more leverage.

So bipedalism goes back a lot further than most people think. If we'd really evolved on Earth, the bones, muscles, ligaments, and discs in our backs would have thickened and strengthened by now, just as they did in the other native hominins. Researchers have discovered that the Neanderthals hardly had any back problems at all, and they're supposed to be our closest relatives. So we either didn't evolve here, or there's something truly bizarre going on.

The Neanderthals' excellent back health was due to a combination of heavier musculature supporting their spines, and lumbar kyphosis,[2-103] which means their lower spines curved the opposite way to ours.[2-104][2-105] Why aren't our spines similarly protected? If we'd evolved on Earth, then we would more than likely have had the same immediate ancestor as them. So it makes no sense that our spines are structured so differently, and are so weak in comparison.

We've already noted that many of us have a small amount of Neanderthal DNA in our genomes. We also apparently inherited some of our susceptibility to diseases and other conditions from them. Researchers believe we inherited some of their robustness too. We must have been a much weaker species before we interbred with them or had sections of their genome spliced into ours. It's a shame we didn't inherit their back health as well.

We're getting taller

The overly nutritious food on Earth has had a significant impact on our development, making us both heavier and taller. This had put more strain on our spines than they were designed to handle. Though it seems they weren't designed to handle all that much in the first place.

Gravity is another factor. It's probably slightly greater on our home planet than it is here on Earth. I'd estimate the difference to be about 5 percent. The higher gravity kept us short, but now that we're on a planet where it's lower, we've grown taller. In some countries, people are still growing taller with each generation – and so quickly that their skeletons and musculature don't have time to adapt.

In most developed nations, our average height increased by about four inches during the 20th century.[2-106] That was mainly because of better nutrition and health care. The switch from having large families to having smaller ones also reduced overcrowding and meant there was less competition for resources.

On the whole, our heights seem to have stabilized now. But the Netherlands is the exception to the rule. During the 20th century, the height increase there was more pronounced than anywhere else in the world. This is thought to be a simple case of natural selection: Dutch women prefer taller men. They're now the tallest nation on Earth, and they're still growing.[2-107]

But there seems to be a natural limit on our heights. Excessively tall people generally have much shorter lifespans. If you look at the list of tallest people throughout history,[2-108] you'll notice that none of those in the top twenty reached the age of sixty, and several died in their twenties.

> Astronauts lose muscle mass and bone density within days of arriving in space, no matter how much they exercise. There's no reason why the reverse shouldn't happen on Earth. But even if that process took a few million years, we shouldn't suffer from bad backs now, whatever sort of lifestyle we have – unless there's something we're overlooking.

OBJECTION!
"Back problems are just a consequence
of our modern sedentary lifestyle."

This is another one of those common misconceptions. If it were true, we'd expect to find fewer back problems in people who lead active lives or do jobs that are similar to those our distant ancestors had: farming, manual laboring, and hunting, for example. But in fact, these are high-risk activities for lower back disorders and musculoskeletal problems. They get *more* back problems, not fewer.[2-109]

Of course, modern farmers spend a great deal of their time driving around in tractors, and they tend to leap down from their cabs without using the steps. So they're more sedentary than ancient farmers, and they're putting greater strain on their backs.[2-110] But manual laborers suffer just as many back problems as those who work in offices.

Modern hunters suffer tremendously from back problems and are often forced to give up hunting because of it. And plenty of elite athletes have had to give up their careers because of back injuries, even when they've had professional coaching. It's clear that our level of activity is only part of the picture. We're highly susceptible to back problems regardless of whether we're active or inactive.

And as we noted earlier, we're a relatively inactive species by nature. It's nothing to do with our modern lifestyles, it's simply who we are and how we've always been.

In our hunter-gatherer days, the men might have rushed out to kill a deer at the beginning of the day. They then carried it home and spent the rest of the day skinning it, butchering it, and cooking it. They ate it in the afternoon, then spent the evening sitting around the fire telling stories and sharpening their spears for the next hunt. If there was enough meat left over, and no hunt was scheduled for the next day, they didn't go anywhere. They didn't know about the value of exercise; their instinct was to conserve their energy. We still have that instinct today. It takes an enormous amount of willpower to get us moving, and it's more willpower than many of us possess. Interestingly though, there are plenty of other creatures on Earth that are far more sedentary than us, and they suffer no ill effects from it.

Anthropologists traditionally blame our poor back health on our bipedalism. As we've seen, they're probably wrong about that. But it's worth pausing here to consider the advantages of bipedalism.[2-111] It allows us to stand tall and see further so we can avoid predators. We can locate food sources that are more distant, and, since our hands are free, we can easily carry it back to our homes. That means we can have a better diet, which in turn leads to better health and longer lives. Being bipeds also means we can use tools. It might also be more energy efficient, and it enables us to regulate our body heat more effectively as we expose less of ourselves to the sun.

OBJECTION!
"Back problems are caused by wearing shoes.
We evolved to walk on grass with bare feet."

That's true to a certain extent. It's worth going barefoot whenever possible at home, on grass, and on the beach. Shoes can interfere with your balance, posture and overall strength. They hold the bones in your feet rigid so they can't move fluidly. As a result, your feet come to rely on your shoes for support rather than supporting themselves.

Studies have shown that athletes suffer fewer injuries if they run barefoot.[2-112] Their feet maintain their proper shape, balance the load, act as shock absorbers, and lessen the impact on their knees.

But we didn't evolve to walk or run on hard surfaces like concrete or asphalt, so we need extra cushioning from properly fitting and supportive shoes on those surfaces.[2-113]

Causes and treatments

As we've seen, lower back pain is a common health problem worldwide, and a leading cause of disability. The main risk factors include bad posture, poor ergonomics in the workplace, depression, obesity, being of above average height, and age. But doctors have been unable to identify any single cause. In most cases, patients don't exhibit just one symptom but a whole raft of them, so pinpointing the origin of the problem is usually impossible.

Back pain is traditionally treated with rest, painkillers, anti-inflammatories, steroids, surgery, and – if none of those work – mobility scooters. But these are only treating the symptoms, not the cause.

Another problem is that drugs are often prescribed long-term, but they're only effective in the short term. It's usually more beneficial to prescribe exercise and posture lessons instead.[2-114] Patients might need some pain relief for the first few weeks as they ease into their exercise regime, but after that, their bodies should begin to regain their former strength and recover their posture, so the drugs can be reduced and eventually stopped.[2-115] Then just keep on exercising.

> **OBJECTION!**
> "Back problems only affect those who are past their prime. They don't affect those who are of breeding age or prevent them from breeding, so the weaknesses get passed on to the next generation and only manifest later in life."
>
> Lower back pain affects people of all ages, from children to the elderly – although it's rare before the age of nine.[2-116]
>
> Although children and adolescents suffer less lower back pain than adults, the rate is rising. It generally increases and peaks during middle age. In older people, most lower back pain is caused by the deterioration of their intervertebral discs.

Interestingly, lower back pain is practically non-existent in some indigenous cultures. They hold their spines in a J shape rather than the more common S shape. This gives them a rather regal appearance, but it takes a lot of strength to hold the shape.[2-117] Most people in developed countries don't have enough muscle tone to be able to do it, but it's possible to develop it with training and exercise.

Many people blame our bad backs on the decline in the teaching of good posture since the 1920s. But that was just a passing trend or fad more than anything. Good posture ought to come naturally. It wasn't taught for most of the 400,000 years or more that we've been on Earth, so it seems highly unlikely that stopping the teaching would have had much effect. We just reverted to our natural S-shaped curved-spine posture. It might be more prone to injury, but it's obviously the way we're meant to stand.

> **OBJECTION!**
> "Our backs are weak compared with other species because we sacrificed strength for dexterity."
>
> You might be right. We certainly have more dexterity than the Neanderthals did, and this is sometimes cited as one of the reasons why the Neanderthals became extinct.[2-118] But I wonder why it hasn't happened in other species.

An alternative theory

Earlier, I estimated that the Earth's gravity is probably about 5 percent lower than our home planet's. But some scientists believe the Earth's gravity is 20 to 40 percent too high for us. As a result, we feel heavy, cumbersome, uncomfortable and unhappy, and we can seriously injure ourselves if we fall over. If the Earth's gravity was only 60 percent of what it is now, we wouldn't have any of these issues. We'd not only fall over less frequently, but we'd do it without causing ourselves any significant injuries – just like most other creatures on Earth.[2-119]

This is certainly an interesting theory, and I'm prepared to accept that mine could be wrong. I'll monitor future developments with great interest. But either way, it's evidence that we're on the wrong planet.

Conclusion

We don't know when we became bipeds on our home planet. It may have been comparatively recently, and it would make sense that we're still adapting to it in that case. But, as we've seen, there are many other factors we need to take into account, including the different levels of nutrition and gravity here.

If we evolved on Earth, our bodies have had up to 7 million years to adapt to being bipedal, so it's bizarre that we're still having major problems with it.

It's important to note that hip, spine and back problems aren't limited to us bipeds. Four-legged creatures can suffer from them too – particularly spinal misalignment. But, once again, the creatures that are worst affected are the ones we've domesticated and selectively bred, and where excessive levels of inbreeding have made them weaker: dogs, cats, horses, donkeys, goats, and so on. The natural versions of these creatures, which evolved on Earth long before we arrived, would have been far more robust and much less likely to suffer from these problems, except through injury or the occasional genetic anomaly.

2.19 Our 25-hour body clock

Our body's natural (circadian) rhythm doesn't match the Earth's 24-hour clock. This is simple enough to prove: you just deprive people of external stimuli, such as daylight and clocks, and let them wake and sleep and turn the lights on and off whenever they like. After about two weeks they'll settle into their body's natural sleep-wake cycle, completely out of step with the outside world, where each day lasts around 25 hours.[2-120]

We aren't usually deprived of external stimuli, of course, and our biological clocks reset each morning as soon as the daylight hits our eyes. But as we're an hour short, we feel pretty rotten when this happens. It's strange that we still haven't adapted to the Earth's 24-hour cycle after all the time we've been here. Even if we only arrived in the last 400,000 years or so, that ought to have been more than enough time to adapt.

Many of us feel a massive resistance when it's time to get up in the morning, even if we've had enough sleep, we're fit and well, and we have something to look forward to during the coming day. Getting out of bed takes an enormous amount of willpower, and forcing ourselves to do it not only makes us feel miserable but can lead to clinical depression.

Sometimes there can be a medical explanation for this. For example, researchers have found that about 10 percent of the population suffers from delayed sleep phase disorder (DSPD). If you suffer from this, the midpoint of your night's sleep is probably between 6:00 am and 8:00 am, whereas it's around 4:00 am for everyone else. If you wake up at what most people regard as the "normal" waking up time, you haven't had enough sleep, and you're in a permanent state of jet lag. There aren't enough hours in the day; you're constantly having to try and catch up but you never quite get there. DSPD seems to be a genetic condition, and although there are ways of managing it – which are essentially just workarounds – there's currently no cure.

DSPD was once believed to be caused by a mutation in the CRY1 gene. But recent research has found that although 1 in 10 Europeans are affected by DSPD, only 1 in 75 of them has the CRY1 mutation.[2-121] So it looks as if more than one gene is involved.

But we should also take experiential evidence into account. You've probably said it yourself: "There are never enough hours in the day." Well, of course there aren't. If we came from a planet with 25-hour days and we now have to try and get the same amount of work done in only 24, is it any wonder that we feel cheated and stressed? If we combine that with all the other effects that stem from our failure to adapt to living on this planet, life can feel pretty intolerable at times.

OBJECTION!
"This is just a factor of our modern lifestyle."

That's partially true. If you're wealthy, retired, or brave enough, it's possible to escape the rat race. You might even have so much spare time that you get bored. But most of us don't have that choice – or aren't brave enough to take that option.

But do you think things were any different for our ancient ancestors? Imagine that you're living in the Stone Age and you have to drag yourself out of bed in time for the big hunt. The deer tend to gather at the watering hole just after dawn, and that's the perfect time to kill them. But you stayed up late last night desperately trying to finish sharpening your spear before the sun went down and you ran out of light. One more hour would have been enough, but you didn't have that hour. This morning you feel exhausted, and your spear still isn't sharp enough. You head out on the hunt, but you don't manage to kill the deer – your spear just bounces off. The deer run away, frightened but unharmed. They won't be back for several days, and that means your family will have to go without meat. You'll just have to hope the women and children can find another source of nuts and berries.

They might blame you, but it wasn't your fault. There simply weren't enough hours in the day to get everything done. And, since this is the Stone Age, you don't have the option of dropping out of the rat race because you're wealthy or retired. There's no such thing as wealth, there's no such thing as retirement, and you probably won't live long enough to retire anyway.

OBJECTION!

"This is simply a consequence of living on Earth for millions of years. Days were much longer in the past."

Days were *shorter* in the past. When the dinosaurs were at their peak 200 million years ago, days lasted just 23 hours. The Earth's speed of rotation is very gradually slowing down and our days are getting longer. That's why we need to add an extra day to our calendar every leap year, and occasionally add an extra second to our clocks. In another 200 million years, days will be 25 hours long. We won't have any trouble adjusting to this, if we're still around then, because our internal clocks are already set for 25 hours. If anything, we'll all feel a lot better.

It's worth noting that researchers sometimes come to different conclusions about the length of our internal sleep-wake cycles. Every test seems to produce a different result. Some people have cycles that are as long as 27 hours. Others have cycles that are as short as 23.5 hours. But the overall tendency seems to be for natural sleep-wake

Humans Are Not From Earth

cycles of about 5 percent longer than 24 hours – which is just over 25 hours.[2-122]

> That figure of 5 percent is important: we came across it earlier when we considered how much stronger the gravity is on our home planet. We'll see it again in Chapter 10 when we look at the other aspects of our home planet's geology.

A study carried out at Harvard University in 1999 found the natural human rhythm to be closer to 24 hours and 11 minutes. But they also discovered that human subjects could be easily trained to follow a 23.5-hour cycle and a 24.65-hour cycle. (24.65 hours – or 24 hours and 40 minutes – is the length of a day on Mars.) Clearly, some people have adjusted to Earth time better than others. And there could be a good reason for it …

Researchers have discovered that they can affect the natural circadian rhythms of fruit flies by modifying their genes. They shortened some to 19 hours and lengthened others to 28 hours. This is interesting and highly relevant to us because there's evidence of considerable external interference in our genome. It's possible that the same thing might have been done to us. Looking at the length of days from the Harvard study above, it's possible that some of us were originally destined to go to Mars not Earth.

> When the space agencies select candidates to go and live on Mars, I recommend they choose people whose natural circadian rhythms are close to 24 hours and 40 minutes – otherwise they might suffer from permanent jet lag.[2-123]

French cave expert Michel Siffre carried out an interesting experiment on himself in 1972. He spent six months underground, completely isolated from the outside world, and he kept a detailed diary of his experiences. He returned to the surface after what he thought was 151 days but was actually 179 days. That means the average length of his day would have been about 28.5 hours. Another underground experiment in 1965 also produced interesting results, with the participants sometimes sleeping for days at a time.[2-124]

Researchers have tested the internal clocks of many of the Earth's native animals and plants. The majority of them are very close to 24 hours. Some coastal creatures synchronize their clocks with the tides, so they operate on 12.4- or 24.8-hour cycles. A few creatures seem to have evolved internal clocks that are slightly out-of-sync with the rest of the world because of the intense competition for food in their niche. If they were to eat at the same time as the other creatures, they'd be less likely to get their fair share. Being slightly out of step means that they've improved their chances of survival.

It wouldn't make sense for us to do that though. We would have begun hunting and foraging for food when the sun rose and stopped when it set. Our internal clocks should, therefore, be closely aligned with the length of a day on Earth. But they're not. Of course, it doesn't help that the Earth has seasons, which means that the sunrise and sunset times keep changing. As we saw earlier, our home planet probably doesn't have seasons, so the sunrise and sunset times will always stay the same.

Biological clocks also play a role in much longer cycles, such as hibernation, migrations, and annual changes in the density and color of fur.[2-125] When an animal's brain registers longer days in the spring and shorter days in the fall, it triggers the release of hormones which influence these events.

Having a scientific mind, I often use myself as a test subject. I've found that wherever I travel in the world, and whichever time zone I'm in, I always naturally gravitate back to the US Central time zone I was born in. That's inconvenient in some places: when I'm in the UK, for example, it means I don't wake up until lunchtime, and I'm not available for morning meetings. For the first few years of my career, I forced myself to adopt the local time zone. But these days I usually choose not to, because (a) it hurts and (b) I have the option not to do it.

I wondered if everyone naturally gravitated back to their home time zone wherever they were in the world, but this turned out not to be the case. My co-writer and publisher, Dave Haslett, was born and raised in the UK, but his internal body clock also seems to be synchronized with the US Central time zone. He loves this as it means he's at his most productive at night, and he can work straight through without getting interrupted. But he says it was a living hell when he had to be at work by 8:30 each morning. I wonder if he might have been a fellow Wisconsinite in a former life?

A reader's comment:
"My day always starts at 5:00 am when I'm woken by my dogs. They wake up at the same time every day, whatever the time of year, and regardless of whether it's light or dark."

That makes sense. Dogs are native to Earth and therefore have an internal 24-hour clock.

Sometimes, when I've been traveling so much that I've gotten completely out of step with the clock, I reset myself. I gradually work my way around the clock, waking and sleeping whenever I feel the need – typically on a 25-hour cycle – until I get back to my starting point (US Central Time in my case). Once I'm there, it takes considerable ...

... willpower to force myself to stay there. After about a week, I usually find I can stick to it. But like most people, I still feel slightly tired and rushed because I'm an hour short each day. Once I retire, I'm going to abandon the clock and switch to my own sleep-wake cycle. I think it'll be much more comfortable and far more productive.

OBJECTION!

"If we had a 25-hour day, wouldn't that mean we'd be on a larger planet with greater mass and gravity, leading to even more back trouble?"

A 25-hour day does imply a larger planet with greater mass and more gravity. But it doesn't necessarily follow. These are separate factors; you can't correlate them. For example, the speed of rotation – and therefore the length of the day – can vary throughout a planet's life. We've already seen that the Earth's speed of rotation is slowing down and its days are getting longer. If our home planet is millions of years older than the Earth – which it undoubtedly is – it may have already slowed down to a 25-hour day. That doesn't mean it's any bigger than the Earth. It might be larger, smaller or the same size. The only way to know for sure is to see it.

But even if we know the planet's size and speed of rotation, we won't necessarily know the strength of its gravity. That would depend on its mass and density. It might be composed of lighter material than the Earth, or have hollow pockets like a sponge, or a much smaller core, any of which would mean it has weaker gravity. On the other hand, it might be denser and heavier than the Earth and have stronger gravity. You'd need to measure these things to find out.

But stronger gravity doesn't automatically mean more back trouble. If we evolved on a planet where the gravity was stronger, we'd have been much shorter, and therefore perfectly able to cope with it. The problems only begin when we're taken out of our natural environment.

When we first arrived on Earth, we were a lot shorter than we are now. We would have been about the same size as the pygmies, who are typically less than 4 feet 11 inches (1.5 meters). The Neanderthals would have been taller than us – which fits with the gravity here being slightly weaker and them having evolved here. Male Neanderthals were typically between 5 feet 4 inches and 5 feet 6 inches (1.64 to 1.68 meters) while the females were between about 5 feet and 5 feet 1 inch (1.52 to 1.56 meters).[2-125a]

If the gravity on our home planet was more than about 5 percent stronger than it is on Earth, we'd be much sturdier, with thicker, denser bones and more muscle strength to support our backs. In fact, we'd have been more like the Neanderthals in that respect – but shorter than modern pygmies.

Interestingly, some people seem to have clock genes that are wired the wrong way around, so they're naturally awake at night and prefer to sleep during the day.[2-126][2-127] I haven't been able to find any figures on this, but it's a big enough issue that pharmaceutical companies are researching ways of switching these people's internal clocks to the regular day-night cycle.

It actually makes good sense that some of us are naturally nocturnal. In ancient times, every population would have needed someone to stay awake and keep watch, keep the fire burning, and ward off intruders and wolves. Today we need night security staff and night-shift workers.

Length of sleep

This has got nothing to do with us being from another planet, but it's an interesting way of rounding off this section.

We sleep less than any other primate.[2-128] We average around 7.5 hours per night, while chimpanzees get 9.7 hours and baboons 10.3 hours. Researchers believe the main reasons for our shorter sleeping period are the increased risk of predators from living on the ground, threats of conflict (because we're inherently violent creatures), and the benefits of increased social interaction.

The animals that sleep the most are little brown bats (19.9 hours), giant armadillos (18.1 hours), pythons (18 hours) and opossums (18 hours).

The animals that sleep the least are giraffes (0.5 to 4.6 hours), horses (2.9 hours), donkeys (3.1 hours), elephants (3.5 hours), sheep (3.8 hours) and cows (4 hours).[2-129]

2.20 We survive, but we don't thrive

It's impossible to be very scientific about this factor as it relies on experiential reports. I'd like to thank the many hundreds of people who reported feeling this way in their reviews, comments, and emails.

They agreed with me that we survive rather than thrive and that we mostly live our lives day to day, getting by – but only barely. Although we've adapted to life on Earth to some degree, and we're continuing to adapt, we're still a long way behind the planet's native creatures.

Bizarrely, many of us live in environments that are bad for us, or at the very least make us feel uncomfortable for part of the year. But worse than that, some of us live in places that make us sick. Most of the Earth's native creatures would die if they tried to do this. So they don't do it; they stick to the environments that suit them best.

As we've already seen, most lizards need to bask in the sun to warm up before they can begin functioning each day. They can't survive in the countries of the far north where temperatures rarely climb above freezing. But you'll find plenty of people there – surviving, struggling, and slowly adapting.

But why do we choose to live in such places when we can live anywhere on the planet? I can accept the fact that we're natural explorers, and we're highly adaptable. And that's fine: there's nothing wrong with exploring these places. But after we've explored them, and we've determined that they're too hot, cold, wet, dry, humid or prone to natural disasters, and they don't make good places to live, we should go home again. It's not as if there's a shortage of space in the planet's most habitable regions.

Most mainstream historians and anthropologists believe we evolved in Africa. There's a long-standing theory that we originated in what is now Ethiopia, although most of the current attention has shifted to Morocco.[2-130] But wherever it was, in Africa or perhaps in the Middle East, that's where we ought to find the majority of people and the largest settlements today. That place ought to be our perfect environment. But it isn't. Not by a long way.

There's certainly plenty of archaeology to be found there. Quite a lot of it dates back more than three million years, although the mainstream scientists would prefer it if I glossed over that. (We'll cover it in Chapter 3.)

About 90 million people live in Ethiopia today, but it's by no means the highly settled, thriving place we'd expect it to be if it was the cradle of civilization. In fact, it's one of the poorest parts of the world. Half the population has no access to clean water, contagious diseases decimate the population, literacy rates are less than 50 percent in many rural areas, and there's a massive shortage of trained health care workers. Things have improved markedly in the last decade, but there's still a long way to go.[2-131]

Ethiopia, and indeed most of Africa and the Middle East, are very definitely not the parts of the world that suit us best. The rest of us might not be thriving, but many of the people who live in those regions are barely even surviving. So what does that mean? Have the scientists got it wrong? Are they covering something up? Did we originate somewhere else? It looks that way.

You might be wondering which countries suit us best. The United Nations publishes an annual list of the best countries to live in, based on things like life expectancy, education, gender equality, and wealth. The current list at the time of writing[2-132] is:

1. Norway
2. Australia
3. Switzerland
4. Germany
=5. Denmark
=5. Singapore
7. The Netherlands
8. Ireland
9. Iceland
10. Canada
11. USA
13. New Zealand
16. UK

It would make much more sense if we'd originated in one or more of these places. And, as we'll see in Chapters 8 and 9, we might well have done. (Sort of.)

> **OBJECTION!**
> "Not thriving is just a consequence of modern living –
> it's our fault for designing it to be that way."
>
> It might seem that way, but take a look at the people in developing countries, or those living in shanty towns and ghettoes in developed countries. With a few notable exceptions, you wouldn't describe their lives as modern. Do they thrive or enjoy their lives? Mostly not, I suspect. They survive, but that's all. Many of them live absolutely miserable lives. They dream of escaping and living modern lives like us. The few that manage it then learn that we're not thriving either. But at least they now stand a better chance of surviving.
>
> And let's also take a look at our ancient pasts, long before what we would call modern times. Did we thrive then? No, we didn't. We barely managed, and we just about got by. Times were hard, the work was hard, the standard of living was appalling, health care was practically non-existent, diseases were rife, there was no health and safety, people died young, there was no such thing as retirement or vacations, and children rarely survived into adulthood. We might not be thriving today, but we thrived an awful lot less back then.
>
> Who among us can say they truly thrive and enjoy their lives today? Not many, sadly.

Of course, there are some exceptions. The lucky few who aren't too hampered by their chronic illnesses, and are retired and wealthy, and have managed to find fulfillment and are living the dream. But that leaves the rest of us, the vast majority, not thriving but surviving, coping, uncomfortable, anxious, slightly depressed, and just about getting by.

2.21 We can't sense natural disasters

Many of the Earth's creatures can sense natural disasters hours or even days before they occur. They can sense things like earthquakes, tsunamis, hurricanes, floods, and so on. If we descended from the ancestors of these creatures, and we're at the top of the evolutionary tree today, we ought to be able to sense them too. After all, the phenomena existed long before any visible life evolved.

But we're completely oblivious to the oncoming danger. The first we know about it is when it hits us – and often kills us. Meanwhile, all the dogs, cattle, birds, toads, and even the spiders have scarpered. They had plenty of advance warning that it was coming and they fled to safety.

So why can't we sense such destructive phenomena when much simpler creatures can? Well, the logical conclusion is that our original home planet doesn't have any natural disasters. It's a reasonable enough assumption. If the crust is one single piece, without any tectonic plates, there can't be any earthquakes or tsunamis. And if there are no seasons and the weather is permanently mild, there should be no hurricanes, cyclones, monsoons, floods or wildfires. So there was never any need for us to develop the mechanisms for detecting them.

2.22 Our poor sense of direction

We lack a decent sense of direction, and this is hard to explain. The Earth has a strong magnetic field, and many native animals use it to find their way around. Salmon can find their way back to their spawning grounds from thousands of miles away. Homing pigeons can find their way back to their roosts from wherever you set them free – even if you take them to another country and keep them in the dark for the whole journey. Migratory birds fly thousands of miles, yet return to the same nesting sites six months later. Even our own pet cats can find their way back to their old homes if they move to new address hundreds of miles away. This both alarms and annoys their owners. Some of them even catch buses and know which ones to catch and where to get on and off. The only cats that can't do this are those that have spent their whole lives indoors. In that case, less than 5 percent are ever seen again.[2-133]

The same can't be said for dogs though. They're poor at finding their way around, but they can memorize a route. They can wander for miles if they're searching for interesting food, looking for stimulation if they're bored, following the scent of a female in heat, or escaping from a frightening or abusive situation. Then they might get distracted, they're not sure where they are, can't remember the way back, and they're hopelessly lost. They're poorly equipped to survive in the wild, and can rarely return home without human help.[2-134] Wolves can find their way around perfectly well, so it seems that dogs must have lost this ability when we domesticated them.

We're aren't too good at finding our way around either, unless it's somewhere we've been before. Most car drivers will recognize the situation where they're driving along an unfamiliar road, desperately looking for street signs that aren't there. Without the signs, we have no idea which way we're supposed to go. We're so bad at it that we had to invent maps and GPS to help us find our way around. And even then, we drive into rivers.

Fortunately, we can always stop and ask for directions. In fact, many anthropologists believe this is why human language evolved.

> Other researchers believe it was our innate desire to gossip that fueled the development of our language.[2-135] They suggest that this led to us developing larger societies than other animals. Most animal groups are no larger than fifty members, but tests have shown that our brains can keep track of 150 people. Gossiping also allows us to keep track of those who are absent from our group, which is something the other animals can't do. There's a theory that our desire to keep track of everyone in our group, and what they're all up to, led to our brains becoming so large.

As we saw earlier, researchers have found a small group of cells in our brains that can detect magnetic fields. We don't seem to be able to use them though, and no one knows why. Some people have suggested that the mechanism may have withered once we developed language and could ask for directions. Another possibility that we looked at earlier is that the magnetic field on our home planet might be much stronger than the Earth's. But there's also an intriguing third option: the mechanism may have been deactivated when our genomes were altered. The big question is: was it accidental or deliberate? Perhaps the extraterrestrials tried to keep us from exploring the rest of the planet. If so, it didn't work.

Like many animals, we can find our way around using the sun and the stars. But it's not an innate skill in us. We can't do it without training – and someone else needs to go first and make a map for us to follow.

There's no evidence that the great apes have any significant navigational skills either, but unlike us, they never stray far from their homes.

All of the migratory species are excellent navigators, of course. But if we include humans on that list – as some people say we should – then we're the sole exception to the rule.

> The latest research suggests that smell might play an important role in navigation too. However, as we'll see later, our sense of smell is becoming weaker and might disappear altogether within the next few generations.

2.23 Lack of defense mechanisms and predators

If we really evolved in East Africa, the big cats that roam there would have been a huge problem for us. We aren't the slightest bit equipped to deal with these beasts. They're stronger and faster than us. They hunt in well-coordinated packs. Some of them can climb trees faster than we can. Some of them can swim just as fast as we can – though they're more likely to just sit and wait for us to come out again. And their teeth and claws are designed for attacking larger, faster, more agile animals than us, and ripping through their flesh and bone.

We have nothing to fight back with except our superior brain power, clubs, and rocks. (And guns of course, but we're talking about when we first arrived.)

This isn't an evolutionary thing. We didn't arrive on Earth equipped with natural defensive mechanisms – sharp teeth, claws, speed, agility, and so on – and then lose them when the need went away. We never had them in the first place.

How could we possibly have survived in East Africa when it was rife with dangerous animals? Bear in mind that the big cat populations have declined significantly. There would have been a lot more of them back in the day, and at some points there might only have been a few hundred of us. The big cats would have outnumbered us, and they could have wiped us out pretty quickly. And there were other predators too, of course, including crocodiles and alligators.

It's far more likely that we originated on a planet where we didn't have any predators. That would explain why we have no way of defending ourselves against them.

We were then brought to Earth and dropped off in various locations around the world that approximately matched the conditions we were used to. We'll look at the most likely locations in Chapters 11 and 12, but one of them appears to have been Israel.

> Israel would have been a wild place too when we first arrived. It had bears, lions, wolves, and leopards. But we quickly hunted most of them to extinction.[2-135a] East Africa, on the other hand, would have been a far more dangerous place.

Early explorers may have ventured from Israel into East Africa. But when they didn't return, or they came back with severe injuries and tales of wild animal attacks, our ancestors probably avoided the place until they'd developed effective weapons. The extraterrestrials may have noticed that the Israeli group was getting wiped out by the big cats. So they may have modified our DNA by inserting genes from the Neanderthals and perhaps even from themselves or other alien species. That would have made us more robust and given us the strength, speed, agility – and above all intelligence – to survive. After that, the big cats didn't stand a chance. And now most of them are either extinct or endangered.

Of course, the fact that we can easily defend ourselves, and we effectively have no predators, is one of the factors that has contributed to our massive overpopulation. We'll look at this in more detail in the next section.

There's another interesting quirk of our design that's worth noting here. We've already seen that our bodies follow the conventional design of herbivores. Yet we have forward-facing eyes that are generally only found in predators. So we're designed to hunt other animals, but we're not designed to eat them.

To me, this suggests that the animals we're meant to hunt (but not eat) are other humans. In other words, we're really efficient soldiers. This fits with our violent natures and war-mongering. We'll look at this in more detail later.

2.24 Overpopulation

A species becomes overpopulated when there's an abundance (or overabundance) of food and a lack of predators. Here on Earth, both of those conditions are met, and our population is spiraling out of control. Biologists say we've long since passed the point where the planet has enough resources to meet everyone's needs. At the time of writing, we apparently passed that point around 2.5 billion people ago – and our population is still growing.

It's not solely due to a high birth rate, of course. More and more of us are living longer, and the death rate is decreasing, particularly in developing countries. When we first arrived, few of us reached thirty years of age. But now that we have abundant food, no predators we can't deal with, and few diseases we can't control, we've infested the planet.

As well as food, we also need drinking water, shelter, fuel, and all sorts of other things that there's a finite supply of. And that means we're depleting the resources future generations will need. We're ingenious and adaptable, though. As one resource dries up, we'll undoubtedly discover or invent something else. But even so, our population can't continue growing forever.

In many countries, it has long been the tradition to have large families, because most children didn't reach adulthood. Most children do survive to adulthood now, yet the tradition continues. The world's governments are waking up to the problem and are starting to legislate against overpopulation. Only China has so far been bold enough to introduce a one-child-per-couple law (in 1979), although this was replaced with a two-child-per-couple policy in 2015.

But our numbers might start falling soon anyway. Male sperm counts have decreased quite significantly over the past few decades.[2-136] This may be a man-made issue, caused by chemicals in our environment, overuse of plastics, hormones from birth control pills in our water, smoking, obesity, and so on. Or it might be Mother Nature trying to take back her planet. Or the aliens might have noticed all the damage we're causing, and they're deliberately reducing our numbers.

People aren't happy about this, of course. Most of us have an inbuilt drive to reproduce. So biologists are trying to counter the problem by developing things like in vitro fertilization (IVF – or test tube babies). But it's an expensive process, and success rates are low.[2-137]

Over the next few decades, we may see more audacious attempts to cull our numbers. In fact, the process might have started already. Our bees are disappearing at an alarming rate. That could have a significant impact on our food supply because we rely on them to pollinate our crops. There have also been several close encounters with asteroids recently, and we didn't even notice some of them until they were already upon us. Either of these things – or something else – could reduce our numbers more effectively than any war, earthquake, tsunami, famine, drought or disease. But we'll no doubt see more of those too.

Back on our home planet, things are probably a lot different. We already suspect the food isn't as nutritious there. That alone would have limited our numbers and lifespan, and probably kept our sperm counts low. With no cold winters to wipe out the pathogens, incurable diseases may be rife, and we might have been on the verge of extinction when the extraterrestrials brought us here. We'll look at this again in Chapter 12.

We've seen in the past that when other species have outgrown the available resources, nature has always found a way of dealing with the problem. That hasn't happened to us yet, but it's probably only because we arrived here so recently.

2.25 Our reaction to carbon dioxide

This is a strange one. Most animals wake up if carbon dioxide levels suddenly rise. This is a useful response as it allows them to flee from things like forest fires. But carbon dioxide has the opposite effect on us: it either sends us to sleep or puts us into a deeper sleep. This is the worst possible response. It's killed millions of people – especially before the advent of smoke alarms. Thousands of people owe their lives to their pets waking them up when their house caught on fire.

No one has been able to explain why we respond this way. I guess it must have something to do with the conditions on our home planet, but I have no idea what it might be.

2.26 Children versus plants

We've already seen that we have the bodies of herbivores. So isn't it bizarre that most of our children hate vegetables? Some of them would apparently prefer to eat nothing at all and starve to death. They have to be coaxed, tricked and threatened into eating their greens. "I can't eat that, it's poisonous!" they yell, spitting out the almost microscopic piece of broccoli you hid in their hamburger.

Studies have found that our children are born with an innate distrust of Earth's plant life.[2-138] This might have made sense in the distant past when many of the plants they encountered would have been poisonous, spiny or covered in toxic hairs. But unless we teach them, they have no idea which ones are safe and which ones aren't. The knowledge isn't inherent in them as it is in other animals. So they play it safe and distrust all of them.

It's ridiculous and bizarre that we don't have an innate sense of which plants are edible and which ones are dangerous. We shouldn't need to be taught this, we should just know it and automatically avoid the dangerous ones. The fact that every other animal can do this from birth suggests that certain plants must be pre-programmed into their brains.

On the other hand, the fact that we *can't* do it suggests that the plants that are pre-programmed into our brains aren't ones that grow on this planet. Since we don't recognize any of them, we have to rely on other people to teach us which ones are safe and which ones are harmful. And we have to develop a taste for the edible ones, which takes time.

When I took my youngest daughter to the park for the first time and tried to lower her onto the grass, she kept raising her legs higher and higher, so she always remained the same distance above the ground. She ended up with her knees next to her ears before I realized what was wrong. She had never encountered grass before, and she was afraid of it.

I had to demonstrate to her that it was safe by sitting on it, running my hand through it and patting the ground. This time she allowed herself to be lowered all the way down, though she was still wary of it at first. Within a minute or two, she was crawling around on it quite happily.

That's true up to a point. But there are plenty of plants we haven't modified – generally the non-food ones – and we still can't tell if they're safe or not. Young children will happily stuff poison ivy into their mouths if we don't keep a close watch on them. (And yet at meal times many of them reject all plant matter.)

Other animals don't seem to have any problems recognizing the plants we've modified. They know which ones they can eat and which ones they can't. And unlike our own children, even the youngest of them automatically avoids the dangerous ones – such as the aforementioned poison ivy.

2.27 Birth issues

Our babies grow way too big inside their poor mothers, who have a devil of a job getting them out. The pelvic opening is barely large enough, and the baby has to rotate in complicated ways to pass through it. If anything goes wrong during this process, both the mother and her baby can suffer serious injury, permanent disability, or even death.[2-139]

No other truly native (non-domesticated*) species has this problem, so something isn't right here.

> This doesn't apply to animals we've modified via selective breeding, such as dogs and cattle. Some breeds of dog are unable to give birth naturally.

In other primates, such as chimpanzees, babies emerge from the birth canal with room to spare. So why don't women have the widest hips possible to allow for easier childbirth? One hypothesis is that our babies only became this large relatively recently. We have no way of proving whether this is true though because their soft skeletons don't survive fossilization. We have no idea what size they were hundreds of thousands of years ago.

> The only other exception amongst the primates is the squirrel monkey. They also have babies with very large heads compared with the size of the females' birth canal, and they can suffer from birth complications just like us.

OBJECTION!
"If women's pelvises were any larger,
they wouldn't be able to walk."

This has been a widely held belief for centuries. But researchers who built an engineering model of the pelvis recently discovered that it could actually be much wider. Women would still be able to walk and run just as well as they can now. They also compared athletes with wide hips against those with narrow ones and found no correlation between hip size and speed or efficiency.[2-140][2-141]

If our babies have only recently become larger, there are a couple of theories about why that might have happened. First, better nutrition; and second, hybridization with another species that increased the size of our brains. We can probably eliminate the better nutrition theory. Babies grow just as large when their mothers live in impoverished countries and are undernourished. In fact, many babies born in developing countries have a higher birth weight than those in developed ones.[2-142]

Historically, women with narrow hips would have died in childbirth. But thanks to modern obstetric care and caesarian sections, even women with unusually narrow pelvises can now give birth safely. As a result, women are unlikely to evolve wider hips than they have now, as there's no natural selection against narrow ones.[2-143] This is an example of how modern medicine is changing human evolution – at least in the developed world.

This hasn't happened in developing countries though. Women in many African nations, where modern obstetric care has been quite limited until recently, have evolved wider hips. This process might be continuing.

Even so, giving birth can still be difficult, exhausting, and excruciatingly painful. In Sub-Saharan Africa, good obstetric care is hard to come by, and women have a 1 in 16 chance of dying during childbirth (compared with 1 in 4,000 in Europe or 1 in 5,400 in the USA). Illnesses or injuries caused by childbirth are also relatively commonplace.[2-144]

The length of the labor is also worth noting. In humans, the average time in labor is about 8 hours, but it can take as long as 18 to 24 hours. In cattle, it's 2 to 3 hours. Apes and chimps take 1 to 2 hours. Dogs take about an hour. Horses take just 30 minutes.

Another issue is that our babies are incredibly helpless when they're born. Chimpanzees are born with brains about 40 percent of their adult size, whereas humans are born with brains just 30 percent of their adult size. Baby chimps are able to cling to their mothers within days of being born.[2-144a] Our babies wouldn't be able to do that for several months; they still have a lot of growing to do once they're born.

But even if the human birth canal was much larger, babies couldn't remain in the womb for any longer. Their energy demands would outstrip their mothers' capacity to supply it.

Interestingly, we have much longer childhoods than other animals. This is thought to be because we need to spend so much time absorbing information and reinforcing the pathways in our brains. This not only gives us our ability to outthink other animals and solve complex problems, but it also allows us to pass information and knowledge to the next generation. And that's what drives our technological development.[2-144b]

You could also argue that we have to learn everything from scratch because everything that's pre-programmed into us – like which plants are safe – is meaningless here.

Let's end this section with a couple of interesting points.

First, it's thought that our heads might become even larger in the future.[2-145]

Second, if you thought we had a bad time giving birth, spotted hyenas have it a lot worse. Don't read this unless you have a strong stomach.[2-146]

2.28 Morning sickness

We don't know why pregnant women get morning sickness. As far as we're aware, it doesn't occur in any other animals. The reason most commonly cited is that it probably flushes out toxins from our diet that would harm the developing fetus.[2-147] But what were the toxins doing there in the first place? This seems to be further proof that the food we eat on Earth isn't what we evolved to eat on our home planet. Our unborn children are rejecting it.

Other hypotheses include:

- A conflict between mother and fetus. That seems unlikely, except where the mother has rhesus negative blood and the fetus is rhesus positive. We'll look at this later in the chapter.

- A sign of genetic interference or incompatibility. That's certainly a possibility. We'll explore this in more detail in Chapter 8.

Experimenting on pregnant women is unethical, so we're unlikely to find a definitive answer soon.

2.29 Concealed ovulation

Human ovulation is entirely concealed, and we're one of the few species where this happens.[2-148] It's impossible to tell whether a woman is ovulating, and even the woman herself generally doesn't know. Her appearance doesn't change. If her smell changes, it's too subtle to notice. And her behavior doesn't change either. Scientists have debated for decades whether men can tell, even subconsciously, when a woman is ovulating, but they haven't come to any definite conclusions so far.

In most other species, the males can easily tell when a female is ovulating. Her body might change – a red, swollen bottom or genital area is common – or she might release pheromones, or engage in mating displays, or alter her behavior in some way.

In most primates, ovulation is semi-concealed. But in chimpanzees, our supposed nearest primate relative, it's clearly advertised.

There's a hypothesis which suggests that women may have begun concealing their ovulation when they became bipeds, because their swollen genitals were no longer on display.[2-149] But this hypothesis isn't fully accepted.

Other hypotheses, which contradict each other, include increasing social bonding, increasing pair-bonding (monogamy), using sex as a reward for bringing food, and reducing infanticide. In this latter hypothesis, the theory is that if a woman has multiple partners, the males competing for her won't kill her children because those children might well be their own.

Another hypothesis suggests that women's bodies mimic a permanent state of ovulation, signaling their sexual readiness at all times. Interestingly, the other mammals that conceal their ovulation (such as dolphins and langurs) are extremely promiscuous.

If we consider this in isolation, concealed ovulation isn't evidence that we're from another planet. It might even be considered something of a red herring. But fully concealed ovulation is rare in primates, and even more so in other mammals. Chimpanzees advertise their ovulation so clearly that even we can't fail to notice it. So I believe it's well worth including alongside the more convincing pieces of evidence.

2.30 Violence

There are only three violent species on Earth: humans, chimpanzees, and dolphins. Violence in this sense means deliberately making trouble and attacking others for the hell of it, rather than fighting over a mate, food or territory, or retaliating when threatened, which many species do.

Let's discuss chimpanzees and dolphins first; then we'll come back to us.

Chimpanzees are known to be extremely violent, and will occasionally kill each other or even wage war. The best-known example of this is the Gombe Chimpanzee War,[2-150] which took place in Gombe Stream National Park in Tanzania between 1974 and 1978. It involved two (and later three) belligerent rival communities.

Six males from one of the groups attacked and killed a male from the other group. Then, over the next four years, they killed *every* male in the other group, as well as one of the females. Two other females went missing, and three were beaten and kidnapped. The victorious group then took over their rivals' territory. But they were forced to relinquish most of it when they were attacked by members of a third group from an adjoining territory.

The attacks were sickeningly violent, with chimps beaten and repeatedly pounded with rocks, strips of skin torn off them, and the victors drinking their victims' blood and eating their young. Researcher Jane Goodall, who was in the park studying the chimps at the time, was shocked and disturbed and took years to come to terms with what she had witnessed.

Dolphins too can be extremely violent killers and rapists. They'll also attack other species, such as porpoise, which they've been known to kill in their hundreds. But these weren't disputes over food or territory. Large groups of dolphins have been seen deliberately hunting, raping and killing porpoise just for fun.[2-151]

But when it comes to violence for the sake of it, humans beat both of them hands down.

Violence has been a feature of human civilization since we first arrived on Earth. It probably was when we lived on our home planet too.

In ancient societies, violence would have been regarded as normal (or at least not pathological). Our ancestors would have been expected to fend off adversaries, secure their desired mate, and get their fair share of the food. If that meant clubbing someone to death, well, that was all part of life's rich tapestry at that time.

Although some capacity for violence was necessary in those days, natural selection meant that the most aggressive members of society got the best mates – and more of them. So they were more successful at reproducing than the less violent ones. Their genes have been passed down to us today, and we still have those traits.

You might think we live in a modern, civilized, peaceful society, but civilization is a very thin veneer. Many of us are just a few missed meals away from reverting to savagery. A day without food would see thousands of us out on the streets rioting and looting, attacking the police, burning cars and shops, storming government buildings, and so on. And, true to form (remember those genes we've inherited), the strongest ones would seize food from the hands of the weaker ones – and probably punch them to the ground for good measure.

But we don't need a good excuse like that to start a riot.[2-152] We'll fight, riot or start wars over things like:

- religion
- racism
- territory and boundary disputes
- oil
- water
- material wealth
- minerals
- spices
- drugs
- taxes
- politics
- anti-government sentiment
- austerity
- poverty

- power
- corruption
- boredom
- drunkenness
- petty arguments
- false beliefs
- misunderstandings
- lies
- jealousy
- envy
- greed
- selfishness
- threats (real or perceived)
- pre-emptive strikes
- perceived shortages
- Black Friday
- sports team rivalry
- terrorism
- gender
- fishing rights
- retaliation
- disrespect
- gang warfare
- rivalry over a potential mate
- declining an offer
- causing offense (whether intended or not)
- revenge
- innate hatred
- ignorance
- seeing the worst in people
- sniping
- spite

- malicious gossip
- failing to hear a warning or answer a question
- … or simply because it's always been the tradition to hate the people in the next village, town, city, school, country, or wherever else, even though they've done nothing wrong.

And then there are the people who don't even need an excuse; the ones who were born (or bred) evil. They'll punch random strangers in the face. They'll shoot random strangers from their car. They'll take what they want, not because they want it themselves but because someone else has it. If anyone stands in their way, they're going down. They'll say things like: "You'll never take me alive," and "If I'm going down, I'm taking everyone else with me."

Interestingly, some biologists believe our violence might have led to something that's given us a massive advantage over other primates: the ability to make a fist.[2-153] This is a controversial theory, but they believe our long, dexterous fingers and uniquely shaped hands, which are useful in so many ways, might have evolved that way so that we can throw a decent punch.

Not everyone is violent, of course. Most people shy away from it, refuse to take part in wars, and suffer from post-traumatic stress disorder (PTSD) if they're forced to join in against their will. It's usually the group leaders and alpha males – and governments – that push everyone else into fighting. Regular citizens are often given no choice, such as when the government introduces compulsory conscription during wartime.

It's also the violent minority that gives the peaceful majority a bad name. And they might have gotten us banished from our home planet.

Earth as a prison planet

There's a popular theory that the Earth is actually our prison and we were brought here as a punishment. According to the theory, we were a violent (murderous, thieving, lustful, vengeful) group of criminals – a menace to society – who were rounded up and transported to a prison planet chosen for its habitable but primitive state and its remoteness from galactic civilization.

The theory suggests that the extraterrestrials who brought us here probably erased our memories, so we had no recollection of the civilizations and technologies we left behind. They then dropped us off on Earth and left us to our own devices. They monitored us to see how we developed and whether our violence genes eventually disappeared. If that happened, perhaps they'd allow us to integrate back into galactic society. But we're still just as violent as we ever were, and we're still here in our prison.

What happened next was probably unprecedented. There were already some hominin civilizations here when we arrived – the Neanderthals, Denisovans, and at least one other species, and perhaps also some older ones such as *Homo heidelbergensis*. The extraterrestrials might have hoped we'd integrate with them. But instead, we may have driven them to extinction.

Then came our unexpectedly rapid development into an advanced society, complete with tools, language, mathematics, science, art, architecture, farming, domesticated animals, and so on. The extraterrestrials may have erased our memories when they brought us here, but they seem to have overlooked the information stored in our genetic memories*. We obviously lived in an advanced society on our home planet. And once we had the foundations in place here on Earth, it didn't take us long to recreate it.

* Our genetic memories are a set of common experiences that are encoded into our genome and are present at birth. They tend to express themselves as feelings rather than knowledge. For example, if one of your parents or grandparents experienced some of the worst atrocities of World War II, you might have an intense fear or hatred of the Germans or the Japanese, even though you've never met one and your relative never spoke about it.

This leads us to the big question: is our innate violence genetic or learned? The answer seems to be both.

Genetic

We seem to be naturally violent right from birth. Babies and young children are innately selfish until they're taught to share and be nice. They'll grab whatever they want, sometimes snatching it out of another child's hand and pushing them if they won't give it up easily.

Learned

Parents who were beaten as children are far more likely to beat their own children. And there's another problem in our society: children are exposed to numerous incidents of violence every day, in cartoons, live action dramas, reality television and news shows. The average American child sees around 200,000 acts of violence on television by the time they reach the age of 18. While it might not cause them to become violent, it desensitizes them to it.[2-154][2-155]

Some people say the 20th century was the most peaceful 100 years since we arrived on Earth. And there were two world wars in that time, as well as numerous lesser ones.

Even when there aren't any wars going on, around 1.6 million people die from violence worldwide each year. About half of that is from self-inflicted violence – suicide – which we'll look at later.

So, is there any sign at all that our imprisonment on this planet is working? Are we becoming even slightly more peaceful? A quick online search makes it clear that we're not. There are forty times more results for anger management classes than there are for assertiveness classes. It will be interesting to compare these results again in years to come. But I'm not expecting them to change much.

I'll leave the last word on our innate violence to the famous British theoretical physicist and cosmologist, Professor Stephen Hawking:

> "It may have had survival advantages in caveman days, to get more food, territory or a partner with whom to reproduce, but now it threatens to destroy us all."[2-156]

2.31 Selfishness and greed

Although we're not the only creatures that exhibit selfishness, most other animals do it as a survival mechanism. But we're *willfully* selfish – and it's all about greed. In our minds, the winner is the one who accumulates the most – and we don't care what it takes to get it. We lie, cheat, steal, put other people at risk, and always look for a fast buck and easy money. There's no such thing as having enough. There can *never* be enough. There's always more – and we want all of it.

This behavior is unique in the animal kingdom, and it's highly destructive.

I hasten to add that not everyone thinks this way. It does seem to be the default though. Those who know what "enough" is, and are willing to settle for it, have usually learned one of life's hardest lessons. They might have witnessed someone destroying themselves or their family through their relentless pursuit of "more." They might have noticed it in themselves and stepped back before it was too late. But many people don't notice it at all – or they just don't care.

If you offer certain businessmen the option of spending more time with their families for the same money that they have now, or less time with their families but an extra digit on their bank balance, they'll take the extra digit. And then they'll push for another digit on top of that. And a fancy car to go with it. And then a boat. And a plane. And then another digit on their bank balance.

There are some interesting examples of selfishness in other animals, such as the flocking, herding and shoaling instinct in sheep and fish. Those on the outside are more likely to get attacked or eaten, so they all try to get on the inside. But of course, this behavior is instinctive rather than deliberate. The intention is that it improves their chances of survival. So it's unfair to call it selfishness, even though that's what it is.

Adélie penguins, which live in the Antarctic, exhibit a fascinating form of selfishness. If they aren't sure whether the sea is safe, they'll shove one of their group into the water and watch what happens. If their chosen victim is all right, the rest of them jump in too.

But we're *motivated* by selfishness and greed, and that leads to things like distrust, envy, spite, hate, and violence. As we saw earlier, some of us are also motivated by a perverse kind of reverse greed, where we don't necessarily want a particular thing, but we don't want the other person to have it either. That sort of thinking can ruin people's lives.

There have been countless financial scandals. The banking industry and Wall Street are often synonymous with greed and excess. This was especially true during the 1980s. Greed is also thought to have caused the global financial crisis that began in 2007 – 2008.

Politicians are frequently involved in financial scandals – among other things. A prime example of this was the UK parliamentary expenses scandal of 2009[2-157] when vast numbers of Members of

Parliament, Ministers and Peers were found to have abused the expenses system. At least eight of them were subsequently convicted of criminal charges, four were imprisoned, and several others resigned, including the Speaker of the House of Commons. Others had to repay thousands, or even tens of thousands of pounds and make public apologies. It destroyed the reputations of many prominent parliamentarians, who not only lost the trust of the British public but lost their parliamentary seats in the 2010 general election.

2.32 Destruction of our resources and environment

We are the only species on Earth that changes (and destroys) its environment through its natural behavior. We're also the only species that recognizes and understands that we're destroying the environment, yet continues to do so.

> **OBJECTION!**
> "Beavers destroy their environment by felling trees, building dams and causing floods."
>
> Tests have shown that the beavers' impact is generally small-scale and localized, and it often has environmental benefits.[2-158] Even when that's not the case, they don't cause harm deliberately or recognize that what they're doing is harmful.

> ## OBJECTION!
> "Elephants damage their environment by felling trees."
>
> When elephants do this, they're actually doing more good than harm. The trees need thinning out, and old and damaged trees need felling so that new ones can grow in their place.
>
> Elephants cause the most harm when they tear down fences around farmland. But they only do this when farmers encroach on their territory or block their routes. We certainly can't blame them for damaging the environment.

There are occasional outbreaks or swarms of creatures that damage the environment – things like locusts or crown-of-thorns starfish, for example. But again, this isn't willful destruction; it's a simple case of overpopulation and an over-abundance of food. Mother Nature has an effective plan for dealing with these outbreaks: the invaders either eat all the food and move on, or they die of starvation, and the environment recovers. Mother Nature hasn't (yet) found a way of dealing with us.

Many people argue that cattle damage the environment, mainly by producing greenhouse gases. But this is another problem that *we* caused. There's only a superabundance of cattle because we breed a superabundance of them. There wouldn't be nearly as many of them if we didn't interfere with nature. So you could argue that it's *us* who are damaging the environment. The cattle are the innocent party here; they have no idea they're doing anything harmful.

You could say the same thing about domestic cats and the huge numbers of wild birds they kill. It's true that they cause tremendous damage, but there wouldn't be nearly as many cats if we didn't insist that (almost) every home should have one. The cats are only doing what comes naturally. We may have domesticated them, but they haven't lost their hunting instincts – and they wouldn't be cats without that anyway.

We've also caused massive problems by taking plant and animal species out of their natural environments. We saw earlier how parasitic worms multiply and grow to enormous sizes when they find themselves in the human gut, which isn't a place they should be. We've done the same thing with species like Japanese knotweed, harlequin ladybugs, cane toads, and many more.

Of course, we did it with the best intentions. For example, we needed to get rid of the aphids that were destroying our plants. Introducing more ladybugs seemed like a natural (and harmless) way of dealing with them. We had no idea they'd also outcompete and decimate the native species. Or perhaps we found some attractive plants while we were traveling, and decided we'd take some home with us. Little did we suspect that once they were outside their natural environment, they'd spread like wildfire and wreak havoc. And in some cases, those attractive plants came with some extra unseen passengers: the larvae of harmful insects. And they ended up in the wrong environment as well.

An article in *National Geographic* magazine (March 2005) confirmed this: "When plant and animal species wind up where they don't belong, they can attack ecosystems and economies with terrible consequences."

So these are cases where we harmed the environment, but it wasn't intentional. But it was still our fault.

You could argue that the same thing applies to us. We've ended up on a planet where we don't belong. And we're causing terrible problems.

OBJECTION!

"Early hunter-gatherer humans were in tune with their environment and did not destroy it."

That's another common misconception. The hunter-gatherers' hunting practices were *highly* damaging.[2-159] They tended to focus on a single species of large mammal or flightless bird and over-hunted it, driving it to extinction or near-extinction – and destroying their own food supply in the process. They then switched to another species and repeated the process.

They also wiped out countless smaller herbivores, which led to the extinction of untold numbers of carnivorous mammals that fed on them.

They also uprooted native plants and deliberately started fires to clear the land. They did this so they could plant the seeds of other species for food – hundreds of thousands of years before the development of agriculture. There's also evidence that they cleared forests at least 30,000 years ago.

So while they might not have *destroyed* their environment, there's no question that they *changed* it dramatically.[2-160]

In the last two hundred years, we've seen the rise of the corporation, consumerism and the throwaway society. We have disposable this and disposable that. We flush things down the toilet without thinking of the consequences. We clear forests. We empty the seas of fish. We strip the planet of its mineral resources.

We have mass advertising, which drives the need to consume and produce more and more, even though we have enough already. We've seen the rise of hoarding. We've also seen the rise of the super-rich. Global corporations have to satisfy their shareholders by continually producing more. They demand big profits at any cost – and never mind what resources they consume or whose lives they disrupt or destroy. They also demand higher yields and less spoilage, and that means using harmful artificial fertilizers, pesticides, and genetic modification.

The seas are choked with plastic and contain ever-increasing amounts of chemicals, and they're becoming more acidic. Coral reefs are getting bleached. Cities are choked with smog, and people can't breathe – Beijing in China is notoriously bad.

Renewable energy schemes give us the means to produce enough power for everyone in the world. But successive governments in several countries have cut the rewards for producing power this way. The oil and coal producers lobby and bribe parliamentarians to support them instead, and they make huge donations to political party funds. So oil and coal get the government's backing.

I should emphasize that most of the damage is being caused by certain wealthy and powerful individuals and their global corporations, not by humans as a whole.

The tipping point

The years 2016 and 2017 seem to have been a tipping point for change, and things are starting to improve. For example, some forward-thinking countries are fully backing renewable energy and are producing significant amounts of it, with the aim of switching to it entirely as soon as they can. The campaigns and efforts to clean up the world's oceans are becoming well supported. Some European countries have said they'll be banning the sale of new non-electric vehicles from 2040. And we're finally starting to make improvements to the environment – though the first step will be to put right all the damage we caused in the first place, and that will take decades.

As far as we're aware, no other species on Earth has deliberately improved its environment, or put right the damage it caused.

You could argue that some creatures improve their environment by eating fruit and berries and excreting the seeds, which helps to spread plants around and fertilizes them. But that's what nature meant to happen. The creatures aren't aware that they're doing it, and you couldn't call it deliberate or willful. Pollination is another example of this. Again, the bees aren't aware that they're doing it; they're just collecting nectar.

Reader's comment:
"The bees are dying out. As they pollinate more than 80 percent of our crops, that could lead to our own extinction."[2-161][2-162]

Well, yes and no. We've recognized the problem, and we've identified what we think are the main issues that cause bees to die. So now we can take steps to address them. But even in the unlikely event that we lose all our bees, we should remember that we're a highly resourceful species and we'll find other ways of pollinating our crops. People are already working on this. One suggestion is that we could use thousands of migrant laborers, who could move from field to field armed with soft paintbrushes. Or we could dust crops with pollen dropped from planes or drones. Or we could build miniature robotic drones to take the place of the bees until their numbers recover.[2-163]

Whatever happens, we aren't going to die if the bees disappear. But you can guarantee that crop prices will rise.

> Reader's comment:
> "We behave more like a virus than a native mammal."
>
> That's true. We're clearly an invasive species that doesn't belong here. Just like a virus, we invade, consume, multiply, destroy and make the planet sick. And antibiotics are useless against us.

Conclusion

Surely Mother Nature would never have created such a destructive species or allowed us to evolve to the point where we knowingly and intentionally cause so much damage. We're obviously in the wrong environment, and our numbers have multiplied out of control. It could well be the case that we didn't evolve naturally at all, on any planet. We could be hybrids created from species from several different places. We'll look at this in more detail in Chapters 5 and 11.

Regardless of where we actually came from, Mother Nature might already have a plan in place to deal with us. Numerous advanced civilizations once existed on Earth and either collapsed or were wiped out. We could be next.

Here's an interesting fact to end this section. Did you know that none of our spacecraft have ever visited the parts of planet Mars that are most likely to harbor life? Astrobiologists imposed a ban on our craft visiting those areas in case we contaminated them.[2-164] We've only been allowed to visit the areas that are *least* likely to harbor life, or that may have harbored life in the past but couldn't possibly harbor it now. No wonder we haven't found anything.

That could be about to change though, because they've finally agreed to allow a craft to visit one of those areas. The joint European and Russian *ExoMars* mission[2-165] is planned for 2020. It will carry a sterile rover that will explore and analyze a region of Mars with a high potential for life.

The issue of contamination also applies when we visit other planets.[2-166] But the aliens who brought us here obviously had no qualms about contaminating the Earth. Perhaps they saw how well we fitted in on our home planet, and how small we were in number, and decided we wouldn't cause any harm if they brought us here.

We now know that they unwittingly added a massively destructive and invasive species to the Earth's ecosystem. We've done similar things ourselves, so it was an easy mistake to make. But the planet would be in a much better shape if they'd left us where we were.

> There is, of course, the possibility that our own planet was dying and we'd have become extinct if they'd left us there. So they may have done us a favor.

2.33 Super-intelligence

When the first hominins appeared on Earth about 5.8 million years ago, their brains were about the same size as a modern chimpanzee's. They stayed that size for the next 5 million years.

Something then triggered a massive growth spurt, beginning about 800,000 years ago and ending about 200,000 years ago. During that time, hominin brains tripled in size and became much more complex.

The hominins we're talking about here, by the way, aren't modern humans but *Homo erectus, Homo heidelbergensis, Homo rudolfensis, Homo ergaster, Homo neanderthalis* (the Neanderthals), *Homo denisova* (the Denisovans) who were the Neanderthals' Asian relatives, and probably one or two other species. Their brains ended up being about the same size as ours, or perhaps even slightly larger.[2-167]

When we appeared towards the end of this period, we already had "full-size" brains. In fact, like the other hominin species, they might have been a little larger than they are now.

> **OBJECTION!**
> "We evolved from one of those earlier hominin species, so of course we would have the same size brains as them."

But we didn't evolve from any of those species. We certainly didn't evolve from the Neanderthals or Denisovans. There was a long-held belief that we descended from *Homo erectus*, but that's now been disproven. The only species we could have realistically descended from is *Homo heidelbergensis*, but even then, the dates don't really tie up and their skulls are completely different from ours. We'll look at this in more detail in Chapter 8. There's also a revised timeline of human evolution in Chapter 12 which explains how everything fits together and where the gaps are.

Some researchers believe the 600,000-year growth spurt in the hominins' brains may have been caused by dramatic climate change. It may have forced them to interact with their surroundings, and with each other, in new ways. The climate was definitely changing quite significantly around that time, so it's a reasonable supposition. But of course, it begs another question: if the hominins' brains needed to expand to cope with the changing climate, why didn't the brains of all the other creatures on Earth also expand?

It's remarkable that the hominins' brains tripled in size in such a short period. If it had happened naturally via natural selection and evolution, it should have taken several million years. It looks as if they may have had some external help – or interference. The extraterrestrials who brought us here might have manipulated their genomes too. Or perhaps they carried out their first hybridization experiments on the hominins before they tried them on us. We'll look at both of those things in more detail in Chapter 5.

2.34 DNA anomalies

Scientists working on the Human Genome Project and other DNA projects have discovered an extra 223 genes (out of a total of about 20,000) in us that don't appear in any other species. Some of these orphan genes (or ORFans)[2-169] may have arisen from non-coding sequences of DNA. This is known as de novo origination. Another possibility is duplication and divergence during a period of rapid evolution. Or they could have come from natural or artificial horizontal transfer from another organism. That organism may have been viral, bacterial or extraterrestrial – though, of course, the mainstream science papers never mention the extraterrestrial possibility.

We can immediately rule out the viral option though. We've already mapped the parts of our genome that came from viruses, and none of the 223 orphan genes were among them. But we did find the complete genome of a functioning virus hidden in there. There are more details about this in Chapter 7, where we'll take a closer look at DNA.

Hybridization theory

Some (non-mainstream) geneticists believe that aliens may have spliced the 223 orphan genes into the genome of one of the Earth's native hominins, such as *Homo erectus* or *Homo habilis*. Those genes may have come directly from the aliens themselves. But some researchers claim there's evidence of *twenty* extraterrestrial species in our DNA.

The geneticists believe this hybridization process created an instant leap from the native hominin to modern humans, with no missing link in between them. We'll come back to the lack of a missing link in the fossil evidence later.

There's plenty of evidence of external interference in our genome. For example, there are hundreds of scars where sections of genes have been duplicated from other genes, had their heads or tails stripped off (which normally disables them), had sections added or removed, or been joined onto parts of other genes. These cuts and splices have been present in our genome for hundreds of thousands of years.

Our own scientists can perform these same processes in their labs today, but they've only had the technology to do it for the last few years.

In the previous section, we looked at the rapid growth of our brains. It's worth taking a closer look at the gene known as HYDIN2.[2-170] This gene is unique to us, and it bears considerable evidence of scarring and external manipulation. This has been of enormous benefit to us though. Whoever carried out the manipulation knew exactly what they were doing.

HYDIN2 is a copy of the HYDIN gene, which is found in many animals and is particularly common in the neurons in the brain. Our HYDIN2 gene has had its head and tail stripped off, and the head has been replaced with a section of the same length from a different gene. This has made HYDIN2 much more efficient than HYDIN. It's replaced HYDIN in our brains, and sped up the actions of the neurons, meaning we can process information – and therefore *think* – much faster than other species.

Another gene that's unique to us is FOX P2, which is also known as the language gene. Some geneticists believe the aliens gave us this gene so we could communicate with them.

I'm not saying this is what happened, but let's just imagine for a moment that the aliens have very large brains. Let's also assume that their large brains are encoded in some of those 223 genes they inserted into one of Earth's native hominins. That could explain the rapid growth in brain size that we saw earlier. Given the large size of their brains, it would make sense if the aliens also had wide pelvises. But for some reason, they either didn't give us the genes for those, or they didn't work in us. That could explain why we have so many problems giving birth.

Many of the factors we've looked at in this chapter, including our intolerance to bright sunlight and so on, could also be explained by hybridization. For example, the native hominins had heavy brows to shield their eyes, but when the 223 genes were spliced in, our craniums grew larger, the bones became thinner, and the heavy brows disappeared. Clearly, the aliens we received the genes from don't have heavy brows. That's probably because they didn't need them on their world. Unfortunately, we *do* need them here on Earth, and it makes no sense that we don't have them.

If we accept that the hybridization theory is correct, that means we're *mostly* native to Earth, but some important parts of us are not. It's also apparent that the hybridization process didn't turn out quite the way it should have done. Since alien abductions are still happening, it may be the case that we're a work in progress and not yet the finished article.

OBJECTION!

"Humans share 99 percent of their DNA with chimpanzees, so coming from another planet or being hybrids of aliens doesn't make sense."

Well, yes and no. Chimpanzees share 96 to 98 percent of their genes with us, but we only share 90 percent of our genes with them. But genes make up less than 2 percent of our DNA. If we look at our DNA as a whole, including the non-coding part, we only share about 85 percent of it with chimpanzees. And some sources say it's just 79 percent.[2-171] We'll come back to this later in the book.

The non-coding part of our DNA used to be called "junk DNA" because geneticists assumed it had no purpose. But we now know it performs all sorts of vital functions. We'll look at this in more detail in Chapter 7.

Here's an interesting point to end this section. The oldest-known *Homo sapiens* (modern human) DNA has been confirmed to be 400,000 years old. Yet mainstream scientists "know" the first modern humans evolved no more than 300,000 years ago. They call the discovery of 400,000-year-old DNA "irritating" because they can't explain it and it doesn't fit their theory of human evolution.[2-172]

That means they're suffering from cognitive dissonance,[2-173] which is the inability to reconcile two apparently contradictory facts. Their "solution" is to cling to their broken theory that we evolved 300,000 years ago. They'd prefer it if everyone just shut up about the 400,000-year-old DNA.

By the way, until June 2017 the theory of human evolution stated that we first appeared 195,000 years ago. Once the mainstream scientists had finally accepted that we'd been around for at least 300,000 years, archaeologists revealed something astounding: they'd been finding evidence which proved this for decades. They'd discovered 300,000-year-old human remains and artifacts all across Africa, but ignored it (or were *ordered* to ignore it) because "it was wrong." Of course, we now know it wasn't wrong at all. I'm staggered (and rather angry) that they ever thought it was. Decades of evidence will now have to be reassessed and textbooks rewritten.

> I wonder how long it will take them to accept that we've been around for at least 400,000 years?

2.35 Rhesus negative blood

Most people have rhesus positive blood. That means their red blood cells have a substance known as D antigen on their surfaces. About 15 percent of people don't have this antigen, and their blood is said to be rhesus negative. The origins of rhesus negative blood are unknown, but it's also commonly known as "alien blood" so that might provide a clue.

The percentage of people with rhesus negative blood varies around the world. It's rare in some places, but most common in the Basque region of Spain and France, where 30 percent of the population has it. Whether there's any genetic advantage in having (or not having) rhesus negative blood is currently unknown. Some researchers suspect that those with this type of blood might be more resistant to parasitic diseases such as toxoplasmosis, but they haven't confirmed it yet.[2-174]

The D antigen could have been lost through genetic mutation or external manipulation. Some researchers have suggested it could have been lost through disease, though no disease has been identified that can strip an antigen from your blood and modify your genes so it isn't passed on to your children. Given the suspicion that its absence protects us from parasites, it could be further evidence that our genome was tampered with to make us more resilient.

If we'd all evolved from a single African ancestor, as mainstream scientists insist, then we'd all be biologically compatible. But we're not, and our scientists can't explain why. People with rhesus negative blood aren't fully compatible with those with rhesus positive blood.

If a woman with rhesus negative blood becomes pregnant with a rhesus positive child, and any of that child's blood gets into her bloodstream, her body will reject any subsequent children that also have rhesus positive blood. Antibodies in her blood will attack the fetus's red blood cells, causing hemolytic disease which leads to anemia and jaundice.

To stop this from happening, women with rhesus negative blood are routinely given an "Anti-D" injection during their first pregnancy. This mops up any D antigens in their bloodstreams that may have crossed over from the fetus, and prevents them from becoming sensitized to it.[2-175]

Since we're not all compatible, this suggests that we aren't just one single species. It also lends credence to the fact that we may be a hybrid race.

You can read more about this in Robert Sepehr's book *Species with Amnesia: Our Forgotten History*.

> Although the rhesus factor is named after rhesus monkeys, it only occurs in humans. Rhesus monkeys were used in the experiments which identified the factor and tested its properties, but they don't actually have the factor themselves.

Interestingly, as well as being nicknamed alien blood, rhesus negative blood is also sometimes known as royal blood. There's reported to be a very high incidence of it in members of the royal families of Western

Europe, and especially in the British royal family. We don't have access to their medical records, so we can't confirm if this is true.

Of course, if you put the two nicknames together you could easily come up with the hypothesis that the original kings and queens of Europe might have been aliens. Unsurprisingly, plenty of people have said exactly that.

2.36 Semi-aquatic features

As we saw earlier, we're the only creatures on Earth that have subcutaneous fat – apart from the marine mammals. So let's take a closer look at the aquatic ape hypothesis.[2-176a][2-177]

This hypothesis suggests that we started out as land-based mammals. Food became scarce on the land for some reason; perhaps a volcanic eruption blanketed the planet in dust and clouds for an extended period. So we began foraging for food in the sea, lakes, rivers, streams, swamps, and other bodies of water. Eventually, we started spending more time in the water than we did on land, and we supposedly adapted to this by becoming semi-aquatic around ten million years ago. Once food became abundant on the land again, we came back out of the water permanently. But we still have the remnants of those aquatic adaptations today.

- It explains our hairlessness, which we have in common with many marine mammals.

- It explains our body shape, which is streamlined for swimming and diving.

- It explains our descended larynx.

- It explains our ability to voluntarily control our breathing.

- It explains our diving reflex,[2-178] which allows us to tolerate a lower level of oxygen when under water and stay underwater for longer. As soon as we put our heads under cold water, our diving reflex reduces our heart rate by 10 to 30 percent. (With training, you can reduce it by 50 percent.) It also constricts the blood vessels that supply our muscles, reducing the blood flow to them while maintaining the oxygen supply to our brain and heart. During the deepest dives, it allows water and blood plasma to leak into our chest cavity and lungs, protecting them from pressure damage. The liquid is quickly reabsorbed when the pressure drops again.

- It explains the size and complexity of our brains, which are much more akin to aquatic mammals than land-based ones.

- It explains why our brains need DHA (a type of omega 3 fatty acid) that's abundant in seafood but rare on land. Our ancestors could only have experienced the rapid growth in brain size we noted earlier if they'd eaten a lot of seafood.

- It explains babies' affinity for water. They can swim underwater almost from birth, and long before they can walk. Baby apes can't swim at all.

- It explains our affinity for water.[2-178a] Most of us love coastal areas, we love looking at water, we love living near it, and we like swimming. Seaside resorts are hugely popular. But apes *hate* water. All it takes to confine them to a particular area is a shallow moat that they could easily wade across. They'll never cross it.

- It explains why we prefer to bathe in water, rather than grooming or taking dust baths. Wild apes never bathe in water.

- It explains why water births are easier and safer than the conventional method of lying on a bed.

- It explains our face-to-face mating position, which is unknown in other land-based animals, but common in marine mammals.

- And it explains why our hearing becomes ten times better under water. The range of frequencies we can hear increases from 20,000 hertz to 200,000 hertz, which is better than some native marine mammals.

> When our heads are under water, we hear via bone conduction rather than air pressure.

The aquatic ape hypothesis also explains:

- Our bipedalism, which forces us to walk upright on land. As we saw earlier, this puts an enormous strain on our spines. But on the other hand, it makes us good swimmers.

- The vestigial webbing that sometimes occurs between our fingers and toes.

- Our kidney structure, which is closer to that of marine mammals than to the apes'.

- Vernix – the waxy coating that covers our babies when they're born. This is unknown in other land mammals but occurs in several sea mammals.

But there's also some significant evidence to refute this hypothesis:

- The structure of our skin is different from the marine mammals. It becomes waterlogged and starts to disintegrate if it's exposed to water for prolonged periods. You can see the beginnings of this if you examine your fingertips after a few minutes in the bathtub.

- All of today's hairless marine mammals evolved tens of millions of years ago, not ten million years ago.

- Although our kidneys are similar in structure to those found in marine mammals, they function differently. Ours are far less efficient at removing salt from our blood. Hence the constant appeals from doctors to reduce our salt intake. In humans, sweating is a more efficient way of getting rid of excess salt.

- We don't know whether any other land mammals can voluntarily control their breath under water.

- It doesn't explain why we have hair on our heads and pubic regions, but that may have appeared after we'd come back out of the water.

- It also doesn't explain why apes have hair and we don't.

As we saw earlier, the first hominins probably split from the ape branch of evolution about 7.2 million years ago. If we'd evolved from semi-aquatic mammals 10 million years ago or more, as the hypothesis suggests, then the apes must have too. They should, therefore, exhibit these same vestigial semi-aquatic characteristics. But they don't. This suggests that we aren't related to the apes at all. Our semi-aquatic period must have occurred back on our home planet.

A related hypothesis suggests that we became semi-aquatic much more recently – within the last three million years, and after the first *Homo* species had emerged.[2-179]

And there's a third hypothesis which suggests that rather than our ancestors becoming semi-aquatic for a time, the aliens might have spliced DNA from a marine mammal into one of the ancient hominins. Why they might have done this is a mystery, but it fits the evidence we've seen in this section.

There is, of course, a fourth hypothesis, which is that we were created by God or some other intelligent designer. We'll come back to this later in the book.

Mainstream scientists reject these hypotheses, mainly on the basis that the evidence is absent from the fossil record. But the fossils *do* exist and can be found quite widely in coastal areas. As so often happens, the scientists have chosen to ignore the evidence because it doesn't fit their theories.

2.37 The shape of our skulls

Our skulls look nothing like those of our supposed ancestors. You can see the evidence for yourself if you look at the official timeline of human evolution.[2-180][2-181][2-182] Even the skulls of our "closest" hominin relatives, *Homo erectus*, *H. heidelbergensis*, and the Neanderthals and Denisovans, look nothing like ours. They're different in just about every respect and have heavy brow ridges. On the other hand, they look very much like the hominins that preceded them. There's no question that these species are related and belong on Earth. But there's every reason to believe we do not.

Chins

We're the only creatures on Earth that have chins.[2-183] The chin is a bony protrusion at the bottom of our lower jaw. None of the earlier hominins had them; they had inward-sloping lower jaws, just like every other creature. No one can explain how we came to have chins or what their purpose is.

2.38 Lack of a penis bone (baculum)

All of the great apes, including chimpanzees and gorillas, have penis bones, as do most mammals. The only primates that don't have them are spider monkeys, wooly monkeys, and of course humans.[2-184] We have to maintain rigidity using blood pressure alone.

So, why don't we have them? No one knows for sure, but as usual, there are several theories:

- If a male without a penis bone can maintain rigidity, it proves he's a good candidate to mate with: he's not too old, sick or stressed (or drunk).[2-185]

- Creatures with penis bones engage in infrequent but lengthy mating sessions. Those without them engage in more frequent sessions but of fairly short duration.

- We didn't need penis bones once we switched to being monogamous. Lengthy mating sessions are intended to prevent the female from sneaking off and mating with someone else. If the male can be sure she won't do that, mating can be a much quicker affair.[2-186] That, of course, leads to another question. Why did we become monogamous? A popular theory suggests that it significantly reduced our chances of acquiring sexually transmitted diseases.[2-187a]

> The aquatic ape hypothesis offers no clues on this. Some marine mammals have penis bones, and some don't.

Happily, the lack of a penis bone means we can bend our penises into all sorts of shapes and angles, even when they're fully erect. That means we can achieve around 250 sexual positions,[2-188][2-189] while all the other land mammals have to settle for just one.

On a related note, although all male mammals have prostate glands, only humans and dogs get prostate cancer.[2-190][2-191]

2.39 Gender identification issues: non-binary

Thanks to recent social changes, people now feel more confident about revealing who they really are. And this has brought to light a considerable (and growing) number of people who are non-binary or intersex. That means they identify as being neither male nor female, or both male and female, or they're biologically neither male nor female.[2-192][2-193][2-194]

It's actually much more complicated than that because there are different types and degrees of being non-binary or intersex. Some people clearly look male or look female (their primary sex characteristics), and they have the appropriate reproductive organs (gonadal sex characteristics) for the way they look. Others look male or look female, but their reproductive organs are less well defined. And some are difficult to classify as male or female from their appearance alone, and their reproductive organs might tell you nothing. If you filled a room with non-binary people, they'd all be slightly different in this respect.

Biologically speaking, there are five components to consider: your chromosomal sex, your gonadal sex, your primary sex characteristics, your sex hormones, and your secondary sex characteristics. These usually all line up in the way we'd expect them to. But that isn't always the case.

Emily[2-195] is non-binary, but chooses to identify as female. Most non-binaries choose to identify as either male or female because life would be even more difficult if they didn't. "Neither" or "Both" aren't recognized options yet. Let's look at Emily's biological profile:

- Chromosomal sex: male

- Primary sex characteristics: female

- Gonadal sex: indeterminate

- Sex hormones: indeterminate – but she takes female hormone replacement pills

- Secondary sex characteristics: would be indeterminate if she didn't take the hormone pills

But even when your biological characteristics all line up, that doesn't necessarily mean you identify as a member of that gender.

There are two stages during a fetus's development where it gets flooded with sex hormones. One of these occurs right at the start of its development, and determines its primary sex characteristics. The second stage occurs later in its development, and this time it's the brain that's affected. It determines which gender you identify with. Usually, this hormone is the same as the first one.

But sometimes the second hormone is the one for the opposite gender, and this is one of the leading hypotheses to explain gay, lesbian, and transgender development.

Very occasionally, the first or second (or both) waves of hormones don't happen at all, or the dosages are smaller than they should be. This may explain what's happened to non-binary or intersex people. But is it a developmental defect or is there a particular reason for it? Could there be a biological advantage? No one knows at this stage, though it's hard to see any advantage in it.

Some non-binaries have said they didn't realize they were non-binary initially; they thought they were transgender. Some of them had hormone treatment and even surgery to become the gender they thought they were meant to be. Then they realized they weren't really that gender either. They were just *themselves*.

Most non-binaries struggle to recognize their place in society. Many of them have found they're not covered by Lesbian, Gay, Bisexual, and Transgender (LGBT) rights, and many countries don't even have *those* rights. Some LGBT rights groups don't allow non-binaries to join. Some are actively hostile towards them.

Many non-binaries, especially the younger ones, reassess the gender they most identify with at intervals throughout their lives. They might decide to stay as they are, or they might decide that at a certain point it would be better to identify as the opposite gender.

The social climate in developed countries has only recently allowed people to reveal their true selves. Gender identity clinics are rare, but the few that exist have reported a dramatic rise in the number of non-binary people coming forward. It's probably safe to say that most of them haven't come forward yet.

There seems to be more questions than answers. We don't know how many cases there are. We don't know if it's a recent phenomenon or one that's as old as our species. And we have no idea whether it's more (or less) predominant in certain races or in certain parts of the world. It seems to be unique to humans, but we haven't really been looking for it in other animals.

Some animals can appear to change their genders, or they deliberately mimic the behavior of the opposite gender. Some fish can actually switch genders. For example, all clown anemone fish begin life as males. If a female dies, the dominant male can become female, and another male takes over his former role.[2-196] But is this a conscious act, or is it instinctive, or is it a purely biological or chemical process that they have no control over? We have no idea. But these are things that benefit their long-term survival. They're unlikely to bear any relation to the issue of non-binary or intersex humans.

A related issue is pansexuality[2-197] or omnisexuality, where someone is attracted to another person regardless of their gender or gender identity. Whether this is the same as bisexuality is hotly debated. Again, more people are coming forward with this issue, probably because they now feel more secure about doing so, rather than there being more cases.

OBJECTION!
"This is just a random developmental defect.
It does not mean we came from outer space."

We have no idea what it is. But it affects a surprisingly large number of people that we didn't previously know about. We also know that our genome has been externally manipulated and things haven't always gone to plan. This might be another one of those instances. For example, the extraterrestrials may have altered a section of our DNA to increase the size of our brains, but accidentally caused our sex hormones to occasionally misfire during our development.

Interestingly, just before this book went to press, Transport for London said they would no longer be using the phrase "ladies and gentlemen" in their announcements on the London Underground. They said they wanted all passengers to feel welcome, so they were replacing it with the gender-neutral phrase "hello everyone."[2-198]

2.40 Our *real* missing link

When you hear the words "missing link" you probably think of the immediate ancestor of both hominins and apes. This may have been *Graecopithecus freybergi*, which was discovered in 2017.[2-199] This ape-like species is believed to have lived throughout the eastern Mediterranean around 7.24 million years ago. The discovery is currently considered controversial. But if it's eventually proven, it will mean that the best-known missing link has been found.

But that's not the missing link I'm referring to. There's another missing link later in our timeline that should connect us to the other hominins. This missing link is much more important than the ape–hominin link because it suggests we didn't originate on Earth.

Let's look at the evidence. The remains of modern humans have been found in Australia and Israel, dating from around 400,000 years ago. Human DNA dating from that period has also been found in Spain. This suggests that our missing link must lie somewhere between 400,000 and 500,000 years ago.

> Interestingly, the famous Piltdown Man forgery[2-201] was said by its creator to be 500,000 years old. That would have fitted neatly into the space in our timeline that we're talking about here. The only problem is that Piltdown Man was meant to be the ancestor of both apes and humans. So it was about 7 million years out.

Several hominin species would have been present between 400,000 and 500,000 years ago. The Neanderthals and the Denisovans were definitely here. Their probable ancestor, *Homo heidelbergensis*, was here too, and perhaps also *Homo erectus*, although there's some doubt about the dates there.

If we'd evolved on Earth, our immediate ancestor would probably be the same as the Neanderthals' and Denisovans' ancestor: *Homo heidelbergensis*. But if we compare the skulls of *H. heidelbergensis* (and *H. erectus*) with those of modern humans, we can see at a glance that there's no way we could have descended from them. They're very different in shape, size, structure, and weight. Their skulls are much more robust than ours, with pronounced brows, and inward-facing lower jaws. If we handle them, the weight difference is immediately obvious: ours are much lighter. Our craniums are much rounder, and the bone is thinner. The sinus structures are totally different too.

There's such an enormous difference between their skulls and ours that I doubt one missing link would be enough. It would have needed several intermediate stages to get to us. We haven't found any signs of any intermediate species, either as physical remains or as remnants within our DNA. In any case, there wouldn't be room for an intermediate species in our timeline.

So we can conclude that:

- the missing link(s) between the native hominins and modern humans never existed

- the leap from the hominins to ourselves is too great to have occurred in a single jump

- we must, therefore, have evolved on another planet or we must have been artificially created via hybridization

2.41 Depression and unhappiness

Take a break from reading for a moment and look at the expressions on the faces of the next ten people who pass you. Choose people you don't know or recognize. What do you see?

I just tried this myself. Four of them looked completely blank and expressionless. Another four looked gloomy with down-turned mouths. They seemed to be having terrible lives. One looked as if he was about to burst into tears. And one had a haunted look. Shiny happy people, they were not. Ten out of ten looked (and probably were) unhappy or depressed. And I'd say there was more than a touch of anxiety in the mix too.

You'll find pretty much the same situation all over the world. There are a few exceptions, of course. But I'd say that significantly more than 90 percent of adults are generally unhappy, with a large subset of them being seriously unhappy or clinically depressed.

OBJECTION!

"This is a result of modern living. We brought it upon ourselves. We spend hours commuting to jobs we hate, we don't get enough sleep, we eat junk food, and even though we hate our jobs, we get upset if we lose them."

That's a reasonable point, and it's something most of us can identify with. Having said that, the ten people who passed me during the above exercise were heading into town in the middle of a weekday afternoon. I'm not sure any of them had jobs. I'd say they were retired, unemployed, sick, or stay-at-home parents. I have no idea whether they were getting enough sleep or ate junk food. And I'm not sure that it would have made much difference to them.

As far as I can tell, there has never been a time in our history when the majority of us were happy. The wealthy and the upper classes – which are often the same thing – have generally made a point of enjoying themselves. But almost everyone else seems to have a pretty gloomy life, interspersed only occasionally with brief moments of joy.

Many workers say they'll only be truly happy after they retire. But if you speak to retirees, many of them are gloomier than those who have to work for a living. Quite a few of them die within a year or so of their retirement. It was the work that was keeping them going – even though they may have hated it.

There could be any number of reasons for this:

- the death of their partner and friends means they're lonely

- their children and grandchildren rarely visit

- old age frightens them

- they don't recognize themselves in the mirror any more

- parts of them are starting to fail

- they're losing their eyesight and hearing and feel cut off from the world

- they ache all the time, their joints are stiff, and they feel the weather more

- they worry about who would take care of them if they were seriously ill

- they're upset that their pension fund wasn't as large as they'd expected, and they don't have the money to do the things they'd wanted to do

- they're bored

- they feel useless because they're no longer contributing anything to the world

- they feel that their time has passed

- they regret wasting so much of their lives

- and so on

And on top of all of that, we age horribly. We'll come back to this point later in the chapter.

> "Life is too long to be comfortable and too short to achieve anything useful." (Anonymous)

Other species don't seem to suffer any of these problems, or at least not to the same degree. Dogs are generally happy unless they're ill or lonely or mistreated, or their companion or owner has died – then they can get depressed. Primates will mourn the loss of one of their group, but they're generally happy. Dolphins always seem to be happy – even when they're killing and raping things. We assume whales are generally happy too, though we have no idea why they sometimes beach themselves.

Most researchers don't believe they're doing it with the intention of killing themselves.[2-202][2-203]

There's a popular expression in Britain: "as happy as a pig in muck." You can watch seals and penguins sliding down ice slopes over and over again – they definitely know how to have fun. Elephants and giant pandas slide down mud slopes too – again, definitely happy. Birds flock around in the sky, weaving in and out and calling to each other – happy as Larry. (Although some researchers believe they might actually be yelling abuse at each other, at least some of the time.)

> Many animals become extremely depressed and unhappy if they're confined to small enclosures, chained up, or mistreated. But that's a different issue. We're focusing here on animals living in their natural environments.

Even our own children are mostly happy – if they're raised in happy homes and aren't abused or bullied. But when they reach adulthood, the realities of life hit them. Nobody ever tells them (or warns them) about this, of course, but somehow, they all succumb to it.

So why are we all so unhappy? It's probably because the Earth isn't our natural environment and the conditions here don't really suit us. We feel out of place, and we have done ever since we first arrived. We've never been able to settle down and call this place "home." After thousands of generations, that feeling has now become deeply ingrained in all of us.

Interestingly (but no less depressingly), Lego, the Danish toy company, has started making its mini-figures (minifigs) "more realistic" by making them look sadder and angrier.[2-204]

It's enough to drive you to drink. Speaking of which …

2.42 Self-destruction

We're the only species on Earth that seems determined to destroy itself. There are constant wars, of course – but there are probably wars on other planets too. But many people smoke cigarettes even though it clearly says on the packet that doing so will kill them. Many of us drink far too much alcohol, even though we all know what the limits are and what it will do to us if we continue. Some of us stuff ourselves with junk food to the point of becoming morbidly obese – and then we still keep stuffing it in.

Why do we do this? Well, it's almost certainly linked to the depression and unhappiness we looked at in the previous section. Because we're on the wrong planet, and we don't feel we belong here, our lives hold little meaning. We don't look after our bodies because we don't care enough about life – ours or anyone else's.

Here are ten pointers to human self-destruction
(courtesy of LiveScience.com)

- Gossiping
- Gambling
- Stress
- Body modification
- Bullying
- Clinging to bad habits
  (smoking, drinking, eating to excess, and so on)
- Cheating
- Stealing
- A craving for violence
- Lying

So where is all of this leading us? Probably not to our extinction. But most researchers believe we'll never reach our true potential as a species – because we'll make damned sure we won't. We clearly have no business being here.

You can easily recognize self-destructive behavior[2-205][2-206] in the people around you – and perhaps in yourself too:

- They over-eat or under-eat to the extent that it becomes a medical issue

- They have a self-defeating mindset

- They fail to take action

- The push people away

- They refuse offers of help

- They make unnecessary self-sacrifices

- They portray themselves as incapable or incompetent

- They self-harm

- They deliberately harm others

- They abuse alcohol and drugs

- They hide from their emotions

- They suffer bouts of self-pity

- They spend too much

- They neglect themselves, both physically and mentally

- They sabotage relationships

- They live recklessly

- They commit social suicide

- They commit actual suicide

We've already seen that many of these behaviors are linked to depression, but that might not be the full picture. There's a Freudian argument which states: "People have an innate death drive that impels them to pursue their own downfall and death."[2-207] How can that possibly be normal? No other species has this death drive. But that's probably because they all belong here and feel perfectly at home.

2.43 Feeling out of place

Do you ever have the feeling that you're in the wrong place? I don't just mean the town or city or state or country you're in. If you moved somewhere else, you'd still feel the same way. The feeling that we don't really belong here is quite pervasive.

According to mainstream theories, we evolved in Africa – supposedly somewhere around modern-day Ethiopia. So that should be the one place on the planet that feels most like home. But I've been there and, believe me, it *really* doesn't.

Do you ever look up at the stars at night and think that it feels more like home up there than it does down here? If you do, you're not alone.

Many of us have a prevailing feeling that we don't belong here and something "just isn't right."

> ### OBJECTION!
> "I'm sorry, but this is just nonsense.
> No one I know feels this way."
>
> Have you actually asked them? After the first edition of this book was released, thousands of people sent me emails or left comments and reviews on websites and forums. Many of them said this was *exactly* how they felt, and it came as a relief to know they weren't the only ones who felt this way. This is what we call empirical evidence.
>
> Some people described it as the type of sadness you feel when you're missing family you haven't seen in a while. Others said it felt like a constant but distant sorrow. A longing for … something … that can never be satisfied. A relationship you yearn for, but you know in your heart it can never be fulfilled. Or the feeling of melancholy that comes from knowing you'll never see your true home again.

Most of us feel a great affinity for our homes – whether that's a building or the town, city, state or country where it is. We feel a sense of nostalgia or longing if we're away from it for very long. It even has a name: homesickness. But these places aren't our *real* homes, they're just our *Earth* homes. They're the best we can do in the circumstances. Our *true* homes aren't on Earth.

This could explain why the fields of astronomy and space exploration are so popular with the public. It's not just about the search for life elsewhere or wondering if we're alone in the universe. Many of us have a feeling, a hope, an optimism, that one day someone might show us where we really come from.

But if we found it, would you want to go back there? Don't make your mind up just yet. In theory, it should be paradise, but there may have been a very good reason why we had to leave. Bear in mind too that we left it hundreds of thousands of years ago. It might be unrecognizable or even uninhabitable by now.

> Many indigenous tribes that have had no previous contact with the outside world point to specific stars and say: "Our ancestors came from there." It's part of their identity and culture. Some of them also have knowledge of advanced astronomy that they couldn't possibly have gained using their own technology. We'll look at this phenomenon in more detail in the next chapter.

2.44 Our innate need to worship deities

We seem to be hard-wired to worship deities. The practice can be found in every culture in the world, even in remote tribes that geographers and anthropologists say have never had prior communication with anyone. We might not agree with the deity they worship, and in some cultures worshipping the wrong one can get you killed. In other cultures, you're fine if you worship the wrong deity while you're alive, but they say when you die you'll go straight to whatever that religion's version of Hell is.

But why do we worship deities at all? Some say it's because we're seeking answers: Why are we here? What's our purpose? Others say the deities sprang out of the ancient morality tales our ancestors made up. These were designed to spread the messages that people shouldn't kill each other, steal each other's possessions or bed other men's wives.

This evolved into the idea that someone is constantly watching us and judging us, which further encourages good behavior. If we behave well, we'll be rewarded with, for example, sunshine and rain at the right times of the year to ensure a good harvest. The idea of a benevolent, nurturing, father-like figure watching over us gives many people a great sense of comfort.

There's undoubtedly an evolutionary advantage in believing in a deity and living by his or her moral standards. For example, if your neighbor believes he and his family will be punished if he kills you, you're more likely to survive long enough to reproduce and raise your children. You will, of course, instill this same belief and moral code in your children, so they'll grow into decent citizens too. Over the course of countless generations, this belief becomes deeply ingrained.

There's an enormous amount about life, the universe and everything else that we don't understand. The origins and complexity of DNA, and indeed life itself, are perfect examples of this. Attributing it all to a deity is an easy way of making sense of the unexplainable. It also gives us someone to blame when something tragic happens. It means we've done something to anger the deity – even if we have no idea what that thing might be.

Unlike other animals, we're also aware of our mortality. We need the comfort of knowing there's a life beyond this one. Otherwise, what's the point of anything?

So the general feeling among most philosophers and theologians is that our deities are fictional creations that evolved from our moral codes and storytelling. The deities gradually took on distinct personas, and their mysticism grew with each retelling. The stories of our deities are now inseparably entwined with our codes of morality and proper behavior, and with tales that attempt to explain our origins and what happens to us after we die.

The many depictions of deities in ancient rock carvings and paintings all over the world are immensely interesting. Many of them look less like deities and more like extraterrestrials or astronauts – or extraterrestrial astronauts. Many of today's religions might be based, at least in part, on the fact that we were visited (or brought here) by "space people" thousands of years ago. But did those ancient space visitors command us to worship them? Or did we just assume they were gods and start worshipping them ourselves?

It's interesting that none of the Earth's native animals build shrines to any deities or acknowledge their existence in any way. It's not that they aren't intelligent enough. If they had any reason to do it, many of them would be more than capable of doing so.

Some people argue that we aren't animals at all, but an entirely separate category of being that sits above the animals.[2-208] They say we're the only beings that were made in God's image, and we alone were granted the ability to worship Him.

But then we have the counter-argument that says: if the compulsion to worship Him is hard-wired into us, why are there atheists and agnostics? No one knows. It's an unanswerable question. In fact, just about everything to do with the deities is unanswerable. And that may be deliberate.[2-209]

2.45 We can mend ourselves (and other animals)

We are the only creatures on Earth that can repair ourselves when we break. I know there are a few creatures that can regenerate lost limbs, but I'm referring to the fact that we can mend broken bones, stitch up wounds, and so on.

These sorts of injuries are often fatal in other animals. Even if they manage to survive, they can be left with a crippling disability or lifelong pain. But as long as an injured person gets help in time, they can usually make a full recovery.

This isn't a miracle of modern medicine. We've long had the ability to splint broken bones and repair open wounds with bone needles and thread. But no other creature can do this.

> The miracle of modern medicine involved giving the patient anesthetic, using sterile equipment, and the doctor or surgeon washing his hands before ministering to you. But that all came much later.

Some of the Neanderthal remains we've found show evidence of broken bones that have healed. They weren't splinted or put in casts; the best they could have done would have been to rest the broken limb – if they understood that it was necessary. But they would have been in a great deal of pain. Open fractures would have become infected, often resulting in death. Even the lucky few whose bones healed might not have been able to use the injured limb properly afterward, especially if the bone was displaced.

> We can, of course, go much further than this these days, and carry out complex and intricate surgery. But this was part of the massive technological leap we went through in the last few decades. We'll look at this in more detail in Chapters 3 and 8.

As well as repairing ourselves, we can also use many of the same techniques to mend other animals. They too can make a full recovery from their injuries. But they couldn't have done so without our help. This could be one of the main reasons why we were brought here.

Interestingly, researchers have discovered that *all* four-legged animals once had the ability to regenerate their limbs.[2-210] We don't know why most of them lost this ability. Geneticists are trying to figure out whether we still have the genes for it, and if so whether they could be re-enabled.

2.46 We go against our natural behavior

We are the only creatures on Earth that go against our natural behavior. In fact, most of us utterly reject our natural behavior.

But what is our natural behavior? It's rather hard to define these days. But anthropologists believe some of the last remaining people to retain their natural behavior are the Bushmen of the Kalahari in southern Africa.[2-211]

Let's take a look at their lifestyle:

- The Bushmen are small communities of hunter-gatherers.

- Some are nomadic, while others live in small villages.

- They hunt with bows and arrows or sometimes use poison darts.

- They are not farmers.

- They wear animal skins or make their own clothes.

- They own few possessions – usually only what they can carry.

- Few of them live beyond the age of 45.

- Those aged over 60 are highly respected.

- They have no access to modern medicine and instead rely on their local shaman.

- Tribal customs are important to them: they engage in dancing, singing and ritual gatherings, and everyone tends to get involved.

- They are skilled artists.

If we contrast this with the way most of us live today, we can see that we've almost completely turned away from that sort of lifestyle.

- The modern trend is for greater urbanization: most of us now live in urban areas (54 percent in 2014, and increasing rapidly).

- Nomadic lifestyles are rare. We have small groups of itinerant travelers who are largely rejected and frowned upon, older people driving around in their motor homes experiencing their last chance of freedom, younger ones backpacking around the world during their gap year, and so on. But the majority of us have settled in one place.

- We usually only fire bows and arrows for sport, and even then, it's not a particularly common one. We also do it during occasional re-enactments of ancient battles. A few people have a go at shooting animals with bows and arrows during survival expeditions and such like. But on the whole, we haven't fired arrows at animals for centuries. The small proportion of people that go hunting generally use guns. Happily, most people don't go hunting any more.

- We've been farming for about 12,000 years. Most of our food now comes from farms.

- Most of us consider wearing animal skins, especially fur, repugnant. You risk being attacked by animal rights protestors if you do it. But tanned animal hides (leather) from sustainable sources is generally accepted.

- Few of us make our own clothes. They can be bought easily, and everyday clothes are affordable. Those who make their own clothes generally do it as a hobby, or to sell to others. On the other hand, millions of people around the world work in clothing factories.[2-212]

- Most of us in the developed world have tons of possessions. Many of us have cupboards, garages, lofts, basements, storage units, and boxes packed full of things we never use. Some of us have so much stuff that we aren't sure what we have or where it is. Hoarding is becoming an increasing problem as we're reluctant to throw anything away.

- Most of us live to about eighty. Living a long life doesn't generally command great respect. Some of those who reach 100 are celebrated, but many elderly people are seen as a problem, a burden, or a nuisance.

- Access to modern medicine and health care is widely available – though not necessarily cheap or even affordable. In a few countries, such as Canada and the UK, it's publicly funded and free to use, but the full range of drugs and equipment isn't always available because the government won't fund it. In some countries, the health care system is severely underfunded. But that's usually a political decision made by the country's government and business leaders.

- We don't have shamans, but we do have independent health practitioners, alternative medicine providers, and natural healing centers. These are usually private practices that operate outside the mainstream health care system.

- We still engage in dancing and singing, though only a small percentage of the population does it regularly. We have ritual gatherings in the form of weddings, funerals and religious ceremonies. A tiny minority celebrate other occasions such as the solstices and ancient harvest rituals.

- We have highly skilled artists, but they're uncommon among the general population. Good ones are highly regarded, and the best can sell their work for high prices. Most homes have artwork on display, but usually in the form of reproductions or prints. Original works are much rarer. Art is considered an acceptable hobby or creative outlet, even for the less skilled. It's taught as a mainstream subject in most schools. There are also dedicated art schools for the more talented students.

But on top of this, we need to consider the many aspects of our modern lifestyle that damage our health. No other creatures on Earth would knowingly and deliberately engage in behavior that could kill them.

As we've already seen, we need to be fairly active, but our inclination is to reject this. Many people reject natural foods too, even though they're widely available and affordable. And people knowingly ruin their health by smoking, abusing drugs, and drinking excessive amounts of alcohol.

While many of these things are recent phenomena, the trend is that we're moving further and further away from what anthropologists recognize as our natural behavior. It probably goes hand-in-hand with the technological leap we've already mentioned – and which we'll return to later in the book.

2.47 We age horribly

As we get older, we don't just become grayer and more wrinkled, as other animals do; our appearance changes completely. If you look at a sequence of photos of someone from their early years, through their prime, and on into their declining years, the changes are obvious – and horrific. If you compare a photo of that person from the prime of their life with one from their final years, you often can't tell it's the same person. The years aren't kind to us. We age horribly. By the time we reach our 90s, many of us look quite decrepit.

But it's not only our appearance that changes; we also become weaker. As our population ages, you've undoubtedly noticed the proliferation of mobility scooters, overcrowded doctors' offices, ever-growing hospital queues, waiting lists for surgical procedures, and so on. Our eyes become weaker too; almost everyone needs to wear glasses by retirement age.

> Some populations have poorer eyesight than others. This is especially the case in East Asian countries. The people of Singapore have the worst eyesight of all.[2-212a]
>
> This is another important indicator that we aren't all the same. We clearly didn't all descend from the same African ancestor, as mainstream anthropologists would like us to believe.

On the other hand, most animals look pretty much the same throughout their entire lives.

There's also the issue that as we get older, our mortality rate increases exponentially. Yet in many other species, their mortality rate decreases as they get older, so the longer they live, the more likely they are to stay alive.[2-213]

This begs the question: are we living beyond our natural limit. Earlier, we met the Bushmen of the Kalahari. They're living what most people would say are natural lives, but their upper age limit is about 45. So the answer has to be yes, most of us are living well beyond our natural limit. Earlier civilizations, dating back to when we first arrived on Earth, would have had an even lower life expectancy – just 35 to 45.[2-214] Many of them wouldn't have made it out of their thirties.

There's undoubtedly an evolutionary advantage in living longer, as we'll see in the next section on Grandparenting. But we have no way of selecting a longer-living partner – and we don't tend to choose our partners because of how old their parents or grandparents are. The only way to find out whether your partner will live a long life is to wait and see if they do. And even if it turns out that they do, you've long since passed the age where you can reproduce, so you can't suddenly start producing long-living children.

All of this means that our increased life expectancy over the last 100 years or so can't be anything to do with evolution. There must be another explanation: better medicine and health care, better hygiene, better food, and better living and working conditions. In any case, evolution would have taken considerably longer than 100 years (which is just four generations) to make any significant changes.

The fact that we can increase our lifespans simply by improving our living conditions raises a further question. Can we do the same for other animals? It turns out that we can increase their lifespans by a small amount if we keep them in captivity. But we certainly can't double their lifespans as we've done in ourselves.[2-215] This suggests that the animals were already living in near-optimal conditions. The fact that we were able to extend our lives to such a degree suggests that our "natural" lives were far from optimal. This is staggering, and a further indicator that we're markedly different from other animals and not originally from this world.

The starvation diet

Here's an interesting note to end this section. You may have heard that it's possible to increase mammals' lifespans significantly by restricting their calorie intake. This system is known as calorie restriction or the starvation diet. As long as they get just enough nutrition – but no more than that – we can increase their lifespans by about 50 percent.

However, most of the experiments which investigated this were conducted back in the 1930s, and they only really worked well on rats and certain other organisms, such as yeast. More recent experiments on rhesus monkeys found that calorie restriction made no significant difference. And while it helped to reduce their incidence of diabetes and heart disease, it also reduced their fertility rates and their ability to fight serious infections.[2-216]

Few people have been willing to try this on themselves, but some tests are ongoing. We obviously won't know the results for decades, as we'll have to see how long the test subjects live for.

In theory, calorie restriction could increase our average lifespan to over 120. But most people probably wouldn't want to live that long if they had to feel hungry the whole time. Maybe it's something you get used to.

But why does it work so well in rats but not in monkeys? It could be something to do with the rats' ability to survive on meager scraps during periods of famine. And if that's the case, calorie restriction probably won't work on us either.

2.48 The menopause and grandparenting

The menopause is the point in a woman's life when she's no longer able to have children. It typically happens around the age of fifty. Her menstrual periods stop, and her ovaries reduce their hormone production.

As far as we know, the only creature that goes through the menopause in the wild is the short-finned pilot whale. But it's been seen occasionally in some captive species, including killer whales (orcas), elephants, rhesus monkeys, and chimpanzees, and rarely in budgerigars, laboratory rats and mice, and one or two species of fish.[2-217]

> Humans, pilot whales, and orcas are the only known species that live beyond their reproductive years.[2-218] Pilot whales and orcas are both marine mammals, of course, which is particularly interesting if you recall our earlier discussion on the aquatic ape hypothesis.

The vast majority of animals can reproduce throughout their lives, although their reproductive cycles may slow down towards the end, making reproduction less likely. Older cats and dogs, for example, are not considered good candidates for breeding purposes, even though it's still possible for them to do so.

Why the menopause occurs in humans is a mystery, but it seems to tie in with us living beyond our natural lifespan. Our natural limit seems to be about 45 years, and if we only lived to that age, we'd be able to reproduce throughout our entire lives, just like other animals.

> It's interesting, and quite incredible, that all women go through the same physical and biological process when they're about fifty years old. At that point, they typically stop acting as parents and become grandparents instead. This is unheard of in all other animals, apart from the two species of whale we saw above.

Although we can't be sure why the menopause occurs in humans, in whales it seems to be to do with competition for resources. Young females can out-compete their mothers for food, and as a result, they produce healthier offspring. So there's a biological advantage if the older females stop reproducing and help to nurture their grandchildren instead. It seems unlikely that this is why it evolved in us though. Food is readily available in most parts of the world, so there's no need to compete for it. And few children would deny their parents enough food.

It's worth remembering that in ancient times, the elderly (the few who made it past the age of 45) were highly respected. They wouldn't have been expected to gather food or take part in hunts. Members of their community would have brought them food and taken care of them. These days, many of the more senior members of our society are left to fend for themselves.

With both their mothers and their grandmothers taking care of them, young whales are more likely to survive into adulthood. Grandmothers have also had the experience of looking after their own children, so they're more likely to do the right things and not make the mistakes that new parents might.

There's also the issue that male whales die much younger than the females. In fact, the males tend to die at around the same time that the females go through the menopause. Most females live for several decades afterward.

Human males generally die younger than females too, though we don't really understand why. In developed countries, the difference is about seven years. Interestingly, about 90 percent of centenarians are women.

We have no idea whether the ancient hominins would have gone through the menopause if they'd lived long enough. I would suggest

Humans Are Not From Earth

not; it's more likely to be a recent phenomenon that only kicked in when we began outliving our natural lifespan. Having said that though, if the few hominins that reached old age did go through the menopause, it could prove our link to the marine mammals.

Of course, the only way we could find out for sure would be to time travel into the past.

2.49 Savant-like skills

Our brains are capable of much more than we once thought. Allan Whitenack Snyder, director of the Centre for the Mind at the University of Sydney, Australia, has been investigating this. He uses magnetism to stimulate volunteers' left temporal lobes, and he's found that this induces savant-like skills in healthy people. They exhibit extraordinary (and previously hidden) skills in things like mathematics, art, memory, and possibly even telepathy.

His experiments have proven that just about everyone has these skills, but in most of us they've been disabled and put out of reach – the connections seem to have been deliberately broken. But, as his work shows, it might one day be possible to reconnect them, triggering another massive leap in our progress.

This ties in with the idea that the extraterrestrials may have erased our memories when they brought us to Earth. Perhaps they deliberately disabled other parts of our brains at the same time, with the intention of keeping us permanently in the Stone Age.

How we escaped from the Stone Age remains a mystery. How did we suddenly acquire new skills, abilities, and knowledge that enabled us to progress so rapidly? Did the parts of our brains that were disabled suddenly become re-enabled? Were the blocks removed or the connections re-established? Did we receive outside help? Or did something else happen? Whatever it was, it seems there are still several more blocks to remove.

2.50 Massive technological leaps

The jump from Cro-Magnon man (*Homo sapiens*) to fully modern humans (*Homo sapiens sapiensis*) is ridiculously short in evolutionary terms. We spent at least 300,000 years using rocks and sticks as our only tools. Then, apparently out of nowhere, we created the modern world: metallurgy, farming, water and sewerage systems, language, art, architecture, medicine, machines, electricity, complex chemistry, nuclear weapons and power, quantum physics, and all the rest of it.

We can identify at least four moments in our recent history where we made sudden leaps in progress. The first was around 12,000 years ago with the introduction of agriculture and fixed settlements. The second was around 5,000 years ago when the Ancient Egyptian, Greek, Roman and Chinese civilizations made massive and lasting contributions to the modern world. The third was the industrial revolution, which began in the mid-18th century, particularly in Britain. And the fourth seems to have followed the alleged UFO crash near Roswell, New Mexico, USA in 1947.

Regardless of whether any UFOs actually crashed at Roswell, a vast amount of new technology became available in the months and years that followed it. Many of these things should have taken decades to develop, yet there's no record of anyone having worked on them before they were made public. No one has ever admitted that they were working on such things before the late 1940s, and there were no patents on that sort of technology – not even classified ones. They all seemed to come out of nowhere, and all at around the same time.

We'll take a more detailed look at the Roswell incident, and the technology that apparently stemmed from it, in Chapter 13.

Humans Are Not From Earth

As well as these major leaps in our development that occurred as part of great movements, there have been numerous others that are no less important. They include:

- the massive amounts of progress we made during (and as a result of) the two world wars, the Cold War, and the space race

- the invention of electricity and electrical appliances, gadgets, computers, and information processing technology

- the revolutions in transport, medicine, and the food supply chain

- and so on

Many people believe that our rate of progress has been too rapid to have occurred naturally. They believe we must have had some outside help or reverse-engineered technology created by extraterrestrial civilizations.

That doesn't necessarily prove we were brought here from somewhere else, but it lends a significant amount of weight to the idea that there is somewhere else out there that we could have come from.

The massive leaps in our progress may have occurred when the aliens who brought us here came back and gave us a nudge in the right direction. Or, perhaps more likely, a different alien race could have done it. We don't know why. As we've seen, there's a theory that they might want our help in a battle with another species. And, of course, there's the theory that the key to our rapid progress was already encoded in our genetic memories. We'll take a more detailed look at each of these ideas later in the book.

2.51 Evolutionary design flaws

We're reckoned to be the most advanced species on the planet, yet our bodies are poorly designed for life here. In fact, they're poorly designed for life on other planets too. To be fair, many other creatures are badly designed too. But you'd think that by the time we appeared, after hundreds of millions of years of evolution, the biggest problems would have been overcome. But they haven't. Has someone been screwing with our design? Are we the result of hybridization experiments that didn't quite work? Or did evolution take a few wrong turns?

Here are some of our most basic design flaws:[2-219]

The pharynx
Like other primates, we use the same anatomical structure (the pharynx) for breathing and for ingesting food and drink. This dual function has caused countless deaths because our airway can easily become obstructed. About 3,000 people die in the USA each year from choking on their food.[2-220a] The figure is about 200 in the UK.[2-221a]

Inability to Biosynthesize Vitamin C
Like many animals, we've lost the ability to synthesize vitamin C. We can only get it from our food – mainly from fruit. If foods that are rich in vitamin C become scarce, our immune systems become weakened. In extreme cases, this can lead to scurvy. We have the gene for synthesizing vitamin C, but it's broken. Biologists suspect this is because we had a high-fruit diet in the past and the ability to synthesize vitamin C became unnecessary. But many cultures in the developed world now consume little or no fruit, even though it's readily available, and they're becoming vitamin C deficient.

Proximity of our genitals and rectum

This is a terrible design. It's aesthetically displeasing and unhygienic and leads to frequent urinary tract infections in women, who have shorter urethras than men. Thousands of women have been rendered infertile or even died from this, especially before the advent of antibiotics. It's astounding that a better design hasn't evolved.

Multi-function genitals

Again, this has all sorts of hygiene issues. Men use their penis and urethra for both intercourse and urination. The penis forces bacteria deep inside the woman's vagina, as well as into her urethra which opens right next to it. Both men and women can contract urinary tract infections and sexually transmitted diseases because of this multi-function arrangement.

The prostate gland

The male urinary tract passes through the prostate gland, which is prone to swelling, especially in older men. This can block urinary function. It would make much more sense if the urinary tract was routed around the outside of the prostate gland and was connected to it by ducts.

Overloaded lower backs

We've already looked at our back problems, and we've seen that there's no good reason why our backs couldn't be significantly stronger. More than 700,000 people in the USA suffer fractured vertebrae each year. Despite what many anthropologists believe, our weak backs are highly unlikely to be the result of our transition from four-legged to two-legged creatures. Five million years is more than enough time for that issue to have been resolved. And we know that the Neanderthals had excellent back health.

Knees and hips

Again, anthropologists point to our bipedalism as the primary cause of the problems in our knees and hips. They say it's because we now have to carry our entire weight on two limbs rather than four. But, as with our backs, more than enough time should have elapsed for those issues to have been resolved. We may be the only species that walks fully upright, but we aren't the only bipeds. Birds have carried their entire weight on two legs since the Jurassic period. Admittedly, most birds don't weigh all that much, but ostriches are much heavier than us, and emus and some species of cassowary weigh about the same as us. Several dinosaurs, including the massive Tyrannosaurus rex, were bipeds.

Narrow birth canal

As we saw earlier, the human birth canal is unreasonably narrow compared with the size of our babies' heads. This leads to prolonged labor, significant pain, and increased risks to both mother and baby. We've seen that this is primarily the result of our brains tripling in size over a remarkably short period. There's no good reason why our pelvises couldn't eventually evolve to accommodate this – except that modern advances in obstetrics have halted our pelvic evolution.

Complicated feet

Our feet are overly complex, with 26 bones in each one. This made sense in ancient times when we lived in trees and needed the flexibility. But we stopped living in trees between 5 and 7 million years ago, and our feet have hardly changed since then. They've become slightly more stable, and developed arches that act as shock absorbers, but the arches are prone to collapse, and our feet twist too much as we walk.

The ostrich is a good example of a bipedal creature with stable feet: its ankle and lower leg are fused into a single structure, and they only have two toes. We might eventually evolve the same sort of structure, but progress in this area seems to be extremely slow. It's likely to take us tens of millions of years to get there. In the meantime, we need to wear shoes.

Sinuses, infections, headaches and joint pain

Our sinuses are the air-filled cavities at the front of our skulls. We have several of them. They're supposed to help drain fluid and mucus, but they're dreadfully inefficient. Fluid and mucus often drain the wrong way or build up, leading to infection, inflammation, and pain.

> We get pressure- and moisture-related headaches and joint pain when the weather changes. We can conclude from this that the weather on our home planet must be much more stable, with no significant pressure changes.

Blind spots

Our optic nerve is in a ridiculous place, almost exactly in the center of our field of view. This leaves a blind spot in each eye that we have to work around. Usually, our brain uses information from the other eye to fill in the blanks. But if we're looking at something closely, the two blind spots can overlap, and we can't see it.

Teeth

We only have a single set of adult teeth, and they don't grow continuously as they do in some animals. Our teeth and gums start to weaken and deteriorate once we reach the age of about 35, no matter how well we take care of them. This is another indication that we're living well beyond our natural lifespan.

Interestingly, most herbivores' teeth grow continuously throughout their lives. This is one of the few instances where we differ from them.

Our fondness for the wrong foods

As we've seen, we probably originated on a planet where food was scarce and not particularly nutritious. As a result, our brains tell us to eat as much of it as we can whenever it's available. Here on Earth – in the developed world at least – it's always available, and it's highly nutritious. We still have the urge to eat as much as we can, and if we give in to that urge, it can damage our health and threaten our lives. Resisting the urge takes more willpower than many of us possess, even when we know it will kill us.

Tribes and clans

We have an inherent need to belong to a tribe or clan. We also have an ingrained distrust or hatred of other tribes and clans. This was undoubtedly an important survival trait in our ancient pasts, but it's stayed with us. In today's world, it causes social problems such as bitter rivalry, prejudice, racism, gang warfare, terrorism, and so on.

Cognitive deficiencies and biases

Our decision-making skills have several glitches that lead us to reach erroneous and questionable conclusions. Many scientists believe this stems from a time when we had smaller brains and were less intelligent. Examples include:

- always agreeing with people who agree with us

- preferring outcomes where things stay the same as they are now, even if something better is on offer

- the gambler's fallacy of basing forecasts on past events

An example of the gambler's fallacy is the assumption that if a tossed coin has landed on "heads" three times in a row, then it's more likely to land on "tails" next time. In fact, the probability hasn't changed.

Hyperactivity

This is another trait that would have been beneficial in the past. An active hunter, gatherer, and fighter who had boundless energy and was always on the go would have been a huge asset to an ancient tribe or clan. In today's world, approximately 5 percent of children have Attention Deficit Hyperactivity Disorder (ADHD). They're seen as problems, and they're often medicated to calm them down.

2.52 Ancient structures and artifacts

There are hundreds of ancient man-made structures all over the world, including many that are now submerged under the sea. They've been dated to thousands, and in some cases millions of years before modern humans supposedly evolved. Countless artifacts have also been discovered that are unquestionably man-made, yet they also date to a time long before anthropologists say we were here. We'll take a closer look at some of these in the next chapter.

As we saw earlier, mainstream scientists and historians ignore these things because they don't fit into their rigid view of human history. If you push them for an answer, they'll insist that they must be more recent than the evidence indicates.

The thing is, most of these things have been dated by multiple experts and trusted laboratories, using approved methods – and the dates still tally. Some of the artifacts were found inside layers of rock that we know are millions of years old.

The people who made these things couldn't possibly have evolved on Earth because they don't fit the evolutionary timeline. The more recent human civilizations, dating from around 400,000 years ago, kind of fit the timeline, but there are still some major discrepancies, including the fact that there's nothing we could have evolved from. The fact that we sort of fit into the timeline could be just a coincidence.

It looks as if the oldest civilizations were part of a series of experiments to see if humans could survive on this planet. Small groups of people would have been brought here from our home planet and dropped off at various locations around the world. They were then monitored to see how well they fared. All of them eventually died out. So the aliens tweaked their genomes to try to make them more robust. They repeated this experiment several times over the course of millions of years.

As part of this process, they appear to have replaced or modified some of our genes using DNA from themselves, other alien species, some of the Earth's native hominins, and some of Earth's marine mammals. Eventually they managed to create a hybrid species that could survive here long-term. And that would be us.

The origins of our modern-day races and cultures

Having finally created a version of the human race that could survive here, the aliens dropped off larger groups at various locations around the world. The first group appears to have been dropped off between 400,000 and 500,000 years ago. Other groups seem to have arrived more recently. The last group probably arrived around 70,000 years ago.

There's evidence that the first of these groups were dropped off in Israel, Spain and Australia.[2-222a] The next groups were probably dropped off in Central or Southern America, India, and China. Around 300,000 years ago the African groups arrived. One was dropped in North Africa (specifically present-day Morocco). The other, which was

Humans Are Not From Earth

by far the largest of all the groups, was dropped in East Africa (present-day Ethiopia, Kenya, Somalia, Eritrea, and Djibouti).

The Israeli group then appears to have migrated north and west and merged with the Spanish group to become the French branch (Europeans and northern Asians). The Africans spread south and east, with the eastern group meeting and interbreeding with the Indian group to create the Middle Easterners.

As these groups spread further across the world, they inevitably bumped into each other and interbred, creating the different races and cultures we see today. For example, the original Australians appear to have interbred with the Chinese – and later also the migrating East Africans – to create the Polynesians[2-223a] and Melanesians.[2-224a]

Mainstream historians and anthropologists don't accept this multi-location theory – or the idea that we could have come from another planet. They will only accept that we originated in Africa – although a small minority have now plumped for Israel instead, based on recent evidence.

They also believe that the first exodus out of Africa, when we began colonizing the rest of the world, only occurred between 60,000 to 70,000 years ago. But there are countless structures, artifacts and confirmed human remains all over the world that are much older than that. For example, modern human teeth that are as much as 125,000 years old have been found in China.[2-225a] We'll look at these issues in more detail in Chapter 9.

2.53 Miscellaneous other factors

- We're the only species in which the female's breasts are permanently enlarged and sexual – meaning they turn men on.

- We're the only species that cries to express emotion. Many animals cry when they're in pain, and we do that too. But we also cry when we're happy, sad, overwrought or feeling empathy. No one knows why we do this.

- We're the only species that kisses (and I mean *properly* kisses) as a way of expressing love (or lust). It's thought to be a way of detecting a potential partner's pheromones to see if they'd make a good parent.

3

The Evidence

In this chapter, we'll take a look at the wealth of evidence that proves we've been on Earth for far longer than mainstream scientists would have us believe. This is important stuff, because if we were here before the native hominins, it proves we can't have evolved here and must have come from another planet.

We'll look at ancient structures, artifacts, and civilizations that fall well outside the conventional timeline. We'll also see some examples of technologies that shouldn't have existed at that time, which implies that we must have had outside help in creating them. And then we'll meet some highly respected and reputable people who've either had encounters with aliens or have inside knowledge of what's really going on.

We'll also take a look at some other interesting theories along the way. For example, did you know that our Sun might be part of a binary star system?

3.1 Out-of-place artifacts

Rather than list pages and pages of evidence here, I'd like to refer you to *Forbidden Archaeology* by Michael A. Cremo and Richard L.

Thompson. In this book, the authors prove, beyond question, that we've been on Earth for at least two million years. It's packed with well-documented evidence, and their research is meticulous and can't be faulted. It's been thoroughly reviewed and fact-checked by hundreds of renowned scholars, who have all given it their full approval. It is of course hated and derided by mainstream scientists who call it "pseudoscience" – though it absolutely isn't.

A typical example of an artifact from this era is a seashell carved with a crude but recognizably human face. It was discovered by geologist Henry Stopes in Suffolk, England in 1881, embedded at the base of a Red Crag rock formation that's at least two million years old [Forbidden Archaeology, 2.15]. Mainstream evolutionary scientists say we didn't acquire the level of dexterity needed to create something like this until about 100,000 years ago, and modern humans didn't reach England until 30,000 to 40,000 years ago.

> The mainstream scientists might be correct in their belief that modern humans didn't start creating detailed artworks until around 100,000 years ago. But they're referring to the groups of humans that were dropped off here within the last 400,000 years. They're deliberately ignoring the much older civilizations we looked at in the previous chapter. We saw that small groups of people were brought to Earth millions of years ago, but they died out fairly quickly. But they clearly possessed advanced skills and knowledge, and left evidence that proves they were here.

Another set of artifacts was discovered a few years earlier, in 1872, by Edward Charlesworth, a Fellow of the Geological Society. He found a set of sharks' teeth with holes bored in them, in a way that suggested they were probably once strung together on a necklace. Again, these were found in a layer of Red Crag dating from 2 million to 2.5 million years ago. When he presented the teeth at a Geological Society meeting, he explained how he'd ruled out natural explanations such as erosion, decay or parasites. No known parasites are able to bore through sharks' teeth. And in any case, the holes were all in the same place on each tooth, exactly where we'd drill through them to make a necklace today. There was also evidence of tool marks. Charlesworth said he'd had the teeth independently examined by a Professor Owen, who'd confirmed the tool marks were definitely made by humans.

> A number of those present at the meeting refused to accept Charlesworth's findings, and stuck firmly to the natural explanations he'd painstakingly ruled out. The independently confirmed fact that the holes were created by humans was too far outside their comfort zone for them to contemplate, so they chose to ignore it. This is called cognitive dissonance. We'll see a lot more of it throughout the book.

These artifacts prove without a doubt that humans were present on Earth at least two million years ago, and therefore couldn't possibly have evolved here. Cremo and Thompson's book lists hundreds of other examples, all meticulously documented and independently verified.

Thousands of other anomalous objects have been discovered, and we'll look at a few of them in a moment. Millions more languish in locked drawers and cabinets in the basements of museums and universities, well away from public view. If you ask to see them, as I've done on numerous occasions, you'll generally be refused access. Sometimes, they'll say they've been lost, or they'll deny ever having them, or they'll deny they exist. They say these things even when presented with copies of official records which confirm they're the registered keepers.

As for the artifacts that *are* available to view, mainstream scientists question both their validity and the qualifications and reputations of those who found them. Many careers have been deliberately ruined when the discoverers "went public" – usually against their colleagues' advice.

We can find evidence of human activity on Earth dating back a lot further than two million years. For example, artifacts have been found in coal and sandstone deposits which are known to be *hundreds* of millions of years old.

These include:

- A piece of zinc-silver alloy embedded in a vase that was found in a mine in Massachusetts, USA in 1851. It was found inside a 500-million-year-old block of coal.

- A cast iron cup or pot that was found in Oklahoma, USA in 1912. It was inside a 312-million-year-old lump of coal.[3-01]

- A piece of an aluminum gear that was found in a coal mine in Vladivostok, Russia.[3-02] The layer of coal it was found in was 300 million years old. The aluminum is 96 to 98 percent pure, which is a level of purity we've only been able to achieve recently. The other component in the alloy is magnesium. An aluminum-magnesium alloy is uncommon now and totally unheard of in the past.

- There's a seemingly impossible bas relief carving of a stegosaurus at Ta Prohm, a Buddhist temple in Angkor, Cambodia. The carving is known to be more than 800 years old. But stegosaurus became extinct 150 million years ago, and the first fossils weren't discovered until 1877.

- The Ica stones[3-03] were discovered in Ica Province, Peru in 1966. These are polished andesite stones that are finely engraved with illustrations, some of which feature dinosaurs. The stones can't be reliably dated, but the first was believed to have been found in a tomb more than 600 years old. This is at least 400 years before the first dinosaur fossils were discovered. More than 11,000 Ica stones have been discovered to date.

> The farmer who found the first Ica stones, and sold them to tourists, was threatened with prosecution for selling archaeological artifacts. To escape prosecution, he claimed they were fakes he'd made himself. Most mainstream reports end there, with the stones confirmed as a hoax. But the farmer later retracted his claim, saying that although he'd made and sold copies of the stones, the originals were genuine. Many independent historians and paleontologists also now believe they're genuine, as they show the correct stance and tail positions of dinosaurs that were only confirmed recently. Despite this, mainstream scientists continue to brand the stones a preposterous hoax.

- Stone tools, utensils, and vessels have been found by gold miners beneath Table Mountain in Cape Town, South Africa. The objects were embedded in rock strata confirmed to be 55 million years old.

- There are unconfirmed reports that stone tools and other artifacts dating from at least two million years ago have been found in Mexico. Information about these objects appears to have been suppressed because they violate the Out of Africa theory.

> Out-of-Place Artifacts are often suppressed. We'll look at the reasons for this in the next chapter.

Let's now look at some of the evidence which confirms that modern humans were dropped off at various locations around the world within the last 300,000 years or so:

- Stone tools have been found in Hueyatlaco,[3-04] near Puebla in Mexico that have been confirmed to be 250,000 years old. According to mainstream anthropologists, modern humans didn't reach Central and South America until around 15,000 years ago.

Virginia Steen-McIntyre, an archaeologist who worked at this site, went against her colleagues' advice and published the results of the team's findings. As a result, she was denied further opportunities to work in that field, and the site was closed off. Team leader Cynthia Irwin-Williams never published the official report into their investigations at the site, and the team members appear to be in dispute about what they found.

> This is almost certainly an attempt to save their careers and reputations after what happened to Steen-McIntyre.

More recent investigations by independent teams have confirmed the original team's findings that the tools were between 220,000 and 250,000 years old. These results have been peer-reviewed and published in mainstream science publications, including the *Journal of Paleolimnology* Volume 36, Number 1, Pages 101-116, July 2006].

- Stone tools have also been found in Toca da Tira Peia, on the Serra da Capivara plateau[3-05] in Brazil, that have been confirmed to be 22,000 years old (7,000 years before humans officially reached that region). In fact, there's evidence that modern humans may have been living on the plateau for 100,000 years.

- Bones of giant sloths, confirmed to be 30,000 years old, have been found in Uruguay. They have tool marks on them, indicating that they were hunted and butchered – almost certainly by modern humans.[3-06]

- The Williams Enigmalith[3-07][3-08][3-09] is, as its name suggests, an enigma. It appears to be a small (0.3 inches, 8 mm) XLR-style electrical plug embedded in a solid granite pebble. Dating tests show that the pebble is around 100,000 years old, which is itself an enigma because granite takes millions of years to form. Researchers have scoured catalogs of electronic components but have been unable to identify the plug.

The Enigmalith was found by American electrical engineer John J. Williams during a hiking trip "somewhere in North America" – he refuses to say exactly where. He has expressed his frustration that not a single mainstream scientist was prepared to take a close look at it, yet they still call it a hoax.

OBJECTION!
"Doctor Silver, you are a scientist, why don't *you* take a look at it?"

I knew you'd say that! But I'm not the right kind of scientist – I study lakes, seas, and our extraterrestrial origins. The Enigmalith sounds genuine, but I've only seen photographs and heard the finder's testimony. I don't have the knowledge, equipment or contacts to be able to test it properly. If no one with the right qualifications is prepared to look at it, then it will have to remain an enigma for now.

- The Antikythera mechanism[3-10][3-11][3-12] – the first-known analog computer – is thought to date from about 205 BC. But it incorporates technologies that were previously unknown until the 14th century AD. It was found in 1902 among objects recovered from a shipwreck off one of the Greek islands.

The mechanism seems to have been made in the region of Corinth, Greece. It may have been designed for calculating astronomical and astrological positions, or as a navigational tool, but the latest theory is that it was probably a teaching aid for philosophers. But how did it come to exist 1,500 years before we developed any comparable technology? Why have no examples of similar technology been found? Why did the technology needed to make it not develop and advance over the following 1,500 years? And how much more advanced would we be now if it had? Was it made by aliens, or did they help us make it?

Although the mechanism seems too complex to have been made by the people of that era, it also seems too crude to have been made by extraterrestrials who were capable of space travel. Perhaps it was simply a toy, or a model, or a gift from the aliens to one of the kings of that period. Or perhaps the aliens met a local engineer, removed the mental block from his brain, and he made this as a demonstration of what he was now capable of.

We may never know the truth. But whatever the case, the stir it's caused in the scientific community continues unabated to this day.

- The Voynich manuscript[3-13] consists of around 240 pages of hand-written and illustrated vellum, although some of the pages seem to be missing. It first came to light in 1912 when a Polish book dealer, Wilfrid Voynich, apparently came across it in an Italian monastery. It's been dated to the early 15th century, and some researchers believe it may have been created in northern Italy, possibly by an Italian Jew.[3-14]

The language it's written in is unknown, although a recent theory suggests it could be an extinct Mexican dialect[3-15] or abbreviated Latin. The characters don't come from any known alphabet, and some researchers say it's just gibberish. It contains hundreds of detailed illustrations of plants, few of which have been identified, along with other objects and diagrams. One researcher suggests it could be a women's health manual, though his claims have been dismissed.[3-15a] Some researchers say the manuscript is probably a hoax, possibly created by Voynich himself, while others believe it's genuine and will one day be interpreted. Intriguingly, at least one of the plants that's been identified in it was unknown until after 1912 when the manuscript first came to light. As for its true origins, I wonder if it could have come from our home planet and offers us a glimpse of what life is like there?

Mainstream scientists cast doubt on the authenticity and origins of all of these artifacts, labeling them hoaxes, jokes, or pseudoscience usually without even examining them. They attempt to come up with rational explanations that rarely make much sense. But there are good reasons for that, as we'll see in Chapter 13. It doesn't mean the artifacts aren't real though.

> If you're interested in finding out more about artifacts like this, visit YouTube and search for "Out of Place Artifacts." You'll find plenty of intriguing videos there. I recommend cross-referencing them with the *Forbidden Archaeology* book I mentioned earlier.

Most of the artifacts are also included in the online encyclopedia *Wikipedia*. But it's important to bear in mind that Wikipedia is an organ of mainstream science. That means the artifacts will be automatically labeled hoaxes or pseudoscience, even when they've been tested and verified by independent researchers.

Discounted anomalies

Several other artifacts often feature in books, articles, and documentaries about anomalous objects. However, I've discounted the following ones as I don't believe they are valid evidence:

- The infamous carved stone panel at the Temple of Seti I in Abydos, Egypt. It appears to depict modern vehicles including a helicopter, a plane and possibly a submarine.

  The image that's most widely circulated has been lit and photographed face-on, so you can't see the depth of the carving. I've examined it in real life, and it looks nothing like the photo. It's small, difficult to see, and sits at the top-right corner of the frame of an otherwise unremarkable internal doorway. It consists of newer hieroglyphs that have been carved over the top of older hieroglyphs, and parts of the panel seem to have disintegrated. They're quite obviously just layered, broken hieroglyphs and look nothing like modern vehicles. If you ever get the chance to go and see it, I wouldn't bother; you'll be very disappointed.

- The Klerksdorp spheres. These are grooved nickel-steel balls, usually slightly flattened or disc-shaped, found in 2.8-billion-year-old rock strata near Ottosdal, South Africa. They closely resemble cricket balls or lawn bowls. Although they look man-made, they're perfectly natural and are formed by concretion in the sedimentary rocks.

- The London Hammer,[3-16] also known as the London Artifact. This was found in London, Texas, USA in 1936. It's a 6-inch iron hammer with a wooden handle that's consistent with tools used in that area in the late 1800s. But it appears to be encased in a 400-million-year-old rock. Although some people consider it a genuine anomalous artifact, most now accept that it was probably formed by limestone concretion around the hammer.

- A similar – and rather humorous – example is the Coso Artifact,[3-17] found in California, USA in 1961. At first, it seemed to be some sort of ancient electrical component embedded in 500,000-year-old hardened clay. But it turned out to be a Champion spark plug, probably from a 1920s-era Ford motorcar.

Other interesting out-of-place artifacts include:[3-18]

- What looks like a microchip. Found in 250-million-year-old rock in Labinsk, Russia.

- What looks like the tracks of a heavy, wheeled vehicle. Found in 14-million-year-old rocks in the Phrygian Valley in Turkey.[3-19][3-20]

- And a screw embedded in a 300-million-year-old stone. Found in Lanzhou, China.

If any of these turn out to be genuine, and they're as old as they appear, I'd say they're more likely to have been left behind by ancient alien visitors than by humans.

Anomalous maps

The final set of out-of-place artifacts I'd like to discuss are the anomalous maps.

The Piri Reis map[3-21][3-22] was created in Istanbul, Turkey in 1513 and rediscovered in 1929. It shows the coastlines of Africa and South America with almost perfect accuracy. That level of accuracy shouldn't have been possible at that time. We couldn't measure longitude properly until accurate marine chronographs were invented in the 1790s.

The map also shows the coastline of Queen Maud's Land, Antarctica, including sections that have been under two miles of ice for the last two million years. And it shows mountain ranges that were only discovered in 1952. As far as we're aware, no humans even saw Antarctica until 1820.

Intriguingly, the map features a level of distortion that matches the curvature of the Earth. You would only see the world that way if you viewed it from some distance away.[3-23]

The map-maker stated that his map was based on more than 20 older maps, some of which were at least 2,000 years old.

The Buache map,[3-24] published in 1737, shows the complete coastline of Antarctica, more than 80 years before the first recorded sighting of it. Philippe Buache de la Neuville was a renowned cartographer, and the official geographer to King Louis XV of France, so his credentials are impeccable. His map also shows the entire coastline of the continent as ice-free. That means he must have based it on an earlier map dating back at least two million years.

Interestingly, although his map shows the coastline of Antarctica with almost perfect accuracy, Buache labeled the continent "conjectured." So it's clear that he never saw it with his own eyes, and he didn't necessarily believe it was there. Another map of his from the same period leaves Antarctica out entirely. Naturally enough, mainstream cartographers and historians label the Buache map "controversial."

The French cartographer Oronce Finé's World Map of 1531 is even more astounding. It shows the *entire* continent of Antarctica as ice-free, with rivers and valleys, and indicates the approximate position of the South Pole. Antarctica was completely buried beneath an ice sheet 15 million years ago.

Other maps that show the Earth as it must have looked in the distant past[3-25] include:

- the Map of the North by Ptolemy, produced in about 150 AD

- the Hamy-King world map[3-26] of 1502 which, among several notable features, shows Indonesia as a large, connected land mass

- the King Jaime World Chart, also from 1502, which shows the Sahara Desert as fertile land with vast lakes, rivers, forests, and cities

So, who created the ancient maps that many of these later maps were based on? Were they drawn by members of ancient civilizations whose navigational and cartographical skills were as highly developed as our own? Or could they have been drawn by aliens?

Of course, the original maps might not be millions of years old. The aliens could have created them more recently and used radar to see beneath Antarctica's ice sheet. That's exactly what we did, and it's how we know the maps are accurate. It's doubtful that any ancient human civilizations could have had that level of technology.

3.2 Ancient advanced civilizations

Carolina, Badplaas, Waterval and Machadodorp
South Africa

The vast complex of stone circles and ruins that can be found across this region may once have been part of a massive metropolis. Dating back as far as 200,000 years, they're considered the world's oldest man-made structures.[3-27]

The Harappan Civilization, Indus Valley
Pakistan and India

The remains of the ancient cities of Harappa and Mohenjo-Daro lie in the enormous Indus Valley. They date back to at least 2800 BC but could be thousands of years older. That's not particularly old on the timescale we've been looking at, but the level of technology and sophistication that can be seen there goes far beyond anything else in the world at that time.[3-28]

The cities are isolated and weren't discovered until the 1800s. Excavations began in 1920. The cities are highly sophisticated and well planned. Archaeologists believe they were probably planned in their entirety before construction began. This is well beyond anything seen even in the Egyptian or Mesopotamian cultures.

The cities are laid out in a grid pattern, aligned with the points of the compass. Public and residential areas are segregated, and the flow of each city was designed to allow easy movement from one neighborhood to the next. There were plenty of wells for drinking water. And they had a sophisticated waste removal system, with each home having its own latrine. Waste from homes, bathing houses and drains was piped into a larger sewer system and then onto the fields to be used as fertilizer. Buildings were constructed from bricks which were all uniform in size.

The Harappa culture remains an enigma, and the city's origins are a mystery.[3-29] Their dialect is unknown, and their writing has proven indecipherable thus far. There are no temples or religious buildings of any kind, although small religious artifacts and seals have been found, and there's evidence of fire altars and possible ritual sacrifice. No differences in social class can be discerned. There are no military monuments or artworks depicting battles, and no fortifications.

While other cities of that era were typically ruled by military leaders, Harappa and Mohenjo-Daro seem to have been ruled by business leaders, wealthy merchants, landlords, or possibly spiritual leaders who controlled vast trade networks stretching from East Asia to the Middle East. The Harappans were noted for their arts and crafts skills, especially in producing fine jewelry. And they had their own system of weights and measures, which were highly accurate.

The Indus civilization is thought to have begun to collapse around 2200 BC because of climate change and drought. By 1300 BC, the cities were overcrowded and suffering from a lack of maintenance, suggesting that the rulers had lost their authority. New cities began to appear from about 600 BC, following the same pattern of sophisticated planning, and the culture was able to continue. Other ancient cities in the Indus Valley have since been discovered but are yet to be excavated.

Tiwanaku, Bolivia

The structures at this ancient ruined site align with astronomical positions as they would have appeared in 15000 BC. This would make it the world's oldest city by a good 7,000 years – at a time when civilization didn't even exist in South America according to mainstream theories.[3-30]

Mainstream archaeologists claim they've now discredited this theory and the site dates from only around 1500 BC. However, several notable researchers have confirmed that the site is at least 12,000 years old, based on data from satellites. This would still make it the world's oldest city. Naturally enough, the mainstream scientists refuse to accept this.

The site is also notable for its perfectly flat 100-ton stones that are arranged so tightly that not even a needle can penetrate between them. No mortar was used to hold them in place. If the site really is 12,000 years old or more, this level of technology shouldn't have existed.

Aboriginal people, worldwide

Aboriginal people around the world have continually stated their belief that we didn't evolve on Earth but were placed here. If you're interested in reading more about this, I can recommend the book *Ancient Aliens In Australia: Pleiadian Origins of Humanity* by Bruce Fenton and Steven Strong with Daniella Fenton and Evan Strong. It includes evidence from indigenous Australians which proves that extraterrestrials visited the Earth up to one million years ago, seeding what would become modern humans.

Other civilizations

There's plenty of evidence that ancient civilizations, including the Egyptians and the Mayans, knew all about our solar system and other stars in our galaxy, long before they were discovered in modern times. There's no record of them having telescopes, so the only way they could have gotten the information is if it was given to them by extraterrestrials. There are countless rock carvings, and stone and pottery artifacts illustrating these visitors. Almost identical carvings and artifacts have been found all over the world. Mainstream scientists claim that the ancient people who created them simply had vivid imaginations.

Deforestation of the Amazonian rainforest has exposed evidence of numerous lost civilizations. Research work carried out by the Russian geologist Dr. Alexander Koltypin[3-31] is well worth following.

Further ancient civilizations and artifacts are being discovered all the time, often in places where they shouldn't exist according to mainstream theories. The evidence continues to build, but the mainstream scientists and historians continue to cling to a version of history that can't possibly have existed.

3.3 Monumental stones

All over the world, we can find examples of ancient civilizations that had the ability to finely cut, move and precisely lay and align massive monumental stones, some of them weighing hundreds of tons. We have no idea how they managed to do this.

These civilizations include:

Sacsayhuaman, near Cuzco in Peru

The largest stones here are estimated to weigh up to 440 tons and are over 28 feet (8.5 meters) high. Some of the blocks have been cut with 12 sides to precisely align with neighboring blocks.[3-32]

Puma Punku, part of the Tiwanaku Site in western Bolivia

The stones here may be up to 15,000 years old and predate the Incas. No one knows their true origins or how the walls were constructed. The massive blocks are finely cut and precisely interlock. They were pinned together with metal clamps, which were formed by cutting grooves into adjoining blocks and pouring molten metal into them.

Similar clamps have been found at several Incan sites, including Coricancha, Ollantaytambo and Ñust'a Hisp'anain in Peru, as well as in ancient Egypt.

The builders must have had highly sophisticated knowledge of stone-cutting, geometry, engineering, and metal smelting. Mainstream researchers say the people of that period weren't capable of generating the high temperatures required to melt metal. So how did they do it? And why did that knowledge die out?

Like the Indus Valley civilizations, Puma Punku had an irrigation system, sewerage pipes, and hydraulic mechanisms, thousands of years ahead of other civilizations.

The Inca Temple of the Sun, Ollantaytambo, Peru

This is an astonishing site, and well worth a visit. Stones weighing up to 70 tons each have been finely cut and precisely fitted together. They were cut from the side of a mountain many miles away and transported to the site, presumably using ramps and rollers.[3-33]

Strangely, many of the stones have protrusions that are similar to what we see when metal is melted and cast in molds. While we have the technology to melt rock today using highly focused sunlight,[3-34] it's doubtful that the Incas could have done it – or at least not without help.

> The stones themselves were cut, not melted, and they bear fine chisel marks. Only the protrusions show signs of having been melted. We have no idea why.

Baalbek (also known as Heliopolis), Lebanon

This site dates back at least 12,000 years, and perhaps as much as 20,000 years. It features important Roman ruins. But it's what lies beneath those ruins that's more interesting to us. They're built upon a massive megalithic mound consisting of stones weighing up to 1,200 tons each. Architects and engineers have no idea where the stones were quarried, how they were brought to the site, or how they were lifted and fitted into such a limited space. Even today we don't have the technology or equipment to be able to do this.

Gornaya Shoria, southern Siberia, Russia

First discovered in 2013, the stones at this site are even more massive than those at Baalbek. Some are estimated to weigh 4,000 tons or more, and they're stacked 130 feet (40 meters) high. Despite their smooth, vertical surfaces, sharp corners, and perfect right angles, many mainstream scientists insist that the stones, and the structure they form, must be natural features, as it would have been impossible for anyone to put stones that large into place. The origins of this site will be hotly debated for many years to come.[3-35][3-36]

Göbekli Tepe, Turkey

This ancient site has been dated to 11,500 to 12,000 years old and has been called the most important archaeological discovery of modern times.[3-37][3-38]

One of its most significant features is a set of twenty stone circles made up of two hundred elaborately carved stone pillars, each up to 20 feet (6 meters) in height and weighing 15 to 20 tons. Their construction would have required advanced knowledge of stone-working and masonry. The carvings on the stones provide an important astronomical record from that time, including comet and asteroid impacts. No one knows who made them. The area is known to have been inhabited by primitive hunter-gatherers at that time, and it's extremely unlikely that they would have had such knowledge.

The Great Sphinx of Giza in Egypt

The sphinx is the subject of enormous debate and conjecture.[3-39] It's commonly believed to be around 4,500 years old, but some researchers believe it could be as much as 12,500 years old. The evidence for this lies in its position in relation to the pyramids, which reflect the alignment of the stars in the belt of the constellation Orion[3-40] as they would have looked in 10,500 BC.

But there are claims that it might be 800,000 years old. These claims are based on what appears to be significant signs of water erosion affecting the lower portion.[3-41] The erosion seems to indicate that the structure was partially submerged for a considerable period of time after it was constructed.

3.4 Why we don't have these ancient technologies now

Many of the ancient technologies used to create the structures and artifacts we've looked at in this chapter have been lost. They no longer exist in our collective memories, and they haven't been recorded anywhere.

A huge part of our history is undocumented – or perhaps it was never ours to document in the first place. But let's assume the technology was ours rather than extraterrestrial. And let's assume that thousands of years ago we could (and did) build well-planned cities, complete with water and sanitation systems, and we could smelt metal, and melt stone, and carve rocks with almost microscopic precision, and move massive stones that we can't move today. What happened to that technology? How did we lose it for thousands of years?

The main problem is that technologies are lost when civilizations die out. In addition, conquerors often destroy the most important parts of the civilizations they take over. We can see the same thing happening today: the self-proclaimed Islamic State of Iraq and the Levant (ISIL) group of militant extremists has destroyed numerous historic buildings and monuments in Iraq, Syria, and Libya.[3-42]

Most of our ancient records were lost when the money to maintain the libraries ran out. They later crumbled, or were torched by conquering forces.

The most ancient civilizations left no records at all, even in the form of rock carvings or cave paintings. They only had oral histories – the stories about their origins – that they once passed down from one generation to the next. When their civilizations collapsed, their histories went with them.

Even when we have records, there's the problem that technologies change over time. It wasn't so long ago that we stored our computer records on magnetic tape reels, paper tape, and cards with holes punched in them. But if you came across any of them today, you'd have a heck of a job reading them. The magnetic data on the tapes probably degraded decades ago. The equipment required to read them and transfer the data into the computer either no longer exists or no longer works. And the software that understood how to interpret the data was probably erased when the outdated computer was scrapped. Some of the data may have been transferred to a more modern medium, but most of it is effectively lost forever, even though it might be less than 50 years old.

When ancient civilizations collapsed, the inhabitants either died or fled for their lives, taking whatever they could carry. Anything they left behind was forgotten. They were more interested in basic survival than saving historic records.

Imagine if our civilization collapsed today. Let's say that a massive electromagnetic pulse has wiped out all our electronic records, and everything printed on paper has been burned. The few survivors have fled into the wilderness. Some of us would know how to create advanced technology – such as computers – but we wouldn't have the tools or materials with which to build them, nor the electricity to power them.

We wouldn't pass those skills on to our children, so the knowledge would be lost. Our great-grandchildren might have no idea such things ever existed.

Let's skip forward three or four generations. Imagine if our great-grandchildren also grew up in the wilderness. One day they go exploring and come across the ruins of our civilization. In one of the semi-collapsed buildings, beneath the layers of debris, they find a computer. It obviously won't work, and they have no idea what it is or what it was used for. They wouldn't believe that their own great-grandfathers used to build and operate such things. And they couldn't contemplate the amazing things they used them for. They'd probably think they were looking at extraterrestrial technology – maybe a collapsed alien base.

Now imagine that those children weren't born just three or four generations after our civilization collapsed, but 20,000 years later. What would they think if they dug into the hardened mud and found an iPad?

This is exactly the sort of thing that's happening today when we uncover artifacts from earlier civilizations. Independent researchers get hugely excited about it. But our mainstream scientists can't seem to get their heads around it.

3.5 Similarities between ancient civilizations

There are striking similarities between the ancient civilizations. They include the Sumerians (in modern-day Iraq); the Incan Empire (in modern-day Peru); the ancient Chinese, Japanese and Indians; the Aborigines (of modern-day Australia); the Malekula people (of modern-day Vanuatu); and more. Their buildings, windows, doors, and pyramids are virtually identical in style. All of them have produced similar-looking carvings and artifacts of what appear to be visitors from space. They're frequently depicted in flying machines or spacecraft, and they're often referred to as "gods."

Modern descendants of dozens of ancient cultures point to the heavens and say: "We came from there." They include the Sumerians, the Egyptians, the Chinese, the Mayans, the Aboriginal Australians, and Native American groups including the Hopi and Cree, among others.

How could these diverse civilizations have produced such strikingly similar structures and artifacts when mainstream scientists say they had no contact with each other?

In fact, there's a simple explanation: the mainstream scientists are wrong. There's plenty of evidence to show that these ancient civilizations *were* in contact with each other. For example, examinations of Egyptian mummies have found traces of things like hashish, tobacco, and cocaine, which could only have come from the Americas. Some researchers believe there might even have been well-established trade routes.[3-43] This would have been more than 3,000 years before the New World was officially discovered, and is another example of how our knowledge of earlier civilizations has been lost.

But if the mainstream scientists don't think these civilizations were in contact with each other, how do they explain the similarities between their structures and artifacts? Well, it's all rather vague, to be honest. They simply claim that the various civilizations must have had vivid imaginations and were attuned to nature. And maybe there was "some sort of synchronicity" involved.

Of course, none of this explains why the ancient civilizations all depicted their gods as astronaut-like figures.

3.6 Our Sun's binary twin?

There's an intriguing theory that our Sun might have a binary twin. If this is true, then its twin must be incredibly distant. But the Sun's orbit seems to be being affected by a weak gravitational force that's consistent with it being part of a binary system. One of the strongest candidates for its binary twin is Sirius – which is itself a binary star.[3-44]

The Dogon people of Mali in west Africa claim to have been visited by alien beings from a planet orbiting the Sirius system.[3-45] Their descriptions match the type of extraterrestrial that we know as the Reptilians. (We'll look at the different types of alien in Chapter 13.)

The Dogon people have also been confirmed to have advanced astronomical knowledge, totally out of place for that sort of culture. How they acquired that knowledge is hotly debated. Some believe they could only have acquired it from an extraterrestrial source, while others believe it could have been passed on to them by French astronomers who visited the region in 1893, or by anthropologists who visited the Dogon elders in the 1950s.[3-46]

Sirius is a young binary star system, no more than 300 million years old. That's far too young for any advanced life forms to have developed there. But the Dogons speak of a third star in the system – a brown dwarf companion – that Western astronomers haven't discovered yet. Orbital irregularities hint that there *could* be a third star in the system, but it must be very small and dim. Researchers say that if this star (putatively named Sirius C) is ever found, it will prove conclusively that the Dogons must have acquired their knowledge from extraterrestrials. It's unlikely that the extraterrestrials came from Sirius themselves though, unless Sirius C turns out to be a much older star. At the time of writing, no planets had been discovered at all in the Sirius system.

> If Sirius is our Sun's binary twin, it's worth noting that it only appeared comparatively recently. The Sun would have been a single star for more than 90 percent of its life.

> If you'd like to learn more about the Dogon people's claims, and the evidence which supports it, I can recommend the book *The Sirius Mystery: New Scientific Evidence of Alien Contact 5,000 Years Ago* by Robert K. G. Temple (Second edition, 1999).[3-47]

3.7 Human–alien hybrids?

Archaeologists and anthropologists have found numerous remains of what appear to be human–alien hybrids. Unfortunately, it's difficult to determine their true origin as the DNA evidence is somewhat scant, and is undoubtedly being suppressed, ignored or confiscated by mainstream organizations and authorities.

Of particular interest are the significant number of elongated skulls that have been found, mainly in Central and South America. Typical examples have been found in Onavas in Mexico and Paracas in Peru.[3-48][3-49]

Some human cultures deliberately splinted and bound their babies' heads so that their skulls became elongated. Why they did this is unknown, but they may have been trying to mimic the appearance of the hybrids or aliens, whom they regarded as gods.

But we can easily tell the difference between humans that have had their heads bound and the elongated skulls that appear to have developed naturally. For example, the ones found in Paracas were 60 percent heavier than human skulls, were structurally different, and had craniums that were 25 percent larger than ours. Researchers managed to extract mitochondrial DNA from them and found mutations which indicated an unknown human-like species that didn't fit the evolutionary tree.[3-50]

Some of the Ancient Egyptian Pharaohs are also thought to have been human-alien hybrids – particularly Akhenaten.[3-51]

3.8 Ancient nuclear explosions

There are signs of ancient nuclear explosions in Rajasthan,[3-52] near Jodhpur in India, and in the Sahara Desert in and around Libya. Several sites in northern India are also contaminated by radiation.

The radioactive contamination in Rajasthan has been dated to about 12,000 years ago, but it could be older. It appears to have been caused by an atomic bomb, equivalent in size to those the US dropped on Japan during World War II. But the radiation level there today is around fifty times higher than at the Japanese sites. Human remains that have been unearthed there show signs of sudden death by a nuclear bomb.

The possible nuclear explosion in the Sahara Desert has been dated to around 28.5 million years ago. It's estimated that such an explosion would have been 10,000 times greater than any atomic bomb we've ever tested. The main evidence for the explosion is the large quantity of dense yellow-green glass[3-53][3-54][3-55] that can be found in wide areas across the desert, particularly in Libya and western Egypt. It formed when the sand was vitrified by the heat of the explosion, and shows definite signs of having been formed by a massive amount of thermal radiation. Similar material formed at other sites during modern-day nuclear testing.

Mainstream scientists are reluctant to accept that a nuclear explosion could have occurred that long ago, and they've been actively pursuing alternative explanations. An asteroid impact has been ruled out as they've been unable to find any signs of an impact crater, even under the sand. In any case, the desert glass doesn't match the tektites that form during such impacts. Some geophysicists are still searching for the elusive crater, but with the idea that it may have been created by a comet rather than an asteroid or meteorite. They're also exploring the possibility of an air burst, similar to the Tunguska event that occurred over Siberia in 1908. But for now, the origins of the glass remains an enigma.

Interestingly, one of the Egyptian pharaoh Tutankhamen's necklaces features a scarab beetle carved from Libyan Desert glass.[3-56]

It's worth noting that a significant part of the Sahara only became a desert quite recently.[3-57] Numerous human settlements lie buried beneath the sand,[3-58] which is over 490 feet (150 meters) deep. The exact timeline is disputed, but up until about 5,400 years ago much of the region was a lush paradise covered in great lakes. Intensive farming combined with a shift in the Earth's axis, which increased the temperature and decreased rainfall, are thought to have caused its abrupt desertification.[3-59]

3.9 Reports from credible people

Several of the people featured in this section waited until late in their lives before coming forward. They'd retired, so their careers weren't at risk, and many of them had no family left, so they couldn't be threatened. They had nothing to lose and nothing to gain, and they no longer gave a damn about their reputations; they just wanted the public to know what *really* went on. Their former colleagues and the media sneer at them – because their secret government-sanctioned protocols say they must. But we should regard these people as heroes for coming forward.

Many other current and former members of the armed forces have said they have important information on UFOs and extraterrestrials. But they've refused to reveal it, having had their reputations and even their lives threatened.

3.9.a World leaders

Two US presidents have openly admitted seeing UFOs:[3-60] Ronald Reagan and Jimmy Carter. Reagan repeatedly tried to talk about UFOs and extraterrestrials while he was in office, but he was shut down. But he gave at least one speech in which he acknowledged that: "We are not alone in the universe." Carter filed two formal reports of sightings while he was Governor of Georgia. During his presidential campaign, he pledged to release all reports and documentation from investigations carried out by the US Government into UFOs and extraterrestrials. He won the election, but nothing was ever released. In fact, witnesses reported seeing him crying at his desk shortly after being briefed on the subject.

Several other presidents pledged to "get to the bottom of it" while out on the campaign trail. But once they were elected they either refused to discuss it or said there was nothing in it – yet gave hints that there was. In 1995, President Bill Clinton said he suspected things were being kept from him, and he believed senior military officials and career bureaucrats were lying to him. He also said there was a "government inside the government" that he was not in control of.

Clinton's wife Hillary said in 2016 that she too would force UFO disclosure if she were elected, suggesting that her husband had already tried and failed when he was president.[3-61] She failed to win her election.

George W. Bush has admitted seeing classified documentation on UFOs and extraterrestrials, but refused to reveal what it said. He said he would take his knowledge of the contents to his grave.[3-62] That suggests it must have been something fairly monumental.

John F. Kennedy was assassinated ten days after ordering all US Government files on UFOs and extraterrestrials to be released. Nothing was released.

> It should be noted that Kennedy was reportedly about to reveal several other Government secrets, all of which have been put forward as reasons for his assassination.

Barack Obama failed to respond to requests for information about his knowledge of UFOs and extraterrestrials. But presidents were reportedly no longer briefed on the subject by the time he took office, so he probably knew no more than the rest of us.

All of this seems to stem from three meetings President Dwight D. Eisenhower is purported to have had with representatives from extraterrestrial civilizations in 1954.[3-63][3-64][3-65][3-66][3-67]

One of these meetings was reportedly held at Edwards Air Force Base (then known as Muroc Field) in California. Another took place at an Air Force Base in New Mexico. According to witnesses, Eisenhower met with representatives of the Nordics (a human-like alien race) but refused to sign a deal with them because he wouldn't accept their terms. Apparently, they wanted the US and other countries to get rid of their nuclear weapons.

At a later meeting, Eisenhower is said to have signed a deal with a different alien race. Most sources say it was signed with the Greys, but it's more likely to have been the Tall Whites. They're now reported to hold a controlling interest in US politics.[3-68]

> The deal is known as the Grenada Treaty.
> The US Government denies it exists.

Although the deal was formally known as a treaty, many commentators say it was effectively a negotiated surrender. The aliens were so far ahead of us, in terms of their technology and weapons, that we had no way of stopping them from doing whatever they wanted.

According to the terms of the deal, the aliens would provide us with advanced scientific and engineering knowledge, which would enable us to make a massive leap forward. In exchange, they wanted to establish bases on Earth, carry out experiments on a limited number of human subjects, and place virtually undetectable implants in them. They agreed not to cause the subjects any physical harm, to erase the subjects' memories of the incident, and to supply the Government with the names of everyone they experimented on. Some researchers believe the aliens were also granted permission to take cattle.[3-68a]

Following his meetings with the aliens, Eisenhower halted all further attempts by US Government agencies to find extraterrestrial life, and all documentation on the subject was classified.

Exact details of what went on in those meetings is almost impossible to come by, and the little information we have is somewhat conflicting, although there were apparently numerous witnesses.

The former Russian President and Prime Minister Dmitry Medvedev has acknowledged that aliens have visited Earth.[3-70]

The former Canadian Minister of Defense Paul Hellyer publicly stated his belief in extraterrestrials. He claimed to have witnessed a UFO and said four alien species had been visiting the Earth for thousands of years.[3-71] He called upon the world's governments to release any information they've been given by extraterrestrials that would help solve the problem of climate change. He also warned that the USA was in danger of leading the planet into an intergalactic war.

3.9.b Astronauts

I believe you can trust the word of an astronaut. Many of them served in the Air Force and made rapid progress through the ranks. They're often highly trained engineers or scientists, and they're skilled observers. They're some of the smartest people in the world. And they don't tend to make mistakes or lie – unless they're forced to. Having said that, several of them have expressed frustration that they're not allowed to talk about some of the things they've seen. Fortunately for us, some of them have breached protocol and spoken about it anyway.

Reportedly the first person to land on the Moon, American astronaut Neil Armstrong is said to have made the following radio report to a medical officer at mission control in Houston, Texas, using the private medical frequency: "They're here. They're right over there, parked on the other side of the crater, and they're watching us. Looking at the size of those ships, it's obvious they don't like us being here."

As this message was sent via the medical channel, it wasn't heard by media broadcasters and doesn't form part of the official *Apollo 11* mission transcript.[3-72] But it was picked up by several ham radio operators. Another message was apparently transmitted to mission control but was screened from the public and omitted from the transcript. Again, it was picked up by ham radio operators. Armstrong is heard to say: "These babies are huge, sir. Enormous. Oh, God, you wouldn't believe it. I'm telling you there are other spacecraft out there. Lined up on the far side of the crater edge. They're on the Moon watching us."[3-73]

According to reports, Armstrong was informed by mission control that NASA was fully aware that the alien craft were there, and he should carry on with his job as planned.

Official sources have (of course) said the whole thing was a preposterous hoax. But the messages were picked up and repeated by so many amateur radio operators that there could well be some truth in it.

Incredibly, NASA says it has "lost" many of the audio, video and telemetry recordings from the Apollo missions, and they can't be recovered.[3-74] The official story is that the tapes were erased and reused, as was the practice at that time. This is beyond belief: many people regard the *Apollo 11* mission as mankind's greatest achievement. It would be reasonable, therefore, to expect every part of it to have been carefully archived. If the tapes were erased, there must have been a good reason for it – and it had nothing to do with saving money on tape. Former US Army Command Sergeant Major Robert O. Dean said NASA had also deliberately erased forty rolls of film taken during the Apollo program. They didn't just lock them away, or mark them "classified" or "top secret"; they made sure the public would never get to see them.[3-74a]

On his return to Earth, Armstrong cooperated with media requests for interviews at first, but he soon became withdrawn and reclusive. In 2009, he initially refused to take part in the fortieth-anniversary celebrations of the Moon landings. Although he was eventually persuaded to do so, he gave a bizarre speech in which he implied that he was only allowed to say what NASA said he could say, and that the words and phrases he should use had been drilled into him – like teaching a parrot.[3-75][3-76]

Armstrong's colleague on the *Apollo 11* mission, Edwin "Buzz" Aldrin, has admitted (on video) that the whole crew saw a light following their craft. After discussing it among themselves, they decided not to report it to mission control as it would have alerted the public and caused a UFO frenzy. Radio records show that they asked mission control if their own Saturn stage 3 rocket booster was nearby, but they were informed that it was 6,000 miles away.

There are reports that they also saw a cylindrical craft, but Aldrin said in his book *Return to Earth* that they concluded it was just a detached panel that had covered the lunar module during launch. There are also reports that the aliens on the Moon were menacing and ordered them away.[3-77]

Edgar Mitchell[3-78] was the lunar module pilot on *Apollo 14*, and the sixth man to walk on the Moon. He became the most vocal of the former Apollo astronauts and revealed a great deal of information about what they had seen. He claimed that alien bodies were recovered and studied,[3-79] that the Pope was aware of the existence of aliens, and that governments were covering up their contact with aliens. He said that following John F. Kennedy's assassination, US presidents were no longer briefed on the existence of UFOs. And he claimed that aliens had been attempting to prevent wars from breaking out, and were trying to bring about peace on Earth.[3-80]

In a radio interview, he said: "I happen to have been privileged enough to be in on the fact that we've been visited on this planet, and the UFO phenomenon is real." NASA said in response that it did not share his opinion.

American astronaut and senator John Glenn admitted he'd also seen things while in space, but he wasn't allowed to talk about them.

Project Mercury astronaut L. Gordon Cooper said he'd seen flying disks when he was a US Air Force pilot in Germany in 1957. He told a United Nations committee: "Every day in the USA our radar instruments capture objects of form and composition unknown to us." He said there was a veil of secrecy – which he'd broken – and he called for investigations to be opened.[3-81]

Former NASA employee Donna Hare revealed that alien spacecraft had been airbrushed out of photos from the Apollo program before they were released to the public.

> There's a 24-hour live video feed from outside (and sometimes inside) the International Space Station.[3-82] But don't expect to see anything except images of the Earth or astronauts going about their business. If anything really interesting happens, the feed is immediately cut – to the intense frustration of UFO-spotters.

Brian O'Leary[3-83] was the only planetary scientist-astronaut in NASA's Astronaut Corps during the Apollo program. He was the first astronaut selected for NASA's manned mission to Mars, which was originally scheduled to follow the lunar missions during the 1980s. He said he believed in an extraterrestrial presence on Earth, and that the aliens had given us the technology to generate free energy, which would potentially transform the world, as well as things like anti-gravity systems. He also said public knowledge of these things was being suppressed by global authorities.[3-84] After resigning from NASA, he lectured widely on this subject.

3.9.c Pilots

Pilots, like astronauts, can generally be relied upon to speak the truth. They're also highly experienced observers and know what should be in the sky and what shouldn't. Tens of thousands of pilots from all over the world have given reliable testimonies of UFO sightings and encounters. These have often been corroborated by their co-pilots and passengers, and are sometimes backed up by radar and visual sightings from the ground.

3.9.d Armed forces personnel

Retired US Air Force airman first class Charles Hall has written and spoken about his encounters with three types of extraterrestrials. He said two of them – the Tall Whites and the Greys – have large bases at Nellis Air Force Base in Nevada. A third species – identical to us but with only 24 teeth compared to our 32 – has a base in Norway.[3-85][3-86]

Retired US Army Sergeant Clifford Stone said he was part of an elite covert unit run by the US Air Force that recovered crashed UFOs, alien bodies, and artifacts. He said extraterrestrials are visiting Earth in spacecraft that bypass the conventional laws of physics.[3-87][3-88]

Other former US military personnel, including Corey Goode and Dan Sherman, have said they were involved in extraterrestrial communications and worked for multiple secret space programs.

3.9.e Scientists and engineers

We've already seen that mainstream scientists point blank refuse to get involved with anything to do with UFOs, extraterrestrials, or human remains or artifacts that fall outside our official evolutionary timeline. We'll look at the reasons for this in Chapter 4. But, happily, some highly regarded scientists are prepared to talk.

Boyd Bushman, a former engineer at Lockheed Martin, revealed that US President Ronald Reagan's Strategic Defense Initiative (also known as the "Star Wars" program) evolved into the secret space fleet program known as Solar Warden.[3-89][3-90] Its existence was confirmed by British computer hacker Gary McKinnon. Bushman said Solar Warden was a black budget program operating under the US Naval Network and Space Operations Command (NNSOC). It has approximately eight motherships that are each as long as two football fields, as well as 43 scout ships. At least 300 people are known to be employed in the program, including several "non-terrestrial officers."

> It might or might not be relevant, but Bushman appears to have suffered from dementia later in life. He gave a "deathbed interview" in which he claimed to have proof of alien life, but then showed a photo of a toy alien. That doesn't mean the information he gave about the Solar Warden program is wrong, of course. It seems credible, but we need to consider other people's testimonies too.

American biochemist Kary Mullis was awarded the Nobel Prize in Chemistry in 1993 for his work on the polymerase chain reaction. He also claims to have had an encounter with a glowing green alien raccoon, suffered from missing time, and suspects he's been abducted by aliens.[3-91][3-92]

Italian electrical engineer Professor Stefano Breccia revealed that aliens are living among us and have underground bases in Italy.[3-93] He personally interviewed many eyewitnesses. He also claimed to have flown on a bell-shaped alien spacecraft. He released details of its propulsion and navigation systems[3-94] and published a book, *50 Years of Amicizia* (Friendship), which includes clear photographs of an eight-foot-tall alien and the inside of one of their spacecraft.

The British paleontologist and evolutionary biologist Professor Simon Conway Morris said aliens are real and look just like us.[3-95]

The Canadian nuclear physicist Stanton Friedman has said we're regularly visited by aliens, and some are living among us. They're prepared to take control and put the Earth into quarantine to prevent us from venturing any further into space.

Theodor C. Loder III, Professor Emeritus of Earth Sciences at the University of New Hampshire, said: "Intelligent beings from other star systems have been and are visiting our planet Earth."

American physicist Dr. John Brandenburg, who worked on NASA's *Clementine* mission to the Moon, has spoken freely about alien life and UFOs.[3-96]

The well-known American scientists Neil deGrasse Tyson and Bill Nye also believe that extraterrestrials exist and are intelligent.

> Neil deGrasse Tyson famously said: "The good thing about science is that it's true whether or not you believe in it."

3.9.f Directors

Ben Rich, "the father of the stealth bomber" and the former director of Lockheed's Skunk Works (their secret research and development division), said: "We already have the means to travel among the stars, but these technologies are locked up in black projects, and it would take an act of God to ever get them out to benefit humanity." He also confirmed that extraterrestrial visitors and UFOs are real.[3-97a][3-97b][3-97c]

Rich's colleague, Don Phillips, a Skunk Works contractor, testified that we have captured extraterrestrial craft and developed advanced technology by studying them.

We'll take a closer look at this technology in Chapter 13.

Joe Firmage, co-founder and CEO of the former internet marketing company USWeb, left the company in 1999 to pursue his interests in extraterrestrials after claiming to have been visited by them in his bedroom.[3-98] He said they'd revealed advanced technologies and details of extraterrestrial civilizations. He aims to expose the Government conspiracy to cover up the 1947 UFO crash in Roswell.

3.9.g Others

Thousands of other highly respected and trustworthy people claim to have had encounters with extraterrestrials, witnessed UFOs, or discovered evidence of our non-terrestrial past. In particular, the word of police officers and professional astronomers can usually be trusted, and plenty of them say they have credible evidence.

US Government adviser and researcher Timothy Good[3-99] and former US Government geologist Philip Schneider[3-100] claimed to have uncovered a secret program, run jointly by the US Government and extraterrestrials, that's attempting to create human–alien hybrids and capture and replicate their souls. Good said the work takes place in a deep underground military base (DUMB) in Dulce, New Mexico. Schneider was one of the structural engineers who helped build the facility, and he confirmed Good's testimony.

Schneider also claimed to be one of only three personnel who survived a military shootout with Grey aliens at the Dulce base in 1979. He was severely injured in the battle: his chest was split open by a "beam weapon" and he lost two fingers. He died in 1996, and although the official verdict was suicide, his widow claims he was murdered for revealing the truth about the USA's involvement with extraterrestrials.[3-101][3-102]

Humans Are Not From Earth

3.10 Conclusion

As we've seen, there's a wealth of credible information available, and thousands of reliable and trustworthy witnesses have given testimonies. Their statements are frequently corroborated by their colleagues, as well as by things like radar, audio and video recordings, photographs, and mass public sightings.

Of course, it's possible that some of those witnesses were mistaken, or hallucinating, or suffering from dementia or some other mental illness. Or perhaps they were lying, or either they or their colleagues or friends faked the evidence for some reason. But these are, on the whole, trustworthy and credible people. There can be no doubt that at least some of them – and I'd say it was the majority – really did have the experiences that they said they did.

These aren't the kind of people that make mistakes either. They knew exactly what they were – and weren't – looking at. They risked their reputations, their careers, and even their lives to say what they'd seen. They could have kept quiet – and I'm sure their managers and colleagues told them to, and wish they had done so.

Some of them are now vilified and ridiculed for "going public" – just as they knew they would be. But, as I said earlier, in my eyes they're heroes who deserve our highest praise and respect.

4

The Cover-Ups

I n this chapter, we'll look at why governments cover up and deny the existence of extraterrestrials and UFOs, and why mainstream scientists refuse to get involved.

There have been dozens of UFO crashes around the world. The Phoenix Project has documented at least 36, and several more are still to be researched.[4-01] The earliest report I could find of a UFO crash was in 1884.[4-02] In several cases, there were credible witnesses, and the incidents were well documented.[4-03] There can be no doubt that at least *some* of these crashes really happened. Numerous other reported encounters with extraterrestrial craft were also undoubtedly real.

Taken en masse, this is extraordinary evidence. And it's therefore reasonable to make the extraordinary claim that extraterrestrials have visited the Earth, are still visiting the Earth, some are living here now, and they're in communication with our governments.

4.1 Why the government doesn't want you to know

There are all sorts of reasons why the governments of the world don't want you to know about this.

The main reason is that the aliens themselves don't want the public to know they're here. You have to remember that the aliens are so far ahead of us technologically that we're powerless to stop them. The only weapon we have is diplomacy. So the governments have to give them what they want and hope they'll go easy on us. If the aliens ever want the public to know they're here, they'll order the governments to make the announcement – and the governments will have no choice but to do so.

All of the world's governments deny the existence of aliens, despite a wealth of evidence to the contrary – much of it collected by the governments themselves. This policy of denial is believed to be part of the Grenada Treaty that US President Dwight D. Eisenhower signed with a race of extraterrestrials in 1954.

It could also be the case that at least some of the world's governments have enough on their hands just dealing with local matters. They don't have the time, money or energy to deal with so-called "alien matters" as well. And in any case, they probably believe the denials issued by larger governments, and repeat them to their own citizens.

If aliens and UFOs ever become an issue, they'll deal with it then, they say. But not until it becomes an issue. That means, of course, that they have no (official) plans for dealing with this sort of thing. If the situation ever arises, they'll either have to make it up as they go along – which could cause problems for the whole world if they get it wrong – or seek advice from other governments.

Another point to remember is that we're inherently violent and our leaders are often warmongers. That could explain why the extraterrestrials brought us here in the first place.

> We'll discuss the prison planet hypothesis in the next chapter.

The aliens might not want us to know they're here because we'd attack them if we found out. That wouldn't be a problem for the aliens, of course; their superior weapons could wipe us all out in a flash – perhaps literally. But it would be a massive problem for us. So the aliens may have instructed the world's governments to keep things quiet for *our* benefit rather than for theirs.

There have already been reports of small-scale battles between humans and aliens.[4-04] The aliens have made it clear that if we attack them, they *will* fight back.

That's not usually the case when we encounter them in the air though. There have been several reports of military jets pursuing and firing missiles at UFOs,[4-05] but the UFOs easily avoided the danger, either by dodging out of the way or by absorbing the missiles harmlessly. There have been very few cases of UFOs firing back. But at least one US jet was reportedly shot down by a UFO, and another pilot lost control of his plane and crashed while pursuing one.[4-06]

There's a popular story that when the American actor Orson Welles broadcast a performance of *The War of the Worlds* on the radio in the 1930s, it caused a nationwide panic. According to the media at the time, millions of Americans believed that Martians really had landed and were killing people. But this story seems to have been nothing more than media hype. Many people who heard the broadcast said they were fully aware it was fictional and the so-called "panic" never happened. Even so, many authorities cite the public's panic in response to this broadcast as a reason for concealing the truth.

I have to be honest here: I have no idea what the public's response to a real alien visitation would be. Would we line up and greet them in peaceful but fascinated interest? Would we experience brain-freeze and gape at them open-mouthed, unable to respond? Would we run at them with guns, sticks, rocks, broken bottles, and whatever else we could lay our hands on? Would there be total panic and worldwide riots? Would all the major religions collapse? I guess it depends on where they land and how friendly they are – or at least how friendly they *look*.

Then there's the issue that knowledge is power. And, of course, where there's power there's often a great deal of money to be made. Many political leaders – and their relatives and friends – are directors, board members, and stockholders of the companies that benefit most from technology derived from extraterrestrial sources. Their true aim, often underlying their political careers, is to exploit and monetize those technologies to the maximum extent – for their own benefit.

Naturally, they lie, cheat, cover up and deny all knowledge of the true source of their wealth. They're all about self-preservation and protecting their income. Of course, if they could make more money from revealing the secret than they could from covering it up, they'd reveal it in a heartbeat, even if thousands of people died as a result.

4.2 How the government covers up the truth

Media cover-ups

The government controls the media, and the media releases only what it's allowed to release or what it's told to release.

Think about the members of the public you've seen in the media who've come forward as witnesses to UFO sightings or alien encounters. Do they seem credible, reliable and trustworthy? No, of course they don't. The media carefully selects them and portrays them as nuts. This is deliberate for two reasons. First, they're following orders from the government, and second, it makes for great entertainment. No matter how busy the day's news schedule is, there's always room for a couple of minutes at the end to laugh at the nut jobs with their whacky story about aliens.

The credible witnesses, on the other hand, don't make it into the news at all – even though they form the majority of cases. They might be sold the story that they're *definitely* going to be featured, and they might even be invited along to a television or radio station. But on the day, more important news items *always* crop up. The story about their UFO or alien encounter gets pushed further and further down the running order until it falls off the bottom and is quietly dropped. The producer apologizes to the witnesses and says: sorry, guys, but that's how the news business works. Their job is to report the big stories first, and if there are *only* big stories – or they can make it *look* as if there are only big stories (and they always can) – they run out of time for the other stuff.

There's also the issue that the majority of credible witnesses won't come forward anyway. They've seen how the media portrays all witnesses as nut jobs. They know that even if they manage to get on the air or in the newspapers with their story, they'll be made fun of. So they keep it to themselves.

Threats, ridicule, and career suicide

Underlying all of this is a more sinister threat, and it's one you're undoubtedly aware of. Do you ever worry about what might happen to you if you came forward as a witness? The government wants you to know that if you say anything publicly, "people" will come after you. Your career, your reputation, your family and even your life could be in danger – or at least that's the implication. In all probability, nothing will happen at all. But there's a chance that it might, and it could be bad. So most people won't take the risk and keep their silence.

We've already seen some examples of this. In the previous chapter, we met Virginia Steen-McIntyre, a member of a team of archaeologists that found legitimate evidence that modern humans were in Mexico 250,000 years ago. Excited by the discovery, she went against her colleagues' advice and published their results. Her career and reputation were destroyed.

Another example is Philip J. Corso, a highly respected colonel in the US Army who worked at the Pentagon. When he wrote about some of the projects he'd worked on, specifically those involving technologies recovered from crashed extraterrestrial spacecraft, his reputation was quickly trashed. His former employers said he'd "become senile" and couldn't be considered a credible person.[4-07] They said his book, *The Day After Roswell*,[4-08] should be regarded as a work of fiction or a literary hoax.[4-09]

Yet if you read his book and check the facts he mentions, you'll find that not only is most of it *highly* credible, it's also verifiable. He really did work on the projects he talks about. I can't vouch for everything he says, as I don't have access to that level of information, but I'd say it was, at the very least, a reasonably accurate account of what happened.

Of course, I can't be certain that he wasn't suffering from a *degree* of mental impairment when he wrote it. But he certainly wasn't *completely* senile, and in all probability, he wasn't the slightest bit senile. His book is most definitely *not* a work of fiction. The only fiction is what people said about him after he wrote it. I only wish I'd been able to meet him before he died.

The Roswell cover-up

The things that happened in the immediate aftermath of the Roswell incident[4-10][4-11][4-12][4-13] illustrate what happens when the government and military stage a cover-up.

William ("Mac") Brazel, a foreman who worked on a local ranch, spotted some clusters of brightly-colored material scattered over the land. He later returned with members of his family, and they gathered some of it up and reported it to the local sheriff. Major Jesse Marcel, a US Army intelligence officer, was then dispatched from the Roswell

Army Air Field to take a look and to gather more of the material. After examining some of the material at the local base, a truck was sent to collect the rest of it from the ranch. It was reportedly sent to the army unit's headquarters, but that was the last anyone ever saw of it.

According to Brazel and Marcel, the debris included thin sheets of an unusual type of super-strong memory metal, along with short lengths of I-beam made from an unknown metal and marked with strange hieroglyphic-like symbols.

Major Marcel was then asked to pose with the debris for press photos at Fort Worth Army Air Field. But the debris he was asked to pose with wasn't the material they'd collected from the ranch. It was just some pieces of a burst weather balloon, or something similar. Another photo shows General Roger Ramey and Brigadier General Thomas DuBose inspecting the same debris.

When the photos appeared in the press, Brazel said they'd been staged by the Army to make him look like an idiot, and the debris in the photos wasn't what he'd found. But as the original materials had been seized by the Army, he had no proof, and he lost all credibility.

The US Army's press releases following the Roswell incident also defy belief and deliberately perpetuated the conspiracy theory surrounding it. Their first press release said that a "flying disk" had been recovered from a ranch. The story was reported in the *Roswell Daily Record* the following day, and quickly caught the world's attention. The Army then issued a second press release saying it had turned out to be just a weather balloon. When witnesses pointed out inconsistencies that the Army couldn't explain away, they issued a third press release "admitting" that the balloon had actually been monitoring nuclear tests. There are still far too many inconsistencies for this to be true, but they've stuck firmly to this story ever since.

The account of the incident on Wikipedia used to match the account I've given here. But just before this book went to press, we noticed that Wikipedia's entry had been substantially altered and now only gives the US Army's version of the incident. It's incredible that this sort of thing is still happening after more than 70 years.

The book *The Roswell Incident* by Charles Berlitz and William Moore gives a more thorough account of what happened. It also says that witnesses were intimidated by the military and Brazel was incarcerated.

You saw nothing

There have been plenty of mass sightings of other UFOs. In some cases, the people who witnessed them received visits from military, police or other authority figures over the following days, telling them they "saw nothing." If they insisted they *did* see something, the message was repeated more aggressively: "There was no incident. Nothing happened. You saw nothing." The visitors then left, leaving an unspoken threat of what might happen if they continued to make their "false" claim.

Those who ignored the warning and continued talking about what they'd seen said it was an empty threat and nothing happened to them. But the visit would have been enough to scare most witnesses into silence.

Of course, no right-thinking person is going to come forward and talk about what they saw after hearing how these witnesses were treated. So, who can you report UFO incidents to? Well, no one really. It used to be the case that you could report them to independent groups such as MUFON – the Mutual UFO Network. But I understand that even this once-respected organization is now under the control of a US Government agency.

Roscoe H. Hillenkoetter, the first Director of the CIA, said in 1960: "Behind the scenes, high-ranking Air Force officers are soberly concerned about UFOs. But through official secrecy and ridicule, many citizens are led to believe the unknown flying objects are nonsense."[4-14]

Need to know

Within the government and the military, things are so tightly compartmentalized that staff employed on secret projects often don't know what the people in the next room are working on. Everything is on a need-to-know basis. Regular employees never get to see the full picture. They're given just enough information and training to do their job, but no more than that. In the USA, it's said that the only people who can see the whole picture are the twelve members of Majestic 12 – a secret committee that doesn't officially exist. Even the President is kept out of the loop these days.

Project Blue Book

Following the Roswell incident, US President Harry S. Truman reportedly formed Majestic 12 under the auspices of the Air Force. The Majestic 12 committee established Project Sign (1947) followed by Project Grudge (1949) and then Project Blue Book (1952). These projects "investigated" reports of UFO sightings and extraterrestrial encounters and were tasked with explaining them away. Staff were instructed to find alternative explanations that didn't involve UFOs.

As we saw earlier, these projects were highly successful – particularly Blue Book. Although it was officially terminated in 1969, its work continues to this day, though the Government denies it.

Representatives from the current project are said to be the people who visit you if you report a credible UFO or alien encounter or you're part of a mass sighting. They're the ones who tell you "you saw nothing." The current name of the project is unknown.

When the CIA reviewed some of Blue Book's early work in 1952, it set up a committee of scientists known as the Robertson Panel.[4-15] The panel recommended establishing a public education program to explain that there were no such things as UFOs or extraterrestrials. They said this would stop the public from swamping the Air Force with reports of sightings. They also recommended monitoring civilian UFO groups.

Although the Robertson Panel reduced the level of concern about UFOs within the Government, most of its recommendations were classified until 1966, so it did nothing to reduce public concern. When its final report was eventually released, it was heavily criticized. Its investigations were superficial and unscientific, and its conclusions appeared to have been predetermined by the CIA.

Official denial

Increasingly, work on sensitive projects is contracted out to the private sector. This means that the government can officially – and truthfully – deny any involvement in them. It also takes the work outside of government control and communication – except for the highest-ranking military personnel. The private companies can, of course, apply their own secrecy restrictions, on the grounds that the projects are "commercially sensitive."

Public skepticism

The rise of CGI – computer-generated imagery – means that just about anyone can now easily fake a UFO or extraterrestrial sighting and make it look convincing. The internet is flooded with fake photos and videos. Any genuine ones just get lost among them and are also regarded as fakes. No one can tell the difference any more, and even the experts struggle and are sometimes fooled. So these images can no longer be regarded as evidence.

All of this means that the public is now incredibly skeptical of anything to do with extraterrestrials and UFOs. They're also skeptical of anything to do with the paranormal. Everything in these fields is now regarded as "pseudoscience" and the people who believe in them are labeled crackpots and nut jobs. And the government couldn't be happier.

Many of the so-called conspiracy theories are absolute bunk, of course. There's not an ounce of truth in some of them. The authorities love them because they muddy the picture and cause the public to be automatically suspicious of everything. Most people's default position is to assume that everything is a lie or a fake. And, again, that means most of the real evidence gets lost in all the noise.

Those who believe that some of the conspiracy theories are true are free to express their opinions, but they can't present a convincing case without evidence. And, as we saw earlier, much of that evidence has been locked away, well out of their reach.

There's also the problem that any evidence that hasn't been locked away will be ignored. As we saw earlier, most mainstream scientists won't even look at it. The few that do will only express the superficial opinion that it "looks interesting." Then they thank you for bringing it in and show you to the exit.[4-16] As John. J. Williams discovered when he tried to get scientists to look at his Enigmalith, finding someone who's actually willing to test it is no easy task. He couldn't find anyone, and, like most people, he eventually gave up trying. We'll look at why that is later in the chapter.

SETI

Interestingly, the US Government is one of the biggest contributors to the SETI project – the Search for Extraterrestrial Intelligence.

There's plenty of evidence that the Government is not only in contact with extraterrestrials but has contractors working alongside them here on Earth. Yet they continue to invest in projects like this, giving the impression that they're still awaiting first contact. It's all smoke and mirrors, designed to cover up what's really going on.

The public space program

The public space program is pretty much the same thing. It's "exploring new frontiers" that the secret space program already explored decades ago.[4-17] The public program is directed to only visit areas where there are no signs of extraterrestrial life. It's banned from going anywhere else.

4.3 What the government is *really* doing

In this section, I'm referring mainly to the US Government. Other governments undoubtedly have their own systems and secret agendas in place too.

Although the Government claims it no longer investigates or has any interest in UFOs or extraterrestrials, there's a wealth of evidence to suggest otherwise. It *does* investigate, and it's *very* interested indeed in valid cases. As we saw earlier, if you report a sighting and you have a significant and credible piece of evidence, you will almost certainly receive a visit from one or more authority figures. Interestingly, it doesn't seem to matter who you report the incident to.

See "Are the Men in Black real?" later in the chapter for details of what happens when they visit you.

There's no question that the Government is developing technology based on material recovered from crashed extraterrestrial craft. The things they're working on now, in secret, are decades ahead of anything the public knows about. There are all sorts of special projects, covering everything from space exploration, aircraft, stealth technology, weapons, science and engineering, transport, robotics, computing, communications, medicine, energy, and more.

Much of this work is conducted by a layer of what might be called the "invisible government": private industrialists, financiers, and contractors who operate outside of government communication and control. Only a select few within the Government and military know they exist, what they're working on, where they're located, who works for them, and how they're funded.[4-18]

As we saw earlier, each project is tightly compartmentalized. You might go to lunch with someone who works in the next room, but you have no idea what he does, he has no idea what you do, and neither of you can discuss it. You're probably working on the same project, but you have no idea which aspect of it the other person is working on, and you aren't allowed to ask, even if it might benefit your work.

Alongside and within the known Government departments are an unknown number of "invisible departments" that most people, including Government employees and politicians, know nothing about. These organizations run black projects, deep-black projects, beyond-black projects, Special Access Programs (SAPs), and Unacknowledged Special Access Programs (USAPs or UNSAPS).[4-19][4-20] The people who work on these programs are not listed as official government employees.

Secret funding

The US Government has an official budget for black projects: in 2015 it was $58.7 billion. But the true figure is almost certainly much higher. The invisible departments and special projects have enormous budgets. The Secret Space Program (SSP-UNSAP), for example, has a budget that dwarfs the $19 billion NASA receives each year.[4-21][4-22][4-23][4-24][4-25][4-26][4-27]

So how are they *really* funded? Well, there's this for a start: the Department of Defense, whose annual budget is well over $500 billion, "admitted" to losing track of $8.5 trillion between 1996 and 2014.[4-28] That's more than $472 billion per year – or almost their entire budget. Can the Department of Defense really be that inept? Of course not; that would be beyond ridiculous. I've spent some time working for the federal government, and I can tell you they just don't operate that way. They know *exactly* where it went. Every last cent will have been accounted for and triple-checked. But you and I will never get to hear about it, and nor, I suspect, will the President.

Other funding allegedly comes from arms[4-29] and drugs sales, donations and project contributions from foreign governments, licensing and royalty fees on classified patents, and all sorts of other things you'll also never get to hear about.

There's even a rumor that the Department of Defense funded some of its black projects by selling Nazi gold they seized during World War.[4-30][4-31][4-32] The sale went unrecorded of course – officially they never had the gold in the first place.

Who is really in control?

Behind all this shadiness lies something potentially even more worrying. The extraterrestrials might be the ones who are really running the show. The world's governments might believe they're in control, but in reality, the aliens could seize power at any moment.

The governments might think the aliens are benign and even helpful, but the aliens undoubtedly have their own agenda. They may have already infiltrated the US Government at every level. They may be already running things, or at the very least *influencing* things, so they proceed in their preferred direction.

4.4 Are the Men in Black real?

There's no doubt that the so-called Men in Black are real. Many reliable and trustworthy witnesses have encountered them, and they've been recorded on CCTV footage.[4-33]

Many people ask whether they're aliens or government agents from top secret black projects. I have no idea. But it's important to remember that black project staff are usually employed by private contractors, not directly by the government, so it's probably wrong to call them "government" agents.

Whatever the case, they're reported to behave and speak rather strangely and stiffly, as if they're not quite human. Some people even suspect they might be robots. In one encounter, one of them appeared to have loose wires hanging out, but that might have been a deliberate part of his disguise. They generally operate in pairs, so I suspect that one of them is an extraterrestrial – probably one of the Tall Whites – while the other is a human from one of the black-budget defense departments. But I haven't yet met any of them in person, and even if I did, I'm not sure I'd be able to tell what they were.

So how do you get to meet them? Well, these days they generally contact you electronically if you've reported a legitimate UFO or extraterrestrial sighting or encounter. As I mentioned earlier, it doesn't seem to matter who you reported it to: the police, the military, or one of the private UFO groups they monitor. They'll find a way of contacting you, even if you're using a private email account that you haven't shared with anyone else. Some people have reported message boxes popping up on their computers.

According to reports from those who've had dealings with them, their initial approach is to establish a rapport with you and chat about the incident. They then try to persuade you that there's a more rational explanation for what you saw. If you insist that the encounter was real and continue to push that point, the discussion will take a more aggressive tone. Most people stop responding to their messages at this point and block their email address so they can't receive any more. I could find no reports of them taking any further action after this. The threat that they might is generally enough.

If, when you reported your encounter, you said you had physical evidence, such as a legitimate photograph or video or artifact, or you were part of a mass sighting and there were multiple witnesses, you can usually expect a visit in person. Again, they'll be able to find you even if you didn't give your address or any other details they could use to trace you.

They generally use the same sort of script that they use when they contact you electronically. But they'll also ask to see any physical evidence you have. If you hand it to them, they won't return it.

Before the advent of digital photography, they'd seize photographs and video tapes and remove the film or tape from your camera. But these days they'll just ask you to delete everything, and they'll watch you as you do it, checking that every last trace of evidence is removed from every device.

As before, they'll tell you that you saw nothing. You'll be warned that if you tell anyone you saw anything, they'll be back, and you'll be in serious trouble. Then they leave.

I could find no recent reports of them taking things any further than this. In the past, they've reportedly made threats against people's lives, livelihoods, family, friends, reputations, and finances. They've also threatened to take people to remote locations and dump them there.

You can read a lot more about this in Nick Redfern's book: *The Real Men In Black: Evidence, Famous Cases, and True Stories of These Mysterious Men and their Connection to the UFO Phenomena.*

4.5 Why mainstream science won't get involved

According to the former Canadian defense minister Paul Hellyer, proof of an alien presence on Earth is overwhelming. Science is at fault for dismissing it.

So why do they dismiss it? There are many reasons.

It all starts with the government, of course. They monitor projects, funding boards and science publications and control what gets approved, funded and published, and what doesn't.

> A book such as the one you're reading now would never be approved, funded or published through the mainstream science channels. While many have criticized me for publishing it independently, there really was no other option.

The next issue is the teaching of science. Some of the topics in fields like genetics, for example, are little more than well-crafted fiction. They're designed to provide students with false – but nevertheless plausible – explanations for things like the hundreds of scars that are evident in our DNA where it's been modified. Genetics students are indoctrinated and brainwashed with alternative explanations that don't make sense, particularly in context with the other topics I've written about.

The students will, of course, challenge what I've written, because they believe the things their professors have told them. And, in fact, their professors undoubtedly believe those things too.

If they examine the evidence I've included to back up my claims, and they discover that it has some merit, it'll cause them to suffer from cognitive dissonance – the psychological discomfort of trying to hold two opposing views at the same time. We'll look at this in more detail later. Most of them won't take that risk, and won't even look at the hundreds of references I've listed in Chapter 15. The few that do will reject them as fake or pseudoscience, ignoring any proof to the contrary, just like their peers.

It takes an enormous amount of inner strength to break free from all the years of indoctrination and learn how to think for yourself again. But we can fix this. Here's what I'd like you to do:

- follow up the links in Chapter 15 and see for yourself what other people have discovered

- ignore what other people say about them – they have their own agendas

- consider their evidence with an open mind

- offer to help them to research it further

- examine the artifacts for yourself and properly test them

- campaign for hidden artifacts to be released

- correct any mistakes in the published works – not with what you've been taught but with your own first-hand experiments and research

- if you're 100 percent sure you're right, discuss it with your peers

- don't be afraid to go public when you have sufficient proof; if your funding is cut you can make even more money from lecturing about it

If you're worried that you'll be labeled a crackpot for doing this, accept the label and wear it with pride. We've already seen that many scientific geniuses of the past were given that label, and they were proven right in the end. Encourage your peers to join you, and let's create a world of crackpots who reject scientific indoctrination and consider the evidence with our own minds.

None of this will happen, of course, because those who have been indoctrinated aren't strong enough to break free from it. Again, it's not their fault, nor is it their teachers' or professors' fault. It goes a lot higher than that.

All of this can be traced back to the shadow government behind the real government.[4-34][4-35] The shadow government in the USA was created by Allen Dulles in about 1961 when he was Director of the CIA. It isn't accountable to either the real Government or the President.

The shadow government established a knowledge filter which states that if something doesn't fit existing theories, it should be denied or covered up. Any anomalous evidence should be hidden, never discussed and never taught.

Unfortunately for the shadow government, there's a wealth of anomalous evidence out there that's still available to the public, and there's no question that it's real. Their crude attempts to deny it and cover it up have led to their exposure.

Governments have another weapon they can use to make sure mainstream scientists stick to the rules. In the US, it's known as the

Espionage Act, and in the UK, it's called the Official Secrets Act. If the government wants scientists to keep quiet about something, they just have to declare it an official secret, and it's immediately covered by the relevant Act. Most scientists will have signed the Act on their first day at work, as will most government employees. If something is covered by the Act, it generally means they can discuss it among themselves if doing so is a necessary part of their work, but they can't discuss it with anyone outside of their department or organization, and they can't disclose it to the public. Anyone who has signed the Act is bound by it for the rest of their lives.

Scientists joining an organization have to follow their managers' orders. Those managers will have been through the same school of indoctrination, and probably additional levels of it too. So they know what's at stake if they try to investigate something that's even slightly outside the mainstream. The penalties include:

- loss of credibility

- loss of funding

- loss of tenure

- ridicule from their peers

- refusal by their peers to review their work

- refusal by mainstream publications to review or publish their work

As a result, mainstream scientists refuse to have anything to do with these things, even if you provide them with irrefutable evidence. They don't want to be associated with it. They see it as potentially career-damaging, and, as we've seen, they label it "pseudoscience" or "yet another stupid hoax" to emphasize their dismissal of it, usually without even looking at it.

> It's interesting to note that they've all been indoctrinated with the late, great Carl Sagan's mantra: "Extraordinary claims require extraordinary evidence." They repeat this endlessly. Ironically, they're forced to ignore the wealth of extraordinary evidence that's staring them in the face because it would damage their careers.

Another problem with scientific teaching is that it follows a single, rigid pathway. Anything that isn't on that pathway "can't possibly be true." If you present a mainstream scientist with what appears to be a two-million-year-old human skull, he instantly dismisses it. It's not on the pathway, so it can't be real. It might *look* real, but it can't be. So he won't investigate it, nor will he test it to see if it's real. Because it can't possibly be real. End of story.

Those of us outside the mainstream have our own pathway, but it's a more flexible one. We would happily accept a two-million-year-old human skull as genuine *if* it were properly examined, dated, and confirmed by scientists. But mainstream pathways are so firmly fixed in place that it takes a metaphorical earthquake to shift them.

If you're interested in learning more about the drawbacks of mainstream scientific indoctrination, it's worth taking a look at Mark Hodges' books: *Textbook Folly: Bias and Indoctrination in College Textbooks* and *Textbook Propaganda: Education or Indoctrination?* These books analyze mainstream science textbooks, looking in particular at how they attack the Bible and Christianity. Although that's not really what we're looking at here, there's a great deal of overlap, and they make interesting and enlightening reading.

Cognitive dissonance

We saw earlier that when scientists are presented with credible evidence that conflicts with their mainstream teaching, they can suffer from cognitive dissonance. This is a term from psychology that refers to the mental stress of trying to hold two or more contradictory beliefs or ideas at the same time. It's deeply uncomfortable and unpleasant and can be traumatic. It can cause confusion, anxiety, depression and in the worst cases, it can even lead to a complete nervous breakdown. So scientists actively avoid any evidence or information that's likely to conflict with what they hold to be true.

Here's a comment on the first edition of this book, posted by someone who's experiencing a classic case of cognitive dissonance: "This load of claptrap is aimed at the unfortunate mass of people who lack the scientific grounding to see the gaping holes in his arguments."

And here's a comment on the same book from someone who's *not* experiencing cognitive dissonance: "In a society where science and empirical testing have taken over as requirements for truth, the idea of there being life on other planets is sometimes thought of as wishful thinking. However, aliens and UFOs have been experienced by countless people since the beginning of recorded history."

And here's another example: "It is beyond any reasonable doubt that man is a completely different species than any other of this planet. Science will have to prove why."

4.6 An example of mainstream denial

In this example, a small team of researchers has just announced its discovery that morning sickness in pregnant women is caused by anomalies in our genomes. They've repeated the test numerous times and always got the same results. They've found that the anomalies are inaccessible through normal reproductive means and are always passed on to the next generation, meaning they could only have got there via external interference.

> This is a fictional example, but I've based it on what geneticists have discovered about spina bifida. We'll discuss spina bifida in more detail in Chapter 7.

The team's discovery and conclusion are obviously not part of the mainstream pathway, so the following events occur:

- Their peers refuse to review their work.

- Their peers report that the results are impossible to reproduce, so they can't be accepted as evidence. (In fact, the results are easily reproducible, and the team included instructions on how to do it.)

- The results are declared invalid because of some technicality. (No matter how meticulously the team carried out their tests.)

- The mainstream science journals reject their report and don't publish it.

- Their results are ridiculed by mainstream scientists.

- The media poke fun at them and their "stupid report about aliens."

- They become pariahs and lose their funding and credibility. All of their previously published studies and results are called into question.

- The original hypothesis – for example, that morning sickness prevents toxins in our diet from reaching the fetus – will be restated as the absolute and unbreakable truth, even though it has never been definitively proven.

Although the discovery in this example was fictional, the events that followed it were real. They've happened to me, they've happened to several of my colleagues and staff, and, regrettably, they'll continue happening. Thousands of major discoveries of global importance have been suppressed using these techniques.

Most of the announcements of these discoveries are freely available for anyone to read – a simple online search will find them. But if you read them, you'll also see the comments that have been left – sometimes by the researchers' peers or rivals, sometimes by uninformed members of the public who think they know better than the researchers, and sometimes by internet trolls. Each discovery will be ridiculed and probably taken out of context. They want you to treat it as a joke. And, sadly, most people who read it will do exactly that.

These highly qualified scientists carried out groundbreaking and faultless work, but because they dared to deviate from the mainstream pathway – even if that wasn't their original intention – they're now ostracized and ridiculed. As a result, they might not be able to secure funding for any future projects, and they may have no choice but to leave the profession. This is an international scandal.

5

Alternative Hypotheses

There are many different hypotheses about how we came to be on Earth. These are the main ones.

5.1 We evolved on Earth

This is of course what most people believe, and what mainstream scientists insist is the only possible truth. But we've already seen how unlikely it is. We're poorly suited to life here, despite being, supposedly, the highest-evolved creature on the planet. And the long-standing theories about us evolving in Africa and migrating to the rest of the world don't stack up. There are remnants of earlier civilizations all over the world, predating the exodus from Africa by tens of thousands of years.

The hominins that were present on Earth before we arrived don't really resemble us. As we've seen, their skulls, in particular, are markedly different from ours. They were also stockier and more robust than us, and much better adapted to living here. It's obvious that we couldn't have descended from them. However, we have a small amount of their DNA in our genomes. That could have come from interbreeding with them.

Ancient hominin DNA in our genomes

About 1 to 2 percent of Europeans' DNA can be traced back to the Neanderthals. But not all Europeans have the same 1 to 2 percent, and some have more than 3 percent. In fact, if you add up all the different bits, it comes to around 20 percent. Benjamin Vernot, a population geneticist at the University of Washington in Seattle, suggests it might even be as much as 40 percent in total. Other studies have suggested that the percentage of Neanderthal DNA in individual non-Africans might be far higher than previously thought – possibly as much as 7.3 percent.[5-01][5-02]

About 6 percent of the DNA of Aboriginal Australians, New Guineans and some Pacific Islanders can be traced back to the Denisovans (a close relative of the Neanderthals). A much smaller percentage, around 0.2 percent, can be found in mainland Asian populations, including the Chinese, and also in Native Americans.[5-03][5-04]

Sub-Saharan Africans have neither Neanderthal nor Denisovan DNA, so we could regard them as "pedigree" humans. This suggests that they're the most recent arrivals on Earth, coming after most of the native hominins had died out. It also suggests that by this time, conditions on Earth had changed and were better able to support us without the extraterrestrials needing to modify our genomes.

However, there's an interesting alternative theory which suggests that the Sub-Saharan Africans might actually be the *oldest* human civilization. This would fit the mainstream scientists' view. And if that were the case, perhaps there simply weren't any other hominins in Sub-Saharan Africa for them to interbreed with.

But there's another theory which suggests that we never interbred with the Neanderthals or Denisovans at all. The researchers who conducted this study concluded that the Neanderthal/Denisovan component of our genome might have come – at least in part – from an earlier shared ancestor, such as *Homo heidelbergensis*.[5-05][5-06] While this is an interesting idea, we've already ruled out *H. heidelbergensis* and the other hominins as our ancestors.

Some human DNA also shows signs of another, currently unknown, species of hominin that may have lived in South-East Asia and interbred with us when we migrated there.[5-07][5-08][5-09]

However, all of these theories overlook the distinct possibility that the hominin DNA may have been spliced into our genomes artificially. We'll look at this in more detail later.

Human–Neanderthal relations

Let's focus on the Neanderthals for a moment. Why would we have interbred with them? There are two possible scenarios, both of which involve Neanderthal men mating with human women.

In the first scenario, the Neanderthals were violent and raped our women. We put a stop to that by driving the Neanderthals to extinction.

In the second scenario, human women (probably teenage girls) mated with the Neanderthal men for a dare or because they were drunk from eating fallen fruit that had fermented.

Either way, most of the resulting pregnancies would have failed because the two species would have been right on the very edge of biological compatibility. Researchers also believe the Neanderthals may have had problems producing sperm.[5-10] But a few children may have been born, survived and gone on to reproduce, passing some of the Neanderthal DNA to the next generation of humans.[5-11][5-12]

In fact, these liaisons could have been relatively rare. Researchers who modeled the spread of Neanderthal DNA in our genomes believe there might have been only a few hundred liaisons in total over a period of 10,000 years, and perhaps only one successful pregnancy every fifty years.[5-13]

5.2 The earlier hominins all died out before we got here

Many diagrams of the human evolutionary timeline show gaps in the sequence. Quite a few of them show a gap of tens of thousands of years between the last of the native hominins dying out and modern humans first appearing. If that were the case, we couldn't possibly have descended from them, or even have interbred with them. We must have been brought here from somewhere else.

However, the data that these timelines are based on is out of date. We've already seen that in 2017 the earliest confirmed date of human evolution was pushed back from 195,000 years ago to 300,000 years ago. In fact, we were probably well established throughout Africa by then. We also saw that human DNA dating from 400,000 years ago was found in Spain, though the mainstream scientists have yet to accept it. There's also evidence of modern human civilizations elsewhere in the world dating from that time.

Several other hominins were present around that time, including *Homo heidelbergensis* and *Homo naledi,* as well as the Neanderthals and Denisovans and that other mysterious species that appears in some of our genomes but is still undiscovered. *Homo erectus* may have been here too, although the date of its extinction is uncertain, ranging from 550,000 years ago to 143,000 years ago. There are even possible *H. erectus* or *H. naledi* remains dating from just 14,000 years ago, but I'd say these are more likely to be from a hybrid species.[5-16]

At any rate, several other hominin species were present on Earth when we made our first appearance, so there are no gaps in that particular part of the timeline, and the diagrams need to be updated. The fact that we bear no resemblance to those other hominins is, of course, another matter. There is definitely a gap, but it's physiological rather than temporal.

5.3 Panspermia

We know that life appeared on Earth almost immediately after the planet formed.[5-17] But, as we'll see in the next chapter, it's pretty much impossible that it could have evolved here naturally.

Panspermia is the theory that life exists throughout the universe and is carried to other worlds by comets and meteorites and so on.[5-18] The specific part of panspermia that interests us here is exogenesis – the theory that life originated elsewhere in the universe and was brought to Earth. This theory was first proposed in 1871 and, although it remains on the fringes of science, it's highly plausible. Francis Crick, one of the co-discoverers of DNA, was a keen supporter.[5-19]

OBJECTION!
"If life can survive the journey through interplanetary space, then space ought to be crawling with life – which it doesn't appear to be."

Space could very well be crawling with life. It could exist, in primitive form at least, on every *habitable* planet in the universe. But we haven't visited any other habitable planets yet. And although we've detected thousands of exoplanets, and we suspect some of them *may* be habitable, we haven't yet confirmed that any of them actually are.

But if you're talking about highly advanced, intelligent life that exists within our timeframe, is within detectable range, and is broadcasting radio signals in our direction, that's a different matter entirely. We'll discuss that later in the book.

We know life can survive in space because certain bacteria have survived outside the International Space Station for extended periods.[5-20]

Bacteria might also have survived for over two and a half years on the Moon. A camera from the *Surveyor 3* spacecraft that was recovered by the crew of *Apollo 12* was found to have dormant Streptococcus bacteria on it.[5-21] Contamination from other sources can't be ruled out in this case though, as inadequate precautions were taken. Procedures have since been revised.

Surveyor 3 landed on the Moon in April 1967, and the camera was recovered in November 1969.

The Sri Lankan-born British astrophysicist Chandra Wickramasinghe has confirmed that the Earth is constantly exchanging organic material, and even living material, with planets around neighboring star systems.[5-22] He said: "This was conjecture in the past, purely theoretical, but now we have evidence for it." He also believes this could explain the origins of certain human illnesses, such as the virus that caused the 1918 flu pandemic.[5-23]

There are several types of panspermia:[5-24]

Directed Panspermia

This is the hypothesis that the Earth was *deliberately* seeded with life about 4.2 billion years ago. Whether or not this was for our benefit, we don't know. The Earth may have been terraformed by extraterrestrials to turn it into a place where we (or they) could survive.

Astrobiologists who collected dust and particle samples from the Earth's stratosphere found that they had also collected microscopic metallic spheres which contain what appears to be organic material.[5-25][5-26] This implies that the Earth is *still* being seeded – and it's clearly deliberate. The big question is: what are we being seeded with? (And who's doing it? And why?)

The 1918 flu pandemic may have been deliberately seeded. But was it an attempt to cull our numbers or wipe us out? Or was it meant to modify our genome without harming us, and did something go wrong? Was it meant for a different species? Or was it something else?

Ballistic Panspermia and Lithopanspermia

When comets and asteroids hit a planet's surface, rocks from that planet are often expelled into space, and some of them could land on other planets. We know this happens because rocks from Mars have been found on Earth.

Those rocks could contain biological material, which is shielded from harm during its journey through space. Again, we know this sort of thing happens because amino acids – the building blocks of life – have been found inside meteorites that have landed on Earth.[5-27] A large meteorite exploded over British Columbia, Canada in January 2000 and fragments containing amino acids were recovered from the frozen surface of Tagish Lake.

Reverse panspermia

This hypothesis suggests that other planets may have been seeded with life from Earth. For example, the asteroid that is suspected to have hit the Earth 66 million years ago, resulting in the extinction of the dinosaurs, could have blasted millions of individual rocks into space. Some of them may have landed on other planets and moons in our own solar system, and a few could have reached planets around other stars. And that's just one example. The Earth has been struck by hundreds of meteorites[5-27a] since life became established here around 4.2 billion years ago. Life that originated here could have been spread all over our sector of the galaxy by now.

Of course, what the theory of panspermia doesn't explain is how life got started in the first place. We'll look at that in the next chapter.

5.4 We are entirely alien

This hypothesis says we evolved on our original home planet and were then brought to planet Earth in stages.

- Stage 1 was around 300 million years ago.

- Stage 2 was around 2 million years ago.

- Stage 3 began at least 400,000 years ago and continued until about 100,000 years ago.

- Stage 4 was around 70,000 years ago.

Let's look at these four stages in more detail.

Stage 1: 300 million years ago
Stage 2: 2 million years ago

These two stages are well backed-up by evidence, some of which we looked at in Chapter 3. The people who arrived in those stages established settlements, some of which we know were architecturally and technologically advanced.

Artifacts from those periods have been found all over the world. Where mainstream scientists have managed to get hold of them, those artifacts are kept locked up and permanently out of view. If they came to public attention and were closely scrutinized, the scientists would have to admit they were real. That would have major consequences. Not only would they have to abandon their long-standing theories of human evolution and completely rewrite the history books, but they'd also have to admit we couldn't possibly have evolved here – which would also prove that extraterrestrials must be real. That latter point is the main problem. As we saw earlier, such a revelation would go against the policy of every one of the world's governments. And that's very likely because that policy was dictated by the extraterrestrials themselves.

> Of course, that isn't how the mainstream scientists explain it. The few who were willing to speak to me told me they're in too deep to backtrack now. Admitting the truth would be too much work (or, more likely, cost too much) and it would make a lot of important scientists look like idiots. So they close ranks, protect each other, and deny the artifacts ever existed. As we saw in Chapters 3 and 4, there are plenty of artifacts they haven't managed to get hold of, but they declare them hoaxes or misidentified natural features without even seeing them.

Ultimately, these two very early human civilizations died out. They were probably small, experimental groups, brought here just to see if survival was possible. It wouldn't have taken much to drive them to extinction, and it's possible that conditions on Earth couldn't sustain human life at that time. They may have been wiped out by disease or famine – most likely as the result of an extinction event that affected much of the planet. They may have been killed by wild animals or by the native hominins. Or, bearing in mind our inherent violence, they may have beaten each other to death in a war over something or other and the surviving population may have been too small to be viable.

When the earliest humans failed to survive, the aliens would have started tweaking our genomes to see if they could find a way to fix the issue. They might have also manipulated the Earth itself: the ecology, geology, atmosphere, flora and fauna, and more. They might even have introduced species from our home planet to make us feel more at home.

Stage 3: 400,000 years ago, continuing to 100,000 years ago

This stage of the hypothesis is the one I'm focusing on in this book, as it explains our origins.

After thousands of years of tweaking our genomes and dropping off small, experimental groups of people on Earth, the aliens came up with something that worked. They finally had a group that could (just about) survive.

Building on their success, they dropped off at least seven much larger groups at locations around the world. Researchers believe there must have been about 20,000 people in each group to make up a viable population. The largest group would have been dropped in East Africa. As we saw earlier, mainstream scientists would like us to believe this was the *only* group, but it definitely wasn't.

Stage 4: 70,000 years ago, continuing to 55,000 years ago

We were all but wiped out by the Toba super-eruption in Sumatra, Indonesia, 75,000 years ago.[5-28] Estimates of the surviving global population range from 3,000 to 10,000 individuals, with as few as 1,000 breeding pairs. The largest group of survivors would have been in East Africa, with small pockets throughout the rest of the world. At this stage, we were critically endangered: there weren't enough of us to maintain a viable population, and there would have been a genetic bottleneck caused by inbreeding as we attempted to rebuild the population.

We desperately needed an influx of new blood – and the aliens provided it. Several thousand more people were dropped off in Sub-Saharan Africa over the next 15,000 years. They bred with the survivors of the Toba extinction event and helped reduce the inbreeding problem.

Although there were still a few Neanderthals and Denisovans around at this time, they also fared badly after the Toba catastrophe and were in severe decline. They would die out completely over the next 30,000 years. So, unlike the Stage 3 group, this new influx of people didn't interbreed with any of the native hominins and have none of their DNA in their genomes.

By around 55,000 years ago our population had fully recovered.

Pure humans?

As we saw earlier, there's an interesting theory which suggests that these most recent human arrivals weren't genetically altered. They were pure humans, in their naturally occurring form, brought straight from our home planet. They could survive on Earth because the conditions here had changed so much since the aliens began their original experiments and most of the predators were gone.

5.5 We are hybrids of ancient hominins and aliens

Could the aliens have interbred with Earth's native hominins, and are we the result? Well, that depends on how hominin-like the aliens were. But let's be realistic here. The aliens would have been an intelligent, technologically advanced, space-faring race. The chances of them being even slightly compatible with stocky, primitive, smelly, heavy-browed Earth creatures are remote at best. I imagine they would also have thought such a thing abhorrent. I think we can safely rule it out.

But they *could* have inserted specific sections of their DNA into one of the hominin species. And they could have used DNA from other alien species too. They may have visited several other inhabited planets and collected samples from them for just such a purpose.

Interestingly, some researchers say there's evidence of twenty different extraterrestrial civilizations in our genomes.

But there could be another explanation. We may have been visited by various alien races, and they might each have made subtle "improvements" to our genome. They might have given us what they regarded as the most useful sections of their own genomes, or that of another species.

Our own biologists developed the ability to do this recently. For example, we can now make bioluminescent rats and mice – and other creatures – by splicing in the relevant genes from fireflies and bioluminescent jellyfish.[5-29] The principle is exactly the same.

We began as pure humans

My own hypothesis, which combines several of the ones we've looked at here, is that we started out as natural hominins that evolved on our home planet, not on Earth. The first groups of us that were brought to

Earth were "pure" unmodified humans. But as we saw earlier, we didn't survive for very long.

So the aliens began tweaking our genome to address the problem. Some of the DNA they used probably came from the more robust Earth hominins. It would have made sense to use them, as they were already here, it would have been easy to harvest DNA from them, and they could obviously survive the conditions of that time.

That didn't work either though – we still weren't able to survive here. So over the next few thousand years, they tweaked our genomes so more, using DNA from themselves and other alien species. Eventually, as we all know, they succeeded.

And that makes us a complex mixture of pure humans from our home planet, with parts of at least one alien species (and probably several more), plus parts of at least one hominin species from Earth.

Why?

But the changes to our genomes obviously weren't too radical. Although there's evidence of hundreds of small modifications, only 223 out of our 20,000 genes seem to have been entirely replaced. At heart, we're still the same species that evolved on our home planet. So when the most recent group arrived after the Toba eruption, and they hadn't been modified at all, they looked much the same as us, and we were still fully biologically compatible with them.

So, why might the aliens have created us as hybrids? Could it have been for our benefit or for theirs? There are *many* theories.

- Some suggest it's entirely for the aliens' benefit because we won't resist if they attempt to take over the planet. I disagree with this on two counts. First, why are we here at all? If the aliens wanted to take over the Earth, they'd have stood a much better chance if we weren't here. It makes no sense to create us as hybrids or bring us here from somewhere else and *then* try to take over the planet. If they really wanted the planet, they'd have taken it before we arrived. Second, we may or may not be hybrids, but if you know anything about human nature, you'll know that we would resist any attempt to take over our planet with every resource we have. The only reason we might lose the battle is because the aliens would have better weapons. But it wouldn't be from lack of trying.

- Another theory is that some aliens only exist in spirit form, and they use us as their physical bodies. Again, this is unlikely: I think we would have noticed by now.

- There's also the opposite theory, that we touched on earlier, which suggests that the aliens are creating alien-human hybrids so that they can capture and replicate our spirits. The theory suggests that the aliens are part of a hive mind and don't have individual spirits – but they would very much like them.[5-30]

- And there's another theory, though much less common, which suggests that our bodies are from Earth, but our spirits or souls are alien.

- I should, of course, mention the Anunnaki – mainly because I'll be criticized for leaving them out if I don't. The ancient Sumerians wrote that the Anunnaki were aliens who came to Earth and created us as hybrids/slaves so we could mine gold for them. Numerous books have been written about this. Personally, I think it's just a Sumerian myth. Gold mines can be found all over the world, and surely the Anunnaki would have wanted to mine the largest of them. There were certainly some rich gold deposits in that area that they could have exploited,[5-31] but there were plenty of much bigger deposits elsewhere that they left untouched.[5-32] There are other issues with this theory too. For example, the Sumerians were the only civilization that ever mentioned the Anunnaki.[5-33] And only a tiny fraction of the human race has ever worked in gold mines.

- Another theory suggests that the aliens were dying out because of some sort of genetic weakness. So they created a race of hybrids (which would be us), based on themselves but without the weakness.[5-34] This enabled them to survive as a species – sort of.

There's a related theory that says these aliens were the Greys.[5-35] But we've already seen how unlikely this is, because the Greys probably evolved from reptiles, whereas we evolved from mammals.

- There's a theory that the first "pure" humans who were brought to Earth were dangerously violent and destructive. So the extraterrestrials created less violent, more caring hybrids to take their place and repair the damage. Again, this theory seems unlikely. It's true that there are plenty of caring, peace-loving people in the world. But they can't keep up with the damage caused by the reckless politicians, corporate polluters, and warmongers. Could it be that the original, pure humans are still here among us, and still wreaking havoc? That could explain why the leaders of our governments and corporations are so out of touch with the rest of us, and appear so cold and uncaring.

> The most recent group of people that arrived on Earth after the Toba eruption were also "pure" humans. Our cold-hearted, profit-driven, warmongering leaders may be their descendants.

- Another theory suggests that today's Caucasians were created as hybrids around 7,700 years ago. That was when the first people with white skin, blond hair and blue eyes appeared. This is one of the few hybrid theories that makes sense. The Caucasians *did* first appear around 7,700 years, and we don't know why. We'd been living in temperate regions including Scandinavia for tens of thousands of years before that time, yet we'd retained our dark skin, hair, and eyes. And it seems we hadn't succumbed to vitamin D deficiency. So the sudden switch to white skin, blond hair, and blue eyes is both unexpected and unexplainable.

Most mainstream biologists say it was a simple genetic mutation that people found attractive. But another explanation is that the Caucasians were hybrids of humans and a type of alien known as the Nordics.[5-36] We'll look at the different alien species in Chapter 13.

> Although they only appeared 7,700 years ago, the Caucasians spread rapidly across the world, from Portugal and Spain in the west, all the way across Europe and Asia to the Pacific Rim. In Siberia and Asia, they were absorbed into the Mongoloid races. This also happened in Japan, creating the Ainu people who are Mongoloid-white hybrids, substantially different from the rest of the Japanese population. The Sumerians were also Caucasian, which is somewhat strange given their location in what is now southern Iraq. Tall, blond Caucasian mummies have also been found in China.[5-37]

- There's also a theory that we were created as hybrids in an alien laboratory, but we escaped. According to the theory, the aliens abducted hominins from Earth and replaced some of their genes.

The new hybrid species was highly intelligent, could speak, and looked different from the original hominins. For example, they had more rounded craniums, shorter arms, and slimmer, less robust bodies. It seems strange that they didn't remove the gene that causes our violence while they were at it. Perhaps that's a difficult thing to do, or it involves multiple genes or our genetic memories. Or maybe it's a function of the human spirit or soul rather than the brain or body.

5.6 The Earth has changed

This hypothesis suggests that we evolved on Earth and were once ideally suited to living here. But then the Earth changed, and we didn't.

The possible changes that have been suggested include the planet gaining or losing mass, which would have affected its gravity; changing the speed or direction of its rotation after being struck by an asteroid; or losing part of its UV shield. As a result, we became cumbersome, disorientated, more fragile, and prone to chronic illness.

But there's no evidence of a significant change in mass or speed of rotation since we arrived on Earth. And as far as we can tell, the level of UV reaching the Earth's surface peaked at 25 to 30 percent above normal during the last thirty years because of damage we caused to the ozone layer. But it's now stabilized and is showing signs of recovery.[5-38]

5.7 The Earth is a prison planet

Many people believe that the Earth is actually our prison, and that we were brought here as a punishment. According to this hypothesis, we were a violent, murderous, thieving, greedy, lustful, vengeful, vain, egotistical group of criminals and outcasts, and a menace to society. A race of space-faring aliens (who might or might not have lived on the same planet) rounded us up and brought us to a prison planet (Earth). They chose this planet because of its habitable but primitive state, lack of tools, and remoteness from galactic civilization. They erased our memories so we couldn't remember how technologically advanced we once were, and then left us to our own devices.

They would have monitored us to see how we developed and whether the violence gene (or genes) ever disappeared. If that happened, we might be allowed to integrate back into galactic society. But, as we all know, it definitely hasn't happened. We continue to lie, cheat, steal, murder, rape, pollute, destroy, and so on. So we're still in prison.

A variation of the hypothesis suggests that we were intended to live alongside the pre-existing Neanderthals, and perhaps integrate with them. Instead, we may have driven them to extinction.

Our unexpectedly rapid development into an advanced society, with tools, language, mathematics, science, art, architecture, farming, domesticated animals, and so on, may have been the result of information stored in our genetic memory. Researchers theorize that the aliens completely overlooked this when they erased our "brain memories."

There's plenty of evidence that the aliens are still monitoring us. They've often interfered with nuclear weapons and power stations, for example. And, as this is a prison planet, they'll undoubtedly prevent us from traveling very far outside the solar system if we ever develop the capability for long-distance manned space flight.

Our attempts to contact other galactic civilizations have failed, and this is probably for two reasons. First, because we're so remote from them, and second, because the few that are within range have undoubtedly been told not to respond to us.

Astronomers have confirmed that we live inside the largest-known void in the universe. Voids are regions of space that have far fewer galaxies, stars, and planets than others. Our void, known as the KBC void, is spherical and 1 billion light years in diameter – seven times larger than the average void.[5-39] That makes it the ideal place for a prison.

Some people wonder why the aliens didn't simply eradicate us instead of going to the trouble of finding a remote but habitable planet and transporting us here. Perhaps it's because the aliens are a lot more humane than we are.

There's a related theory which suggests that rather than being in prison, we're being held in quarantine, so we don't contaminate other worlds.

OBJECTION!
"Earth is too beautiful to be a prison."

The Earth is certainly beautiful when seen from space, and parts of it are beautiful close up too. Most parts are just about passable. Some parts are downright awful. And the place is generally made worse by our presence. But beauty doesn't really matter in this context. What matters is that the Earth is remote enough from the other galactic civilizations that we're completely isolated from them.

OBJECTION!
"We aren't all violent, we are different individuals, not a collective being."

That's a fair point. But there are plenty of schools where the policy is to put the entire class in detention if just one student misbehaves. And countries such as North Korea (if it still exists by the time you read this) punish an entire family if one of its members defects. This could be exactly the same principle.

The aliens would also have based their decision on what our distant ancestors were like hundreds of thousands of years ago. Perhaps one of your ancestors was so violent that he and his entire family were brought to this remote prison planet. And, of course, it wasn't just your ancestor, it was mine too. It was all of our ancestors.

While most people claim they aren't violent, events like Black Friday tell a different story. You've undoubtedly seen news coverage of hundreds of "not violent" people brawling with each other to get a half-price television.

You're just as capable of violence as everyone else; it's human nature. It's in our genes, and there's nothing we can do about it. I'm not violent either – normally. But if someone attacks my child, they're going down.

Civilization is a thin veneer. It's said that we're only nine missed meals – or three days – from total anarchy.[5-40]

5.8 Experiment hypothesis

This hypothesis suggests that we're here because the aliens want to see how well we develop in this environment. We can't make contact with extraterrestrial life on other planets because the aliens don't want any outsiders interfering with their experiment.

5.9 Collection hypothesis

The collection hypothesis or zoo hypothesis, is closely related to the experiment hypothesis, except that it applies to every species, not just us.[5-41] It suggests that all of the species on Earth may have been collected from different planets, and brought here to form someone's private collection.

You could think of it as a giant-sized wildlife park, with humans from one planet, equines from another, felines from a different one, canines from yet another ... and who knows where those weird octopuses came from? And here we are, all living together on one planet.

This isn't a recent collection though. The first invertebrates may have been brought here during the Cambrian era around 500 million years ago. Other species arrived much later as the collection developed and expanded.

The first humans look to have been added to the collection a few million years ago but – as we've already seen – they failed to thrive. After several further failures, a genetically altered version was brought here around 400,000 years ago. We still weren't perfect by any means, but at least we were now able to survive and reproduce.

400,000 years later and we still haven't really adapted to the environment – in fact, we've adapted the environment to suit us – and it's made us all chronically ill. We're also in danger of stripping the planet of its resources. So we may have to be culled at some point to save the rest of the collection.

The collection is probably still being monitored, maintained and added to today. Every year we discover hundreds of new species we've never come across before. And they aren't all in remote forests, oceans, swamps or mountainous areas; some are in our own backyards. Have they always been here and we've just not noticed them? Or are they recent additions added by The Great Collector?

And just who or what is The Great Collector anyway? Is he an individual extraterrestrial, a supernatural being, or a deity? Or is he a whole race of aliens?

5.10 We are digital simulations or holograms

Scott Adams, the American cartoonist and blogger who created *Dilbert*, believes there's a greater than 50 percent chance that we're all just bits of programming code running inside a computer simulation of Earth.[5-42] If you know anything about computer programming, the clues are all there. Take all those coincidences and feelings of déja vu, for example: they're just loops of programming code repeating themselves – a clear sign of lazy programming. And there are far too many coincidences for it to be a coincidence.

Elon Musk, the American billionaire entrepreneur behind Tesla, SpaceX, PayPal and Hyperloop, also supports the computer simulation theory. He suggests that we're either the first civilization in the universe that's advanced far enough to create realistic worlds in virtual reality, or we're already living in a virtual world that's indistinguishable from reality.[5-43][5-44]

It might seem rather unbelievable, but even the mainstream scientists are taking this seriously.[5-45]

Theoretical physicist Juan Maldacena has proposed a model of the universe that's comprised of thin vibrating strings which exist in nine dimensions of space, plus one dimension of time. He says this universe of strings would be merely a hologram; the real action would play out in a single-dimensional cosmos where there's no gravity. Again, it sounds unbelievable, but there's compelling evidence that it could be true. It also solves the apparent inconsistencies between quantum physics and Einstein's theory of gravity.[5-46]

There's another clue that things aren't as they should be: the universe seems strangely uniform when it ought to be chaotic.

And, of course, if we lived in a computer simulation, the aliens could easily switch shape at will, even appearing as humans. They could then walk among us completely undetected. Plenty of witnesses say they already do.

5.11 The Greys were here first

There's an interesting hypothesis which suggests that the type of aliens we know as the Greys were on Earth before we were. The really ancient civilizations that we can find remains of all over the planet might actually have been built by them rather than by us. Some researchers have attributed them to humans, but as the artifacts are millions of years old, or even hundreds of millions of years old, they seem astonishingly early. This could be a reasonable explanation.

5.12 We were created in God's image

According to some interpretations of the Bible (The Book of Genesis), we were created by God and placed here on Earth about 6,000 years ago, on the sixth day of creation.[5-47]

In fact, there are *two* creation stories in the Book of Genesis, and they conflict with each other.

There's also a related theory which suggests that Adam and Eve weren't the first humans, but they were the first to be given souls. Some scholars believe the earlier humans, referred to as "wanderers" in the Bible, didn't have souls.

There's also a theory that the wanderers were Adam and Eve's descendants. But I can't see any merit in that one.

5.13 Miscellaneous other hypotheses

There are lots of other hypotheses that try to explain our origins. Some of them are rather obscure. Here's a small sample of them:

- Adam and Eve were aliens who were sent to Earth. They may have had their memories erased, so they didn't realize they were aliens. They may have thought they were hominins like those around them. They bred with the native hominins and the resulting children were the first modern humans.

- Several pairs of aliens, each named Adam and Eve, were sent to different parts of the planet to breed with the hominins and early modern humans who'd begun migrating from Africa.

- We already existed on Earth, but on the sixth day of creation, God gave us souls.

- We evolved in Australia, not Africa, and we were seeded by aliens from the Pleiades.

- Our home planet was dying, and we needed to find a new one. The Earth was just about good enough.

- Early hybridization experiments didn't turn out too well. Planet Earth was where they dumped all the failures. The successful ones went somewhere else.

- The aliens aren't extraterrestrials, they're humans from the future.

- We were caused by a genetic defect in apes.

5.14 The digital dormancy hypothesis

There's one other hypothesis that's worth mentioning, if only for its entertainment value. It's nothing to do with our evolution, but it explains the so-called Fermi paradox.[5-48]

> The Fermi paradox says there's a contradiction between the massively high probability of extraterrestrial civilizations existing versus the fact that we've never made contact with any, and nor do we have any evidence that any exist.

The digital dormancy hypothesis suggests that the extraterrestrials have all become digital entities inside computers. And they've put their computers into hibernation mode until the universe gets much colder. The reason we can't find any evidence for them is that they're all currently dormant.[5-49]

In billions (or trillions) of years' time, when the temperature of the universe is barely above absolute zero, their computers should operate blisteringly quickly (up to 1030 times faster than is possible today). They'll then be able to get much more done, so they'll wake themselves up.

It's difficult to believe that *every* extraterrestrial civilization in our sector of the universe has become digital and gone into long-term hibernation. In any case, we have a wealth of evidence that aliens not only visit us regularly but are living among us right now.

6

The Origins of Life

No one knows how life originated – on Earth or any other planet.[6-01]

There are three main schools of thought:

- **Nature**
  Life formed naturally via a chain of fortunate coincidences when exactly the right chemicals randomly bumped into each other and joined together.

- **Chemistry**
  Life is an inherent part of chemistry, and always self-forms if the right mix of chemicals and sunlight are present.

- **Intelligent design**
  Some form of intelligence made it happen. This is a fundamental aspect of most religions.

As we saw in our earlier discussion on panspermia, once life formed on one planet it could have spread to others if it was struck by a comet or asteroid. Planets might also have been deliberately seeded with life by extraterrestrials. But what everyone really wants to know is: how did life form in the first place?

> Some people have speculated that life on Earth could have been started by an alien race.[6-01a] They may have assembled the RNA of the first life forms to appear on Earth and left the rest to evolution. We might do the same thing ourselves on other planets one day.
>
> But this only shifts the problem back a level. Who or what created life on the planet the aliens came from? Perhaps it was a more ancient alien race. In that case, who or what created life on the planet *those* aliens came from? We can keep going back like this, step by step, until we reach the beginning of the universe. But we still don't have an answer.

6.1 Simulating nature

Chemists have carried out experiments that simulated the atmospheric chemistry of the early Earth and then added electricity to simulate lightning strikes. The best known of these (the Miller-Urey experiment)[6-02] was performed in the early 1950s by Stanley Miller at the University of Chicago. His chemical mix of methane, ammonia, hydrogen and water vapor was slightly off, but it produced amino acids – the building blocks of proteins. Since then, a more accurate record of the atmospheric chemistry of the young Earth has been obtained by analyzing rocks which formed at that time. Repeating Miller's experiment with this chemical mix also produces amino acids.

Another experiment found that a type of pre-RNA could have formed spontaneously when molecules of barbituric acid and melamine combined with ribose (a sugar) in water.[6-03] The molecules bonded – weakly at first – but were then joined by another molecule and formed a stronger bond. They then entered a sort of positive feedback loop that encouraged more molecules to join together. The researchers believe the molecules could have eventually formed a long strand of polymers that could catalyze its own components. They could even have self-organized themselves into the ladder-like structures we see in RNA and DNA.[6-04][6-05]

> RNA, like DNA, is a nucleic acid that's involved in the coding, decoding, regulation, and expression of genes.[6-06] RNA is a simpler single-stranded form, whereas DNA is more complex and takes the form of a paired double strand.

That's still a long way from creating life, though. And we have no idea whether any of these experimental processes even slightly resemble what actually happened.

In fact, the odds against such a thing happening naturally are astronomical. It's improbable that it could have happened in the entire 4.5 billion years since the Earth formed. The fact that it apparently happened within the first 200 million years is either mind-blowing or completely ridiculous – I'm not sure which.

6.2 The improbability factor

The biologist and paleontologist Professor Andrew Knoll of Harvard University discusses this in his book *Life on a Young Planet: The First Three Billion Years of Life*. He believes that in order to prove this is what happened, we need to look for some kind of molecule that's simple enough that it could have been created by physical processes on the young Earth, but complex enough that it could take charge of reproducing itself.

That's a huge ask. The Swiss mathematician Charles Eugene Guye calculated the odds of such a thing happening as 1 in 10^{160} (10 followed by 160 zeros), which to my mind means it's all but impossible.

American Scientist magazine agreed: "From the probability standpoint, the ordering of the present environment into a single amino acid molecule would be utterly improbable in all the time and space available for the origin of terrestrial life."

The Nobel Prize-winning British researcher Francis Crick, who co-discovered the structure of DNA, also agreed. He said: "There is no possible way that the DNA molecule could have kick-started on Earth. It must have originated from elsewhere." He also said the chances of life forming from molecules randomly crashing into each other were about the same as a hurricane hitting a junkyard and assembling a jumbo jet from random pieces of debris.[6-07]

Scientists who contributed to the book *The Evidence of God in an Expanding Universe* (edited by John Clover Monsma) also considered the odds improbably slim. They said: "The amount of matter that would need to be shaken together to produce a single molecule of protein would be millions of times greater than that in the whole universe."

> It should be noted that the scientists who contributed to that book were what we would now call creationists. But their point is still a valid one.

> Creationism is the religious belief that the universe and life came about through divine creation rather than forming through natural processes. We'll be discussing creationism a number of times over the next few chapters. I'm not a creationist myself, and most of their claims are complete nonsense. But I'm including it in the ...

> ... discussion because a few of their claims – such as the one above – seem to have a degree of merit. They could fill the gaps in our knowledge that mainstream science has been unable to explain. As always, the only way we'll make progress is if we consider these things with an open mind.

Of course, there's an incredibly remote possibility that life really did evolve by itself in this part of the universe, and in the manner that the evolutionary scientists propose. Otherwise, how did any of us get here? But bearing in mind how unlikely it would be to evolve even once, I can't believe it also evolved anywhere else in the universe.

That doesn't mean we're alone though. There are undoubtedly other star systems with inhabited planets nearby (in astronomical terms). We've already seen that life can travel to nearby star systems via panspermia, and planets can be deliberately seeded. But unless our more advanced galactic neighbors have seeded other parts of the universe (perhaps by traveling through wormholes, which we'll look at in Chapter 11) there's a distinct possibility that life only exists in this region of our galaxy, and nowhere else at all.

> If life only evolved once, and our galactic neighbors are more advanced than us, then life must have evolved on their planet, not on ours.

6.3 What happened next?

Let's assume that the processes demonstrated in the simulation experiments are what actually happened: amino acids *may have* formed when lightning interacted with simple chemical compounds. Protein chains *may have* then formed spontaneously from those amino acids, particularly in geothermal pools but perhaps also around hydrothermal vents on the ocean floor. Those protein chains *may have* occasionally stuck together randomly, very occasionally creating enzymes. Over the course of millions of years, the oceans *may have* become full of these protein chains and enzymes. Some of them *may have* become trapped inside naturally occurring lipid spheres, together with different combinations of chemicals. The lipid spheres *may have* acted as the first, primitive cell walls. The first genetic blueprint that formed *may have* been the simpler RNA rather than the more complex DNA.

There are an awful lot of "may haves" in that explanation, and the likelihood that this chain of events actually happened is minuscule. And it still doesn't explain how the first organisms came to life.

No one knows how that happened, so let's skip that part for now and jump ahead to the stage where the first organisms have formed and are now alive. Mainstream science says evolution then took over, creating the incredibly diverse range of flora and fauna we see today. But that isn't necessarily what happened either. As we'll see in Chapter 8, there are some *serious* problems with the theory of evolution.

6.4 The theory of self-organization

American physicist Jeremy England of the Massachusetts Institute of Technology (MIT) has proposed a controversial and highly speculative new theory. He suggests that simply applying heat and light to a bunch of atoms will cause them to self-organize themselves in order to use or dissipate the energy. This, over time, *could* lead to the development of life.[6-08][6-09][6-10]

6.5 Designing life

As we'll see in the next chapter, the genome of even the simplest pond slime is incredibly complex. Tens of thousands of molecules of exactly the right type all have to come together in exactly the right order to form a long strand. And even then, all we have is a long strand of molecules. It isn't a cell, it can't reproduce, and it can't be said to be alive.

The next step would be for this proto-life form to begin reproducing itself. And for that to happen, it would need to somehow start catalyzing chemical reactions.

6.6 How to build a living cell

Here's how to make a basic living cell (courtesy of the *How Stuff Works* website.[6-11]) In this case, it's an *E. coli* bacterium,[6-12] which is about as simple as it's possible to get today while still being classed as "alive."

The absolute minimum requirements for a living cell are:

- A cell wall, to contain everything.

- A genetic blueprint (RNA or DNA). Even the simplest form of *E. coli* has over 4,000 genes and over 4 million base pairs.
  (We'll look at what these are in the next chapter.)

- An enzyme that can read the genetic blueprint and use it to make proteins and other enzymes.

- An enzyme that can make new enzymes.

- An enzyme that can make cell walls.

- An enzyme that can make an exact copy of the entire genetic blueprint so that when the cell splits in half (which is how it reproduces), it creates two identical but fully independent living cells.

- One or more enzymes that can complete the process of reproduction by moving the newly copied genetic blueprint to one side of the cell, along with half of the cell contents, while the original genetic blueprint and the other half of the cell contents move to the other side of the cell. The cell wall then splits down the middle to create two separate cells, and their walls seal up to fully enclose their contents.

- Enzymes that can convert food molecules into energy to power all of the above enzymes

In addition, the living cell needs to be able to:

- ingest food molecules, which involves detecting whether or not a molecule is food, creating a temporary hole in the cell wall, pulling the food molecule in, and sealing up the hole again

- maintain and expand its cell wall (so it can grow)

Of course, the very first living cells were almost certainly nothing like the ones we see today. They may have been so different that we couldn't even begin to imagine them.

6.7 Intelligent design theory

Intelligent design is the theory that some form of intelligence caused life to happen. And while the theory stops short of saying it was a deity (or god), that's what is ultimately implied. It certainly couldn't have had a physical form.

Intelligent design theory is part of creationism.[6-13] As I said earlier, we'll be discussing various aspects of it over the next few chapters. Some of them have merit; many do not.

Literal creationists, also known as Young Earth creationists, go much further than this. They not only reject the theory of evolution in its entirety but insist that the Earth is no more than 10,000 years old. This is obviously absurd.

But there are parts of progressive creationism[6-14] that *could* have merit, and such is the case with intelligent design theory. After all, if we've ruled out Mother Nature and random chance, what are we left with?

Unsurprisingly, Wikipedia labels every aspect of creationism, including intelligent design, as "pseudoscience" – though it has a surprising amount to say about it.[6-15] Mainstream scientists say intelligent design "isn't science" – mainly because the possible supernatural origin of life can't be tested. Several US states have outlawed any teaching of it, while others used to *insist* on teaching it instead of the theory of evolution. Other countries, including the UK and Australia, allow it to be debated in religious classes but don't allow it to be taught in science classes, although teachers can answer students' questions about it. Some Islamic countries place it on an equal footing with evolution.

Interestingly, the theory also states that the entire universe shows signs of having been intelligently designed. But that's beyond the scope of this book.

For now, the best summary of intelligent design is the "God of the gaps" argument:

1. There's a gap in our scientific knowledge (i.e. where life comes from).

2. The gap *can* be filled by an act of God (or an intelligent designer), which therefore proves the existence of God (or an intelligent designer).

Perhaps one day we'll be able to fill the gap using science alone and rule out the need for an intelligent designer. I can't see that happening any time soon though.

Opponents of intelligent design theory claim that if life had been intelligently designed, all of our enzymes would function correctly. That means we'd be able to produce our own vitamin C and so on. And all those annoying imperfections we looked in Chapter 2 wouldn't exist.

They also ask why there are parts of the world that are perfect for certain life forms, yet no examples of those life forms live there. And would an intelligent designer *really* have made us so inherently violent? The only possible conclusion, they say, is that everything must have evolved that way.

They may be right, though we're not really considering the evolutionary aspects of the theory right now. We're more interested in how life got started. And for that part at least, the theory does have some credibility.

Computer simulations revisited

In Chapter 5, we looked at the hypothesis that we're all computer-generated simulations living in a virtual, computer-generated world. In that case, the intelligent designer might not be a god but a computer programmer or a video game-player.

The computer we're running on might be in an enormous air-conditioned warehouse somewhere. The person or intelligence that programmed us might have died years ago – perhaps millions or even billions of years ago. Perhaps no one is in charge of us now, or even knows how to operate the ancient machine we're running on. There might be a faded note taped to it saying: "Do not touch, do not switch off." And we're left to our own devices, hoping no one ever resets, reboots or erases us.

Of course, that still doesn't answer the question of who created the computer, the programmer or the gamer ...

6.8 The case for God

Whether or not you believe in God, none of the ideas in this book disprove His existence.

He may have created Heaven and Earth, as the Bible says. And He may have created mankind in his image. But He didn't necessarily create those things in the same place. He may have put us somewhere else originally – on our home planet, for example. Earth and mankind are now together, of course. But whether that's what He intended, and whether He's happy about it, whether He knows about it, and whether He even exists, we'll never know.

Millions of people believe in God and believe He created the Earth, the people, and all of the different types of plants and animals. There are plenty of scientific theories which disprove some of that, but there are also plenty of unexplained gaps in those theories. So we can't completely rule out God and his work. He may have initiated things, set everything in motion, and then left evolution to carry on with the rest. Or not. As we'll see in Chapter 8, the theory of evolution is starting to fall apart. And that means God could still be manipulating things today. Or He might not exist, and the theory of evolution might be falling apart for some other reason.

> ### OBJECTION!
> *"Humans invented God."*
>
> That's certainly one theory. Although, over the millennia, we've created written, pictorial and sculptural records of countless gods. Were they entirely invented? Were some of them real? Were they alien visitors? No one knows.
>
> Every civilization on Earth speaks of, or worships, some form of God, or their own local deity (sometimes several of them). Even isolated civilizations that have had no prior contact with the rest of the world do this. The same thing might be happening on every other inhabited planet. Although we have no way of knowing whether they're all referring to the same God.

As far as we're aware, no other creatures on Earth have invented any gods, created any religions, are aware of the existence of any deities, or worship any. The general consensus is that they lack the level of intelligence and self-awareness to be able to do so. A few of them *are* highly intelligent and self-aware, but presumably not to the required level. The concepts of God and religion appear to be too complex for them to understand. The thought that there might be a God has never even occurred to them.

Having said that, you might recall that in Chapter 2 we learned that some people don't consider us to be animals at all. They say we're a higher category of being, created in God's image, possessing human essence and divine spirits, and able to recognize and praise His great works – and perhaps even programmed to do so.

> **OBJECTION!**
> "I doubt many scientists have even heard of God, or read the Bible."
>
> That is categorically not the case. I'm sure every one of them has heard of God. I could tell you the names of many respected scientists who are highly religious and regular churchgoers. And I'm sure that the proportion of scientists who have read the Bible is about the same as it is for the rest of the population. They may, of course, have read it with a more analytical mind. (I initially wrote "with a more open mind," but that's clearly not the case.)

6.9 The human soul

According to some researchers, the human soul is, like matter, impossible to destroy. They say that when our host body dies, our soul reincarnates into another one, usually after a period of recovery, debriefing, judgment, and adjustment. Or, if we've learned all the lessons that can be learned in the physical realms, we move to a higher plain of existence. Some believe this higher plain is billions of miles from Earth, in a separate part of the universe.[6-16]

We have a wealth of evidence for reincarnation. Dr. Ian Stevenson, a psychiatry professor who worked at the University of Virginia School of Medicine for fifty years, investigated thousands of cases of people who claimed to be able to remember their past lives. Ninety percent of their memories from their past lives turned out to be accurate. He recorded some of those cases in his book *Children Who Remember Previous Lives: A Question of Reincarnation*, and he wrote several other books on the subject. Numerous studies by other researchers have produced similar results.

> I have first-hand experience of reincarnation in my own family, so I'm a firm believer in it. There's no question that it's real.

> If you're interested in learning more about how souls are created, reincarnated, or move to the higher plain, I can recommend Michael Newton's books *Journey of Souls: Case Studies of Life Between Lives* and *Destiny of Souls: New Case Studies of Life Between Lives*. Newton is a hypnotherapist who specializes in past-life regression.

Weighing the soul

Another way of proving that we have a soul is to weigh it as it leaves our body when we die. This is what Dr. Duncan MacDougall of Haverhill, Massachusetts did in a series of experiments in 1907. With their agreement, he placed dying patients on a bed attached to a scale and watched to see what happened at the moment of death. He found that the body suddenly lost around 0.75 ounces (21 grams). He carefully checked that he'd taken into account every other possibility, from evaporation to evacuation of the bowels (which would have remained on the bed anyway and not affected the weight). But he could find no other explanation. He concluded that the 0.75-ounce loss had to be the weight of the soul as it departed from the body.[6-17][6-18]

Interestingly, a small amount of weight loss continued after the sudden 0.75-ounce loss. In some cases, it took fifteen minutes after the patient's death for the scales to settle.

Unfortunately, his sample size was too small for us to be able to draw any real conclusions. He only carried out six experiments on people, and he was forced to discount two of them. In one case, the patient died before he'd finished calibrating the scale. In another case, observers interfered with the equipment. I could find no records of anyone else conducting the same experiment.

Mainstream scientists rejected his experiment, despite it being something they could easily repeat and the result something they could physically measure. We saw earlier that they refused to accept the possible supernatural origin of life on the basis that they couldn't measure it. But in this case, they have no such excuse. Could it be that they're *afraid* of confirming it?

When Dr. MacDougall carried out the same experiment on dogs, he saw no loss of weight at all. He therefore concluded that dogs (and perhaps all other animals) don't have souls.

That would fit with us being a separate class of being, and the only one to have a divine spirit. It doesn't rule out dogs having individual personalities, of course, because we know they do. But it suggests that their personalities may be physical functions of their brains rather than a separate divine essence like ours.

Closing thoughts

Before we move on, I have a couple of thoughts about human souls.

First, what happens if someone dies and they're frozen in the hope that they might be returned to life in the future? Does their soul stay with them? Dr. MacDougall's experiment suggests not. It seems unlikely that they'd get their original soul back; it may have been reincarnated into someone else. Perhaps God or the universe has allowed for this eventuality and can supply a spare soul to fill the void. But that means the reanimated person wouldn't be the same person who died, they'd just have the same body.

On the other hand, if they aren't given their original soul *or* a spare, the reanimated person might be a real-life zombie – literally a person with no soul.

> Not to be confused with the fictional "living-dead" zombies, which are basically mobile corpses with a hunger for human brains.

My second thought is: if we're from another planet, or if we're hybrids, what does that make our souls? Are they human, alien, hybrids, or something else?

Philosophical questions like these keep me awake at night.

6.10 Was Jesus an alien?

This may seem a bizarre question, and we're going off on another tangent here, but so many people asked this when commenting on the first edition that I decided to answer it as best I could.

The official account of Jesus's conception and birth, as recorded in the Bible, states that he was a hybrid of a supernatural deity (God) and a human (Mary). So, no, he wasn't an alien.

But having said that, he might not have been a hybrid either. There are some major inconsistencies in the Bible, along with several more rational explanations. Most of them point to him being a regular human.

Let's look at some of the alternative explanations for Jesus's conception and birth:[6-19]

1. **Mary and Joseph were Jesus's parents.**

   Joseph denied this and Mary was apparently examined and declared to be a virgin. The hymen doesn't always break during intercourse, so she could have given the appearance of being a virgin even though she wasn't one. If they really were Jesus's parents, both of them lied about it and invented a preposterous tale to cover it up. Why? Perhaps Mary was underage.
   Conclusion: Jesus was human.

2. **Joseph could have unknowingly fathered Jesus.**

   He and Mary could have engaged in heavy petting, and his semen could have leaked into her without either of them being aware of it. Mary would still have been an intact virgin, and they would have been speaking the truth when they said they hadn't had intercourse.
   Conclusion: Jesus was human.

3. **Another man could have been Jesus's father.**

   Mary could have had a secret lover. Or she might have been raped by a Roman soldier, possibly while drugged, so she had no recollection of it. That doesn't fit with her being a virgin though, and rape would almost certainly have ruptured her hymen. So we can probably rule that out.

Conclusion: Jesus was human.

4. **Mary had a phantom pregnancy.**

The Bible states that Mary suffered no labor pains and there was no placenta or afterbirth. Combined with Joseph's denial of being the father and Mary's purported virginity, this suggests her pregnancy may have been a phantom one, perhaps brought about by suggestion. Someone could have placed a baby next to her while she was sleeping, and she woke up believing she'd given birth to it.

Conclusion: Jesus was human, and his real parents are unknown.

5. **Biblical inconsistency 1.**

The Bible states that Mary was an eternal virgin. It also states that Jesus had brothers and sisters who were not children of God. Mary and Joseph must, therefore, have had other children after Jesus was born.

Conclusion: Mary couldn't have been an eternal virgin.

6. **Biblical inconsistency 2.**

Elsewhere in the Bible, it states that Mary and Joseph are Jesus's parents. It also states that he can trace his lineage back through Joseph to King David and Abraham.

Conclusion: Jesus was human.

7. The text of the Bible could have been mistranslated from Hebrew. It may have said Mary was a "young woman" not a "virgin."

8. Some people believe Jesus's body was human, but he was given a divine soul.

So the most likely explanation is that Jesus was human. He definitely wasn't an alien, and it seems unlikely he was a hybrid deity either. But witnesses saw him performing miracles, so we can at least elevate him to sainthood.

Also, as you probably know, his name wasn't really Jesus. He was Yeshua (or in English: Joshua).

***

Earlier in the chapter we looked at the creation of an *E. coli* cell. There are several different types of *E. coli*, some of which are harmless and some of which can cause severe food poisoning. About 2,000 people are hospitalized in the USA each year because of E. coli infections.[6-20]

Under ideal conditions, an *E. coli* bacterium can reproduce every twenty minutes. If the resulting "children" bacteria also reproduce every twenty minutes, and the process continues unhindered, a single bacterium could (theoretically) become 4.7 sextillion bacteria within 24 hours. That's about 5 million times more bacteria than there are cells in the human body. They'd also weigh more than 450 tonnes. Of course, you'd be dead long before they reached those kind of numbers.

Fortunately, the human body *doesn't* represent ideal conditions for *E. coli*. It quickly begins attacking and killing the bacteria, and increases the temperature above their optimum range, slowing and eventually reversing their spread. Most people fully recover from an *E. coli* infection within a week. The first few days can be pretty awful though.

7

DNA

7.1 Introduction

Almost every cell in every living organism on Earth contains DNA. But DNA is probably not unique to Earth. It almost certainly exists elsewhere in our galaxy, and it might even be universal.

DNA is basically a script – a universal recipe for life. It's made up of genes (sections of DNA that perform a particular role) and non-coding sections. The genes are the parts that most interest us here.

If you want your life form to have four legs, for example, you give it the 4-legs gene (*not its actual name). If you want it to have fur, you give it the fur gene, and so on. Of course, it's a lot more complicated than that: there are multiple genes for fur. They determine things like its type, density, and color; whether it grows continuously (like the hair on our heads) or falls out and gets replaced (like the hairs on our bodies and limbs); and so on.

We share many of our genes with every living thing because they're necessary for life. These are the genes for things like basic cell function and growth, respiration, converting sugars into energy, and thousands of other functions. That's why we share around 15 percent of our DNA with grass and 50 percent with bananas.[7-01] Evolution likes to preserve genes that work, so we still have them today, and they perform the same functions – although most of them now do it in an entirely different way.

As we work our way up the evolutionary tree, the number of shared genes increases. We become increasingly similar to the creatures near the top. But, as we've just seen, some of those genes can be traced all the way down the tree too, right back to the single-celled organisms. We'll look at the specific percentages later.

Our complete set of genetic material is called our genome, and it's *huge*. The human genome contains more than 3 billion base pairs.[7-02] If you printed it out on regular printer paper using a regular-sized font, it would fill a million pages. If you printed it on both sides of the paper, it would make a stack 82 feet (25 meters) tall.

We share 99 percent of our DNA with each other. The 1 percent difference (10,000 printed pages) accounts for all the differences between you and any other person on the planet, including all the different races.[7-03] All of the different races are biologically compatible and can interbreed with each other.

7.2 What is DNA?

DNA is short for deoxyribonucleic acid. You can find it in the nucleus of almost every cell in every living organism. Every cell contains a copy of that organism's entire genome. You can also find it in some cell organelles, such as mitochondria. Some organisms, such as bacteria, don't have nuclei or organelles. Their DNA is in their cytoplasm.[7-04]

> DNA is present in every cell that has a nucleus. The vast majority of the cells in our body have nuclei. But there are a few that don't, including our red blood cells.

DNA forms two long strands of molecules, twisted into a double helix, with both strands carrying the same information. Most organisms have multiple sets of strands, known as chromosomes. They control everything about that organism, including what it is, what it looks like, its growth and development, its everyday functioning, and its reproduction.

Each chromosome contains multiple genes and non-coding sections. Simple things like bacteria only have one chromosome, whereas we have 46, made up of 23 pairs. Apes have 48 chromosomes in 24 pairs.

As we've already seen, a gene is a section of DNA that determines a specific property or function, such as the organism's gender, height, skin color, hair color, and so on.[7-05] Some properties and functions are more complex and are spread across multiple genes. Those genes may be on separate chromosomes, so finding them and identifying their purpose isn't easy.

We each have about 20,000 genes. This is far fewer than expected. When biologists first started looking, they thought there would be at least 100,000, and some thought there might be as many as 2 million.

About 10 percent of each organism's genes are considered essential for survival. In our case, that's about 2,000 genes. These control things like basic cell function, brain development, blood circulation, breathing, digestion, and reproduction.

Most of an organism's DNA is non-coding.[7-06] In our case 98.8 percent is non-coding, and only 1.2 percent is made up of genes. The non-coding part used to be called "junk DNA" as it was thought to do nothing at all. But at least 80 percent of it has now been found to have a purpose. This includes protecting genes from mutation and disruption, acting as switches to determine where and when genes are expressed, regulating the expression of genes (i.e. to what extent they're expressed), controlling the flow of information from DNA to messenger RNA (mRNA), and several more minor functions.

So instead of needing 100,000 genes (or even 2 million), we can get by with just 20,000, and use the non-coding parts to vary their activity and strength. We could get the same result by having a lot more genes that each had fixed functions, but having fewer of them means there's less to go wrong. It's actually rather clever. It's almost as if someone deliberately designed it that way.

7.3 Where did DNA come from?

You're probably familiar with the riddle that asks which came first, the chicken or the egg? (It's the egg, by the way.) But now we have to ask: which came first, DNA or living organisms. And the answer to this one is *RNA* – probably.[7-07]

RNA (ribonucleic acid) has a much simpler structure than DNA, so it's easier to build. For example, it only has a single strand compared with DNA's double strand. Most scientists believe that RNA-based life forms evolved first, and those organisms then created the first DNA. They eventually switched to storing their genetic information in their DNA because it was more stable.

Whichever came first, RNA or DNA (or perhaps both for a time), we're still left with the question: where did it come from? How did those separate molecules join together into a structure that could store biological information? How did they create long chains that exactly encoded the various characteristics and processes of a living organism? And, once a suitable chain somehow formed, how did that lead to a living organism being created?

In the previous chapter, we saw some experiments which showed how amino acids may have formed on the primitive Earth. Similarly, chemists from University College London believe they're close to showing that the building blocks of DNA can also form spontaneously. Again, they're using chemicals that they think were present on Earth shortly after it formed. So far, they've managed to synthesize two of the four nucleotides that make up DNA. They're still working on the other two. If they succeed – and they're confident that they eventually will – it will prove that the molecules that make up RNA and DNA *could* also form, more or less spontaneously, on other planets. This could imply that life is universal – although proving this isn't their intention.

Other researchers have found that sections of DNA, once they've formed, seem to recognize similar sections and combine with them, even if those sections are some distance away. The researchers describe this ability as "telepathic." Mainstream scientists call it "chemically impossible."[7-08]

Of course, this still doesn't explain how the RNA (or DNA) managed to organize itself into the complete genome of the very first, simplest living organism. It would have taken thousands and thousands of molecules, all of exactly the right type, coming together in exactly the right order, to form complex units. Even if one gene formed, it couldn't have done anything on its own. It would have needed hundreds more, each controlling one or more vital functions of that first organism. If just one of the essential genes was missing, the organism couldn't have survived. This implies that all of its essential genes (10 percent of its entire genome) must have formed at the same time. And that – as even the mainstream scientists must admit – is totally impossible.

So what does that mean? Well, we're either back to intelligent design again, or some other process was involved.

Given the extremely short timescale of around 200 million years, the first living organism to appear on Earth (which was most likely a primitive algae) almost certainly formed somewhere else. It must have arrived in a comet or meteorite, or the Earth must have been seeded with life by a much older alien race.

But once again, all we've done is moved the whole process back a level. We still don't know how RNA or DNA formed on whichever planet that organism came from. And we still don't know how the RNA or DNA became a living organism.

7.4 Extraterrestrial influences on our DNA

We can find plenty of evidence that our DNA has been interfered with. It bears numerous scars where sections have been chopped out, and other sections have been spliced in. This is covered in detail in the book *Everything You Know Is Wrong: Human Origins* by the late American writer and researcher Lloyd Pye. He carried out extensive research on this subject, and his findings have been validated and verified by others.

Mainstream geneticists, on the other hand, would prefer you to believe that the DNA scars were caused by natural processes such as aging, stress, trauma and radiation damage. They also blame them on contaminated samples, even though different researchers keep finding the same scars. The researchers who discovered the scars were also able to prove that their samples had been collected and handled properly, and repeated tests showed the same results. There's no question that the scars are there.

It's true that DNA can be damaged by natural processes. But we would expect everyone's DNA to be damaged in a slightly different way. As we age, tens of thousands of mutations occur in our DNA each year. So young children should show hardly any evidence of scarring at all. But that's not what we see.

Many of the scars occur in the same place in *everyone*, including new-born babies. There are certain scars that everyone of a particular race has, and some that everyone in the world has. These obviously can't be blamed on aging or radiation or stress or trauma or disease. And there's no way that every single DNA sample could have been contaminated in exactly the same way.

Why spina bifida shouldn't exist

Some genetic defects prevent people from reproducing. Spina bifida is one such condition.[7-09] Since people with spina bifida can't reproduce, no one with the condition can pass it on to the next generation. That means it should have been quickly eradicated from our genome and no longer exist. Sadly, that hasn't happened.[7-10][7-11]

So what's going on? Well, two things. First, non-sufferers must be passing it on. Second, the genetic defects that cause spina bifida must be in sections of our genome that evolution can't get at. The only way they could have gotten there is if they were spliced in artificially – possibly by accident when the aliens were trying to manipulate something else.

It's highly likely that the majority of us carry the genes that cause spina bifida. They might even be present in all of us. It's only when they're expressed in a specific way – in about 1 in every 1,000 births – that the defect becomes active.

As we've just seen, the expression of genes is regulated by the non-coding sections of our genome. It's taken us decades to work out what all the genes do, and that's only 1.2 percent of our genome. Working out what all the non-coding sections do will be a much greater challenge, and one I certainly wouldn't relish. It's almost certainly beyond our current technology.

Eventually, it might become possible to treat spina bifida using gene therapy. But eradicating it altogether, or at the very least preventing it from being passed on, is unlikely to happen within our lifetime.

In the meantime, all we can do is try to reduce the number of cases. That means screening for the disease during pregnancy and offering a termination to those affected. Folic acid (vitamin B9) has also been found to reduce the incidence of spina bifida, and it's now added to many cereal products in the developed world.

It might have been better for us if spina bifida was a much more common problem. The aliens would then have spotted the error they'd made, and they could have corrected it.

7.5 Could we repair and improve our own DNA?

As we've just seen, the only way we'll ever be able to completely eradicate genetic conditions like spina bifida is by editing our DNA ourselves. We can already do this to a limited degree thanks to the latest CRISPR/Cas9 technology.[7-12]

The problem, of course, is knowing which sections to edit. In cases such as spina bifida, where the problem almost certainly lies in the non-coding sections of our genome that haven't been mapped yet, that's a huge task.

But other genetic conditions may prove easier to repair. In fact, it might have happened already. Some genetic research laboratories operate outside of the mainstream and are funded by secret black budgets. They're decades ahead of anything that's been made public. They tend to pursue military, defense and space applications before anything else, but their work often leads to applications that have public health benefits too.

Extraterrestrials may be helping with this work. Which is only fair, since they almost certainly caused the problem in the first place.

Interestingly, the 2015 Nobel Prize in Chemistry was awarded to an international group of researchers for their study of the mechanisms of DNA repair.[7-13]

7.6 Life on other planets

As we've already seen, it's highly unlikely that life could have evolved on Earth. That means it must have come from somewhere else. But if it reached this planet, it could also have reached thousands of others planets. Most of them wouldn't have been habitable, but a few of them might have been, and it would have kick-started evolution there too.

We've already seen that certain molecules seem to attract each other in almost telepathic ways. This suggests that evolution probably follows a fixed pattern. So it's highly likely that life on those planets evolved in much the same way that it did here.

We certainly wouldn't see the exact same species on every planet, but we should expect to see the same classes of organism. That includes the protozoa, algae, mosses, ferns, flowering plants, cartilaginous fish, bony fish, amphibians, reptiles, birds, mammals, primates, and hominins.

If evolution happens the same way everywhere, we should be able to trace everything back to a single ancestor. We would also share our ancestry with life on all the other planets that were seeded from the same source as us.

Some of those planets might not have had extinction events. Their version of the dinosaurs might have ruled for a much longer period, and their version of the hominins may have evolved from them rather than from the mammals. We think this is how the Reptilian extraterrestrials evolved.

> There are many different reptilian races. We'll look at them in Chapter 13.

On planets which had extinction events, and where the environment was similar to the Earth's, the mammals may have become the dominant class. In that case, their most advanced hominins probably look very much like us. According to Walter H. Andrus, Jr., the director of

MUFON (the Mutual UFO Network) from 1970 to 2000, about one-third of extraterrestrials resemble us. The others evolved from other species, with the reptiles being the most common.

If DNA is a universal recipe, and evolution went through the same set of processes on other Earth-like planets (including our home planet), we could be biologically compatible with the human-like mammalian races that evolved there.

In fact, if they're bipedal, upright, mostly hairless, highly intelligent and self-aware, they might be closer to us biologically than the chimpanzees are on Earth. At the very least, their DNA should look familiar, and we can expect to see similar (or even identical) protein sequences and enzymes. Any biological differences could be easily addressed with a little gene manipulation. Some of these races will be millions of years ahead of us, so doing something like that would be child's play to them.

And so we come back to the ideas we discussed earlier, where the aliens can replace sections of our genome with their own or other species' to make us more suited to life on Earth.

If they're millions of years ahead of us, they've probably modified their own genomes too. They may have eradicated all genetic conditions, genetically inoculated themselves against all diseases, cured aging, and made themselves stronger, faster, more intelligent, and so on. You might be able to buy pills on their planet that permanently change the color of your eyes, make you taller, make your hair grow back, and so on.

> The aliens may have taken us from our home planet and dropped us off on other habitable planets too. Conditions on each planet will vary, so each group probably needed modifying in different ways to help them cope with their new environments. Within our own Milky Way galaxy, there are an estimated 40 billion habitable …

... Earth-sized planets.[7-14] About 11 billion of them orbit Sun-like stars. At the very least, the aliens will want to monitor all of those planets, even if they don't actively interfere with them. That should keep them busy!

OBJECTION!
"The formula for DNA might be the same everywhere, but the planets have very different environments. So the aliens would be strange creatures and wouldn't look like us."

That will be true of some planets. But there are billions of planets, and we can expect a significant number of them to have similar environments to the Earth's. If there are mammalian hominins on those planets, they could be just like us. Alien species such as the Nordics and the Tall Whites are almost indistinguishable from us; they can only be identified as non-humans if you know the specific signs to look for.

You could certainly call the reptilians strange creatures, and they can be easily distinguished from humans. But they probably evolved on planets that are remarkably similar to ours. The key difference is that their planet didn't have the extinction event that wiped their dinosaurs out.

Most of the aliens that have reportedly visited the Earth seemed to be able to breathe the air here perfectly well. So even though they didn't all look like us, they must have come from planets with similar atmospheres.

But there will undoubtedly be planets where the environment is so different from ours that their species will be completely unrecognizable. As far as we know, none of them have ever visited the Earth.

Amino acids

Although there are around two hundred possible amino acids, life on Earth is based on only twenty of them. Presumably, that combination is the best one, and it happened for a good reason rather than by accident. If that combination is always the first to form, or if it's the most stable in the long term, we'd expect to see the same thing on other habitable planets. And the same would apply to the nucleic acids, monomers, sugars, polypeptide chains, and so on.

Life on some planets might be based on other combinations, but it's unlikely that we're the only ones to use this particular combination.

Interestingly, about three billion years ago, when our DNA reached the point where it could use those twenty amino acids, it appears to have stopped evolving.[7-15] Geneticists have no idea why this happened. But it lends credence to the idea that those twenty are the best combination. In theory, our DNA could have continued evolving to use up to 63 amino acids. The geneticists are now looking at ways to artificially increase the number – though I'm not sure how they think that will benefit us.

7.7 How much of our DNA do we share with other species?

This is the question I'm asked most frequently, but it's horrendously difficult to answer. Few organisms have had their entire genomes sequenced. Different species have different amounts of DNA, different numbers of genes, different numbers of chromosomes, and the chromosomes break off at different points, so you can't really make a direct comparison.

There are also two ways of looking at the data:

- from the human perspective – the amount of our DNA that we share with an organism

- from the other organism's perspective – the amount of DNA it shares with us

These aren't the same thing. For example, 67 percent of our DNA can be found in mice, but mice can find 88 percent of their DNA in us.

We can conclude from this that we have more DNA than mice. But if you want to know how much DNA we share with them, which figure should I give you: 67 percent or 88 percent?

Personally, I'd be more inclined to choose the human perspective and tell you it's 67 percent. But other people might tell you the true figure is 88 percent and accuse me of not knowing what I'm talking about.

Another problem is that when the geneticists worked out how much of our DNA we share with other species, they thought the non-coding sections were junk and only looked at the genes. Since then, we've discovered that the non-coding sections have a biological purpose and should have been included as well. So the geneticists will have to work it out all over again, and the results will be different this time around.

Most people want to know how much of our DNA we share with chimpanzees. Again, I can give you several different figures. From the human perspective, looking only at the genes, it's about 90 percent. But from the chimps' perspective, it's 96 to 98 percent. From the human perspective, looking at the entire genome including the non-coding sections, it's about 79 percent.[7-16] And from the chimps' perspective it's about 85 percent.

> When I say we share parts of our DNA with different species, I'm actually referring to the species on our home planet, not the ones on Earth. But as both planets undoubtedly have the same classes of organism, the figures should be roughly the same.

Here's a typical list of the amount of DNA we reportedly share with other organisms.[7-17][7-18][7-19] Other lists give different values, so you should only consider these figures a rough guide:

Grass:	15%
Cress:	18%
Yeast:	18 – 26%
Grape:	24%
Rice:	25%
Roundworm:	38%
Honey bee:	44%
Fruit fly:	44 – 60%
Banana:	50 – 60%
Chicken:	60 – 65%
Mouse:	67 – 88% (see the text above)
Platypus:	69%
Rat:	69%
Fish:	73%
Dog:	82 – 84%
Cow:	80 – 85%

Cat: 90%
Chimpanzee: 79 – 98% (see the text above)
Human: 97.0 – 99.9% (see the text below)

All humans have the same genes, but their sequence of base pairs varies. No one has the same set of sequences as anyone else, even if they're identical twins.[7-20] It'll be pretty close, but never a perfect 100 percent. In the case of the twins, most of the differences will come from mutations caused by their lifestyles and environments, and the differences will become more pronounced as they get older.

In theory, we share at least 97 percent of our DNA with every other member of the human race. But in practice, it's well over 99 percent.

> You might be wondering where that theoretical figure of 97 percent comes from. Researchers have identified a possible 88 million points of difference in the sequence of three billion base pairs that make up our complete genome. That's a maximum difference of three percent. But 12 million of those 88 million points cover all of the most common variants, and that makes a difference of just 0.4 percent.[7-21]

Most people are very similar to each other. For example, the genetic difference between a Caucasian and an Asian is only about 0.04 percent.[7-22]

7.8 How to make a human

Step 1
Humans are living organisms, so we first need to collect together all the genes that control basic cell function, brain development, blood

circulation, breathing, digestion, and reproduction. These are common to every multicellular organism. We'll also need some genes that determine where all the bits are supposed to go.

Step 2
We then need lots of supporting genes: for example, the digestive system will need genes for the number of stomachs, the length of the intestine, the strength of the stomach acid and bile, and so on. The digestive system begins at the mouth, and for that, we'll need genes for things like the shape and strength of the jaw, the number of teeth, the type of saliva, the size and shape of the tongue and the number of taste buds on it. We'll continue following along the length of each system, adding genes to make them function the way we need them to. Most of these genes are common to all herbivores.

Step 3
Now we can start adding the things that make us land animals rather than, say, fish. We've already got a gene for breathing, and we've selected the one for lungs rather than gills. We breathe through our mouths and noses, and while that's not ideal, the majority of land animals use that system, so we'll use their genes.

> A blowhole would be entirely separate from our digestive tract and would probably work much better, but that isn't what the recipe calls for.

We'll need the gene that makes us warm-blooded. We'll also need one that gives us mammalian skin, including a layer of subcutaneous fat underneath it, and a light covering of body hair. The genes for skin and hair are available in different colors, but we won't worry about that here. We also need the gene that gives us four limbs. And the gene for eyes, which are also available in different colors. We'll need to refine our reproductive system, so it has all the relevant appendages and hormones. And we want to give birth to live young rather than laying eggs, so we'll select the genes for those that too.

Step 4

So far we've managed to make a fairly advanced mammal. Now to make it look more like a human. To save time we'll just copy the recipe for a chimpanzee and work from there.

*Step 5

We've made a chimpanzee. So now we just need to refine it.

First of all, we need to check that we're still using the herbivore recipe, and make any necessary corrections. We also need to use a significant part of the marine mammal genome that we looked at earlier. That will take quite a lot of work.

Next, we'll select genes to make the brain bigger, and the cranium big and round. And we need to lose the chimpanzees' brow ridges for some reason, even though it would be more beneficial to keep them. Our recipe calls for agility rather than robustness, so we'll choose genes that make the body as light as possible. We'll also select the genes for bipedalism and uprightness. Chimps have long arms, but we need shorter ones, so we can either replace their arm-length gene with our own or use some of the non-coding DNA to regulate the arm gene.

There's too much body hair, so again we can either switch to the gene that gives us less hair or regulate its length with non-coding DNA. The recipe says we have to keep the gene that lets us grip with our feet, even though we don't climb trees. But we can use the non-coding DNA to reduce some of the flexibility. We'll also need the genes that enable us to speak and understand language.

*Some of the genes needed for Step 5 might not be available on Earth and may have to be imported from another planet.

Step 6

There are just a few minor adjustments to make now, such as switching off the gene for the penis bone, but otherwise we're pretty much there. In upgrading from a chimp to a human, we've replaced around 2 percent of the genes and 15 percent of the non-coding DNA.

Step 7

With the bulk of the DNA now in place, our human is virtually complete. We just need to select a race and make some slight refinements to the sequence of base pairs.

If this is the first time you've tried making a human, you've probably made several mistakes, and it might not survive for very long. This is normal: the environment on Earth can be tricky. You'll just need to practice a few more times until you get it right.

When you're happy that you've finally got it right, try experimenting and making small changes to see what happens. There are all sorts of problems with the original recipe so you might like to see how many of them you can fix.

7.9 How to make an alien

Method 1

Human-like aliens

If your alien looks like a human, repeat steps 1 to 6 above, then make any final alterations in step 7 to bring out the differences. If it looks exactly like us, reproduces in the same way, eats the same things, and can survive on Earth, then its DNA should be practically identical to ours. It's a standard, universal recipe after all. It might even be just about biologically compatible with us, in the same way, that the Neanderthals may have been.

Hominin aliens

If your alien doesn't quite look human, follow steps 1 to 5 above (or save time by starting with a chimpanzee) and then fix the fine details in steps 6 and 7. At least 97 to 99 percent of its DNA should still end up being identical to ours.

Reptilian and other aliens

If your alien doesn't look human at all, follow steps 1 and 2 as above, then switch to a different recipe. If your alien evolved from reptiles, for example, follow the recipe for the closest living reptile species – let's say a lizard – and refine that into your alien. In this case, it certainly won't be biologically compatible with us, but as long as it can survive on Earth and live on the land, it will probably share at least 75 percent of its DNA with us.

Despite its reptilian origins, it will probably share its basic skeletal structure with us – for example, walking upright and having two arms and two legs. It will probably have a large brain, and therefore a large, rounded cranium. It makes sense if that's at the top of its body – if nothing else it will make balancing and walking easier. It will undoubtedly have dexterous hands that can grip, hold tools and manipulate things with great precision – it can build and fly spacecraft after all. It will probably have two eyes because that format evolved on Earth multiple times. There are no vertebrates with more than two eyes.

> Some lizards have an extra light-sensing organ on their heads, but it's not strictly an eye.

All of this implies that the layout of your alien's internal organs will be very similar to ours, if not identical. And each of these features increases the percentage of DNA it shares with us.

> As was the case when we tried to make a human, some of your alien's genes might not be available on Earth. Your nearest supplier of extraterrestrial genes is (probably) located in the Alpha Centauri B system. While you're waiting for delivery, you might like to have a go at making your own versions using the latest CRISPR/Cas9 genome editing system.

Method 2

Capture an alien and take a sample of its DNA. The alien can then be released. Determine the differences between human DNA and alien DNA and isolate those sections, then splice them into a human embryo.

Beware of infringing interplanetary regulations that your government may have signed without telling you.

> Your alien might or might not have hair. For some reason, most images of aliens seem to show them without hair, but the two that I've met (a male tall white and what I believe was a female reptilian-human hybrid) both had hair just like ours.

> I'm sure you have many questions about the two aliens I've met. I'm not going to say where I met them, except that one was in the US and one was in the UK. I didn't get to speak to them or take any photos.
>
> The tall white male looked fine and healthy and was mixing with other humans perfectly happily. Everyone treated him with great respect, just as he did them. He seemed friendly, but there was no doubt that he could handle himself in a fight. He looked to be in his mid-forties.
>
> But the reptilian-hybrid girl was clearly not thriving. She seemed to be wasting away, had a haunted look, and shunned company. As she was part-human, she probably wouldn't thrive on the reptilians' home planet either, even if she had the opportunity to go there. She looked about seventeen, and I fear her life will be short and horrible. Her limbs were incredibly thin. I was amazed that she was able to walk around without them breaking – until I realized how little she weighed.

7.10 Why are aliens so interested in our DNA?

Extraterrestrials seem to have an unusual interest in our DNA. Hence the huge number of alien abductions and medical experiments that have been reported. They also seem to be implanting monitoring/tracking chips in those they abduct. As we saw earlier though, the number of abductions has fallen sharply in recent years. It looks as if they've gotten most of the DNA and data they need for now.

So why were they doing it?

- They may have been harvesting our DNA to insert into other hominins on other planets. They may have been trying to increase their brain size or improve their reasoning skills, or make them more agile or better able to survive on a new planet they were being moved to.

- They may have been harvesting sections of our DNA to enhance or repair their own.

- They may have been checking up on the results of their DNA manipulation, to see how it's fared after hundreds of thousands of years of evolution.

- They may have been looking for any mistakes they made – such as accidentally causing spina bifida – and trying to find ways to fix it.

- They may have been looking for signs that other extraterrestrial species have been meddling with our genome. If that's the case, the other species may have left messages (or graffiti) there for them to find.

Or they might have had something much more sinister in mind that had nothing to do with DNA. We'll look at that in Chapter 13.

7.11 Horizontal gene transfer

A significant percentage of our DNA didn't come from our ancestors but from viruses, bacteria, and fungi. How this happened is currently unknown.[7-24]

About 8 percent of our DNA came from invading viruses. Their entire genomes have somehow become encoded within our genome, with the result that they can now manifest in our bodies as if from nowhere. This is a particular problem for those with weakened immune systems, such as HIV patients and those undergoing bone marrow transplants. Even if they're isolated from all possible external sources of infection, the viruses lurking in their genomes can still infect them.[7-25][7-26]

This process, known as horizontal gene transfer, also happens in many animals – perhaps all of them – though it's only recently been discovered in us. It has, without a doubt, affected evolution. For example, some beetles have acquired genes from bacteria that enable them to produce the enzymes they need to digest coffee berries. Nematode worms have acquired genes from microorganisms and plants. And some researchers believe that molecules from the virus remnants in our genome could help our embryos develop. They might even be essential.[7-27]

Horizontal gene transfer might also help to explain how bacteria manage to evolve resistance to antibiotics so quickly.

7.12 The future of DNA (and mankind)

As we saw above, geneticists have recently begun editing our DNA. There will undoubtedly be a huge number of edits to come. Eventually, we should see the eradication of conditions like spina bifida that we can't get rid of any other way, as well many other problems that conventional medicine can't treat.

But why stop at fixing genetic conditions? Once we fully understand what we're doing, it should be possible to modify absolutely anything, provided we do it at the embryo stage. That means we could take the genes for regenerating limbs from lizards and splice them into ourselves. We already have those genes, but ours aren't active, so it might simply be a case of replacing like for like. In a few generations time, losing a limb might no longer be a life-changing issue – you'll just sprout a new one. The same thing might happen with our teeth. We should also be able to prevent or reverse aging by extending the length of our telomeres – geneticists have already had some success with this. And we might even be able to redesign our bodies. That could include rerouting the male urethra around the prostate gland rather than through it, and modifying the throat, so we no longer risk choking if we swallow and breathe at the same time.

There are two parts to this process, of course. First, we need to understand how to fix the problem. Second, having fixed it, we need to ensure the modified genome gets passed on to future generations. Actually, there's also a third part, which we saw in the section on spina bifida, and that's making sure we don't accidentally cause another problem while we're fixing things – even if it only occurs in 1 in 1,000 cases.

So before we start meddling with anything, we need to fully understand exactly what each gene does, and how it interacts with other genes, and how each gene is regulated or modified by the non-coding sections. It's also important to bear in mind that some genes may have more than one function, so fixing one problem might cause several more.

Many people will object to these changes. We've already seen mass protests over the use of genetically modified organisms (GMO) in food crops. The reality is that they haven't been altered all that much, and they pose no greater risk to us than regular crops that nature has modified. But people are concerned about them nevertheless, and they're banned or restricted in several countries.[7-28]

In the future, this could lead to two separate human species: those who welcome and embrace all the changes and thus become superhuman; and those who resist them and insist on remaining pure. I can foresee the superhumans out-competing the pure ones, whose numbers will dwindle as a result until they become extinct. This may have been what happened when we arrived on Earth and drove the Neanderthals to extinction.

But alongside the rise of the superhumans, we'll also have the rise of intelligent machines. So we can expect to see brain-machine interfaces, cyborgs (people who are part machines), and robots running human brain software as their operating system. That will make things like deep space exploration a lot less complicated. Intelligent robots might also replace us on Earth, becoming soldiers, miners, doctors, surgeons, maintenance staff at nuclear power stations, and more. They'll be better at it than us, and they'll be able to go into situations that would harm us.

> We'd also need to figure out whether our souls are separate from our bodies, as many people suspect, or an integral part. If they're integral, and the robots are using our brain software as their operating system, they might end up with souls too. So we'd then need to figure out whether or not that was a good thing – and how to remove their souls …

> ... if we decided it wasn't. We'd undoubtedly learn an awful lot about our own souls in the process.

But this raises a number of questions. Will they eventually be treated as a species in their own right? What happens when their brains become superior to ours? That's only a matter of time. Will they take control of the world and enslave us? Or will we put mechanisms in place to prevent it? Science fiction is full of warnings, so let's hope the governments and robot-builders of the world take heed of them.

We'll also have to worry about rogue states like North Korea. They'll be fully aware of the warnings, but they'll almost certainly go ahead anyway.

7.13 Interesting things about DNA

- If you laid out all the DNA from a single human cell, it would measure about 6 feet 6 inches (2 meters). Yet somehow it all fits into the nucleus of a cell just 6 microns across. (For comparison, the width of a human hair is about 75 microns.)

- The organism with the longest DNA on Earth (that we've discovered so far) is a plant: *Paris japonica*.[7-29] If you stretched out all the DNA from one of its cells, it would measure more than 300 feet (91 meters). Candidates that might have even longer DNA are currently being studied. One possibility is *Polychaos dubium*.[7-30]

- As far as we know, the organism with the most chromosomes is also a plant: the adder's tongue fern, which has about 1,440 chromosomes in 720 pairs. (Humans, you'll remember, have 46 chromosomes in 23 pairs.)

- We have about 20,000 genes. Viruses can have just two. Plants tend to have a lot more: rice, for example, has about 46,000.

There are several reasons why plants have more DNA than us.

  o They need to be more resistant to disease and attack because they can't move away from danger.

  o Some of them have backup copies of their DNA – grapes have three copies.

  o Mistakes can occur during cell division (meiosis) when the two strands of DNA separate and the cell splits into two. Sometimes both strands can end up in the same cell, which then has twice as much DNA as it's supposed to. In regular cells, that's not usually a problem. But if it's a sex cell – a spore or pollen or egg – and it combines with a sex cell from another plant, the resulting child plant could end up with a double-dose of DNA in *every* cell. The chances of this happening are minimal, but over millions of years, it might happen a few times and even spread throughout the entire species. This can't happen in animals though as they have mechanisms which prevent it.

  o Plants with large genomes seem to be less able to tolerate extreme weather conditions, they're less well adapted to living in polluted soil, and they're at greater risk of extinction.

- Human chromosome number 2 seems to be made from ape chromosomes 2A and 2B which have fused together. There's also an extra piece of DNA at the site of the joint that isn't found in apes.[7-31]

- There are about 5 million types of gene on Earth, and they can be combined in different ways to make every living organism.

- DNA can create organisms that are astonishing in their complexity and variation. It can create every living thing, from pond slime all the way up to modern humans. It can create insects with multiple legs or snakes with none; spiders with multiple eyes or blind cave fish and worms with none; lobsters and crabs with blue blood; poison and venom; and so on. It created everything that lived on the Earth in the past, including the dinosaurs, and it will create everything that will live on the Earth millions of years from now – and who knows what the heck that might look like?

- Our height is encoded in our DNA, but we haven't found out where it is yet. So we can't tell how tall a person is from their DNA alone. We know our height is encoded in our DNA because tall parents are more likely to have tall children. That doesn't mean they'll definitely be tall though. It's only an increased likelihood, not an absolute guarantee.

- Similarly, our level of intelligence must be encoded in our DNA somewhere because very intelligent parents are more likely to produce very intelligent children. Again though, it's only an increased likelihood, not a guarantee.

- Organ transplants from other animals to humans always fail because of genetic incompatibilities. For example, medical researchers have tried transplanting organs from baboons and pigs into people. Although the organs worked well initially, they were always rejected and attacked by the patients' bodies eventually, no matter how many anti-rejection drugs they were given. With our current level of technology, the only way we can make animal-to-human transplants work is by stripping the transplanted organ of its genetic material. It can then be used as a skeleton or framework on which the patient's own biological material can grow. Over the next few years, new gene-editing techniques might be able to overcome this issue.[7-32]

- As we saw earlier, you can find DNA in almost every cell in every living organism. You have around 8 ounces (200 grams) of DNA in your body.[7-33]

- All of the DNA on Earth adds up to around 50 billion tonnes.[7-34]

8

Evolution

Once life got started on Earth, the theory of evolution kicked in, and it chugged along quite happily for the next four billion years. Evolution eventually led to a set of universal, optimal patterns. So just about every vertebrate ended up having eyes, for example, even if they got them via a different route than other creatures. Eyes evolved independently multiple times. So did flight. And just about every vertebrate has pentadactyl limbs.

We can expect evolution to have progressed along similar lines on other planets too, which means we should see the same patterns and features. Their flora and fauna might look a little different from the ones on Earth, and they might have some species that we never had, and vice versa. But they'll almost certainly have the same orders, classes and family groups that we have on Earth. Many of the planets will have hominins that evolved from mammals, and some will have advanced hominins like ourselves. Again, they might not look quite like us, but they'll be similar enough, and we'll be able to recognize what they are. On a few planets, they might even be so similar that they're biologically compatible with us.

But there are many things about human evolution that don't make sense. For example, once we arrived on Earth, our development progressed really slowly for the next 300,000 years. We don't seem to have been that much more advanced than the hominins that were already here. We were probably a little faster in our thinking and slightly more agile on our feet, and that seems to have given us a big enough advantage to out-compete them. But given our faster brains and better agility and dexterity, we ought to have advanced far more quickly than we did.

We have to accept, of course, that we were newly arrived on the planet and the extraterrestrials who brought us here had probably erased our memories. We had no recollection of living in the advanced technological society we almost certainly came from. And we didn't have the knowledge, skills or materials to rebuild it. So we were functioning in "survival mode" – purely on instinct – at least initially.

But, knowing how good we are at making connections and solving problems, logic suggests we should have overcome those early difficulties pretty quickly. Our brains were at least as big as they are now. According to some theories, they were even a little bigger. Yet it seems to have taken us more than 200,000 years to even think about wearing clothes – despite the fact that we were as hairless then as we are now. We ought to have figured that sort of thing out within a few weeks at most. There's evidence that we were killing animals for food from the moment we arrived. But apparently, we never thought about wearing their skins – or at least there's no evidence of it. We might have been living in Africa (and other warm parts of the world) but it still gets cold some of the time. The fact that we managed to survive is incredible. As I said earlier, all of this makes me wonder whether our brains might have been deliberately handicapped to prevent us from making progress.

Equally surprising is our recent rapid development. In the space of a few hundred years, we went from being farmers and hunters living in caves and primitive mud huts to living in purpose-built houses in large, urban communities, building machines, developing electricity, inventing computers and satellites and planes and traveling to the Moon. After 300,000 years or more of being hunter-gatherers living on the savannah, operating in survival mode, and making little or no progress, this sudden turnaround seems just as implausible as life evolving on Earth within 200 million years of the planet forming. To my mind, it looks as if someone removed the handicap that was holding us back, and gave us a helping hand to make up for lost time.

But who could have done this? Presumably not the extraterrestrials who brought us here; it looks as if they wanted us to remain primitive. So there must be another alien faction that not only opposes the first lot but thinks it would be to their advantage if we made rapid progress.

It's strange that there are no other hominins on Earth any more. We've already considered the idea that we may have out-competed them, leading to their extinction. But other species developed alongside the hominins, including the advanced primates that came from the same evolutionary branch: the apes, chimpanzees, gorillas, orangutans, gibbons, and so on. We didn't out-compete them or drive them to extinction; they're still here. So, what's the difference?

> Some people believe there are still a few hominins on Earth: the yeti, bigfoot, sasquatch, and so on. We occasionally see evidence of them, but we've never caught one. I wonder if we ever will?

We can see some astounding examples of evolution at work. For example, some creatures are fantastic at camouflaging themselves. Others perfectly mimic unrelated species in their quest to eat them or avoid being eaten. There are plenty of examples:

- lizards and insects that are indistinguishable from dried up leaves

- caterpillars that look like snakes or twigs or leaves

- octopuses whose skin can match the exact color and texture of the sea bed beneath them

- stick insects

- ant-mimicking spiders

- butterflies with large eye patterns on their wings – most notably the owl butterfly

- leaf fish

- and hundreds more

8.1 Oxygen

Oxygen is a byproduct of life, not a prerequisite. (So is soil.)

Oxygen is now considered essential to life, but it wasn't always that way. During the Earth's early years, oxygen was a byproduct given off by anaerobic cyanobacteria as they photosynthesized – and it was toxic to every living thing. In fact, the bacteria produced so much of it that it caused Earth's first mass extinction event.[8-01]

When plants came along, they raised the oxygen levels even higher, to the point where massive wildfires would break out every time there was a lightning strike. But those fires were an essential evolutionary step, as they changed the composition of the atmosphere. If the level of oxygen in the air had remained as high as it was, it's doubtful whether many animal species would have evolved; it would have been too toxic for them.

High levels of oxygen are toxic to us too.[8-02] The air we breathe is roughly 79 percent nitrogen and 21 percent oxygen, plus a trace amount of other gases including argon.

Many people wrongly believe that divers' air tanks are filled with pure oxygen. In fact, that would kill them. For regular dives, their tanks contain pretty much the same mix of nitrogen and oxygen that we breathe on land. For deeper dives, the oxygen can be increased to a maximum of forty percent and helium is added to the mix.[8-02a] But that requires special equipment and training and is only used by professional divers.

Does the same thing happen on every planet that has life? Perhaps it does. But even if it only happens on a few of them, with 100 billion planets in our galaxy alone, a few is all it takes.

8.2 How we know evolution is real [8-03]

- If we observe the development of the human embryo, we see that it goes through several stages where it matches the embryos of other species. For example, in the early stages, it closely resembles the embryo of a fish, complete with a tail that later develops into limbs. The embryos of most other animals resemble fish embryos too at that stage. Even a trained biologist would find it hard to tell which species it might develop into: it could become a human, or a fish, a lizard, a bird, a rabbit, or something else.

- Animals (and plants) share traits with their common ancestors.

- We can also find vestigial traits, where something that was useful in an ancestor species still exists in its descendants even though it no longer serves any useful purpose. We have many vestigial traits ourselves. But that doesn't mean we must have evolved on Earth; it just means we inherited them from our ancestors. Our ancestors would have been the earlier hominins who evolved on our home planet. We'll take a closer look at our vestigial features later in this chapter.

- Some people say our imperfections are a sign of evolution. If we were created by a god or an intelligent designer, we should have no imperfections at all. In fact, as we saw in Chapter 2, we have lots of them.

- We can actually see evolution happening*. For example, bacteria are evolving to become resistant to antibiotics. We've also seen many creatures evolve in response to environmental changes.

- We can model evolution accurately on computers and watch it play out in the real world, exactly as predicted, with consistent results.

> *We've only ever seen things evolving within their *own* species. We've never directly witnessed anything evolving into a *different* species. Some people doubt it's even possible. We'll explore this further at the end of the chapter.

8.3 So who or what did we evolve from?

For decades, mainstream scientists believed we evolved directly from *Homo erectus*, and the question was considered settled once and for all. But we now know that this isn't the case. There are considerable doubts about whether *H. erectus* was still around when we first appeared. And, as we saw earlier, it looked nothing like us, particular in the shape of its skull.

Dr. Etty Indriati of Gadjah Mada University in Indonesia, who investigated potential *H. erectus* remains there, said: "*Homo erectus* probably did not share habitats with modern humans." He went on to say that *H. erectus* had been extinct since at least 143,000 years ago and probably more than 550,000 years ago.[8-04]

Evolutionary scientists then turned their attention to *Homo heidelbergensis*, and once again convinced themselves that it must be our direct ancestor. They theorized that *H. heidelbergensis* was the descendant of *H. erectus* (which is a reasonable enough assumption) and that *H. heidelbergensis* was not only our direct ancestor but the direct ancestor of the Neanderthals and the Denisovans too.

There's no question that *H. erectus, H. heidelbergensis* and the Neanderthals and Denisovans were closely related. The timeline fits, the DNA fits (what little we've found), and their skulls show a steady progression with no awkward jumps or gaps.

It's uncertain whether the Denisovans were an offshoot of the Neanderthals or perhaps vice versa, but we don't really need to concern ourselves with that here. The latest findings indicate that Denisovans were already living in Spain before the Neanderthals evolved – which has upset the Neanderthal fans somewhat.

But the link between *H. erectus, H. heidelbergensis*, and modern humans doesn't work at all, despite what the mainstream evolutionary scientists would like us to believe. The timeline sort of fits, and there's not enough DNA evidence to prove things either way, but the most damning evidence is the shape, size, and structure of their skulls. They don't resemble ours at all.

We then need to factor in all the evidence we looked at earlier in the book, and in other books such as *Forbidden Archaeology*:

- The staggering amount of evidence that proves we don't belong here and can't have evolved here.

- The mass of evidence that proves we were present on Earth, as fully evolved modern humans, multiple times throughout history and prehistory, even before the ancient hominins evolved.

- The unexplained technological and astronomical knowledge that ancient people possessed.

- The sudden leaps in our own technological progression.

- And the testimonies of respected and trusted individuals who've confirmed all of this, risking or even destroying their careers and reputations in doing so.

The only logical conclusion is that we didn't evolve on Earth but were brought here from another planet, not all at once but in multiple stages throughout history. I've listed the approximate dates and locations in the timeline in Chapter 12.

Once we reached Earth, a small number of Europeans may have interbred with the Neanderthals shortly before they became extinct, and a small number of Asians may have interbred with the Denisovans.

It's said that everyone who's alive today can trace their mitochondrial DNA back to a single female ancestor known as "Mitochondrial Eve" who lived in Africa about 200,000 years ago. Mainstream scientists say this proves we evolved in Africa. But it doesn't.

We've already seen that our genome has been interfered with. Geneticists can plainly see the scars where our genes were cut, duplicated, modified, and replaced. This is, without a doubt, the source of the mitochondrial DNA we see today. The new sections were probably harvested from an individual female hominin who lived in Africa and exhibited the characteristics the aliens were looking for.

Once they'd inserted the new genes into our DNA – probably at the embryo stage – the extraterrestrials would have confirmed that it produced the required results and would be successfully passed on to subsequent generations. This process would have taken decades. Then, once they were satisfied, they began dropping us off on Earth.

This explains why we all seem to have the mitochondrial DNA of an African woman, even though we aren't originally from Earth and our ancestors might have been dropped off in South America, Asia, Israel, Australia, or somewhere else, and have no African roots at all.

There's a common misconception that we descended from the Neanderthals. This definitely didn't happen. If anything, the Neanderthals would be more like our sister group, where we both descended from the same parent – such as *Homo heidelbergensis*, as we saw above.

If that were the case though, the Neanderthals would be at the same level as us on the evolutionary tree. So it's strange that they seem so much more primitive. This is further evidence that we aren't a part of that evolutionary timeline.

We've already seen that the Neanderthals were more robust than us and didn't suffer from all the back problems that affect us. But it goes much further than that. If we cut a cross-section through a Neanderthal femur (thigh bone) and a modern human femur, they look nothing like each other. The human bone is smaller and tubular with a large chamber for the bone marrow. The Neanderthal bone is thicker, and solid nearly all the way through.

8.4 What happened to the Neanderthals?

The Neanderthals became extinct around 40,000 years ago, but no one really knows why.[8-05][8-06]

But the fact that they died out within 5,000 years of us arriving in Europe is probably the biggest clue. The humans of that era (the Cro-Magnons) would have easily out-competed them for resources using their superior intellect; fast, agile bodies; and well-coordinated pack-hunting skills. They might have also brought diseases and parasites with them from Asia that the Neanderthals would have had no immunity to.

Some researchers theorize that they may have died out because the climate in Europe had become much colder, and they were already in decline before we encountered them. That seems unlikely; they were robust and well adapted to living in cooler climates. The fact that we replaced them so quickly seems to rule this out: we were not only less robust but came from a warmer climate. So the cooling climate may have contributed to their extinction, but it couldn't have been the primary cause.

There's another theory that we may have deliberately driven them to extinction because they were unable to resist our women. They may have become uncontrollably violent and "rapey" when human girls were around.

Some researchers have speculated that their demise might have been brought about by volcanic activity in the Phlegraean Fields near Naples, Italy. We know it erupted between 37,000 and 39,000 years ago. But the latest evidence suggests that the Neanderthals had already died out at least 1,000 years before the eruption occurred.[8-07]

8.5 Why nature doesn't do perfection

As we saw earlier, our imperfection is often put forward as proof that evolution is real – because God wouldn't have made us imperfect. But why doesn't nature "do" perfection? There are actually some very good reasons.[8-08]

For example, the environment is constantly changing. While it might suit some members of a particular species right now, it probably doesn't suit all of them. It suited different members of the species a century ago, and it will suit a different set in a century's time. And that's how evolution works. As the environment changes, those that are best suited to it thrive, while those who are least suited to it don't. The best-adapted ones reproduce more and have stronger offspring who are also well-adapted to the new conditions – some more so than others. And so the process continues.

If every member of that species were perfect for the conditions right now, they'd have no way of adapting if the conditions changed. None of them would find the new conditions more suitable, and they might all die out. So a *good* fit for the environment is better than a *perfect* fit. Perhaps God knew what He was doing after all.

Having said that, some species haven't changed a jot in millions of years. So I guess we could, at the very least, call them *near*-perfect. These are things like mosses, ferns, tortoises, turtles, alligators, and crocodiles. The immortal jellyfish can revert to polyp form upon reaching sexual maturity. Tardigrades (also known as water bears) may be the most resilient animal on the planet. They can survive just about anything, including radiation, extremes of temperature, and even space. If conditions become too severe, they shut down until things improve, then revive themselves.

But just because they've been that way for millions of years, that doesn't mean they're all the same. It also doesn't mean they're bound to remain that way forever. A virus that infects another species might mutate and start attacking them at any moment. It might wipe most of them out, but there will usually be a few survivors: those that have some degree of natural resistance to the virus. If they reproduce, their children should also have some of that natural resistance. If enough of them have survived to maintain a viable population, then the species will also survive. Eventually, their numbers will recover and they'll be more resistant to the virus if it strikes again.

We can take a different approach, of course. While some of us might be more resistant to a virus than others, we can sometimes use medical technology to make *everyone* resistant. For example, we can develop antiviral drugs that cure those that have been infected and prevent anyone else from becoming infected. In other words, we can wipe out some viruses before they wipe us out. We've already done this with viruses such as smallpox. There was no need for any evolution to take place in this case; we did the job ourselves, and millions of times faster.

There's a problem with this approach though. If some of the viruses don't get wiped out by the drug (meaning they have a degree of resistance to it), they can quickly rebuild their population, and all of them will now be resistant to it. If we run out of drugs that work, the virus becomes untreatable. We've already seen this in bacteria. Some of them are now resistant to all of our antibiotics.

And that takes us back to evolution again: only those with some level of natural resistance to a particular virus or strain of bacteria will survive and reproduce. If no one has any resistance, the whole population could be wiped out.

We aren't perfect – and that's a good thing

You could argue that humans are the perfect species. We sit at the top of the evolutionary tree, and we seem to be what the other species aspire to – at least in evolutionary terms. But we've already seen that we're far from perfect.

- Who in their right mind would put a collapsible tube (the male urethra) right through the middle of an organ that's prone to expansion (the prostate gland) and can block the flow of urine, requiring surgical intervention?[8-09]

- And what about brow ridges, which all of our supposed ancestors on Earth had, but we don't? We've already seen that we'd be much better off if we had them. The fact that we don't is quite bizarre. If we're from Earth, we seem to have evolved *away* from perfection.

- Another factor is our skull, which is too thin to provide our brain with adequate protection. Each year about 1.7 million people in the United States suffer a traumatic brain injury that requires hospital treatment, and about 52,000 of them die.[8-10] In the UK about 1.4 million people require hospital treatment for head injuries each year.[8-11] Brain injury is the leading cause of death and disability worldwide.

We've abandoned nature – and to some extent evolution too – and become a technological species that can't survive in the wild. We nurture our sick and disabled, including those with genetic faults and diseases, and many of them go on to reproduce. As we've seen, this has the unfortunate effect of propagating those weaknesses and diseases rather than eradicating them, as would have happened if we hadn't intervened. So our species is becoming weaker, not stronger.

So we'll never reach perfection. And, as we saw above, we must hope we never do, because it would almost certainly mean the end of us. But if we continue the way we are, interfering with nature and propagating weaknesses that should have been weeded out, that could spell the end of us too.

Many of the people who commented on the first edition of this book agreed that evolution doesn't lead to perfection. For example, they suggested that perfect dolphins and whales would have gills. They'd then be able to breathe underwater, rather than having to return to the surface every few minutes. So let's think about that for a moment.

Why don't dolphins and whales have gills? [8-12]

I know we're going off on a tangent again, but lots of people asked the question, and this is my area of specialism. Feel free to skip to the next section if you aren't interested.

- You don't *need* gills to live underwater. Gills are one of nature's solutions; lungs and blowholes are another. They both work just fine – within reason.

> Blowholes are basically nostrils.

- But gills can't extract the amount of oxygen from the water that large, fast-moving, warm-blooded mammals need. Gills work perfectly well in small-to-medium-sized cold-blooded fish. Larger fish, like sharks, have to limit their movements most of the time. Gentle oscillations of their tails and fins are the order of the day. They can move quickly when they need to, and occasional lunges and attacks are fine. But they soon run out of oxygen and have to return to making gentle movements until their blood-oxygen level has recovered.

- The amount of oxygen in the water reduces as you go deeper. Whales can operate at great depths, but they have to carry their oxygen supply with them. As well as having lungs and blowholes, they also need muscles that are absolutely packed with myoglobin.

> Myoglobin is the primary oxygen-carrying protein in muscle. The more of it you have, the longer you can hold your breath.

- Deep-sea fish live at those depths, but they're incredibly sluggish and, like sharks, they keep their movements to an absolute minimum. And that makes it much easier for the whales to catch them.

- Dolphins and whales are already at the tops of their respective food chains. They're highly successful in evolutionary terms – and, as we saw earlier, nature doesn't tend to fix things that are already working.

- Gills wouldn't re-evolve in dolphins and whales because it wouldn't give them an evolutionary advantage. In fact, as we've just seen, it would be a great disadvantage. The only reason it might happen is if the oxygen levels in the sea rose significantly. But that would have so many other repercussions that it could cause another global extinction event.

8.6 Our vestigial features

Our vestigial features are our body parts, mechanisms and behavioral traits that we inherited from our ancestors but no longer have any use for. We have lots of them, and we inherited them not only from the hominins that preceded us but from creatures further down the evolutionary tree.

In our case, of course, those hominins and lower orders of creatures would have lived on our home planet. But as we've already seen, they would have been remarkably similar to those on Earth – but probably several million years ahead.

Non-vestigial features

Appendix

If you ask people to list our vestigial features, the appendix will usually be the one they come up with first. But the appendix *isn't* a vestigial feature. It (probably) doesn't serve the same purpose that it was designed for, but it *does* have a purpose.

The appendix was thought to be the diminished remnant of the long caecum, which herbivores have to help them digest cellulose. We've already seen that we're herbivores at heart, but we don't need to digest cellulose, so the appendix was considered redundant in us. But researchers have discovered that our appendix has taken on a new role: it stores beneficial gut bacteria. Diseases such as cholera and dysentery can kill off these bacteria in the main digestive/fecal stream, but those in the appendix are safely out of harm's way. And that means they can repopulate the digestive system once the pathogen has passed.

We can survive perfectly well without an appendix, but those who have had theirs removed may suffer an increased risk of conditions such as colitis.[8-13]

> Since the appendix no longer serves its original purpose, vegetarians and vegans don't gain any additional benefits from having one.

Coccyx

The coccyx is the remnant of a tail – and it's often known as the tailbone. But it's not as useless as many people believe. In fact, it works with our pelvis, acting like the third leg of a tripod, to help bear our weight when we sit down, especially when we lean back. It's also an important anchoring point for several muscles, including the pelvic floor, as well as tendons and ligaments. We can get by reasonably well without one, as long as the surgeon takes care to protect the muscles, tendons, and ligaments that were attached to it. But those who have had theirs removed may have an increased risk of a hernia because of a weakened pelvic floor.[8-14]

Hiccups

Hiccups were once thought to be the vestigial remnant of the mechanism that makes fish push water over their gills and amphibians gulp air. In mammals, the mechanism appeared to have been rewired incorrectly, so it just made the diaphragm spasm. But a 2012 study found that hiccups helped young mammals coordinate suckling and breathing, and helped to get rid of air trapped in their stomachs. The incidence of hiccups diminishes as we get older, which supports this theory.[8-15]

Junk DNA

As we've already seen, junk DNA is more properly known as non-coding DNA. It's the part of our DNA that doesn't encode protein sequences or genes. Although the term junk DNA has been popular since the 1960s, geneticists now know that at least 80 percent of it has a biological function – and they're still working on the rest. Its primary purpose is to protect the genes, switch them on and off, regulate them, and pass messages.[8-16]

Actual vestigial features

Auricular muscles

These are the muscles that allow us to move our ears. Some people can move their ears a little, and some can't move them at all. In the distant past, we'd have been able to move our ears to help us hear predators. But as we no longer have any predators, we've lost most of that ability, and the auricular muscles are basically non-functioning.

Aversion to high-pitched sounds

Fingernails on a chalkboard, cutlery scraping on a plate, a knife dragged across a bottle … just thinking about these sounds can set your teeth on edge. This is probably a remnant from a time when there were dangerous predators around. They might be similar to the sounds the predators made, or they may have been a warning. For example, fingernails on a chalkboard sound very much like the warning cry of a macaque monkey.[8-17]

Darwin's tubercle

This is the slight thickening some of us have on the helix of our ears, about two-thirds of the way up. It's a remnant from a time when our ancestors had pointed ears. The incidence of this varies: it's only present in 10 percent of Spaniards, 40 percent of Indians, and 58 percent of Swedes.[8-18]

Raising our feet when we're scared or anxious

You may have seen this behavior in cartoons such as *Tom and Jerry*. A mouse or a rat scurries across the floor, and the lady of the house immediately leaps onto a chair. If you see one of these creatures in your own home, your first instinct is usually to raise your feet and tuck them up under you out of harm's way. This is thought to be a remnant from a time when we climbed trees if we felt threatened.

Genital features

Both male and female human genitalia have vestigial organs, ducts, and appendages.[8-19]

Goose bumps

These are the small bumps that appear on our skin when we're cold or experiencing strong emotions. They tend to be most noticeable on our arms. They're caused by the erector muscles attached to each hair follicle contracting. In fur-covered mammals they make their hairs stand on end, so they look bigger and scarier, which helps them to ward off potential threats. The erect hairs also help wet fur dry more quickly, by increasing the rate of evaporation. They also increase the amount of insulation the fur provides if the animal is feeling cold. The same mechanism raises porcupines' quills. As we don't have much body hair, the mechanism serves no real purpose in us.[8-20]

> This mechanism supposedly causes the hair on our heads to stand on end when we're frightened. You can sort of feel it happening, but I'm not sure it's visible to anyone else. I've only ever seen it happen in cartoons and movies. The only thing I know that causes our hair to stand on end in real life is static electricity.

Infant swimming

Most babies make swimming motions when placed in water. They also instinctively hold their breath underwater. They stop making swimming motions when they're around six months old unless they've been taken swimming regularly.

> They can't actually swim at this age because they aren't strong enough yet.[8-21]

L-gulonolactone oxidase

This gene produces an enzyme that synthesizes vitamin C. Most mammals have it, and it's functional in them, but our copy is non-functioning. We have to obtain all of our vitamin C from our food.

Levator claviculae **muscle**

This is a rare skeletal muscle in the posterior triangle of the neck. Most mammals, including gibbons and orangutans, have it. But it has all but disappeared in us. Only about two to three percent of the population is believed to have it, and it's probably even less than that. No one knows why.[8-22]

Lip twitching when we're angry

This is a remnant from a time when our ancestors bared their teeth at those who threatened them or intruded into their territory. It demonstrated that they were aware of the intrusion, they recognized them as a threat not a friend, and they were primed to attack and drive them away if they didn't leave immediately. Teeth baring can still be seen in wolves, dogs, cats, bears, and chimpanzees.

Humans Are Not From Earth

Male nipples

Male nipples are considered semi-vestigial. They don't serve any real purpose, and it's thought that men only have them because women have them, and all human fetuses are female in the early stages of their development. Biologists believe they would have disappeared by now if women had actively selected against them or expressed a preference for smaller nipples when choosing a mate. But that hasn't happened so far.[8-23][8-24]

People sometimes have extra pairs of nipples, or even breasts, lower down their chest. This is similar to what you see in mammals that have multiple pairs of nipples.

Palmar grasp reflex – also known as the infant grasp reflex

Babies automatically squeeze your finger if you place it in their hand. (It also kind of works with their feet.) They lose this reflex by the time they're about six months old. This stems from a time in our distant past when babies clung to their mother's body hair. It allowed mothers with infants to move around easily, or climb trees to escape from danger, while keeping both hands free.

Palmaris longus muscle

This muscle looks like a tendon that protrudes from the inside of your wrist when you clench your hand. To see it, touch your thumb and smallest finger together on your strongest hand (that's your right hand if you're right-handed) and look at your wrist. If you can't see anything, try bending your hand towards you slightly. 14 percent of people don't have one, so if you still can't see anything you may be part of that group.

Plantaris muscle

This leg muscle allows apes to grip and manipulate objects with their feet. In humans, it's superficial and serves almost no purpose. It might help slightly with flexing the knee and ankle, but we can get by perfectly well without it. Surgeons routinely harvest its tendon to graft into other parts of the body that have been injured. About nine percent of people are currently born without it, and that number is expected to rise in future generations.[8-25]

Plica Semilunaris

This is the tiny fold of skin in the corner of each eye. It's the remnant of the nictitating membrane (third eyelid) that we looked at in Chapter 2. It used to protect our eyes from being dazzled by the sun, as well as from things like dust and sand. Many creatures still have theirs, so it's strange that we lost ours. We must have no longer needed it when our home planet clouded over.

Polarized light vision

We can see polarized light, but not terribly well. Here's a quick test to demonstrate it. Open up a blank word processing document or a notes app on your computer, tablet or smartphone. Anything that makes most of the screen go white should work. Stare at the middle of the screen and tilt your head to one side. You should see a faint yellow smear or bow shape. That's polarized light.[8-26]

   The image fades after a few seconds. If you want to see it again, just tilt your head to the other side.

Some people also see a blue shape or smear. This is produced by your brain, which wonders where the yellow came from and tries to cancel it out with a negative image. When I tried the test, I saw the yellow smear, but I didn't see the blue one.

Our ability to see polarized yellow (and sometimes blue) shapes on LCD screens is of no use to us whatsoever. But all sorts of animals, including insects, octopuses, cuttlefish, and many birds, use polarized light to help them navigate.[8-27]

Pyramidalis muscle

This is a small, triangular muscle in the abdomen that attaches to the pelvis. Its purpose is to tense the *linea alba* – a fibrous structure that runs down the middle of the abdomen. Around twenty percent of the population doesn't have one, so we clearly don't need it.

Sense of smell

Our sense of smell isn't vestigial yet, but it seems to be heading that way. It no longer serves the purpose it does in other animals: mainly finding food, avoiding predators, and detecting scent markings at territorial borders. These days we only really use it to detect toxic fumes or tell when food has gone off. We don't choose our partners on the basis of how good their sense of smell is. And having a poor sense of smell, or none at all, doesn't prevent us from reproducing. So biologists think we may eventually lose this sense entirely.

Some people argue that we need a sense of smell to detect pheromones in potential partners. But there's a counter argument that says our pheromones are also vestigial, or very close to becoming so.

Ultraviolet vision

The blue light receptors in our retinas can actually see UV light better than they can see blue light. But the lenses in our eyes block UV. If a lens is removed or replaced with a synthetic one that allows UV light to pass through, a whole new world opens up to us.

> This is something to think about if you ever need cataract surgery. You can ask for replacement lenses that don't restrict UV.
>
> If you don't ask for them specifically, you'll be given the sort that blocks UV and restores your original sight. But older synthetic lenses didn't block UV, so some of you reading this might be able to see it.[8-28]
>
> The artist Claude Monet[8-29] had cataract surgery and could see UV afterward. You can see this in some of his paintings.[8-30]

Most animals, including insects, fish, reptiles and amphibians, birds, and many mammals such as hedgehogs, cats, and dogs, can see UV light. But not primates.[8-31][8-32][8-33][8-34]

Vomeronasal organ

This is also known as the auxiliary olfactory sense organ – basically a second sense of smell. It's involved in detecting chemical messages and pheromones. Most animals have it. We develop it while we're fetuses, but it usually disappears again before we're born. A few people may have one, but it's hard to detect and appears to be totally non-functioning.[8-35]

Whisker muscles

About 35 percent of the population shows signs of sinus hair muscles and *vibrissal capsular* muscles in their upper lips. These are a remnant from a time when our ancestors had whiskers.

Wisdom teeth

These are our third set of molars. They enabled our ancestors to chew fibrous plants. But those ancestors had larger jaws than us. Now that we have softer diets and cook our food, our jaws have become smaller, and our wisdom teeth have become vestigial. Many people don't have enough space in their mouths for their wisdom teeth, and they become impacted and have to be removed. About 35 percent of people never develop wisdom teeth at all these days, and it looks as if they'll eventually disappear entirely.[8-36]

Evolutionary leftovers

As well as our vestigial features, we also have features that are hangovers from our distant past, when our lifestyles were significantly different from the way we live today.[8-37] For example:

- Our feet evolved for tree-climbing, and still retain elements of that flexibility. This makes them unstable when we walk, run or jump on the ground. Sprained and twisted ankles are common injuries.

- Our immune systems evolved to cope with all manner of parasites. There are far fewer of these in the developed world, where most of our food is washed, sterilized, pasteurized or cooked before we eat it. As a result, we get allergies and autoimmune diseases because our immune systems overreact to harmless things.

- We crave fat-rich and calorie-rich food to save ourselves from famine. Famines are rare in the developed world, but the craving is still there. This can lead to obesity and all the harmful conditions that go with it, including heart disease and diabetes.

8.7 The original humans

Based on what we know about the Earth and human evolution, we can come up with a pretty good idea of what our ancestors looked like when they lived on our home planet.

- We know they must have had large heads with no brows, and wide pelvises.

- They would have been shorter and stockier than us, with stronger backs.

- They would have been hairless and naked, only wearing clothes or paint or flowers for decoration or out of prudishness.

- Their skin was probably similar in shade to our own. Those living in the tropics would have had dark skin while those in the temperate regions would have had lighter skin. But they would have been able to stay out in the sun without needing sunscreen because of the lower level of light reaching the surface of their planet.

- They almost certainly had a lower sperm count than us because there was less food available and it was less nutritious than it is here. As a result, they would have reproduced in smaller numbers and lived well within the available resources of their planet, rather than multiplying out of control and completely infesting the place as we've done on Earth.

- They would have been highly intelligent with a well-developed language.

OBJECTION!
"Our bodies contain all the minerals
that can be found on this planet."

That's mostly true. Fortunately, most of them are only found in minuscule quantities, because several of them are highly toxic.

The minerals are in us because we breathe them in and eat them in our food. Our bodies also contain lots of other things that don't belong there, such as pesticide residues, chemicals that have leached out of plastic, and animal hormones from the meat we've eaten. If we lived on another planet, its minerals would be in us. If we went to Mars and took off our helmets for a few seconds, some of the dust in the air would get into us. We might still be able to detect it in our bones months or even years later, but it doesn't mean we evolved there. So the claim that we could only have come from this planet because its minerals are inside us isn't really a valid one.

The materials from which the planets are made formed naturally as part of the nuclear fusion process in stars, and all of the rocky planets are somewhat similar in composition. The mineral composition of our home planet will be similar to the Earth's, and similar to most other rocky planets. We evolved to depend on some of those minerals.

Where rocky planets vary in composition, it's usually nothing to do with what they were originally made from. They were all made from the same stuff but in varying quantities. The difference comes from the processes that affected those minerals after the planets formed. For example, volcanism (intense heat and pressure), water activity, and exposure to solar radiation. These change the structure of the minerals and form new ones, or bond them together into different compounds.

As a result, the proportion (and presence or absence) of particular minerals varies from planet to planet. This allows us to tell rocks that originated on one planet from rocks that originated on another.

In Chapter 2, I said everyone on Earth is chronically ill. That may be because a mineral we depended on when we lived on our home planet is missing here, or is found in much smaller quantities. Or, conversely, there might be too much of it here.

OBJECTION!

"I'm not from another planet – I was born in New York."

New York is a great place to live. But we're talking about your very (very) distant ancestors, going back over 300,000 years or more, not you personally.

I'm sure Charles Darwin got a similar response when he claimed that everyone was descended from the same evolutionary branch as the apes: "That can't be right! None of my family are monkeys!"

Of course, we now know that while the Earth's native hominins descended from that evolutionary branch, *we* certainly didn't. It was a reasonable enough assumption at the time though.

Did the different human races come from different planets?

It's a possibility, though as we're all so similar, it's also highly unlikely. It's more likely that the different races came from the same planet but at different times, perhaps tens of thousands of years apart. They might also have had their genomes altered to suit the particular regions of the Earth they were dropped off in. The Earth is not our ideal planet (it scores less than 83 percent on the habitability chart), so several compromises had to be made. We can still see these today even though most of the original races have interbred to create new ones.

8.8 Are we still evolving?

Yes and no. We're definitely still responding to changes in our environment and evolving. Or at least that's what most biologists think. But we're talking about tiny evolutionary changes that will take hundreds of years at the very least.[8-38][8-39]

Elisabeth Bolund of Uppsala University in Sweden confirmed this: "We are still evolving. As long as some individuals have more children and other individuals have fewer children than others, there is potential for evolution to take place."

In the developed world, we're seeing a shift towards later reproduction, and Dr. Bolund expects to see a genetic response to this. She believes it will lead to women finding it easier to reproduce later in life. She also thinks some people will become less inclined to develop cancer and heart disease, and as a result will live longer and our species will become more robust.

We're becoming more resistant to other diseases too. A 2007 study uncovered 1,800 genes that only became prevalent in us in the last 40,000 years. Many of them were found to fight diseases such as malaria. People living in cities were found to have become more resistant to diseases such as tuberculosis and leprosy than those living in rural areas. Resistance to HIV also seems to be increasing.[8-40]

Evolution can sometimes backfire. West African yam farmers inadvertently changed their environment so it supported malaria-carrying mosquitos. Some people turned out to be immune to malaria, and they survived and had children. Unfortunately, the reason for their immunity was that they carried the sickle-cell allele, which causes sickle-cell anemia. That disease is now widespread throughout their population.

As we saw earlier though, our practice of allowing (and sometimes helping) people with genetic weaknesses to reproduce is propagating those weaknesses further. This will almost certainly have to change one day when the weaknesses become so widespread that our entire future is threatened. There will be massive protests when this happens. It won't happen within our lifetimes though.

American evolutionary biologist Professor Stephen Stearns of Yale University believes the changes we've made to the world might be speeding up our evolution: "We see rapid evolution when there's rapid environmental change, and the biggest part of our environment is culture – and culture is exploding." He adds that "we can't see it because we're stuck right in the middle of the process."

Professor Stearns is also concerned about the number of couples in the developed world who are electing not to have children. In effect, they're choosing to prevent their genes from surviving beyond them.

But Professor Steve Jones, a geneticist from University College London, takes the opposite viewpoint: "The bulk of medical and other technological developments which protect us from our environment have come in just the past century. So in the developed world today, what is there left for natural selection to act on? Natural selection, if it hasn't stopped, has at least slowed down."

We've certainly stopped evolving in some aspects. We saw earlier that women in developed countries won't evolve wider pelvises to help them give birth to children with large heads. Modern obstetrics has put a stop to that. Even women with narrow pelvises can now give birth in complete safety. And that means their narrow pelvises will be passed on to their children.

Other recent changes

We've already noted that about 35 percent of the population no longer develops wisdom teeth. This process began around 10,000 years ago when we started cooking our food and shifted to a softer diet. It's thought that eventually, no one will have them.

We've also noted that people in the developed world have been getting taller in recent decades, although in most countries the rate of growth is now beginning to tail off.

Another change we've seen in the last few thousand years is the increase in lactose tolerance. More than 95 percent of people living in the West can now drink and digest cow's milk.

In fact, all of us are born with the ability to digest lactose because it's present in human breast milk. But historically, once we were weaned off breast milk, that ability shut down. Over the last 3,000 years, that shut-down has gradually been halted because cow's milk gave those who drank it a nutritional advantage over those who didn't. As a result, lifelong tolerance of lactose has gradually become incorporated into our genes. It's still largely absent from those living in the East though, where cow's milk and other dairy products are absent from their diet.

Some of the evolutionary changes we're seeing are quite surprising. For example, heart surgeons who routinely use X-rays to help them guide catheters through their patients' blood vessels are evolving the ability to withstand radiation. Researchers have found fundamental changes in them at the cellular level, as well as raised levels of glutathione (an antioxidant that protects against cell damage) and an enzyme in white blood cells that kills off any damaged cells.[8-41]

Our shrinking brains

When we discussed the Neanderthals earlier, we noted that they had slightly larger brains than us. The difference would be even more pronounced today, because our brains have been shrinking for the last 30,000 years, from 1,500 cubic centimeters to about 1,260 cubic centimeters. The amount of brain matter we've lost would fill a tennis ball.

There are two main theories as to why this has happened.

The first concludes that we're becoming dumber. We don't need to be massively intelligent to live in modern societies, and we don't need to hunt to survive, so our brains don't need to be as complex as they once were.

The second theory is more positive. It suggests that our brains are smaller now because the distance between our neurons has shortened. As a result, electrical and chemical signals can travel between them more quickly, and that means we can think faster. So we're actually *more* intelligent than those with bigger brains who came before us.

> The renowned theoretical physicist Albert Einstein's brain was a little smaller than average – though still within the normal range. But its structure was extraordinary.[8-42]

There's also a third theory that fits with the prison planet hypothesis we considered in Chapter 5. It suggests that our smaller brains are an evolutionary advantage because they make us less aggressive.

According to the theory, we've become less intelligent, and that means we're forced to work together to solve problems. And if we're working together, we aren't tearing each other to shreds.

This also fits the theory that intellectually and technologically advanced humans lived on the Earth millions of years ago.[8-43]

Humans of the future

Dr. Alan Kwan, an expert in computational genomics, has a different theory.[8-44] He believes our brains will continue to grow bigger, resulting in larger heads – and, most notably, larger foreheads. He also thinks we'll evolve larger eyes (unnervingly so by today's standards) as we begin colonizing dimmer worlds that are further from the Sun. And, similarly, he believes our skin will darken and we'll develop thicker eyelids to protect us from UV as we leave the safety of the Earth's ozone layer.

Other changes we can expect from living off-world include thicker hair, and larger nostrils for easier breathing.

Looking further into the future, he expects genetic modification to take precedence, with our faces moving towards what we consider the "perfect" standard: regal lines, straight nose, perfect symmetry, and so on.

Parents will be able to design their children's faces (and bodies), selecting the best features they like in each other, and changing other features to make them more attractive.

And then we'll almost certainly go beyond natural perfection. For example, we might give ourselves enhanced low-light vision, which would make our eyes appear to shine. We could also restore the nictitating membrane (third eyelid) that evolution took away. As well as protecting us from dust, sand and sun blindness, it would give us an eerie sideways blink.

Beer goggles

I'm grateful to the person who commented on the first edition of this book that "mate selection still applies unless we get drunk." I imagine a huge number of pregnancies have resulted from drunken sexual encounters when the "beer goggles" were firmly in place. Many of us wouldn't be here today if it weren't for alcohol.[8-45]

> Beer goggles refers to the strange effect that alcohol has on our visual perception. The more alcohol we drink, the more attractive the people around us seem to become. We may end up sleeping with someone we wouldn't normally find appealing.

8.9 Intelligence

If we'd evolved on Earth, we'd certainly deserve our place at the top of the evolutionary tree, and we could rightfully consider ourselves the most intelligent creatures on the planet. But, as we've already seen, we're comparative newcomers. We may have been at the top of the evolutionary tree on our home planet, but whether we're also at the top here on Earth is the subject of considerable debate. It turns out that we might not be the most intelligent creatures here after all.

In their book *The Dynamic Human*, researchers from the University of Adelaide in Australia, argue that we aren't that much smarter than other creatures. In fact, some of them might even be smarter than us.[8-46] But, of course, it depends how you define "smart." We aren't necessarily *more* intelligent than other animals, we're just *differently* intelligent.

The main thing that distinguishes us from most other animals is our ability to reason. So perhaps we should really be asking why more animals haven't developed this ability. Or maybe we should be asking why several animals already have this ability, but it's taken us until now to realize it.

Ravens, for example, use logic to understand and interact with their environment. Their ability to do this might even surpass the great apes. Their close relatives the crows have also been found to be incredibly smart.[8-47]

Dolphins are renowned for their intelligence. And their brains are not only 15 percent larger than ours, they're also more complex. We now know that they're structured for awareness and emotion.[8-48] Lori Marino, a dolphin expert from Emory University in Atlanta, Georgia, USA said: "If human standards for intelligence are applied to non-human animals, dolphins come very close to our own brain aptitude levels."

Pigs might be the smartest domesticated animals on Earth. They've been found to have the same intellectual capacity as three-year-old children. They can quickly be trained to perform tricks such as jumping through hoops. They often try to outsmart and deceive other pigs to get a bigger share of the food. They understand how mirrors work and they can use them to help them find food. And they can play video games by moving joysticks with their snouts.[8-49] Chimpanzees can also play video games, but pigs learn to play them just as quickly.

When it comes to language, several animals have that ability too. Dolphins and killer whales have a complex language, and we know that dolphins have individual names.

Dogs can understand up to 250 words – again, the same as a three-year-old child – and they learn quickly. But, like dolphins, dogs' brains are structured for emotional intelligence – which is what makes them man's best friend.

Bonobos, gorillas and other great apes can understand our language and learn to use sign language and symbols. A notable example is Kanzi, a bonobo who uses a board covered in symbols to talk to researchers. He's even invented his own symbol combinations so he can express his thoughts. Another example is Koko, a western lowland gorilla who understands about 2,000 spoken words and can use sign language to communicate more than 1,000.

In the invertebrate world, the octopus is thought to be the smartest creature. Again, they have highly evolved emotions, they're highly intelligent, and they're good at solving logic problems. They can also work in teams, with each member demonstrating individual responsibility. The octopus is especially interesting because most of its neurons are in its tentacles, not in its brain. But if you add up all the neurons, they're right up there with the smartest creatures on the planet.

The trouble with intelligence

So why haven't more animals developed a greater degree of intelligence? Well, for one thing, we might not allow it. This is another topic that's the subject of considerable debate. One side believes we'd encourage it, continually test their intelligence, and hopefully, one day be able to communicate with them in meaningful ways. The other side believes that if they could compete with us on our level, they'd take our jobs, or even become our predators, finding ever more cunning ways of stealing our young, destroying our possessions, and so on. So, naturally, we'd drive them to extinction.

> Some people have similar concerns about the rise of intelligent machines.

And it turns out that being intelligent isn't necessarily the best thing in the world anyway.

For example, it takes a vast amount of energy. Our brain uses twenty percent of our body's energy, even though it only makes up two percent of our weight.[8-50]

High intelligence only really benefits those living in social groups in the developed world. If we lived in poverty, we'd be operating in survival mode, just as many other animals do. We wouldn't need much intelligence. And if we lived in isolation, we wouldn't need much intelligence either, as there would be no one to interact with.

> You could argue that we were operating in survival mode in the days when we were hunter-gatherers. That could explain why our intelligence seemed to stagnate for hundreds of thousands of years.

Intelligence is useful for hunting, but most of us don't do that any more. We can easily get all the food we need without having to think too hard about it. So our brilliant hunting skills, and the brain power that developed along with them, no longer give us an evolutionary advantage.

And there's another huge downside to Intelligence. It can lead to boredom, disputes, violence, battles over territory, and so on. All of these could prove fatal, especially as we invent more and more harmful ways of damaging each other. I'm sure most of the nerds reading this have been singled out and bullied for being "too intelligent" and "different."

Here's an interesting fact to end this section. Most of our intelligence (or "smartness") seems to have developed after we migrated to the cooler northern climates. I wonder if there's a connection?

8.10 Interesting facts about evolution

Here are the basic principles of evolution:[8-51]

- An organism's DNA must be able to change or mutate.

- The changes or mutations will be beneficial, harmful or neutral.

- Over a long period, the changes or mutations will result in the formation of a new species.

DNA mutations are the driving force of evolution, and they generally happen in response to environmental changes. But they can also be caused by things like X-rays, cosmic rays, nuclear radiation, and random chemical reactions in cells.

Many scientists believe evolution is messy and inefficient. That might not be correct because until recently they also believed that evolution often resulted in DNA sequences with no function – the so-called "junk DNA." The discovery that at least eighty percent of it actually has a biological function has changed that belief somewhat.

One of the biggest factors that influenced our evolution was learning how to make and control fire. This enabled us to cook our food, which made it easier to chew and digest. And this in turn led to significant changes in our teeth, jaws, and guts.

> There's some evidence that *Homo erectus* could control fire 780,000 years ago, and confirmed evidence dating from 600,000 years ago.[8-52] So we could probably do it too from the moment we arrived. It wouldn't have taken us long to learn how, even if our memories had been erased.

As we saw in Chapter 3, there's evidence that modern humans have lived on Earth multiple times throughout history. There's a wealth of evidence dating from around two million years ago, indicating that there were several well-established, technologically advanced civilizations around the world at that time. There's also a smaller amount of evidence from much earlier in history, some of it hundreds of millions of years old.

Mainstream scientists say this is impossible: there were no hominins here then that we could have evolved from. But they're wrong. You can see well-defined hominin footprints preserved in the rock alongside dinosaur tracks in places like Dinosaur State Park in Glenrose, Texas, USA; Dinosaur Flats in Canyon Lake, Texas; and Kughitang-Tau Plateau in Turkmenistan.

It may be impossible according to mainstream science, but dinosaurs and hominins (not necessarily humans) clearly both existed at the same time, hundreds of millions of years before the hominins "officially" evolved.

In fact, there's evidence that the hominins might even have been here *before* the dinosaurs. A footprint that is quite obviously from a hominin has been found in 290-million-year-old rock in New Mexico, USA.[8-53] The first dinosaurs didn't appear until 60 million years after this.[8-54] Paleontologists describe this piece of evidence as "problematic," but they seem to have made no attempt to debunk it. The few who have visited the site reportedly said: "Yes, it definitely looks like a hominin." And that was their only comment on it.

Mainstream scientists claim to have proven that at least some of the "so-called hominin footprints" were left by dinosaurs.[8-55] Those who claim otherwise are immediately dismissed as religious fundamentalists or scientific creationists. It looks very much as if we're being lied to. One has to wonder why.

I've seen the footprints at Glenrose with my own eyes, and they are unquestionably hominin – or incredibly hominin-like – though significantly larger than our own. Could some of the dinosaurs have had exactly the same type of feet as us? It's hard to believe, but some mainstream scientists are now pursuing that possibility.

Another possibility is that the hominin footprints were left by time travelers who visited the distant past to see the dinosaurs. Though I'm not sure why their feet would have been so much bigger than ours, or why they were walking around barefoot – unless they were trying to leave their footprints deliberately, knowing that they would one day confuse us.

We should also consider the possibility that they're extraterrestrial footprints, and weren't left by hominins at all.

Numerous skeletons of giant hominins have been found around the world.[8-56][8-57][8-58] So it's possible that the first hominins the aliens brought here were a race of giants. This would not only explain the large footprints but the skeletons too. And, to be fair, it's the only explanation that truly fits the evidence.

It's important to exercise caution when examining photos of the skeletons of giant hominins – and any other photographic evidence in fact.

Websites such as DesignCrowd have hosted contests in which skilled photo manipulators submitted highly realistic images of giant skeletons. Some of these ...

... images were later picked up by other websites and newspapers and recirculated as "proof" that the giants existed.[8-59]

The only way to be sure is to track down the real artifact, which is usually held by a reputable museum. Go and see it with your eyes, speak to the curators, and examine the results of any scientific analyses they've carried out. I've done this, and I'm satisfied that some of the giant skeletons are unquestionably real.

Some final interesting facts about evolution

- Although other primates have opposable thumbs, we can also flex our ring fingers and little fingers towards the base of our thumbs, and even touch them. This gives us lots of dexterity and a much more powerful grip and allows us to use tools effectively and efficiently.

- Biologists estimate that the first life forms had spontaneous mutation rates 4,000 times faster than we see today.[8-60] Professor Richard Wolfenden of the University of North Carolina said: "At the higher temperatures that seem to have prevailed during the early phase of life, evolution was shaking the dice frantically."

- 99.9 percent of all the species that ever existed on Earth are now extinct.[8-61]

8.11 The big problem with evolution

Just as we were finalizing this chapter for publication, Turkey announced that it was removing evolution from its school curriculum.[8-62] This was enormously controversial and sparked a public outcry about the country moving backward. But it's actually not an unreasonable step. The theory of evolution is full of holes, and I think most scientists only adhere to it out of a sense of duty, or because they can't face the alternatives. I expect more countries will follow Turkey's lead as people open their eyes to the evidence.

So, what's the big problem with evolution?

We need to take a brief jump back into intelligent design and creationism here. As I said earlier, we shouldn't write all the creationists off as nut jobs just yet, because they do seem to have at least a few valid points.

As I'm sure you know, many creationists don't believe that evolution ever happened. Young Earth creationists rule it out entirely. They say it was all God's work, the Earth is no more than 10,000 years old, and all fossils are fakes. I'm not terribly interested in those people.

But some of the progressive creationists believe that evolution happens *within* species. So each species starts out as a primitive version of itself, and it evolves into a more advanced form. It might even evolve into several advanced forms, each adapted to a different environment. But they don't believe that one species can evolve into a different one.[8-63] Mainstream scientists will never admit it, but the weight of evidence supports the creationists on this point.

At the DNA level, there are fundamental differences between one species and the next: different numbers and types of gene, different numbers of chromosomes, and so on. We've already seen that apes have 24 pairs of chromosomes, while we have 23. If we gained a chromosome from somewhere, it would give us Down syndrome. You just can't do that sort of thing. We've always had 23 pairs of chromosomes, and we always will. If we evolve into different forms of human hundreds of thousands of years from now, those different forms will *still* have 23 pairs of chromosomes, and they'll *still* be fundamentally human. They *have* to be; it can't work any other way.

If we look at the fossil record, we ought to see millions of transitional species, where one species evolved step-by-step into the next one along the evolutionary chain. There should be numerous steps between each species, not abrupt leaps from one to the next. But the transitional fossils just don't exist. Archaeologists *think* they *may* have found a few – though Wikipedia only lists six, and they're all somewhat questionable.[8-64]

To my mind, the creatures that Wikipedia cites as transitional species are just primitive versions of species that would later evolve into more advanced forms of that same species. Some of them appear to have become extinct before they reached the more advanced stage.

The archaeopteryx is commonly cited as a transitional species between feathered dinosaurs and birds. But we haven't found any fossils that represent the intermediate steps between feathered dinosaurs and the archaeopteryx. Nor have we found any fossils that represent the intermediate steps between the archaeopteryx and birds. If those fossils don't exist, the archaeopteryx must be a species in its own right, with no predecessor and no successor. And in that case, a large part of the theory of evolution is immediately disproven, and the progressive creationists are right.

> The implication is that something (a deity, intelligent designer, extraterrestrial, computer programmer, or something else) must have placed primitive versions of each species on the Earth. They can't have evolved from earlier species.

Archaeologists have found plenty of primitive versions of each species. There are fossils of the first known ants, bees, bony fish, seahorses, lizards, dinosaurs, and so on. They evolved into the modern species we know today (except for the dinosaurs of course). But what came before them, and where are all the fossils of the in-between species? We haven't found a single one. Admittedly, the conditions under which fossils form is relatively rare. But even so, if we've found the first, primitive versions of so many species, we ought to have found at least a *few* that were in their intermediate stages. The fact that we've found precisely none speaks volumes. Each species seems to have appeared fully formed. And although they evolved to become more advanced members of that species, they didn't go any further than that. They certainly didn't become other species.

We can find further evidence of this if we examine the Cambrian rock strata. It's full of fossils of fairly advanced invertebrates, but none of the transitional species that should have come before them. But that's fair enough; everything that came before them must be in the next layer down, right? Not so. The Pre-Cambrian layers contain almost nothing: just some bacteria and a few primitive worms and jellyfish-like creatures. There's nothing there that the invertebrates in the Cambrian layer could have evolved from, and no primitive invertebrates in their intermediate stages. When we got to the Cambrian era, the invertebrates just ... appeared.[8-65][8-66][8-67]

Naturally, I tried asking my acquaintances who work in evolutionary biology to explain this to me. They didn't have any meaningful answers.[8-68] And like many others who work in mainstream science, they stopped answering my emails or returning my phone calls.

I'm not saying the theory of evolution is entirely wrong, because it clearly isn't. And I'm not saying the creationists are right, because some of them are obviously nut jobs. But if we take a piece of one and a piece of the other and we put them together, things start to make a lot more sense.

> If you're open-minded enough to be able to handle the ideas the progressive creationists are putting forward, they make fascinating reading, and they neatly fill the gaps where the theory of evolution falls down. Their theories might not be correct, but until we come up with something better – or we find the missing transitional fossils – this could be as close to the truth as we can get.

It's worth repeating the "God of the gaps" argument from Chapter 6, as it neatly summarizes what we've just been looking at.

1. There's a gap in our scientific knowledge.

2. The gap *can* be filled by an act of God (or an intelligent designer).

   But one day we might be able to fill the gap using science alone.

9

Out of ... Africa?

The classical Out of Africa theory[9-01] states that modern humans (*Homo sapiens*) evolved in Africa about 120,000 years ago, from an earlier species, *Homo erectus*. About 60,000 years ago we began colonizing the rest of the world, superseding the other hominin species.

9.1 What's wrong with the theory?

Not one of those things is true.[9-02]

Let's take them in turn:

- **We evolved in Africa.**

   Much older human remains have been found in Israel, Spain and Australia. Examining the teeth of early Europeans shows that they most likely came from Asia. The humans in Africa undoubtedly played a significant role in helping to colonize many parts of the world. They were also probably the only group of any size that survived the near-extinction events. But they certainly weren't the first to appear.

- **We evolved 120,000 years ago.**

Again, we have confirmed evidence that modern humans were in Australia and Israel 400,000 years ago, and 400,000-year-old human DNA has also been recovered from remains found in Spain. Mainstream scientists now agree that humans lived in Morocco 300,000 years ago. In fact, they were probably widespread throughout Africa by then. Confirmed human remains dating from 250,000 years ago have also been found in Mexico.

- **We evolved from *Homo erectus*.**

Quite a few mainstream scientists have now ruled this out. *H. erectus* may have died out as long as 550,000 years ago, which would make our evolution from them physically impossible. *Homo heidelbergensis* is a better fit for the timeline and may have evolved from *H. erectus*. But as we've already seen, the shape of their skulls was entirely different from ours. At the very least, there must have been an intermediate species between *H. heidelbergensis* and ourselves. But if it exists, we haven't found it – it's the modern version of the missing link. In any case, there's no room on the timeline for another species between *H. heidelbergensis* and ourselves. In other words, we don't fit into the Earth's native hominin timeline.

- **We began colonizing the world 60,000 years ago.**

There was certainly an exodus from Africa around that time – though it probably happened a good 10,000 years earlier. But there was also an earlier exodus from Africa about 125,000 years ago. A large group set off along the Arabian coast to India and then on to the South China Sea and into Australia. A 90,000-year-old human

Humans Are Not From Earth

bone has been found in Saudi Arabia.[9-03] And human colonies appeared in China between 80,000 and 120,000 years ago. Intriguingly, there's also evidence that modern humans were living in Brazil around 100,000 years ago. But they must have belonged to a different group.

So there's more than enough confirmed evidence to disprove the Out of Africa theory in its entirety. And there are plenty of alternative theories that make much more sense. Yet the majority of mainstream scientists still cling to it doggedly.

9.2 What are the other theories?

There are three main alternatives to the classical Out of Africa theory that attempt to work around the problem areas:

- The Multiregional Model

- Humans are not from Earth

- The Assimilation Model

9.2.a The Multiregional Model

Just to confuse things, there are several versions of this theory.

1. Modern humans evolved more or less simultaneously in several parts of the world.

2. We evolved from *Homo erectus* (now disproved), with the original Australians evolving from the *H. erectus* population in southeast

Asia, the Chinese evolving from the *H. erectus* population in China, and so on.

3. We originated in Africa but spread around the world much earlier than the Out of Africa theory suggests. We then interbred with the *Homo erectus* populations in different parts of the world, giving rise to the version of us that exists today.

None of these versions seem particularly accurate. We certainly didn't evolve from *Homo erectus*. And even if they were still around, researchers believe we would have had very little interaction with them. The same applies to *Homo heidelbergensis*: they were definitely around when we first arrived, but there's no evidence that we interacted or interbred with them. DNA evidence suggests that we probably interbred with the Neanderthals and Denisovans. But as we saw earlier, the level of interbreeding was minimal, and it may have been rather violent.

The Multiregional Model also suggests that our body and facial features may have evolved in different places. Our high foreheads may have developed in one region, and our chins in another. They then spread across the world when neighboring populations met and interbred, and we all ended up with more or less the same features.

According to this model, we didn't evolve in any one particular place. One group evolved in Africa, and some of them later migrated to the Middle East, Asia, and Australia. So there was an Out of Africa exodus of sorts. But other groups evolved elsewhere in the world, and they did exactly the same thing. For some reason, the Out of Southeast Asia theory and the Out of Mexico theory never get mentioned, even though they may have been more significant than the two known African exoduses. The Asia-to-Europe exodus was *enormously* significant, though it probably happened much later.

Both the Out of Africa theory and the Multiregional Model have mainstream supporters and opponents. The Multiregional Model seems slightly closer to the truth than the Out of Africa theory. As we'll see later, both are mostly wrong, but they're also both partially correct.

9.2.b Humans are not from Earth

This is the only theory that makes sense and fits all the evidence. It also incorporates all the evidence that the mainstream scientists and historians have tried to suppress or deny.

Here's a brief summary, as we've already covered most of this, and the rest will be covered later in the book:

- We couldn't have evolved from any hominin on Earth, but we did evolve from a hominin on our home planet. Our home planet is considerably older than the Earth, and its various civilizations would have been (and might still be) more advanced than ours. Evolution proceeded on our home planet in much the same way as it did here. There probably weren't as many extinction events as there were on Earth, but there must have been one that impacted the dinosaurs and allowed the mammals to become dominant.

> There's also the creationist theory that we may have been placed on our home planet already fully formed. If that's correct, then we didn't evolve from an earlier hominin.

- Extraterrestrials collected several groups of people from our home planet and brought them to Earth millions of years ago. They repeated the exercise/experiment numerous times over an extended period. The groups were probably left to their own devices and had to build their civilizations from scratch. They may have had their memories erased, but apparently retained their genetic memories. None of these groups survived long-term. But they left behind artifacts which we've found during deep-earth archaeological digs and when mining.

- Extraterrestrials brought some other groups of people to Earth more recently. They modified their DNA to make them more robust and more suited to life here. They may have spliced in genes from themselves or other alien species, as well as from Earth's native hominins. The first of these groups arrived about 400,000 years ago and were dropped off in Australia, Israel, and Spain – and perhaps other places too, though we haven't found their remains yet. The next group arrived in North Africa more than 300,000 years ago. Another group was dropped off in Mexico 250,000 years ago. Other groups have arrived since then, most notably in China and Brazil, with an East African group arriving 195,000 years ago. These groups barely survived three near-extinction events. The East African group fared slightly better than the others – though even they would have been considered critically endangered for a while. Most of the groups outside Africa were reduced to small, isolated pockets.

- From this point on we can more or less switch back to the mainstream theories. We recovered from the near-extinction events, and the various groups began colonizing the world, superseding the other hominins and occasionally interbreeding with them, and also cross-breeding with each other. The African groups would have led the spread because they were the largest surviving population after the extinction events and would have been the quickest to recover. So to that extent, the Out of Africa theory is partially correct. The small populations in other parts of the world also gradually recovered, and they began to spread as well. So the Multiregional Model is also partially correct.

9.2.c The Assimilation Model

The assimilation model doesn't say how we got here, but it offers a possible explanation as to how we superseded the other hominins. Rather than rapidly replacing them, the model suggests we steadily interbred with them, creating a hybrid species (or cross-species) that incorporated some of their features and some of our own. The hybrid species is what we now know as fully modern humans (*Homo sapiens sapiens*).

There's a huge problem with this model though. We've already seen evidence that Europeans may have interbred with the Neanderthals and Asians may have interbred with the Denisovans. But Sub-Saharan Africans show no evidence of having interbred with any other species. Yet they're physically identical – and more or less genetically identical – to everyone else. They're also 100 percent biologically compatible with everyone else. So it's unlikely that any assimilation actually occurred, and the amount of interbreeding with other species must have been minimal.

The amount of Neanderthal DNA in Europeans' genomes today would have only required a single human-Neanderthal birth once every fifty years. So I'm sticking with the theory that over the course of about 5,000 years we out-competed the other species for food and resources, took over their habitats, and possibly drove the remainder to extinction when they became violent.

We probably also gave them diseases and parasites they had no immunity to.[9-04] We would have brought things like tuberculosis, various types of herpes, and stomach ulcers with us when we migrated into Europe from Africa, the Middle East, and Asia. We would also have brought intestinal parasites such as tapeworms. The Neanderthals wouldn't have encountered any of these before.

9.3 Why the Out of Africa theory doesn't make sense

Why would we have left Africa in the first place?

We know the first groups to leave Africa headed east initially. That makes sense as it would have still been warm, bearing in mind we probably didn't wear clothes then.

But what about the groups that headed north and south? That makes less sense; they were living in the middle of an ice age, and they were naked. They would have been freezing cold, and there would have been little food available during the winter months. If they started traveling to those areas, they would almost certainly have been forced to turn back – or perish.

This suggests that maybe they *didn't* travel to those areas after all. They may have been there already because that's where the aliens dropped them off. And, despite what the mainstream timeline says, they must have worn clothes, even if they were only animal skins, or they couldn't possibly have survived. As we've already seen, their genomes had most likely been modified to make them robust enough to survive in that climate. The Neanderthals were already living in Europe, so the essential genes could have been harvested from them.

9.4 Interesting facts about the Out of Africa theory

- We seem to have been pretty determined to leave Africa. While it would have been a warm and comfortable place to live most of the time, it wasn't always the case. Droughts and famines are a particular problem there, especially in East Africa. At times, conditions would have been harsh, and food would have been scarce. People living in that region today often struggle to survive and have to rely on foreign aid. Yet this is the part of the world we're supposed to have evolved in.

But you have to wonder why, as there are plenty of places around the world where the conditions would have suited us much better, and our evolution and survival would have been more likely: Central America, northern South America, and southeast Asia, for example.

And, in fact, this is precisely what we see: remains of human civilizations have been found in Central America and northern South America that are much older than the East African ones.

- If Africa is truly our birthplace, then it ought to be the environment on Earth that suits us best. The people living there now should, therefore, have the lowest incidence of things like back problems, cataracts, skin cancer, chronic illnesses and so on. And again, this is indeed the case. But it can also be explained by the fact that they have the world's lowest life expectancy, and most of them don't live long enough for these issues to emerge. So it might actually be the environment that suits us *least*.

- Modern humans weren't the first people to leave Africa. *Homo erectus* did it 1.8 million years ago and went on to colonize Europe and Asia.

- Researchers from the Massachusetts Institute of Technology (MIT) have found that the majority of Y chromosomes in African people seem to have come from Asia. They suggest that after the initial migrations out of Africa there must have been a significant reverse migration back to Africa between 10,000 and 50,000 years ago.

There's also evidence that groups of Europeans and Asians migrated back to Africa more recently; probably around 3,000 years ago. They then headed south between 1,000 and 2,000 years ago. Anthropologists carried out two studies on isolated Khoisan tribes in southern Africa in 2012 and 2014. The tribes were thought to have descended from the original Africans, and researchers believed they'd had no contact with people from other continents. But the two studies proved otherwise. The tribes' DNA closely matched that of Eurasian people, and they even had some Neanderthal DNA even though the Neanderthals never lived in that part of the world.[9-05]

- The team from MIT also disproved the theory that we all descended from two individuals in Africa, traditionally known as Mitochondrial Eve and Y-chromosome Adam. They found that modern humans actually descended from a population of about 10,000 people, and there must have been a roughly equal number of men and women – about 5,000 of each. These would have been the survivors of the most recent near-extinction event (the Toba super-eruption in Indonesia). Such a small population would have suffered from severe inbreeding, and that may have led to many of our current weaknesses and chronic illnesses.

10

Our *Real* Home Planet

So, where did we *really* come from? In this chapter, we'll look at the most likely stars that our home planet might orbit, and we'll think about what our home planet might be like. One thing we know for sure is that our home planet must lie outside our current solar system. It's almost certainly within our Milky Way galaxy, though, and almost certainly in our local section of it.

10.1 The most likely stars that our home planet orbits

Before we can begin compiling our list of candidate stars, we'll need to make a few assumptions. Let's start with the assumption that the extraterrestrials who brought us here can travel at near light speed, but they can't take shortcuts through wormholes or use warp drives.

> In reality, they might well be able to do this. It would enable them to travel faster than light and potentially give them access to the entire universe. But in that case, the list of candidate stars wouldn't fit in this book – by a considerable margin.

Let's also assume that our bodies continued to age during our journey to Earth. If some of us needed to be capable of bearing children by the time we arrived, that would limit the traveling time to about forty years at most. If the journey took forty years, the people selected to give birth (probably to implanted fetuses) once they reached Earth would have been young children when they set off from our home planet. The adults who traveled with them would have been quite elderly by the time they arrived.

In reality, the aliens probably put our bodies into suspended animation, so we wouldn't have aged physically during the journey. Most of the people the aliens brought to Earth probably traveled as frozen embryos. Both of these factors would have extended the possible journey time considerably.

I also doubt that the embryos would have been implanted into the small number of children and adults who made the journey. There would only have been a few of them, but thousands of embryos. It's more likely that the embryos were implanted into the native hominins who were already here. We'll look at this again in the next chapter.

But of course, we also need to take into account the aliens themselves. They would have aged during the journey too. Let's assume they live about as long as we do. If they were adults in their twenties and thirties when they set off, and it took them forty years to reach Earth and another forty years to get home again, they'd have died of old age before they made it back to their planet. Did they volunteer for a one-way journey and settle on the Earth too? Did they put themselves into suspended animation for most of the …

... journey? Or did they use a warp drive to cut the journey time to just a few days?

If we stick to those assumptions, it's reasonable to assume that our home planet is no more than 40 light years from Earth.[10-01][10-02] Listed overleaf are the most likely stars within that range that might have life-supporting planets orbiting them, along with their distances in light years. A light year is about 6 trillion miles (10 trillion kilometers), but we're more interested in the traveling time, as that's the limiting factor, not the distance. So I've also given the traveling time at various speeds.

The traveling times don't allow for acceleration time after leaving our home planet and deceleration time on the approach to Earth. These would extend the actual traveling time considerably, as the G-forces would have to be kept within safe limits.

Just for fun, I've also included the traveling time at warp factor 2. That equates to ten times light speed according to *Star Trek: The New Generation*'s revised warp speed calculation system.[10-03]

At the maximum warp speed of 9.99 (7,912 times light speed), a journey of 40 light years would only take two days. But again, if you allow for acceleration and deceleration, it would take much longer. And on such a short journey, you probably wouldn't get anywhere near maximum speed before you needed to start slowing down again.

Alpha Centauri A

Constellation:	Centaurus
Age:	4.4 billion years
Distance:	4.3 light years
1/2 Light Speed:	8.6 years
1/10 Light Speed:	43 years
Warp Factor 2:	5 months

Alpha Centauri B

Constellation:	Centaurus
Age:	6.5 billion years
Distance:	4.3 light years
1/2 Light Speed:	8.6 years
1/10 Light Speed:	43 years
Warp Factor	2: 5 months

Epsilon Eridani

Constellation:	Eridanus
Age:	360 – 720 million years
Distance:	10.5 light years
1/2 Light Speed:	21 years
1/10 Light Speed:	105 years
Warp Factor 2:	1 year

Tau Ceti

Constellation:	Cetus
Age:	5.8 billion years
Distance:	11.9 light years
1/2 Light Speed:	23.8 years
1/10 Light Speed:	119 years
Warp Factor 2:	14 months

Kapteyn's Star

Constellation:	Pictor
Age:	11 billion years
Distance:	12.8 light years
1/2 Light Speed:	25.6 years
1/10 Light Speed:	128 years
Warp Factor 2:	15 months

Wolf 1061

Constellation:	Ophiuchus
Age:	unknown – a few billion years
Distance:	14 light years
1/2 Light Speed:	28 years
1/10 Light Speed:	140 years
Warp Factor 2:	17 months

Gliese 832

Constellation:	Grus
Age:	9.2 billion years
Distance:	16.2 light years
1/2 Light Speed:	32.4 years
1/10 Light Speed:	162 years
Warp Factor 2:	1 year & 7 months

Gliese 682

Constellation:	Scorpius
Age:	unknown
Distance:	16.6 light years
1/2 Light Speed:	33.2 years
1/10 Light Speed:	166 years
Warp Factor 2:	1 year & 8 months

61 Cygni A

Constellation:	Cygnus
Age:	6.1 billion years
Distance:	17 light years
1/2 Light Speed:	34 years
1/10 Light Speed:	170 years
Warp Factor 2:	1 year & 8 months

61 Cygni B

Constellation:	Cygnus
Age:	6.1 billion years
Distance:	17 light years
1/2 Light Speed:	34 years
1/10 Light Speed:	170 years
Warp Factor 2:	1 year & 8 months

Epsilon Indi A

Constellation:	Indus
Age:	1.3 billion years
Distance:	20 light years
1/2 Light Speed:	40 years
1/10 Light Speed:	200 years
Warp Factor 2:	2 years

Gliese 667 C

Constellation:	Scorpius
Age:	2 – 10 billion years
Distance:	23.6 light years
1/2 Light Speed:	47.2 years
1/10 Light Speed:	236 years
Warp Factor 2:	2 years & 4 months

Gliese 180 (GJ 180)

Constellation:	Eridanus
Age:	unknown
Distance:	38 light years
1/2 Light Speed:	76 years
1/10 Light Speed:	380 years
Warp Factor 2:	3 years & 9 months

TRAPPIST-1

Constellation:	Aquarius
Age:	3 – 8 billion years
Distance:	40 light years
1/2 Light Speed:	80 years
1/10 Light Speed:	400 years
Warp Factor 2:	4 years

The traveling time will, of course, be significantly longer if the aliens can't travel at or near light speed. If they can only reach half light speed, for example, it would take them 76 years to travel from GJ 180, which would put it well outside the range we're considering. If they can only travel at one-tenth light speed, then Alpha Centauri would be the only system within range. If the aliens come from a different planet than us, it would have to be another planet within that system. At the time of writing, no habitable planets have been found orbiting Alpha Centauri A or B – but that doesn't mean they aren't there.

It's worth noting that Alpha Centauri A/B and 61 Cygni A/B are binary star systems, and there are strong indications that our home planet orbits a binary star. In fact, binary star systems might be more common than single stars.[10-04] And Earth-like planets which orbit binary stars might also be common.[10-05]

My initial thought was that a planet orbiting in a binary system would be unable to support life. The stars' gravity would sometimes combine and sometimes oppose each other. I thought this might strip the atmosphere away, cause huge tidal surges, and there might be constant volcanic eruptions. But when I discussed it with an astrophysicist, his opinion was that the gravitational pull would be too weak to have any serious impact. This would especially be the case if the planet's crust were solid, with no tectonic plates – which is what we suspect, given our inability to sense earthquakes and other natural disasters.

If our planet were as close to its two stars as the Moon is to the Earth, it would obviously be a different matter – the planet would be ripped apart. But that's not the case here. Our planet will be in the habitable zone, tens of millions of miles from the nearest star, and perhaps hundreds of millions of miles from its binary twin. So there's no reason why it couldn't have two suns and still be perfectly habitable.

As Alpha Centauri[10-06] is the nearest binary system to Earth, it makes sense to begin our search for our home planet there. If it's located there, the likelihood is that it orbits the B star. It might even be a *superhabitable* world, as some astronomers predict there could be one orbiting that star.[10-07]

This would be a world where the gravity is around 25 percent higher than on Earth. Most plants would hug the ground, and land-based animals would be short and stocky. The air would also be denser than on Earth, meaning that heavier creatures would be able to fly.

Looking at the ages of the stars, Alpha Centauri B is about 6.5 billion years old, whereas our Sun is only 4.5 billion years old. It's mind-blowing to think that the people living on our home planet now might be two billion years ahead of us. It's also apparent that Epsilon Eridani and Epsilon Indi A are too young for advanced life forms to have evolved, so they should be discounted.

There are lots of other stars within 40 light years of Earth that I haven't included on the list. None of them are likely to have planets capable of supporting human life. But life of some kind might exist there, or may have existed at some point.

10.2 Other stars and recent discoveries

If we go beyond 40 light years, we can find exoplanets that would definitely support human life. For example, KOI 3456.02, which is over 1,400 light years away, scores significantly higher on the University of Washington's habitability index[10-08] than the Earth does.

Habitability index of planets

Ideal home planet	1.000
KOI 3456.02	0.955
Kepler-442b	0.836
Earth	0.829
Mars	0.422

When we looked at the prison planet hypothesis, we considered that the Earth might have been chosen as our new home because it's so remote. We wouldn't be able to contact or interfere with any of the other civilizations in our galaxy. If that's the case, our home planet might be much closer to the galactic center, along with most other civilizations, and the journey here may have taken considerably longer than the forty-year maximum ...

> ... we're considering here. (Or, more likely, the extraterrestrials used a warp drive, wormhole, or other advanced technology to shorten the journey time.)

There was great excitement in 2016 when the exoplanet Proxima b was discovered orbiting the star Proxima Centauri.[10-09][10-10] It was dubbed a "Super Earth" and was considered a strong candidate for intelligent life. But later studies found that it was blasted by solar winds with a pressure 2,000 times stronger than on Earth. So it's highly unlikely to be habitable.[10-11]

Proxima Centauri is a distant, dim companion to the binary stars Alpha Centauri A and B and I've never considered it a suitable candidate for our home planet. Some astronomers consider it to be a member of the Alpha Centauri system, which would make it a triple-star system.[10-12]

There was more excitement in 2017 when seven Earth-sized planets were discovered orbiting the ultra-cool dwarf star TRAPPIST-1, which is 40 light years from Earth. In theory, at least six of the planets could be temperate and have liquid water. Three of them are in the conventional habitable zone. But they're all very close to their star, and they may be tidally locked. If that's the case, one side of the planet would always face the star, so it would be too hot to support life, and the other side would be too cold. But there could be a narrow band of habitability on the boundary between the light and dark faces.[10-13]

Another problem with being so close to their star is that the planets are probably being hit by solar flares, which will strip away their atmospheres. If any of them still have atmospheres, they probably suffer from massive geomagnetic storms that are hundreds or even thousands of times more severe than the ones we get on Earth.[10-14]

That's pretty much all we know about the TRAPPIST-1 system at the time of writing. The next step will be to try to detect whether any of the planets have atmospheres, and if so, whether they contain any gases that could indicate biological activity. The chances of this are looking increasingly slim though.

Another recent discovery is also causing excitement: the so-called Super-Earth planet LHS 1140b,[10-15][10-16][10-17] in the constellation Cetus. Again, it's about 40 light years from Earth. It orbits a type of red dwarf star that emits less high-energy radiation than other red dwarfs. The planet lies in the star's habitable zone, and is about the same age as the Earth. Its radius is reported to be about 1.4 times greater than the Earth's, but its mass is nearly 7 times greater. This suggests it's a rocky planet with a much larger iron core. Astronomers have already detected that it has an atmosphere, and they consider it a good candidate for life.

But I wonder if its gravity might be too high to support the kind of intelligent land-based life we'd recognize. The most advanced life forms are likely to be found in shallow seas and the upper levels of the oceans, where the water would support their weight and the pressure wouldn't be too great. I'll be monitoring the astronomers' progress on this with great interest.

And the discoveries keep on coming – which is why this book will quickly become out of date. Just as we were about to go to press, two more potentially habitable Super-Earths were discovered around the star Tau Ceti, which is just 11.9 light years away. Tau Ceti was already on my list of candidate stars, so I'm delighted that these planets have been found. But let's keep searching for habitable planets around Alpha Centauri B.

10.3 Which planet should we look for?

We need to look for planets that are within their star's habitable zone – also known as the Goldilocks zone (not too hot, not too cold, and not so close that it gets blasted by solar flares and solar wind). The size of this zone and its distance from the star varies according to the size, type, age and brightness of the star. The Earth is in the center of the Sun's habitable zone. Mars also lies well inside the zone. Venus is on the borderline, but is considered to lie within it.

The planet needs to be rocky and approximately Earth-sized. It needs to have liquid water. And it needs an atmosphere containing gases that either indicate the presence of life or are compatible with life.

Some astronomers believe that stars with more than one planet in their Goldilocks zone might be the best place to look for extraterrestrial life.[10-18][10-19] In fact, there's a good indication that most life-bearing planets come in pairs. This would mean that microorganisms on one planet would be able to migrate to the other planet if disaster struck. For example, if their planet was hit by an asteroid or comet, they could hitch a ride on the ejecta – the material that was ejected into space. Only a tiny percentage of that material might land on the other planet, but as long as that planet met the conditions for life, it should be enough to kick-start life there.

Observed Super-Earths

Gliese 832 c

LHS 1140 b

Tau Ceti e

Tau Ceti f

Wolf 1061 c

Stars with potential Super-Earths

Alpha Centauri B

Stars with confirmed exoplanets in their habitable zone

Gliese 682
Gliese 667 C
GJ 180
TRAPPIST-1

10.4 Ancient cultures

Several ancient human civilizations revered the star Sirius, the constellation Orion (especially the belt region), and the Pleiades star cluster. Some civilizations even claimed to have come from one of those places, though they more usually claimed that their gods had come from there.

> Their gods may well have been extraterrestrial visitors.

- Sirius[10-20][10-21] is the brightest star in the sky, as viewed from Earth, and it's revered by indigenous cultures all over the world. Its English name is the dog star, and most cultures associate it with dogs, though no one knows why.

But it's a very young star system, only 200 to 300 million years old. It took that long for life to get started on Earth – and that was virtually impossible. So if there's any life there at all, it's barely getting started. Our home planet certainly won't be found there, and no extraterrestrial visitors could possibly have come from there either.

The ancient civilizations who revered it probably singled it out for its brightness, and invented their stories about it. That's doesn't mean they weren't visited by extraterrestrials though. They may have misunderstood what the extraterrestrials were saying, or the extraterrestrials may have pointed at the star as a marker, meaning that they came from that general direction. Or perhaps the extraterrestrials were deliberately misleading them.

- The three great pyramids of Giza in Egypt align exactly with the three stars in Orion's belt.

> Interestingly, some historians believe there might once have been a fourth pyramid, and it may have been black.

- The Pleiades is particularly revered by the indigenous Australians. They claim that extraterrestrials came from there one million years ago to seed the Earth with what would become modern humans.

Like Sirius though, the Pleiades is very young. The oldest stars in the cluster are no more than 150 million years old, which is far too young for any advanced life forms to have evolved. Even if life is common throughout the universe, it's doubtful that there's any life there at all yet.

10.5 Could we have come from Mars?

Geologically speaking, Mars is a good match for what we might expect our home planet to be like. At times, it's our closest planetary neighbor (although Venus is usually closer). Its association with Mars, the God of War, also fits our violent natures.

We know that Mars has plenty of water underground, and it once had flowing rivers and lakes. There's still a small amount of water flowing on the surface. If it once had vegetation (which is doubtful), it may have looked like Earth's twin. And it's a popular choice with the public. If you ask people where humans really come from, many of them will say Mars – including some scientists.

Mars is smaller than the Earth, but it spins more slowly. A Martian day is forty minutes longer than an Earth day. That makes it closer to the 25-hour day that our body clocks are programmed for.

Thus far, we've found no evidence of life there, even on a microbial level. Or at least that's the official word. As we saw earlier though, spacecraft that have been sent to Mars on publicly announced missions were ordered to keep away from places where life was most likely to be found in case they contaminated it.

There's no evidence of any civilizations on the surface of Mars. There are many intriguing-looking artifacts, but none of them have been linked to any kind of civilization. They're almost certainly examples of pareidolia, where our brains detect recognizable patterns when they don't actually exist. Other examples of pareidolia include shapes and faces in clouds and images of Jesus on toast.

As we've already noted, Mars appears to have been struck by a massive object about 3.8 billion years ago. It destroyed the planet's magnetic field and exposed it to solar winds which stripped away its atmosphere and most of its water. Life would have been wiped out before it evolved beyond primitive microbes, and only primitive microbes could possibly survive there today.

So, no, we *didn't* come from Mars – or anywhere else in our solar system.

10.6 So why are we on Earth?

We've already seen that the Earth might be our prison, and if that's the case, it was likely chosen for its remoteness from other galactic civilizations. Its environment is probably close enough to that of our home planet: it's not identical, and it's not perfect, but it *is* habitable. There was already life here, which saved the aliens from having to terraform the planet, kick-start evolution, and wait several billion years. There's fresh water. The food is edible. And there are enough resources to sustain billions of us. So it seems a reasonable choice.

But we know there are other planets out there that are more habitable than the Earth. So why are we *here* and not *there*?

Well, the thing is we *might* be there as well. In fact, we *might* be on lots of planets. The aliens may have dropped us off in several different places – some of them more habitable than others – to see what happened. They might even move us around from time to time. Around one million people disappear from the Earth each year. Some of them return – and a few of them claim they were abducted by aliens – but many of the missing are never seen again. They might be living on one of those other planets now. And if the planet they're on is more habitable than the Earth, they might be feeling perfectly at home for the first time in their lives. Some of them might even have been taken back to our original home planet.

But if the aliens are moving people from one planet to the next, they're probably bringing people here from the other planets too. These people will be our distant relations. They'll look like us, and they'll be biologically compatible with us, so we won't notice anything amiss. They'll almost certainly have had part of their memory erased, so they won't remember living on whichever planet they've just come from. They may have been given false memories of living a hard life in another country on Earth. They might even have been programmed to say (and believe) they're refugees or immigrants.

The aliens seem to be highly adept at erasing certain things from our memories, and it looks as if they've been practicing it for millions of years. They might be equally skilled at implanting or transplanting memories from other people. You might have been born on one of those other planets, or you might have a recent ancestor who was, yet you'd know nothing about it.

Do you remember coming to this country from somewhere else? Do you have a strange sense of not really belonging here, or anywhere else on the planet? Do you have ever look wistfully at the night sky and wonder where home is?

10.7 What is our home planet like?

Let's now think about the most likely geological and environmental conditions we might expect to find on our home planet. What follows is based on our own physiology and how well – and how badly – the Earth fits our needs.

The Earth must have been chosen as our new home for a good reason. As we saw in the previous section, it must have many similarities with our home planet:

- a reasonably familiar environment

- a similar chemical and mineral composition

- a similar atmosphere

- similar gravity

- similar light levels and temperatures

- other life forms that are already well established

- a plentiful supply of fresh water

- and a ready supply food – even if it isn't what we're used to and we don't particularly like it in its natural form

We've already established that the length of a day on our home planet will be closer to 25 hours. This means that:

- our home planet is slightly larger than the Earth but spins at about the same speed

- or it's about the same size as the Earth but spins more slowly

- or it's slightly smaller than the Earth and spins even more slowly

Any of these could be true, but the first one is the most likely. There's a good chance that our home planet is between 5 and 13 percent larger than the Earth and its speed of rotation is about the same. This would fit with the facts we established earlier: that our home planet's gravity is higher and it has a stronger magnetic field. Both of these could be explained by our home planet having a larger iron core than the Earth.

The higher gravity on our home planet would prevent us from growing overly tall, as we do on Earth. When we lived there, we'd have been shorter and stockier. And, sure enough, anthropologists believe that's exactly what we were like when we first arrived on Earth.

Intriguingly, it would also make sense if the gravity on our home planet was *lower* than it is on Earth. We'd weigh less, so we wouldn't put as much stress on our backs, hips and knees. We wouldn't hurt or damage ourselves so much if we fell over. And our heights would probably be constrained by the relative scarcity of nutritious food there, as we discussed in Chapter 2.

But whether the gravity on our home planet is stronger or weaker than it is on the Earth, we're clearly poorly adapted to it. And that's almost certainly because we haven't been here for long enough.

OBJECTION!

"If the gravity on our home planet were much different from the Earth's, we'd be a completely different shape."

If it were *much* different then yes, absolutely. If it were much higher, we'd probably be four-legged and hug the ground. But we're only really talking about a difference of between 5 and 13 percent. This ties in with the size difference we noted earlier: our home planet is probably between 5 to 13 percent larger than the Earth. It isn't a massive difference, but it would make a noticeable difference to our bodies over thousands of years of evolution.

In Chapter 8 we saw evidence that a race of giants lived on the Earth in the distant past. Where did they come from? It's unlikely that they evolved here naturally. Their remains are human-like, so they may have originated on our home planet, just like us. But they couldn't have been brought directly to Earth or they'd have been the same size as us.

(We saw earlier that although we've grown markedly since we arrived, our heights have now mostly stabilized.) This suggests that before they were brought here, they may have spent several hundred thousand years on another planet where the gravity was much lower. And again, this ties in with the aliens moving us around from planet to planet.

As we saw earlier, we have cells in our brains that can detect magnetic fields, but they don't seem to work here. This suggests that our home planet must have a stronger magnetic field than the Earth has. And it might have been hugely important to us. If the planet was permanently covered in cloud, and we couldn't see our local star or any other stars, it may have provided us with our only means of navigation.

Since we can't detect the Earth's (apparently weaker) magnetic field, many of us have tremendous difficulty finding our way around unfamiliar areas without signs, maps, compasses, satellites or spoken directions. If we were at sea or in the middle of a desert, and we had none of those things to guide us, and there were no landmarks in sight, and we couldn't see the sky, and we lost our bearings, we'd be hopelessly lost. This would have been a serious problem in the past: thousands and thousands of people must have died.

The stronger magnetic field on our home planet can be explained by it having a larger solid inner core, composed mainly of iron, surrounded by a molten liquid metal outer core. The relative movement of these cores, as the planet rotated, would generate a strong magnetic field. We've already noted that the planet must be slightly larger than the Earth, so this fits the theory.

Let's now look at the light level on our home planet. Our lack of heavy brows suggests there's no direct sunlight to dazzle us. Again, that may be due to permanent cloud cover. The level of light is probably also more consistent than it is on Earth, so we wouldn't see periods of intense, direct sunlight followed by gloomy periods where the sun can't break through the clouds.

Here on Earth, millions of people living in the temperate regions suffer from SAD (seasonal affective disorder) every winter because of the lack of sunlight. Clearly, we're used to a more even level of light throughout the year. As we've already seen, our home planet probably has little or no seasonal variation. That also fits with it having a consistent level of light. And, as we've already seen, it suggests a fairly circular orbit and an axis with little or no tilt.

The amount of light reaching the surface of our home planet is probably around 13 to 15 percent less than reaches the surface of the Earth. As we saw in Chapter 2, this figure fits with the level of UV protection offered by the blackest shade of human skin. If everyone living in the tropics on our home planet has deep black skin, nobody would need sunscreen.

Apart from the permanent cloud cover, the lower level of light might be caused by our home sun being 13 to 15 percent dimmer than the Earth's Sun. Or it might be that much smaller than the Sun, or our home planet might be further away from it.

If our home planet is in a binary star system, as we suspect, the other star will obviously contribute some of the light (and heat). But it's probably not as much as you might expect. For example, if our planet orbits Alpha Centauri B, Alpha Centauri A would only contribute about 1/400th of the light. That's about the same amount of light as reaches Uranus from our Sun.

> There's a theory that our home sun might be a brown dwarf. I don't support that theory. It would be significantly dimmer than the Sun so our home planet would have to be much closer to it. As we saw earlier, that has all sorts of consequences – solar flares, high-pressure winds, and so on – that don't fit the evidence.

All of this means we'd be able to stay out in the sun for as long as we liked, at any time of the year, without any risk of UV damage, sunburn or skin cancer, while still getting enough vitamin D. And there would be no harsh glare, and consequently no sun blindness.

OBJECTION!
"If the sky was permanently cloudy there, how did we know that space existed?"

We might not have known. We didn't travel here by ourselves. The aliens who brought us here were clearly an advanced space-faring race, so they may have come from a different planet that had clear skies.

On the other hand, we might have known quite a lot about space. There may have been occasional breaks in the cloud. Or there might have been a mountain – let's call it Space Mountain – whose peak was above the clouds and we could see space from the top. Or we might have used rockets or probes to find out how high the clouds went and whether there was anything above them. So we could have discovered space that way.

But if the cloud cover was solid and permanent, most people wouldn't have seen the sun, and they'd know nothing about space. They might have no idea these things even exist.

OBJECTION!
"The levels of light are consistent in Africa, which is our natural habitat. The problems only started when we migrated out of the tropics."

Well, yes and no. The light levels are more consistent in the tropics, but we've already established that Africa – and the Earth as a whole – is not our natural habitat. We may have evolved in the tropics on our home planet, so that would be our *true* natural habitat. But it's in our nature to roam, so we wouldn't have stayed there for very long. Much of the planet, apart from the polar regions, would have soon become our natural habitat. Our skin tones probably lightened as we migrated to the more temperate regions. But with no seasons and permanent cloud cover, light levels there would have been consistent too.

But having no seasons comes with its own set of problems. There will probably be large areas of desert where it never rains, and large areas where it almost never stops raining. The constant rainfall in those areas would wash away the topsoil and leach nutrients deep into the ground where plants' roots can't reach them. This would significantly reduce the amount of land available for farming – and thus habitation. This could explain why food is less abundant on our home planet.

We noted earlier that the crops on our home planet probably aren't as nutritious as they are on Earth. One reason for this is that most of the staple crops on Earth require cold winters to help break up the soil and kill off the pests and pathogens. Our home planet probably doesn't have winters – or any other seasons. So we can expect to see poor crop yields and higher mortality rates.

It would take a huge area of land to support a small number of people – and there might not be that many huge areas of land. So we can expect the population density to be much lower than it is on Earth. Small, scattered, rural settlements may be the norm, rather than big cities.

The people on our home planet are almost certainly herbivores, so they wouldn't have any livestock to feed. Everything they grow will be for ourselves.

Unless we received outside help when we were on Earth, we must have brought some knowledge of science and technology with us, encoded in our genetic memories from when we lived on our home planet. If we lived in small, rural communities there, and we didn't have a large global population, things like agriculture, science, and technology would have progressed at a much slower rate.

But we also know that our home planet must be much older than the Earth. It might have taken them hundreds of thousands of years longer to develop those things, but it looks as if they managed it by the time we left and came to Earth. This explains why they were encoded in our genetic memories.

The extraterrestrials may have been monitoring our home planet, never expecting the people who eked out an existence there to develop a technologically advanced society. When they surprised the aliens by achieving it, the aliens may have nipped things in the bud by removing the most intelligent members of their society and shipping them to Earth – and wiping their memories, of course. Those most intelligent members of their society may have been our ancestors. Perhaps they weren't all violent criminals after all.

There are other issues that may have slowed down the rate of technological development on our home planet. For example, many of the developments we made on Earth during the Industrial Revolution were driven by our need to find new and better ways of keeping warm in winter. With no winters on our home planet, there would have been no need for this. This potential lack of motivation to develop new technology has further repercussions. The space-faring aliens who brought us to Earth couldn't possibly have come from the same planet; they would have been far more advanced than us.

It's likely that when we left our home planet, the level of scientific and technological achievement there was roughly equivalent to where the developed nations on Earth were at the beginning of the twentieth century. They wouldn't have been anywhere close to becoming space-faring yet, but the progress they were making might have been more than enough to worry the extraterrestrials.

Of course, in the 300,000 years or more since we left, things could have moved on considerably – assuming anyone left behind survived. If there was no Industrial Revolution, technological progress was probably driven by agriculture.

No seasons means no growing season and no harvesting season. Plants' growth might not be synchronized with the planet, the weather, or other plants – even those of the same species. They might all grow and ripen in their own time. That would, of course, make fertilization extremely difficult. It's likely that the plants have evolved some other mechanism for fertilization. They might also have evolved their own form of synchronization, perhaps using pheromones, so that all the plants of the same species grow and ripen at the same time.

By now, the people on our home planet may have discovered how to create their own planting, growing and harvesting seasons. One way of doing this would be to collect seeds and store them in the dark until they were needed. They could then plant them all at the same time, thus synchronizing each crop's growing cycle. That would make farming far more efficient. And that, in turn, could have led to other technological advances, and eventually to the development of a recognizable modern world.

They might also have found ways to boost crop yields, eliminate pests, irrigate the arid zones, build giant roofs over the wet zones, build floating farms that could be relocated to higher or lower latitudes to create artificial seasons, and who knows what else. The population might have ballooned by now, and they might have large cities – and even space ports.

When we arrived on Earth, we were apparently naked. But were we naked when we lived on our home planet? Did the aliens take away our clothes – and our memories of wearing clothes – when they brought us here? We don't know, obviously. But let's assume we were naked on our home planet too, even though that seems highly unlikely in an advanced society.

If we were naked, that means the temperature must be consistently mild. Again, that might be to do with living in a binary star system. Nights might be much shorter than they are on Earth, and sometimes might not happen at all. Days may be longer and, depending on how far away the two stars are, potentially much warmer.

But if one of the stars is a considerable distance away from our home planet, its impact might be negligible. This is the case on Earth, where some astronomers believe that Sirius might be our Sun's binary twin. In that case, day and night on our home planet might be very similar to what we see on Earth, and there may be other mechanisms keeping our planet warm. As we've already seen, the planet's crust might be thinner than the Earth's, and the surface might be warmed from within.

In fact, this is more likely than our home planet having shorter nights or (sometimes) no nights. Experiments have shown that people who sleep in rooms that have even a small amount of light are more likely to suffer from eyesight problems than those who sleep in the dark. Low light sources such as night lights and LED clocks can be enough to cause problems. This suggests that the nights on our home planet must be at least seven or eight hours long and completely dark.

The plant life on our home planet should look similar to that on Earth, though they will obviously be different species. Earlier in the book, we noted that the edible plants must be naturally delicious, but less nutritious than those on Earth. It seems that sometimes they must be in short supply too. Both of these things explain our compulsion to grab as much food as we can whenever it's available. With no seasons, we might expect crops to be available all year round, so the scarcity issue is harder to explain. It may come back to the fact that the growth cycle isn't synchronized and there are no cold winters to kill off the pests.

> As we saw above, the people living on our home planet now have probably resolved these issues. I'm talking about the situation as it was when we left around 300,000 to 400,000 years ago.

Some types of plant might be completely absent – sugar cane and sugar beet, for example. When we discovered it on Earth, we fell in love with the stuff and began craving it – which is a shame because it's so harmful to us. That craving must have come from somewhere though. It's likely that our home planet had a much less nutritious and much less harmful alternative, perhaps similar to stevia. This plant would have provided the level of sweetness we like, but without any of the harmful side-effects. Stevia is only just beginning to gain widespread popularity in developed Western countries, though nutritionists must wish we'd discovered it much sooner.

The animals on our home planet should look similar to those on Earth too, but, as with the plants, they'll be different species. Some of the similarities will be striking though, as certain features and organs will have evolved independently on both planets via the principle of evolutionary convergence.

As we saw earlier, eyes evolved independently on Earth about seven times. Wings evolved at least three times: in birds, insects, and bats. Pterosaurs also had wings, but biologists aren't sure whether to class them separately or consider them distant ancestors of the birds. Intelligence evolved at least three times – in the primates, corvids (crows, ravens, rooks, and jackdaws) and cetaceans (marine mammals such as dolphins).

The same types of animal evolved independently too. For example, wolves can be found in Europe, Asia, and North America, but not in Australia. But a wolf-like creature – the thylacine or Tasmanian wolf (or Tasmanian tiger) – evolved there from the marsupials. It wasn't related to the wolves in any way, yet it looked remarkably like them. Sadly, the last thylacine died in 1936, and the species is now extinct.

Researchers from the University of Cambridge have cataloged hundreds of other examples of species that look similar but are unrelated.[10-22]

As well as evolutionary convergence, we can also see optimal patterns and repeating patterns in nature – such as the Fibonacci series. It's reasonable to expect to see the same thing on every other planet where there's life. Everything will converge on the optimal:[10-23] the shapes and sizes of limbs, the layout of internal organs, and even things like hormones, enzymes, and DNA. In fact, life on our home planet might be so similar to that on Earth that only a biologist could tell the difference.

If we wound the clock back to the time when the Earth first formed and let evolution run again, would we get the same species as we have now? The British evolutionary paleontologist Simon Conway Morris concludes that at the very least we'd end up with the same broad categories, because convergence is the dominant force in evolution. And the same thing would happen on other planets where conditions are similar.

So it's reasonable to assume that our home planet – and many others – once had dinosaur-like creatures. There's a remote chance that they're still there if they haven't been wiped out by an extinction event. But it's more likely that our own distant ancestors wiped them out. They would have been too dangerous to have around. And they might have tasted delicious – as many of the Earth's reptiles reportedly do.

> On planets where the dinosaurs survived, they would have eventually evolved into the reptilian extraterrestrials. We'll take a closer look at all the different types of extraterrestrial in Chapter 13.

The lack of seasons would affect the animals too. They probably wouldn't have distinct breeding seasons, as many of Earth's native creatures do. They're more likely to have their own internal breeding cycles, like dogs, cats, apes, and humans do.

We've already noted that we can't detect natural disasters on Earth, but many native creatures can. From this, we can conclude that our home planet probably doesn't have any natural disasters. This is easy enough to explain: if the crust is one solid piece, as it is on Mars, rather than separate plates, as it is on Earth, there won't be any earthquakes or tsunamis. Without seasons, there's nothing to drive extremes of weather, so there won't be any hurricanes, cyclones or tornadoes. The only thing we might expect to see that could be classed as a natural disaster would be volcanos, because of the thin crust.

> As we'll see in Chapter 12, volcanos might be essential on inhabitable planets.

> A happy side-effect of the lack of seasons and weather extremes is that our home planet wouldn't experience significant changes in air pressure. That means we'd get far fewer headaches than we do on Earth. And the lack of glare from direct sunlight would remove another common cause.

Our home planet's chemical and mineral composition is probably very similar to the Earth's. Salt is obviously abundant there, since we crave it. This may be connected with our marine mammal genes, and possible marine ancestry, that we looked at in Chapter 5. But something seems to have happened to us since we came to Earth, because we can't get rid of excess salt as efficiently as we should be able to. Our mechanism for getting rid of it is missing.

The most likely reason, as we've seen several times now, is that the aliens who brought us here replaced some of our genes with those from

Earth's native hominins. It was almost certainly done with the best of intentions: to help us survive here. But the hominins seem to have lacked our craving for salt, and therefore had little need to get rid of it. Consequently, we lost that mechanism too – with disastrous consequences.

The main problem with salt is that it makes our bodies retain water. That raises our blood pressure, which puts a strain on our heart, arteries, kidneys, and brain. And that can lead to heart attacks, kidney disease, aneurysms, strokes, and dementia.[10-24] Billions of people have died from these causes since we first arrived on Earth, and they continue to do so at an alarming rate.

There must be a lot of water on our home planet – almost certainly more than on Earth.[10-25] Again, this ties in with our possible marine mammal ancestry. It also fits in with us being well adapted for a seafood diet.

10.8 Conclusion

Our home planet will be both similar to and different from the Earth. It will have a familiar feel to it. Things will be recognizable, but they'll seem slightly "off." It will probably have less nutritious crops that give poorer yields, more disease, a higher mortality rate, and a much lower human population.

But we're a highly ingenious species, and the planet is undoubtedly older than the Earth, so we've had plenty of time to find ways around these issues. Even so, I doubt the aliens who brought us to Earth came from there. They would have been much further advanced.

We ought to give our home planet a name. It obviously has one, and somewhere in our global consciousness, we might already know what it is. But for now, since it appears to have suited us so perfectly, I suggest we call it "Eden." It has more of a ring to it than something like Alpha Centauri B c.

The Bible tells the story of how Adam and Eve – and therefore all humans – were banished from the Garden of Eden. But could the Garden of Eden have been a reference to our home planet? And when we were banished from it – to a place where there were hominins but no other humans – could that place of banishment have been the Earth?

11

How on Earth Did We Get Here?

In this chapter, we'll consider the mechanisms the aliens used to bring us here. Many of the ideas stem from a conversation I had with an esteemed professor of astrophysics, who wishes to remain anonymous. I'm enormously grateful to him for his advice and friendship.

We've already established beyond any reasonable doubt that we were brought to Earth from another planet. And we're assuming that the aliens who brought us here probably here came from a different planet that was far more advanced.

> By the way, the idea that extraterrestrials intervened in human history is also known as Intervention Theory.

11.1 Why are we here?

- Perhaps we were removed from our natural environment because of the problems we were causing: violence, destruction, over-consumption of resources, driving other species to extinction, and so on.

- Perhaps the aliens thought the Earth lacked a dominant species and they felt the need to add one.

- Perhaps we were brought here as a natural predator to help cull a species that was getting out of control. We've driven plenty of species to extinction since we arrived, so if that was the plan, then it seems to have worked. I wonder which species we were meant to cull?

I doubt that the aliens ever envisaged we would take over the planet to the extent we have. Unfortunately, the time could be drawing near when they decide that we also need culling. As we saw earlier, they could do this simply by introducing a virus that we have no immunity to. In fact, they might have already tried this several times; hence the numerous plagues, and viruses such as AIDS and SARS that apparently sprang out of nowhere. We survived those – as a species at least – but there could be worse to come if they decide to try again.

11.2 Did we arrive as fully-grown adults?

We would have needed a minimum breeding population of at least 2,000 people. 10,000 would be a more realistic number to avoid too much inbreeding. 20,000 would be even better. But that number of people would have required a massive spacecraft, or several of them. Depending on the distance we traveled, and the time it took to reach Earth, the aliens might have had to cryogenically freeze us or put us into some other form of suspended animation. All of this would have been a terrible waste of resources.

It makes sense that they would have brought along a *few* adults. They would have become our guardians when we reached Earth. But I suspect that most of us probably arrived as frozen embryos. Thousands of us could have been stored in a few small canisters, well insulated and shielded from radiation.

When we reached Earth, we would have been defrosted and implanted into whichever native hominins were here at the time and were most compatible with us.

> We wouldn't have been implanted into the adult humans who traveled with us. There would only have been a few of them, but thousands of embryos.

Our most likely surrogate parents would have been *Homo heidelbergensis*. But the aliens might also have used some of the Neanderthals and Denisovans, or even *H. erectus* if they were still around. In fact, the aliens may have chosen the dropping-off sites specifically because there were already native hominins living there who could become our surrogates. The aliens may have genetically altered those hominins ahead of our arrival so that their bodies would accept us as their own embryos. Once we were born, the hominins may have raised us as their own children – at least for a while.

The small number of guardians who traveled to Earth as adults were almost certainly monitoring us throughout this period. They would probably have been instructed (or programmed) to gather us all together when the time was right.

If no adult humans traveled with us, we might well have done this for ourselves as soon as we were old enough. It wouldn't have taken us long to realize that we weren't like our "parents." We would have found others living nearby who were exactly like us. We'd have befriended them and played with them for a while, and eventually established our own separate communities with them, away from the hominins.

Of course, if we'd arrived as embryos we wouldn't have had any memories to erase, so the aliens could have skipped that step. Any adult guardians who traveled with us would undoubtedly have had at least part of their memory erased. We may have lived in advanced modern societies on our home planet, but none of us knew about that any more, and there was no one here who could teach us about it. So we returned to the Stone Age for a few hundred thousand years.

But as I mentioned earlier, the aliens seem to have overlooked our genetic memory. They may have forgotten about it, or they might not have known about it. The aliens might not have a genetic memory; perhaps no other species has one. So they would have had no reason to look for it. Perhaps they knew about it but decided it wasn't important enough to bother with. Or perhaps they didn't know how to erase it. Maybe you can't erase it without damaging our genome – though they would only have found that out by trying. Whatever it was, they ended up leaving it intact, which was good news for us.

Our genetic memories enabled us to gradually re-establish our societies and then make rapid technological progress. Although, as I mentioned earlier, it's likely that we had some additional help with that from another race of extraterrestrials. We'll explore this further in Chapter 13.

Genetic memory allows memories to pass between generations. Events which affected earlier generations and shaped their behavior can be passed on to us.[11-01] Some organ transplant patients seem to be able to recall their donors' memories. This is particularly the case in those who have had heart transplants. Their personalities and tastes can also change.

Mice have been taught to fear certain smells, and their children and grandchildren also fear those smells, even though they've never encountered them before.[11-02] Interestingly, some scientists believe that our genetic memories might also pass phobias from one generation …

... to the next. Children may inherit some of their ancestors' experiences, in the form of feelings and emotions, rather than their actual memories. Many researchers believe this explains why some people have irrational phobias of things they've never experienced themselves.[11-03]

Other researchers believe our irrational phobias may stem from things we experienced in our past lives. But that's beyond the scope of this book.

11.3 Space travel, propulsion systems, and fuel

Spacecraft

Extraterrestrial spacecraft come in all shapes and sizes. Thousands of them have been seen in our skies, and many have been photographed or recorded on film or video. Some have crashed, and they've then been reverse-engineered and studied in secret by government engineers and scientists. Some may have been captured after they landed, and the extraterrestrials aboard them may be being held as prisoners, or they may have agreed to pass on information about their technology in exchange for certain privileges.

It's likely that most of the captured aliens are collaborating with our governments and scientists and providing them with advanced knowledge. In return, several credible people say the aliens have been allowed to build bases here.

We rarely see the largest type of spacecraft, known as motherships. These can be as large as cities. According to UFO researchers, motherships don't usually come any closer than Jupiter when they're in this solar system. But they have, very occasionally, ventured closer to the Earth.

The craft that are most commonly seen are much smaller ones, probably planet-hoppers. These are intended to fly the short journeys between the motherships and local planets. They rely on the mothership to transport them through interstellar space. The planet-hoppers can be spheroid, saucer-shaped, cigar-shaped or tubular, or triangular. Their shapes reflect the propulsion systems they use.

If we were brought to Earth as embryos, the embryos were probably created on board a mothership in the solar system where our home planet is located. The eggs and sperm used to create them would have been harvested from abductees from our home planet, and any genetic manipulation would have taken place there too. The embryos would then have been allowed to develop for a while to ensure they were viable before they were brought to Earth.

Harvesting the eggs and sperm probably took place on one of their larger planet-hoppers that had its own operating theater. Otherwise, they would have had to ferry each abductee all the way to the nearest mothership, which wouldn't have made much sense.

Let's have a look at the most commonly sighted planet-hoppers.

Spheroids

Spheroid-shaped craft are reported to use two or more counter-rotating magnetic disks or drums as an anti-gravity generator. A UFO that crashed in Germany was reported to have a rotating high-voltage electromagnetic propulsion system that also acted as a defensive shield.

This system is also believed to be the basis for Germany's infamous World War II experimental spacecraft known as Die Glocke[11-04] (The Bell). Some researchers speculate that Die Glocke wasn't a spacecraft at all but an attempt to generate free energy. But it certainly seemed to have anti-gravity properties, and reportedly had to be tethered to the ground. So it may have been capable of flight, even if it wasn't possible to control it in the air. It would have been fascinating to see how it developed. But apparently, the Germans destroyed it towards the end of the war to prevent the Allies from capturing it. Most mainstream scientists deny it ever existed – although the framework that once housed it can still be seen.

Black triangles

Black triangles are amongst the most commonly sighted UFOs these days. They reportedly generate their own anti-gravity fields.[11-04a][11-04b]

We now have our own versions, which were almost certainly reverse-engineered from captured alien craft. They include the TR-3 Black Manta[11-05] and the TR-3B Aurora.[11-06][11-07][11-07a] Both are believed to have been developed for the US Military by Northrup Grumman. They're currently classified and their existence is officially denied, but they're regularly spotted all over the world. This suggests that their developmental phase has ended and they're now in operational use. The lack of the letter "X" in their model numbers further indicates that they're no longer in their experimental phase.

Their anti-gravity field is reportedly generated by putting mercury under high pressure and accelerating it with nuclear energy to produce a plasma. There are conventional thrusters (probably hydrogen-powered) on the three tips of the craft, making it highly maneuverable.[11-08]

> Some sources put forward alternative methods for generating the anti-gravity field.

Many people get over-excited when they spot one of these craft, and they call the police, armed forces and media thinking they've seen a genuine UFO. They almost certainly haven't. Most of them (perhaps all of them these days) are our own craft, and we've had them for decades. Unsurprisingly, the armed forces aren't interested in hearing about them. They used to pretend to investigate reports of sightings, but they don't bother any more. The media is usually interested though. It's not really news – and I'm sure they know that – but it helps sell newspapers, and it excites viewers and listeners, which helps generate advertising revenue.

Saucer-shaped and cigar-shaped craft

Saucer-shaped craft probably have doughnut-shaped magnetic rings – toroids – around their perimeters that hold antimatter in suspension. Cigar-shaped craft may have their own onboard antimatter generators that can extract fuel from space while traveling. Both of these types of craft would be capable of interstellar travel as well as planet hopping.

Antimatter as a fuel

Antimatter is regarded as the perfect energy store. It's 100 percent efficient: all of its energy is released when it comes into contact with matter.

We first created antimatter on Earth in 1955, at the Fermi National Accelerator Laboratory (Fermilab) in Illinois, USA. It was created in the Tevatron – a 4.26-mile particle collider – similar to the Large Hadron Collider at CERN in Switzerland.

Using our current technology, it would take us 100 million years to produce a single gram of antimatter. But we're bound to develop more effective ways of producing it in years to come.

Once created, antimatter has to be stored in such a way that it can't come into contact with matter. Otherwise, it will cause an explosion. It's therefore held in magnetic suspension in a toroid (a doughnut-shaped accumulator). In saucer-shaped spacecraft, the toroid is almost the same diameter as the craft itself. But cigar-shaped craft that generate their own antimatter can get by with much smaller toroids, as they only need to store a tiny amount.

There's some dispute about how much antimatter we'd need to travel in space.

- Some sources say a gallon of antimatter would take us 25 billion miles (within galaxies) or 40 billion miles (between galaxies). We'd need 125 gallons to travel 1 light year, so about 500 gallons to reach Alpha Centauri B which is 4 light years away. And of course, we'd need the same amount again for the return journey. By way of comparison, the fuel tank on a Boeing 747 jet plane holds more than 48,000 gallons,[11-09] so 1,000 gallons is practically nothing.

- Other sources say a single gram of antimatter would be enough to power a spacecraft from Earth to Alpha Centauri B in 25 years. That's if we use conventional methods of space flight and go in a straight line. We saw in Chapter 10 that there are much faster ways to travel, and we'll examine these in more detail shortly.

Spacecraft fueled by antimatter would need onboard antimatter reactors that combine antimatter with matter in a controlled way. The resulting blast of energy would generate thrust, and could also be used for other purposes such as powering the craft's electronics, defense shields and weapons systems (if it has them). It could also open and maintain wormholes, power a warp drive, and run a cloaking device that effectively renders the craft invisible.

Depending on its size, a spacecraft could easily carry several tons of antimatter, enabling it to travel vast distances. The only problem is producing enough antimatter and keeping it all in suspension.

The extraterrestrials, being millions of years ahead of us, can probably produce millions of tons of antimatter per day. As we've just seen, they might even be able to produce it themselves while they're traveling. This would significantly reduce the amount they need to carry and give them practically infinite range.

Collecting antimatter from space is possible if you go fast enough. Space isn't quite the empty vacuum that most people think it is. It contains billions upon billions of tons of matter and antimatter, along with gas, dust and dark matter. But it's at such a low density that it behaves much like a vacuum – at normal speeds. But when you approach light speed or even go beyond it (warp speed), so much material is forced into the craft's intake nozzles that collecting enough to fuel the craft isn't a problem. The main issues then are separating the matter from the antimatter and storing the antimatter in such a way that it can't come into contact with any matter – including the spacecraft itself – until it's needed.

Spacecraft carrying more than a few grams of antimatter wouldn't be allowed anywhere near inhabited planets because of the amount of damage they'd cause if they crashed.

If it came into contact with matter, just two kilograms of antimatter would create an explosion equivalent to that produced by the Tsar Bomba – the largest nuclear device ever detonated on Earth. It produced a yield of about 57 megatons of TNT on the one and only occasion that it was tested. That's more than 3,000 times more powerful than the blast that flattened Hiroshima, Japan in 1945.[11-10][11-11]

Hydrogen

For spacecraft that use conventional fuel, hydrogen is a good choice. It should be readily available in most solar systems. Most of them will have gas giant planets that could be used as refueling stations. There are reports that extraterrestrials are using Jupiter for this very purpose. This makes sense as Jupiter is not only the largest gas giant in our solar system, it also has the highest concentration of hydrogen in its atmosphere – about 88 to 92 percent.

The right propulsion system for the job

Spacecraft will use different propulsion systems in different parts of space. When planet-hopping within solar systems, they'll use anti-gravity systems and thrusters when they're flying close to a planet, and magnetic field-based systems and thrusters when traveling between the planet and the mothership. Medium and large-sized spacecraft and motherships which travel through interstellar space will use antimatter-based systems that not only provide them with vast amounts of energy but could be used to open up wormholes and run warp drives.

11.4 Why genuine UFOs are rare

You're unlikely to ever see a real UFO. As we've seen, most of the extraterrestrials will be from planets that are millions or even billions of years ahead of us, and their technology will obviously reflect that. Their craft will have cloaking systems that change the wavelength of light reflected from them, rendering them invisible to our eyes.

They'll also use advanced stealth technology that renders them invisible to radar. Military radar systems, if they can detect them at all, generally treat them as large birds and filter them out before they appear on operators' screens. Civilian radar systems can't detect them.[11-12]

Pilots and alien abductees have occasionally reported encountering genuine UFOs without their cloaking systems engaged. There can be only one reason for this: the extraterrestrials wanted to be seen. UFOs that do this are almost always reported to be acting aggressively and seem to have hostile intentions.

The simple rule of thumb is: if you can see it, and it's not threatening you, it's probably one of ours.

> Even if you *can't* see it, it might still be one of ours. The military won't reveal how advanced their own cloaking systems are. But you can bet they're decades ahead of anything they've announced publicly.

11.5 Warp drives and wormholes

We've looked at the conventional straight-line method of traveling through space, where we're limited to traveling at the speed of light. But let's now consider some much faster alternatives.

Warp drives

A warp drive compresses space-time in front of the craft and expands it behind it.[11-13] In other words, the spacecraft's engine literally *warps* space.

Warp drives are common in science fiction, most notably *Star Trek*. They enable spacecraft to travel at many times the speed of light. The craft in *Star Trek* are capable of traveling at a maximum of slightly less than 8,000 times light speed. Anything beyond that would be impossible as it would require an infinite amount of power.

Until 1994, warp drives were considered impossible and purely fictional, especially since they'd require unimaginable amounts of energy. But the Mexican theoretical physicist Miguel Alcubierre then came up with a possible solution, known as an Alcubierre drive.[11-14] This could achieve faster-than-light travel without breaking any of the laws of physics. His system uses large amounts of matter with negative mass.[11-15] This is different from antimatter, which is considered to have positive mass. And it wouldn't have antimatter's 100 percent efficiency, so spacecraft would need to carry a significant amount of it.

> In 2017, scientists from Washington State University in the USA produced matter with *negative-effect* mass[11-16] for the first time. It was widely misreported that they had produced matter with negative mass, as required by the Alcubierre drive, but it isn't the same thing at all. But at least it's a step in the right direction.[11-17]

In 2012, American researcher Harold White proposed a modified theory that would need much less negative energy to operate. NASA engineers are currently conducting studies to see if his system would be feasible.

A spacecraft equipped with a warp drive could reach any of the planets in our solar system in just hours. If we built a spacecraft the size of a cruise liner, with a crew of several thousand and all the amenities you'd typically expect to find on board such a vessel, tens of thousands of stars could be within reasonable traveling distance.

The craft would have to be built in orbit though. We wouldn't be able to launch something that big from the surface. A space elevator would be useful – or even essential – for that kind of project.

As we've already seen, some stars are much older than our Sun. If extraterrestrials came from a planet orbiting Alpha Centauri B, they could be two billion years ahead of us. They could have achieved this level of space travel hundreds of millions of years ago. And if they couldn't get warp drives to work, they've had plenty of time to come up with alternative solutions.

Wormholes

Wormholes are tunnels through space-time.[11-18] They're really useful if you fold (or bend) an area of space-time so that the distant point you want to travel to is brought closer to where you are.

You could think of space-time as an enormous open book. Let's say you're near the outer edge of the front cover and you want to travel to a place that's near the outer edge of the back cover. That's a heck of a long way – it could be billions of light years. But it's a much shorter journey if you simply close the book. Now you're only separated by the thickness of the pages. If you tunneled through them – via a wormhole – it would be a journey of just a few miles, it might only take a few minutes, and you'd arrive in an entirely different part of the universe.[11-19]

There are two stages to this problem. The first is making the fold in space-time (or closing the book). To do that, you need an enormous mass, such as a neutron star. The second stage is opening the wormhole (or tunneling through the pages) and forcing it to stay open long enough to travel through. And that takes an unimaginable amount of energy.

Wormholes remain hypothetical for now, but they're entirely consistent with Einstein's general theory of relativity. Some scientists speculate that there might be one at the center of our galaxy – and indeed most galaxies.[11-20][11-21] But Einstein's theory also suggests that wormholes might be highly radioactive, prone to sudden collapse, and might bring the objects passing through them into dangerous proximity with exotic matter that could destroy them.

There are theories that microscopic wormholes might spontaneously open and close naturally throughout the universe, perhaps in interaction with dark matter. But these are obviously of no use to us. We need wormholes that we can open and close at will, and where we know, or can determine, the start and end points. They'll need to be large enough for spacecraft to pass through safely. And we'll need to be able to guarantee they'll remain open long enough for the craft to complete its journey.

More advanced extraterrestrial civilizations may have found ways to do this, but I doubt we'll be able to do it for millions of years. Even if we knew how to do it, opening and maintaining a wormhole of that sort of size might take as much energy as the Sun produces. A good starting point might be to find an existing wormhole and try to work out how to enlarge it and stabilize it to prevent it from collapsing. Scientists are currently exploring this idea.

Interestingly, since time and space are so closely interrelated, wormholes could also be used for time travel. But that's another thing that's beyond the scope of this book.

11.6 Navigation and GPS

Despite their ability to travel unimaginable distances through space, the extraterrestrials seem to have had an incredibly hard time navigating around the Earth once they got here. Numerous UFO crashes have been reported since the 1940s, and there were a few that were even earlier than that. Why they had such a problem is a mystery. Perhaps there's something unusual about the Earth's gravity or magnetic field.

However, since the introduction of the Global Positioning System (GPS), no major UFO crashes have been reported. As we'll see in Chapter 13, it's highly likely that the extraterrestrials gave us the technology to create the GPS system. But it seems to have been as much for their benefit as it was for ours.

Since there were so many UFO crashes from the late 1940s onwards, they may have given us the GPS technology decades ago. But we didn't have the skills to build it until the 1970s.

11.7 Teleportation

Several people who commented on the first edition of this book wondered why the extraterrestrials would have bothered with spacecraft at all. Why wouldn't they have simply teleported[11-22] us here?

We know very little about teleportation, outside of fiction at least. It may be that the extraterrestrials have never managed to develop a long-range teleportation system.

Even if it's possible, several other issues need to be taken into account when teleporting physical objects – especially living things. For example, it's vital that the landing area is clear. That's easy enough to achieve in a laboratory. And if you're teleporting someone onto a spacecraft there's probably a dedicated teleportation hub – just as there is in *Star Trek*. But if you're teleporting someone down to Earth and you can't see the landing site, you might drop them into the middle of a tree, or a vehicle, or a river, or another person.

You'd also need to know the exact height of the landing area. Otherwise, the person might end up planted in the ground. And they wouldn't be able to just pull themselves out; their feet and legs would actually be part of the ground.

The best solution would be to set up managed teleportation hubs around the planet. If these exist already, then they must be in secret laboratories and military facilities, and they might only be for extraterrestrial use.

Over the last few decades, millions of people have gone missing. It's possible that a considerable number of them may have been teleported onto extraterrestrial spacecraft. Numerous abductees have reported being teleported onto craft that were hovering a few feet off the ground. Many of them then report being returned to Earth a few hours later, usually to the same spot that they were abducted from. This seems to indicate that the extraterrestrials are using a short-range teleportation system. As far as I'm aware, there have been no credible reports of long-range teleportation.

Here on Earth, our scientists have managed to teleport energy and photons of light,[11-23][11-24] but they haven't yet been able to do it with physical objects. (Or at least they haven't admitted to it publicly.) Those I've spoken to don't believe it will ever be possible to teleport anything more than microscopic particles – certainly nothing as large as a person. But perhaps if we ask them again in 100 million years, they might give us a different answer.

12

The Revised Timeline of Human Evolution

I must admit I thought that this would be one of the easiest parts of the book to write. After all, the timeline of human evolution is pretty well established now, right?

Wrong.

In fact, there are multiple mainstream factions, and there's little agreement between them. Several hominin species haven't been investigated in any real detail. And, as we saw earlier, at least one of them is yet to be discovered, so it's missing from the timeline.

> We know it must have existed because some people have a small amount of its DNA in their genomes.

Large parts of the official timeline are based on scant evidence, such as a single tooth or bone fragment. There are anomalies all over the place. And there's a significant missing link in our section of it – though mainstream scientists deny there are any gaps at all.

The multiple factions have each compiled their own versions of the timeline, and as I compared one against another, I found some astonishing differences.

It quickly became apparent that the "official" timeline is based on:

- a few facts, but not as many as most people think

- a lot of guesswork

- a lot of wishful thinking

- a lot of "forcing the evidence to fit" – in places where it clearly doesn't

- and a lot of "ignoring the troublesome bits"

It's been staggeringly difficult to compile a timeline that truly fits the current evidence, but in this chapter, I present my best attempt. I needed to make hundreds of revisions to it while I was writing the book, and I have no doubt that many more will need to be made in the future.

> For the purpose of this timeline, I've assumed that our home planet orbits one of our nearest stars, Alpha Centauri B. I've also assumed that life evolved there at the same rate as it did on Earth. Although if it did, the extraterrestrials living there now must be two *billion* years ahead of us. That's pretty mind-blowing; we couldn't even begin to imagine what that must be like. Having said that, several of the other candidate stars we looked at in Chapter 10 are even older.

12.1 The Timeline

6.5 billion years ago
Alpha Centauri B formed.

6.45 billion years ago
Our home planet formed (assumption).

6.1 billion years ago
The first life forms appeared on our home planet (assumption).

4.6 billion years ago
The Sun formed.

4.543 billion years ago
The Earth and the other planets in the solar system formed.

4.4 billion years ago
Alpha Centauri A formed.

4.2 billion years ago
The first life forms appeared on Earth.[12-01]

Many people, including some scientists, have suggested that the first life forms may have arrived here from Mars. As Mars formed at about the same time as the Earth, that makes no sense at all. It's more likely that life arrived here on a comet or meteorite, or on material ejected from another planet outside of our solar system. It's pretty much impossible that life could have evolved on Mars – or on the Earth for that matter – such a short time after they formed.[12-02]

3.5 billion years ago
The first single-celled organisms appeared on Earth.

2.45 billion years ago
The Great Oxygenation Event.[12-02a] One of the most significant extinction events in the Earth's history. Oceanic cyanobacteria began producing excessive amounts of oxygen as a waste product, and it escaped into the atmosphere. All life on the planet was anaerobic at that time, and the oxygen was toxic to it.

2.3 billion years ago
Snowball Earth I – the whole planet froze over. This may have been caused by a lack of volcanic activity.

> We need volcanos! But having too many of them can be a bad thing too. See Snowball Earth II (717 million years ago).

2 billion years ago
The first hominins evolved on our home planet (assumption).

2 billion years ago?
Eukaryotic cells – cells with internal "organs" (organelles) appeared on Earth.

1.99 billion years ago
A species equivalent to modern humans was living on our home planet (assumption).

As they're nearly two billion years more advanced than us – which is a *heck* of a big gap – these could be the extraterrestrials that brought us here. I very much doubt they're the same species as us though. We might have been an inferior species that lived on the same planet. Or they may have brought us here from another planet that was less advanced than theirs, but more advanced than the Earth.

If they're two billion years ahead of us, we might seem like rodents to them – or even less than that. Let's think about what the Earth was like two billion years ago. There were only single-celled organisms back then. It would be another 1.5 billion years before any visible signs of life appeared. So we might seem like nothing more to them than a particularly itchy rash. Or maybe some irritating worms.

That could explain how we ended up on Earth: they may have rounded us up, stuck us on a spacecraft, and blasted it towards the nearest vaguely habitable planet. Of course, they would only have put a few thousand of us on the spacecraft – most likely in embryo form. There would have been millions of us back on our home planet, most of whom were presumably exterminated. Let's hope they did it humanely.

If they chose to send some of us to Earth so our species survived, rather than driving every last one of us to extinction, we should take that as a positive sign. But we haven't evolved very far since then, so I guess they still think of us in the same regard: nothing more than some ...

> ... irritating worms. No wonder they don't seem to have any qualms about experimenting on us. *We* experiment on worms all the time and think nothing of it.

From this point on, the timeline refers entirely to the Earth.
Most of these events would have also happened on our home planet, but around 2 billion years earlier.

1.5 billion years ago
Eukaryotic cells split into three separate lineages that would later become the plants, fungi, and animals.

600 – 900 million years ago
The first multicellular organisms appeared.

717 million years ago
Snowball Earth II[12-03] – the planet froze over again. Unlike Snowball Earth I, this may have been caused by too many volcanos. It's thought that a massive chain of them erupted, sending an enormous amount of sulfur dioxide into the air. This reflected sunlight back into space, preventing it from heating the Earth's surface. When the planet thawed around 650 million years ago, the mass of crushed rock released minerals into the oceans. This caused an algal bloom that is believed to have "terraformed" the planet.[12-03a][12-03b]

590 million years ago
The bilateria (primitive animals exhibiting bilateral symmetry) split into the protostomes (which would become arthropods, worms, etc.), and the deuterostomes (which would become the vertebrates).

565 million years ago
Animals developed the ability to move under their own power.

540 million years ago
Animals with a primitive backbone first appeared.

530 million years ago
The first true vertebrates appeared.

*500 million years ago
The oldest known non-natural artifact on Earth. Zinc-silver alloy embedded in a vase inside a block of coal (discovered in Massachusetts, USA in 1851). If this is artifact is genuine, it could have been left by time travelers or it may have come from a crashed UFO. No one could have lived here yet, as there was nothing to eat.

489 million years ago
The Great Ordovician Biodiversification Event began. Many new species appeared.

465 – 470 million years ago
The first land plants appeared: mosses and liverworts.

400 million years ago
The first insects appeared. Plants evolved woody stems.

*400 million years ago
Non-natural artifact: the London Hammer – an 1800s-era iron hammer encased in rock (discovered in London, Texas, USA in 1936). This artifact was almost certainly formed by concretion in modern times. It's included here for completeness, as some people think it's genuine and significant.

397 million years ago
The first four-legged animals appeared.

385 million years ago
The first trees appeared.

320 million years ago
The pelycosaurs, a large group of lizard-like reptiles, appeared and dominated the land until 250 million years ago. Many were small, herbivorous and quite mammal-like, but some were large, predatory and carnivorous. (They weren't dinosaurs.)

*312 million years ago
Non-natural artifact: an iron pot inside a lump of coal (discovered in Oklahoma, USA in 1912). This may have been made by the first group of humans to be dropped off on Earth. If so, they didn't survive the Great Mass Extinctions.

*300 million years ago
Non-natural artifact: a piece of aluminum gear embedded in coal (discovered in Vladivostok, Russia). This may have come from a crashed alien spacecraft or a broken scientific instrument. Or it may have been created by another group of humans that were dropped off here. Again, if this was the case, then they didn't survive the next extinction event.

252 million years ago
The first Great Mass Extinction – also known as the Great Dying.[12-04] This was caused by a series of volcanic eruptions. 90 – 96 percent of life was wiped out, and it took around 1.3 million years to fully recover. Dinosaurs would become the dominant species for the next 185 million years.

Humans Are Not From Earth

200 million years ago
The second Great Mass Extinction. The Triassic period ended. The first mammals appeared.

150 million years ago
The first bird-like creature (archaeopteryx) appeared in Europe.

*150 million years ago
The stegosaurus became extinct. Intriguingly, the first fossils weren't discovered until 1877, yet there's an 800-year-old carving of one at Ta Prohm in Angkor, Cambodia.

140 million years ago
The first marsupials appeared.

130 million years ago
The first flowering plants appeared.

100 million years ago
The dinosaurs were at their peak.

93 million years ago
The oceans became starved of oxygen. 27 percent of marine invertebrates were wiped out. The cause is unknown, but it was most likely a huge undersea volcanic eruption.

75 million years ago
The first rodents appeared.

70 million years ago
The first grasses appeared.

66 million years ago

The Cretaceous-Tertiary (K/T) extinction. All of the giant reptiles, including the dinosaurs, were wiped out. This cleared the way for the mammals to dominate the planet. The extinction is believed to have been caused by an asteroid measuring 6 to 9 miles (10 to 15 km) in diameter, which hit the Gulf of Mexico.

63 million years ago

The proto-primates split into the haplorhines (dry-nosed primates) and the strepsirrhines (wet-nosed primates). The haplorhines evolved into monkeys, apes, and hominins (including humans, according to mainstream theories).

55 million years ago

The Paleocene/Eocene extinction. A sudden rise in greenhouse gases sent temperatures soaring. Many deep-sea species were wiped out as the oxygen levels plummeted.

55 million years ago

The first true primates appeared.

*55 million years ago

Non-natural artifacts: stone tools, utensils, and vessels embedded in rock strata beneath Table Mountain in Cape Town, South Africa. The extraterrestrials appear to have tried dropping off groups of humans again after a significant break. But once again, they didn't survive.

47 million years ago

The first whales appeared.

40 million years ago

The first simians (higher primates) colonized South America.

Humans Are Not From Earth

35 million years ago

Mass extinction of lizards in Australia as the country became completely cut off from the supercontinent Gondwana, and the Earth's climate cooled.[12-04a]

34 million years ago

Antarctica began to freeze over. By 15 million years ago, the whole continent was covered by a thick ice sheet. Most of it has remained covered ever since.[12-05]

30 million years ago

Primates began living in groups, establishing friendships, rivalries, and hierarchies; brain power increased.

*28.5 million years ago

Nuclear explosion in the Libyan Desert.

25 million years ago

The first apes appeared after splitting from the Old World monkeys.

18 million years ago

Gibbons appeared.

14 million years ago

Orangutans appeared.

7 – 8 million years ago

Gorillas appeared.

7.2 million years ago

The ape and hominin lineages diverged. The last known ancestor of both branches, *Graecopithecus freybergi*, lived in the eastern

Mediterranean area around this time. Fossils have been found in Greece and Bulgaria.[12-06] This species could be the famous "missing link."

5.8 million years ago
Possibly the first hominin to walk upright: *Ororin tugenensis*.

4.4 million years ago
Another primitive hominin, *Ardipithecus ramidus*, lived in Ethiopia. Fossils were discovered there in the 1990s. Its pelvis was adapted for both tree climbing and walking upright. The position of its skull on its spine indicates it was bipedal.

4 million years ago
The Australopithecines appeared. They were the first hominins to live on the savannah.

2.9 – 3.9 million years ago
Australopithecus afarensis appeared. Fossils have only been found in East Africa so far. This species is believed to have walked upright, but might have also spent some of its time in trees. The famous skeleton of "Lucy" belongs to this species. She lived in Hadar, Ethiopia 3.2 million years ago.

3.66 million years ago
The oldest known set of hominin footprints that mainstream scientists accept as genuine. Left by *Australopithecus afarensis* at Laetoli in northern Tanzania.

3.3 million years ago
The hominins began losing their body hair (reason unknown), and their skin became dark.

2.8 – 3 million years ago

The first members of the *Homo* genus appeared, and hominins experienced a significant increase in brain size. A fossil (LD 350-1) found in Ethiopia in 2013 is thought to be part of a jaw bone from an intermediary species between *Australopithecus* and *Homo habilis*.

2.8 – 3 million years ago?

Homo naledi first appeared in South Africa. *H. naledi* may have been the first of the *Homo* species, but its age is currently undetermined, and it may be younger. It was certainly one of the earliest, and still existed 2 million years ago. It had a mixture of primitive and modern features, including small, modern-looking teeth and human-like feet, but a small cranium and primitive fingers. It was probably better at walking than we are: its outward-flared pelvis shifted the hip muscles away from the joints, giving it more leverage.[12-07]

Professor Chris Stringer of the Natural History Museum in London confirmed that *Homo naledi* was around 3 million years old, based on specimens found in a cave in Africa in 2015. "What we are seeing is more and more species of creatures that suggests that nature was experimenting with how to evolve humans, thus giving rise to several different types of human-like creatures originating in parallel in different parts of Africa. Only one line eventually survived to give rise to us."

H. naledi also showed signs of ritual burial – something that wasn't recognized in modern humans until around 50,000 years ago.

*2 – 2.5 million years ago

Non-natural artifact: shark teeth with holes bored in them – probably for stringing on a necklace (discovered in England in 1872). If these were created by modern humans, their civilization didn't survive.

2.1 million years ago

Homo habilis appeared. It had a larger brain and smaller teeth than the Australopithecines, but also retained primitive features such as long arms. Around this time hominins also started using stone tools. Some became scavengers and ate meat-rich diets, which gave them more energy for less effort. This is thought to have led to the evolution of larger brains.

*2 million years ago

Non-natural artifact: a seashell with a carved, crude human face, embedded in rock in Suffolk, England. (Discovered in 1881). The human civilization that created this did not survive.

*2 million years ago

Non-natural artifacts: stone tools and other artifacts dating from this era were found during an archaeological dig in Mexico. This discovery was highly controversial – we discussed it in Chapter 3. Yet we now know that the hominins were using stone tools by this period: see 2.1 million years ago.

*2 million years ago

The Piri Reis map and other maps apparently created in the 16th – 18th centuries show the coastline of Antarctica as it would have looked at this time.

1.9 million years ago

Homo erectus and *Homo ergaster* appeared in Africa. They're either closely related to each other, or they both evolved from a common ancestor. *H. erectus* is thought to have been the first true hunter-gatherer, and the first to migrate out of Africa in large numbers (see 1.8 million years ago). We haven't been able to extract any DNA from *H. erectus* specimens, so we don't know what percentage of its DNA (if any) we have in our genomes. We may have lived alongside them, and even interbred with them, as we did probably with the Neanderthals. There's no evidence that we descended from them. *H. erectus* had bodies that were almost indistinguishable from ours, but they had smaller brains and a more primitive face. *H. ergaster* is also known as the African *Homo erectus*. It lived in eastern and southern Africa.

> Interestingly, *Homo erectus* means "upright man," but we now know that hominins had been walking upright for at least four million years before this.[12-08]

1.9 million years ago

Homo rudolfensis appeared in Kenya around the same time that *H. erectus* and *H. ergaster* appeared elsewhere in Africa, but it had a flatter face. Little is currently known about this species. The main evidence is a skull (KNM ER 1470) and a handful of fossils found in 1972 by a team led by Richard and Meave Leakey.

1.8 million years ago

The first known wave of migration out of Africa (by *Homo erectus*). They went to Europe and later spread into Asia.[12-09][12-10]

1.6 million years ago

The first possible use of fire. Charred deposits dating from this period have been discovered in Kenya. (See also: 780,000 years ago.)

1.3 million years ago
Homo ergaster died out.

1.2 million years ago
The first of three modern near-extinctions.[12-11] The worldwide hominin population may have collapsed through over-breeding, or it might not have become very large in the first place. The total global population around this time was about 26,000, with a breeding population of about 18,000. By modern standards, we would consider this "endangered." There were numerous, isolated, very small groups all over the world. The more remote ones eventually died out, leaving only the core groups in Africa. Interestingly, this pattern would repeat itself when we arrived.

1.2 million years ago
Homo antecessor appeared. This is believed to be the first European hominin, and it also lived in the UK.

1.2 million years ago
Stone tools found in Turkey have been dated to this period, indicating that early humans had reached there from Europe and Asia.[12-12]

800,000 years ago
The oldest known set of hominin footprints outside of Africa that mainstream scientists accept as genuine. Discovered in Norfolk, England in 2014, and thought to have been left by *Homo antecessor*.[12-13]

800,000 years ago
Homo antecessor died out.

780,000 years ago

The first convincing evidence of man's use of fire. Complex stone tools appeared.

600,000 years ago

Homo heidelbergensis appeared in Africa, Europe, and western Asia.[12-14] This species is considered by many mainstream anthropologists to be the direct ancestor of the Neanderthals, Denisovans and possibly modern humans – although the link to humans seems dubious.

550,000 years ago

Homo erectus may have died out by this time.
(See also: 143,000 years ago.)

500,000 years ago

The first evidence of man-made shelters appeared: wooden huts near Chichibu, Japan. Speech first began to develop.

430,000 years ago

Possible DNA evidence of Neanderthals (or maybe Denisovans) in Spain. This suggests that the split from the ancestor of the Neanderthals and the Denisovans (either *H. heidelbergensis* or *H. erectus*) may have happened as much as 750,000 years ago.[12-15][12-16]
(See also: 600,000 years ago.)

400,000 – 500,000 years ago

Missing link. This is where the hominin that comes between modern humans (*Homo sapiens*) and native species such as *Homo erectus* and *Homo heidelbergensis* should fit on the timeline. There's no evidence that such a species ever existed.

*400,000 years ago
Human DNA dating from this period has been discovered in northern Spain.[12-17]

400,000 years ago
Evidence of humans living in Israel.[12-18] In 2010 archaeologists from Tel Aviv University who were investigating the Qesem cave near Rosh Ha'Ayin found modern human teeth along with evidence of the use of fire, hunting, and the mining and cutting of flint to make tools.

400,000 years ago
DNA mutation rates of Australian Aboriginal people indicate that they have been present there since this time. This is evidence that Australia, Israel, and Spain (see above) were the first places where modern humans were dropped off by the extraterrestrials.

400,000 years ago
Homo rhodesiensis[12-18a] first appeared in Africa. This appears to be the African variant of *H. heidelbergensis*. Many mainstream scientists consider this species our direct ancestor in Africa. But, as with the other hominin species of that era, it looked nothing like us. It had a thick skull, sloping forehead, and huge brow ridges. In any case, we were already present on Earth by this time.

400,000 years ago
The first evidence of hunting with spears. The first evidence of cooking. The Denisovans may have appeared in Europe (but see 200,000 years ago).

300,000 years ago
Modern humans confirmed to be living in Morocco,[12-18b] and possibly throughout Africa. This suggests that we first appeared on Earth much

earlier than this. This would have been the second main group to be dropped off by the extraterrestrials, and the largest up to that point.

200,000 – 300,000 years ago

Homo naledi died out.[12-19] The last known remains were found in a cave in South Africa in 2015.

280,000 years ago

Complex stone blades appeared. Stone-tipped spears from this era have been found in Ethiopia.

270,000 years ago

An early exodus of humans from Africa. They traveled to Europe and appear to have interbred with the Neanderthals.[12-20][12-21]

250,000 years ago

According to mainstream scientists, the Neanderthals (*Homo neanderthalensis*) first appeared and spread throughout Europe.[12-22] (But see 430,000 years ago – they had already been here for about 200,000 years.) They were shorter and more muscular than humans, but had slightly larger brains. They almost certainly evolved from *H. heidelbergensis* or possibly *H. erectus*. Humans may have interbred with them, but couldn't possibly have descended from them. In fact, if they didn't appear until this later date, there's an extremely remote possibility that they could have descended from *us*.

*250,000 years ago

Stone tools attributed to modern humans and dating from this era have been found in Hueyatlaco, near Puebla in Mexico. Mainstream anthropologists say we didn't reach Mexico until 12,000 to 15,000 years ago. This appears to be the third main group that was dropped off by the extraterrestrials, but it seems they didn't survive for very long.

200,000 – 250,000 years ago

Homo heidelbergensis died out.[12-23] The oldest known specimen has been dated to 259,000 years ago.

208,000 years ago

Y-chromosome Adam appeared. (See also: 170,000 years ago.)

200,000 years ago

According to mainstream anthropologists, the Denisovans[12-24] appeared in Asia, possibly having split from the Neanderthal lineage, although this is currently undetermined. In fact, the Denisovans might be considerably older than the Neanderthals, and they may have originated in Europe. 430,000-year-old mitochondrial DNA from a femur found in Spain seems to be a much closer match to the Denisovans than to the Neanderthals or *Homo heidelbergensis*.

195,000 years ago

Modern humans, who had already been in Morocco for at least 100,000 years, were confirmed to be living in other parts of Africa too. They quickly began migrating across Asia and Europe. (Mainstream anthropologists dispute the dates. See also: 120 – 130,000 years ago.)

The remains of the earliest people from this group were found in Ethiopia in 1967. When they were discovered, they were thought to be the first-ever modern humans. But much older remains and artifacts that had been found all over Africa had been (incorrectly) recorded as belonging to other hominin species because no one believed we could have evolved that early.

This may have been the fourth modern group to have been brought to Earth by extraterrestrials, and it was by far the largest of all the groups.

170,000 years ago
Mitochondrial Eve, said to be the direct ancestor to all of today's living people, may have lived in Africa.

150,000 years ago
The second of three modern near-extinctions. This one was caused by glaciation. The worldwide population may have been reduced to as few as 600 people, meaning we were critically endangered. The main group of survivors lived in South Africa.

143,000 years ago
The latest evidence indicates that *Homo erectus* was extinct by this time.[12-25] They might actually have died out more than 550,000 years ago. (Or a few may have survived. See 14,000 years ago.)

140,000 years ago
The first evidence of long-distance trade.

*131,000 years ago
Possible evidence of humans living in what is now San Diego, California, USA. The remains of a mastodon were found buried alongside what appear to be stone hammers and anvils.[12-26][12-27] No human remains from that period have been found so far. Researchers have no idea who these people were or how they got there. This group may have been part of a previously unknown failed colonization event, or they may have been dropped off there by aliens. But more likely they were the last survivors of the Mexican group (see 250,000 years ago). They probably died out soon after this.

130,000 years ago

The earliest known sea crossing: modern humans reached Crete. There's also evidence of a second exodus from Africa, this time along the Arabian coast into India, eventually reaching Australia where there was already a small Aboriginal population.

120,000 – 130,000 years ago

According to mainstream anthropologists, modern humans evolved in Africa. If that were the case (it isn't), our supposed immediate ancestors *H. erectus* and *H. heidelbergensis* may have already died out 13,000 years and 70,000 years respectively before this date (and probably much earlier), making our evolution from them impossible. As we've already seen, we bore little resemblance to them anyway, so we couldn't have descended from them directly. Most anthropologists now accept that this date is wrong, and that we were in Morocco 300,000 years ago.

> There was a definite influx of new blood around this time, so this probably marked the arrival of the fifth main group to be dropped off by the extraterrestrials. Presumably, they were brought here to raise our numbers following the near-collapse of our species in the near-extinction event 150,000 years ago.

125,000 years ago

Another early migration from Africa is thought to have stalled around Israel. Tools from this era have also been found in Arabian archaeological digs.[12-28]

120,000 years ago

Homo rhodesiensis became extinct. At one time, this species was a potential candidate for being our direct ancestor.

80,000 – 120,000 years ago

Modern humans were living in caves in China.[12-29][12-30] As this precedes the largest exodus out of Africa by 50,000 to 60,000 years, this suggests that the extraterrestrials dropped off a sixth group of us there. As with the fifth group, they were probably brought in to raise our numbers following the near-extinction event 150,000 years ago. The aliens seem to have been experimenting with new habitats for us, as almost all the other groups had died out.

*100,000 years ago

Evidence of modern humans living on the Serra da Capivara plateau in Brazil. Mainstream anthropologists say we didn't reach South America until 12,000 to 15,000 years ago. It's unlikely that we had the technology to cross the Atlantic at this stage. It's also unlikely that we'd have made it that far if we'd crossed the land bridge across the Bering Strait. It's possible that this was the Mexican group migrating south. But as the worldwide population was dangerously low at that point, and the Mexican group had probably long since died out, it's more likely that the extraterrestrials dropped off a seventh group there as they continued to experiment with more diverse habitats.

*100,000 years ago

Non-natural artifact: the Williams Enigmalith – a modern-looking electrical plug embedded in a solid granite pebble. Discovered in North America in the 1990s and dated to this period.

72,000 years ago

Clothing and jewelry were invented.

70,000 years ago

The third of the three modern near-extinction events: the Toba super-eruption in Sumatra, Indonesia. This caused six years of winter, and our global population collapsed yet again, to between 1,000 and 10,000 people.

> If the extraterrestrials cared about our progress they must have been tearing their hair out at this point (if they had any hair). They'd now dropped off at least seven groups of us in modern times, plus several more in prehistoric times, and almost none of us had survived. We were now critically endangered and clinging on by a thread. They may have finally given up, as there's no evidence that they brought any more of us here after this. Fortunately, we somehow staged a remarkable recovery and they didn't need to.

65,000 – 75,000 years ago

The famous "Out of Africa" exodus that all the history books say happened around 60,000 years ago. In fact, it almost certainly happened around 10,000 years earlier, when the remaining African groups went in search of new food sources following the Toba super-eruption. An unknown number of people left Africa, traveled north to the Mediterranean, and then turned east and went to Asia, replacing other hominin species.

> It's worth noting that there were numerous human settlements around the world at this time, but their surviving populations would have been tiny. They would have been in a desperate and precarious state.

65,000 years ago

A smaller migration from Africa to the Middle East.

65,000 years ago

Aboriginal people confirmed to be living in Australia.[12-31]

50,000 – 60,000 years ago

Modern humans were living in Laos.

55,000 years ago

According to mainstream anthropologists, the first Aborigines colonized Australia. But DNA evidence shows that Aboriginal people had already been living there for 350,000 years. Hardly any of them would have survived the modern near-extinction events though, and they were probably reduced to a few isolated communities.

50,000 years ago

The Great Leap Forward – a cultural revolution: ritual burying of the dead, clothes-making, and complex hunting techniques.[12-32]

10,000 – 50,000 years ago

A significant number of Asians returned to Africa. The reasons for this are unknown, but we've tracked their movements through their DNA.

40,000 – 50,000 years ago

The first evidence of modern human behavior and cognition: abstract thinking, deep planning, art, ornamentation, music, and blade technology.[12-32a]

43,000 – 45,000 years ago

European early modern humans (the Cro-Magnons[12-33]) appeared. They were genetically identical to modern humans, but were physically more robust with slightly larger craniums. They are thought to have split off from the Asian group. They appear to be the first group of modern humans to develop blue eyes. (See also: 7 – 10,000 years ago.)

40,000 years ago

The Neanderthals became extinct.[12-34] Until recently it was thought that some of them may have survived until about 28,000 years ago, but this has now been disproven.

40,000 years ago

A significant migration of humans from Africa to Europe. The Neanderthals had apparently managed to keep most of us out of Europe, but now that they had died out, we seized the chance to expand into their former territory. We then joined forces with the Cro-Magnons.

35,000 years ago

The first known cave art was created.

*30,000 years ago

Bones of giant sloths in Uruguay show tool marks from hunting and butchery.

24,000 years ago

According to mainstream theories, humans crossed the Bering Strait land bridge (Beringia) from Asia into North America for the first time.[12-35] The bridge was covered by the sea about 11,000 years ago.

18,000 years ago

Homo floresiensis ("Hobbit people") lived in Flores, Indonesia.

14,000 years ago

A thigh bone from a species resembling *Homo habilis* or *Homo erectus* was found in a cave in China in 2015 and dated to this period. Both species were believed to have been long extinct by then. Some researchers speculate that it may be a hybrid of a modern human and an ancient hominin, or perhaps a previously unknown *Homo* species.[12-36]

*12,000 – 15,000 years ago
The world's first city was established at Tiwanaku, Bolivia.

12,800 years ago
The Younger Dryas impact.[12-37][12-38][12-39] A probable comet impact in North America is thought to have lowered temperatures in the northern hemisphere by about 6°C (11°F) for 1,200 years. This is believed to have caused or contributed to the extinction of the Clovis people (an ancient Native American society), but led to the establishment of the first Neolithic civilizations elsewhere.

12,000 years ago
According to mainstream theories, the first modern humans reached South America.

*12,000 years ago
Nuclear explosion in Rajasthan, India.

11,500 – 12,000 years ago
The Mesopotamian civilization was established. Göbekli Tepe was established in Turkey. Beer was invented.[12-40]

10,000 – 12,000 years ago
Agriculture began.

10,000 years ago
The first fixed communities (villages) were established. The domestication of dogs began.

5,700 – 10,000 years ago

Over-intensive farming and climate change led to the desertification of the Sahara.

7,700 years ago

People with white skin and blue eyes first appeared in northern Europe.

6,000 years ago

A massive leap in knowledge: writing, mathematics, architecture, pyramid-building, science, astronomy, modern societies, money, elections, sanitation, and more – including the invention of wheeled vehicles.[12-41] These all apparently sprang up out of nowhere, in multiple places at the same time.

6,000 years ago

The first modern civilization appeared in Sumeria, Mesopotamia (now Iraq and the surrounding area).

5,500 years ago

The Bronze Age began. We began smelting and working copper and tin.

5,100 years ago

The Ancient Egyptian civilization was established.

5,000 years ago

Construction of Stonehenge began.

5,000 years ago

The tallness gene suddenly appeared, and humans were no longer short.[12-42] The first known writing appeared.

4,800 years ago

The Indus Valley civilization (India/Pakistan) was at its peak.

*2,200 years ago

The Antikythera mechanism – the first-known analog computer – was made. It incorporated technologies that were previously unknown until the 14th century. It was recovered from a shipwreck in Greece in 1902.

2,000 years ago

The Roman Empire was established.

700 years ago

The Renaissance: a 200-year-long surge in art, literature, and learning. It began in Florence, Italy, but with a considerable amount of help from the Chinese.

600 years ago

The Aztec and Inca Empires were established.

500 years ago

The modern era of human civilization began.

250 years ago

The industrial revolution began.

60 years ago

The space age began.

> * Entries marked with an asterisk (*) are usually left out of the official/mainstream versions of our timeline. I explained why in Chapter 4.

12.2 Comments on the Timeline

- There are still quite a few anomalies and mysteries in our timeline, including several that might never be solved. For example, as soon as we appeared on Earth we seemed to know exactly what to do with the planet's resources. Where did we get that knowledge?

- We were totally different from any hominin that came before us. This is one of the reasons why our evolution on Earth makes no sense. There's no place for us in the standard hominin lineage. Yet it all makes perfect sense for the hominins that actually belonged here.

- We have 23 pairs of chromosomes, whereas all the other primates have 24. We have no idea how many chromosomes the hominins such as the Neanderthals and Denisovans had. Mainstream scientists say it's most likely to be 23, but they don't have any firm evidence for this. In fact, there's a strong indication that the Neanderthals didn't have a Y chromosome.[12-43] If that were the case, they would have been biologically incompatible with us. How in that case did their DNA get into our genomes? It couldn't have happened through interbreeding because every pregnancy would have miscarried. It could only have been spliced in artificially.

- The oldest known human mitochondrial DNA is 200,000 years old. The oldest known skeletal evidence is 300,000 years old.

- Many people say the beginning of the space age was a direct result of the reported UFO crash near Roswell, New Mexico, USA in 1947. Although we suspect that extraterrestrials have intervened in our lives many times throughout our history, their intervention on this particular occasion was almost certainly unplanned and unintended.

12.3 Can we ever return to our home planet?

Almost certainly not. For a start, we don't know exactly where it is. We don't have the technology (publicly at least) to be able to send manned spacecraft out of the solar system – and extraterrestrials may be monitoring us to make sure we never do. Our home planet will have changed significantly in the thousands of years since we left it. And our DNA has been modified to make us more suited to life on Earth – and that implies that we're now less well-adapted for life on our home planet.

So although we might feel a strange longing to return to our home planet, after all this time away from it we'd probably find it a strange, alien, and perhaps inhospitable place. We might not even be able to survive there any more. And we have to remember that we left it (or were perhaps forcibly removed from it) for a good reason. The current inhabitants might not want us back. Or there might be nothing left for us to go back to.

12.4 Important Links

- Image of the hominid timeline [12-44]

- Image of the timeline of hominid evolution [12-45]

- Human Evolution Timeline Interactive [12-46]

- Timeline: Human Evolution [12-47]

- Becoming human: A timeline of human evolution [12-48]

- The 15 Tweaks That Made Us Human [12-49]

- An Ancient, Mysterious Scrap of Human DNA [12-50]

13

What We Know About Aliens

I n this chapter, we'll look at the main types of extraterrestrial that people claim to have encountered.[13-01] We'll also look at some of the advanced technology that the extraterrestrials may have given us. Many people believe there must be inhabited planets throughout the universe, yet researchers say they've never found any proof of life out there. So we'll also take a closer look at this discrepancy.

13.1 The main types of extraterrestrial

The most common extraterrestrials are those that evolved from reptiles. They're generally known as the reptilians or reptoids. They evolved into many different species, some of which have been seen on Earth.

The fact that most extraterrestrials evolved from reptiles should come as no surprise. Evolution would have followed more or less the same process on every planet where life became established. Giant reptiles – the dinosaurs – were the dominant creatures on Earth for 185 million years, and they would have remained so had they not been wiped out in the K/T extinction event around 66 million years ago. The K/T event enabled the mammals to take over, and they later gave rise to the higher mammals including the primates and hominins.

Our home planet almost certainly suffered a similar extinction event, so the mammals became the dominant class there too. They may have eventually given rise to us. But most planets wouldn't have had that sort of extinction event, and the giant reptiles would have continued evolving. Eventually, they would have gained most of the features we recognize in ourselves: walking upright, high intelligence, communicative abilities, manual dexterity, and so on.

Let's take a closer look at the main types of extraterrestrial you may have heard about.

13.1.a The Greys

Most people will recognize the Greys[13-02] from the reports of the UFO crashes near Roswell, New Mexico, USA in 1947. They've also featured in numerous photos and "alien autopsy" videos. I have no idea whether these are real or fake, but they're all remarkably consistent.

> The strange thing is that the extraterrestrials involved in the Roswell crash *weren't* Greys. They were taller and slenderer, their faces were more humanoid, and they had small, sunken eyes. Researchers class them as Roswell Humanoids.[13-03]

Most people know what the Greys look like and could draw a picture of one. They're gray-skinned humanoids, usually reported as being 3 to 4 feet (0.9 to 1.2 meters) tall, although some of them (perhaps a sub-species) are reported to be as tall as us. They're particularly noted for their large, almost-bulbous heads and black, almond-shaped eyes that have no discernable irises or pupils.

As we noted earlier, the black parts of their eyes are probably protective membranes. Researchers were able to remove them easily.

They have nostrils, but no nose, and they have ear openings, but no external ears. Their mouths are small. They have no external sex organs, and they're completely hairless.

Their skulls are huge in proportion to their bodies, implying that they may be significantly more intelligent than us. There are claims that they might even have telepathic abilities. They're also reported to be far less emotional than us, to the extent that they'd be classed as autistic if they were human.

As they're largely unemotional, they're reported to have little or no interest in things like stories, humor, film, television, music, friendship, and sex (other than for reproduction). But they're said to express considerable interest in things like science, engineering, language, mathematics, medicine, and psychology. Some researchers have said they don't appear to exhibit fear, and they might not be able to feel it. This would make them fearsome adversaries in battle.

When questioned, they reportedly say they're from the fourth planet of one of the stars in the Zeta Reticuli binary system.[13-04] But there are conflicting theories about their origins. While most researchers believe they're the modern descendants of a reptilian race, others say they might be humans from the distant future who have traveled back to our time.

I don't believe the Greys can possibly be humans from the future. According to reports, their DNA doesn't resemble ours at all, and they aren't biologically compatible with us. I could understand the Nordics being humans from the future, but it makes no sense to say that the Greys are.

The Greys might actually be several different species or sub-species, some of whom are friendly or benign and some of whom are hostile or predatory. The friendly ones are reportedly helping us to advance our knowledge and technology. The hostile ones apparently claim to "own" us and our planet and are seen as a massive threat to our future.

The main group of Greys that have visited the Earth are reported to be in a Cold War-like battle with the Nordic extraterrestrials. There are newspaper accounts of aerial battles between UFOs over Nuremberg, Germany in 1561; southern France in 1608; and the USA in April 2008. Numerous eyewitnesses have reported dogfights between individual UFOs over the USA and Russia in recent years.

The Greys are reported to have at least one base on Earth, and possibly more, and at least one underground base on Mars. In fact, they seem to prefer living underground.

13.1.b The Reptilians

The reptilians[13-05] are said to look like half-human, half-reptilian creatures, though they're generally reported to be much taller than us. Some researchers say some of them can shape-shift between their two forms, sometimes looking exactly like us. They're thought to have been visiting the Earth for thousands of years, though sightings have increased in recent years.

Some reptilians are believed to have psychic powers,[13-06] and many are reported to be hostile towards humans, feeding off their negative energies including fear and hatred.[13-07]

Many of the people who claimed to have seen "demons" in the past might actually have seen these aliens. And the Aztec deity Quetzalcoatl (meaning "feathered serpent") may have been a reptilian.

13.1.c The Nordics

The Nordics[13-08] are virtually indistinguishable from Scandinavian humans. They're noted for their blond hair, blue eyes, pleasing appearance, and especially for their height. They're also believed to have telepathic powers.

The Nordics are reportedly benign, friendly and spiritual, concerned about the Earth's environment, and interested in bringing about world peace. They mingle freely with people on Earth and go unnoticed. Some of them act as our mentors, passing on their knowledge.

Some of them have reportedly said they come from the Pleiades star cluster.[13-09]

> This is incredibly unlikely; the Pleiades is very young. The oldest star in the cluster is no more than 150 million years old, and most are younger, averaging 100 to 115 million years old. If any planets orbit these stars, the chances of life appearing there so soon are pretty remote. Even if life is present, there's no possibility whatsoever that anything other than primitive microbes could have evolved.

The Nordics are our closest extraterrestrial relatives. Their DNA is said to be very similar to ours, and they're biologically compatible with us. Some researchers believe that human Caucasians originated as hybrids of humans and Nordics.

13.1.d The Tall Whites

The Tall Whites are remarkably similar in appearance to the Nordics – and to us – but researchers say they're unrelated. In fact, a reptilian species is thought to have created them by splicing biological material from the Nordics into Tall Greys.

Again, this seems unlikely. The Nordics are said to have similar DNA to us, meaning they must have evolved from mammals, while the Tall Greys would have evolved from reptiles and wouldn't be biologically compatible with them. But if the reptilian race that created them is billions of years ahead of us, I guess they may have found a way of doing it anyway.

13.1.e The less-common extraterrestrial races

Other extraterrestrial races that have reportedly visited Earth include:[13-10]

The Insectoids

These resemble praying mantises. They're almost certainly a reptilian species that just happens to look like insects. It's doubtful that they could have evolved directly from insects.

Insectoids were reportedly seen in Nevada, USA in 1977 and in Poland in 2001.

The Shapeshifters

These have the ability to change their body shape to mimic other species – including humans.

13.2 The "known" extraterrestrial species

The former Canadian defense minister Paul Hellyer claimed that there are about eighty known extraterrestrial species. Of these, at least four have been visiting the Earth for thousands of years.[13-11] His claims were corroborated by his colleagues.

He also claimed that at least two Nordic aliens, who easily passed for humans, were working closely with the US Government.

Extraterrestrial researchers claim there are considerably more than eighty known species. They've interviewed witnesses and read thousands of pages of testimonies and reports of sightings, and gathered details of more than 250 separate species. I'll list these in a moment.

Most extraterrestrial species are reported to be benign and benevolent, and their reason for visiting Earth is to help. They're concerned about the damage we're doing to the environment, our high level of violence, and the amount of money we spend on the military instead of feeding people in poorer countries.

Most of them adhere to a code of conduct that forbids them from meddling in human affairs unless they're invited to do so. But at least two species are reported to have their own agendas and pose a serious threat to us. All of the extraterrestrial species that currently visit (or live on) the Earth are said to be monitoring us. Presumably, they're also reporting their findings back to their home bases.

Here's the list of "known" species that extraterrestrial researchers have compiled. Describing each of these in detail would fill an entire book. But if you're interested in finding out more about them, please follow the links I've provided.[13-12][13-13][13-14]

Animal-like aliens

- Alien Dog / Delta Aliens
- Bigfoot / Sasquatch

- Chupacabra
- Jawas
- Mook

- Felines / Lion People
- Mammalian Humanoid
- The Wadig

Cyborgs and Robotic Aliens

- Androids
- Eva-Borgs
- Synthetics

- Draco-Borgs
- Robots

Greys

- Airk
- Archquliod
- Biave / Biaviians
- Blues
- The Dow
- Grails
- Greens
- Indugutk
- Jefok
- Killimat-Arr
- Large Nosed Greys / Orions / Tall Greys
- Lyrans

- The Alcyone
- Axthadans
- Black Greys
- Browns
- Ebans / Ebens
- Graysli
- Gypsies
- Insect-Eyed Greys
- Jighantik
- Koshnak
- Maitre (extremely hostile)

- Markabians / Marcabians
- Mazarek
- Railoid
- Rumardians
- Tall Whites
- Verdants

- Matrax
- Oliverian
- Reticulans
- Solipsi Rai
- Tanzany
- Yukonadious Greys

Humanoid Aliens

- The 2017
- Acartitians
- Afim-Spiantsy
- Alabram
- Aldebarans
- Allmahulluk-Strat-163
- Alt
- Anabua
- Ancients
- Antarctican
- Apuians
- Arcturas / Arcturians
- Atlans
- Bawwi
- Bernarians

- Acali
- Aenstria
- Agharians / Aghartians
- Alcohbata
- Al-Gruualix
- Alpha Centaurians
- Altimarians
- Anakim
- Andromedans
- Antarieans
- Aquatic Humanoids
- Arians / Aryans
- Baavi
- Benevolents
- Blue Arcturians

- Blue People
- Centaurians
- Clarion
- Dals
- Deros
- Dorsay
- Dropas
- Ectom
- EL-Manouk
- Elffaf
- Elohims
- Eridanians
- Eternals
- Gizan / Gizahn
- Hyadeans
- Lang
- Lemurians
- Moon-Eyes
- Neonates
- Norcans
- Nors
- Onoogie
- Pleiadeans / Pleyadiyans
- Puritav-Illumu

- Caraveldi
- Cetians / Tau Cetians
- Cyclops
- Deneb
- Dorians
- Dries
- Dwarfin / Dwarfs
- EL's / EL Hybrids
- Elegant Humanoids
- Ellina
- Engan
- Errans
- Fomalhaut
- Hairy Dwarfs
- Korendian
- Lanolus People
- Little Green Humanoids
- Mythilae
- Nep-4
- Nordics
- Octolimb
- Pegasians
- Procyanans
- Raelains

Humans Are Not From Earth

- Ramay
- Rigelians
- Saami
- Shining Ones
- Smad
- Sons of Darkness
- Spicans
- The Stygian
- Telosian
- Thiaoouba
- Ummites
- Vegans (from the star Vega)
- Very Tall Race
- Wrinkled Faces
- X–1Z
- Zombies

- Red Giants
- Roswell Humanoids
- Santinians
- Sirians
- Solarians
- Sons of Light
- Strange Red Giants
- Taygetean
- Teros
- Ulterran
- Urantia
- Venusian
- Vinnytvari
- Xilox
- Zeti

Hybrid Aliens

- Harus
- Hybrid Greys
- Meta-Terrestrial
- Positive / Negative Hybrids
- Re-Brid

- Hu-Brid
- Hybrid Reptilians
- Nordic Clones
- Quadloids

Insectoid Aliens

- Ant People
- Depanoid
- Mantis Beings
- Skreed

- Cassiopeians
- Insectoids
- Negumak
- Trantaloids

Light-based Aliens

- Petal
- Ultrons

- RA
- White Brotherhood of Light

Plasma Life forms

- Plasma life forms

Reptilian Aliens

- Allgruuk
- Altairians
- Bellatrax
- Booteans
- Buttahs
- Carians

- Alpha-Draconians
- Anunnaki
- Bellatricians
- Burrowers
- Cappellans / Capellans
- Chameleon

- Chitahuli
- Crill / Krill
- Dinosauroids
- Dragon Worms
- Hydra Reptilians
- Ikels
- Kurs
- Lacertian Reptilians
- Leviathans
- Luciferians
- Mothmen
- Nefiilim
- Philadelphia Project Aliens
- Serpentine Reptilians
- Sirius Reptilians
- Subterranean Reptilians
- Tisar-3
- Ciakar
- Deviants
- Draconians / Dracons
- Hav-Musuvs / MuSuvians
- Iguanas / Iguanoids
- Indigenous Reptilians
- Kyllimir-Auk
- Leverons
- Lizzies
- Magell
- Nagarian / Nagas
- Orangean
- Phoenians
- Serpents
- Skril
- Targzissians
- Vampuria Reptilians
- Water-Dwelling Reptilian Humanoids
- Winged Draconians

Water-based Aliens

- Amphibians
- Cetaceans
- Caponi
- Cygnusians

- Frogmen
- Nommo
- Sirius Beings

- Mintakans
- Nyptonians

Type Unknown

- Amoeba-like Creatures
- Archons
- Conformers
- Giant Brains
- Heplaloids
- Invisibles
- Para-Terrestrials
- Tadpole Aliens
- Tengri Tengri
- X5-Tykut

- Apparitions / Holograms
- Cessna
- Energyzoa
- Hathor
- Interdimensional Entities
- Ishnaans
- Stinky Blobs
- Tarice
- Tubes / Rods / Skyfish

13.3 If the aliens are out there, why can't we detect them?

Much is made of the fact that our radio and television broadcasts have been radiating into space for more than a century. Since this is the case, why aren't similar signals radiating from other highly developed planets? If they were, then surely we could detect them.

You have to remember that the universe is enormous, and our radio signals will have only reached the stars and planets within 100 light years or so of Earth. If there are inhabited planets on the outer limits of that range, and they've started broadcasting radio signals back to us, they won't reach us for another 100 years. Signals from those within 50 light years of us would only just begin reaching us now. But the galactic authorities have almost certainly instructed them not to respond.

Another issue is that this sort of transmission probably only exists for a brief period in a planet's history.[13-15] Here on Earth, they're unlikely to exist for more than another decade or two. We're rapidly reaching the point where all our broadcasts will be via cable, the internet or low-power wireless signals that extend no more than a few miles from the nearest radio mast. These signals won't be broadcast into space, and they'll probably be undetectable from outside our atmosphere. So, as far as radio emissions are concerned at least, the Earth will appear to "go dark" within the next generation.

If technological progress runs at the same rate on other planets, and if they developed even a few decades ahead of us, they won't be broadcasting any radio signals at all by now. Their radio era will have ended, and there will be nothing for us to detect.

Of course, they might not have had a radio era at all. They may have stuck with cables and low-power wireless towers, and skipped high-power transmissions entirely. Or perhaps they used some other form of communications technology: infrared, lasers, fiber optics, microwaves, or something else that we don't even know about. They might have shared details of a more efficient system with each other, but deliberately kept us out of the loop. And if they're using a system that somehow operates faster than light, it will be invisible to us.

Our only real hope of spotting them is if they're deliberately broadcasting radio signals or lasers into space. They might do this if they want to be found by highly developed species on other planets. We've spotted powerful light pulses coming from some of their star systems. These may be natural phenomena – although scientists don't have an explanation for them if they are. But it could be a sign that they're communicating with each other or powering their spacecraft. We'll look at this in more detail below.

We haven't detected any non-natural radio signals from planets within range of us. So if there are advanced civilizations near us, it seems they don't want us to know about it. Again, that could be because the galactic authorities have instructed them not to contact us. (Remember, the Earth might be our prison.)

We know they're out there somewhere. The Earth clearly isn't our natural environment so we wouldn't be here if it weren't for them. There may be a tiny element of doubt as to whether they're out there *now*, but it isn't because they *never* existed, it's because they might *no longer* exist. They may have died out, for any number of reasons.

Another likely possibility is that we're in a quiet corner of the galaxy; one where there are no other civilizations within thousands of light years. We've already seen that we're in an enormous void. Most of the intelligent civilizations in our galaxy probably live much closer to the galactic center, in what's called the galactic habitability zone.[13-16] This zone lies between 13 and 19.5 light years from the galactic center. It's also slightly above and below the galactic mid-plane, where the danger of extinction events caused by exploding supernovae is significantly reduced.

Our solar system is about 27,000 light years from the galactic center, so the galactic habitability zone is well beyond our range. Our earliest radio and television signals won't reach it for another 26,900 years. And even when (or if) they do, they'll be almost imperceptible against the background noise. And, of course, in the unlikely event that someone sends a reply, we'd have to wait another 27,000 years for it to reach us. Our civilization – if it even exists – will have changed beyond all recognition by then.

But even though we haven't (officially) detected any non-natural signals from other planets, and the civilizations living near the galactic center can't possibly have detected any signals from Earth yet, that doesn't mean we haven't been visited by extraterrestrials.

There's a wealth of evidence that indicates they've been coming here for thousands (and more likely millions) of years. We ourselves are evidence of their visits, as we couldn't have got here any other way. There's evidence that they've made secret deals with various governments; most notably with US President Eisenhower in the 1950s. And there's plenty of evidence that some of them now reside on Earth and have bases here.

There are almost certainly several highly advanced civilizations living much closer to us than the galactic center. It's possible that some of them might be within just four or five light years of us.

Over the last few years, astronomers working on the Sloan Digital Sky Survey[13-17] have analyzed more than 2.5 million stars and galaxies looking for tell-tale signs of intelligence. In particular, they looked for super-fast pulses of light emitted at regular intervals, that would be produced by massively powerful lasers. The pulses might be being used to communicate between civilizations or (more likely) to push spacecraft along at incredible speeds. We have several lasers of this type here on Earth, and we're looking at using them for this very purpose.

Interestingly, 234 of the stars they analyzed *were* found to be producing this type of signal.[13-18] The astronomers are now carrying out follow-up observations and analyses, trying to discover whether they're being produced by extraterrestrial civilizations.

13.4 Have aliens given us advanced technology?

According to many researchers, and former government contractors who claim to have worked alongside aliens, yes, they absolutely have.

But it wasn't just advanced technology, it was also *really basic* technology. You might recall from earlier chapters that we spent more than 250,000 years living as fairly primitive hunter-gatherers – Stone Age cavemen. Apart from the occasional extinction event, things were pretty stable technology-wise.

> Given our brain power, it seems incredible that we didn't figure out some things for ourselves. As I mentioned earlier, we may have been deliberately held back or handicapped.

And then something changed, and we started to make progress. Our progress became more and more rapid, and it's hardly stopped ever since. So, what changed? I'd suggest it was almost certainly an alien race giving us a jump start.

This may have taken two forms. First, they must have removed whatever was limiting our brainpower, and second, they must have taught us how to do a few basic things. With our brains now running on full power, a few simple lessons may have been all that we needed. Over the next few thousand years, we made astounding progress.

But I believe the same alien race has given us a few more jump starts since then. Each time we demonstrate that we have the capability to progress, they seem to show us something new that we wouldn't have come up with on our own. Understanding that technology and building our own version of it takes us further forward and enhances our skills even more. And that gives us the capability to understand and build the next thing they show us. There's no question that our technology has advanced thousands of times faster than it would have done if we'd been left to discover everything for ourselves.

But we've undoubtedly also worked out how to create some of these technologies for ourselves. For example, there are numerous reports that we've examined and reverse-engineered crashed extraterrestrial spacecraft. We'll see some of the technologies that resulted from that in a moment.

Those who claim to have worked with extraterrestrials say they'd share even more of their technologies with us if we were less violent and less likely to use it to develop new weapons.

Naturally, they refuse to share with us anything that would allow us to beat them in a war – or even come close to doing so.

13.5 What technologies have the aliens shared with us?

The following technologies are reported to have been developed or discovered as a result of information given to us by extraterrestrials:[13-19]

- The Global Positioning Satellite System (GPS/Sat Nav)

- Medical scanners, including CT and MRI

- Titanium

- Moscovium – chemical element 115 (apparently used in UFO propulsion)

- Memory metal

- Kevlar

- Bullet-proof vests

- Remote control systems

- Holographic displays and touchscreens

- Nano technology

Many believe the following technologies also have extraterrestrial origins:[13-20]

- Heart pacemaker

- Communications satellites

- Cordless power tools

- Computer mouse (unlikely in my opinion)

- Charged-couple device (the light-sensitive arrays used in digital cameras)

- As I mentioned in Chapter 11, during World War II, the Germans reportedly built an anti-gravity device based on a rotating high-voltage magnetic field. Some reports say they learned how to build it by studying two extraterrestrial craft that crashed in the Black Forest in 1936 and 1938.

- The transistor is reported to have been developed as a result of studying an alien craft that crashed in Cape Girardeau, Missouri, USA in 1941.

> It seems unlikely that the extraterrestrials would have used transistors in their spacecraft. They're much more likely to have used an advanced form of quantum microprocessor. The engineers who studied it ...

> ... wouldn't have had a clue what they were seeing or how it worked. A more realistic explanation would be that one of the extraterrestrials explained the principle of how transistors work.

The following technologies are said to have been developed as a result of studying three extraterrestrial spacecraft that crashed near Roswell, New Mexico, USA in 1947:[13-21a]

- Microprocessors and integrated circuits

- Fiber optics

- Lasers

- Particle accelerators and particle beam weapons

- Microwaves

- Night vision systems

- Stealth technology

- Cloaking technology

- Unmanned aerial combat vehicles (drones)

- The US Space Shuttle

- The US Strategic Defense Initiative ("Star Wars")[13-22] (now Solar Warden)

Many historians hypothesize that extraterrestrials must have had a hand in building the numerous pyramids around the world. Some of them also believe that the largest pyramids could only have been built with the assistance of an anti-gravity device. Even if they didn't actually help us build them, the aliens might have designed them and given us detailed instructions. They undoubtedly also told us about the special benefits and powers they would bring. As well as the traditional four-sided pointed pyramids, there are distinctive stepped and flat-topped pyramids all over the world, from Mexico to China. The ancient people who built them all followed a similar set of designs. There's some evidence that these civilizations were in contact with each other – although some historians still doubt it.[13-23] But we don't know why they all felt the need to build their pyramids in this specific style. Perhaps they were common on our home planet, and the details were stored in our genetic memory.

13.6 Suppressed technologies

The following technologies are reported to have been suppressed:
[13-24][13-25][13-26][13-27]

- Pyramids are reported to have remarkable regenerative powers, as well as the ability to generate free energy. If that's the case, you have to wonder why we aren't still building them today. Well, as we saw earlier, if there's any truth in it then it's probably being suppressed by the global authorities. Why give everyone free energy if people are willing to pay for it? There's money to be made!

- Another technology that's reportedly been suppressed is electrogravitics.[13-28][13-29a] This is the ability to generate a localized gravity that's independent of the Earth's gravity. It's extremely useful for things like space travel. We know it was being developed at Wright Patterson Air Force Base in the USA in the 1950s. Some of the information on it was even declassified. But details of any further development have been withdrawn from the public domain.

- Space travel has also been suppressed. As we saw earlier in the book, we've reportedly developed craft that can go a lot faster and a lot further than most people realize. Contractors and former employees who worked on them have confirmed they exist, and they say the Secret Space Program has been using them for decades. The TR-3 black triangles we looked at in Chapter 11 are an example of this type of suppressed technology.

> The last official manned mission to the Moon was in 1972. But contractors and former employees say we've been back several times since then. The "canceled" Apollo missions 18, 19 and 20 apparently went ahead, though later than originally planned, in July 1973, February 1976 and August 1976 respectively. Details of these missions remains suppressed. The official word is that they were canceled and never took place.

- Many people say the aliens would have given us the cure for cancer if they'd visited us. They cite this as evidence that we can't have been visited. Sadly, it's been reported that the aliens *have* given us the cure. But it's another technology that's been suppressed. Pharmaceutical companies and medical researchers make a lot more money from treating diseases than from curing them. The pharmaceutical companies, in particular, are enormously wealthy. They can afford to make huge donations to political parties and key individuals, and employ hundreds of highly persuasive lobbyists to make sure things stay that way.

- Several free-energy systems (also known as over unity generators) have reportedly been developed. These too were quickly suppressed by the authorities, this time to protect the interests of the power companies. The same thing applies here as it did for the pyramids: people are willing to pay for their energy, so let's take their money!

Evidently, plenty of politicians and their family members sit on the boards of power companies. There have even been cases where people have been sued by the government for going "off-grid" and generating their own power.[13-28a] That says it all.

- We've also reportedly developed working anti-gravity systems, stealth technology, cloaking shields, and both hot and cold nuclear fusion (clean energy) systems that go way beyond anything that's been revealed to the public. All of these have apparently been suppressed as well.

13.7 Why the aliens share their technologies with us

Some researchers say the extraterrestrials are doing it to help us. Others say there's no such thing as a free lunch and we'll end up paying for it in the end. Here are the most common opinions:

- They're doing it willingly, for altruistic purposes. They want to nurture us, and to wean us off nuclear power, coal and oil which damage the environment. They want to help us improve our health care and balance the wealth more evenly, so there's no longer such a thing as rich countries and poor countries. They see us suffering from diseases and other issues that they eradicated centuries ago. And they see no harm in lending a helping hand.

- It's to their advantage. Some technologies may help them as much as they help us. We've already seen that the Global Positioning System (GPS) has eliminated UFO crashes. Some people believe they might be recruiting us as allies in an upcoming battle against one or more of their rival races. They need us to have competent vehicles, weapons and training. Or they might be using us as a deterrent: their rivals won't attack them because the fury of the Earth would be unleashed upon them and they'd be destroyed.

   We used a similar tactic ourselves during the Cold War. This was the principle of mutually assured destruction, where the nuclear powers built ever more powerful, fully autonomous weapons that would destroy whichever country attacked them, even if there was no one left alive to launch them. Fortunately, this principle works: no one ever attacked and the weapons were never used. Interestingly, both the Greys and the Nordics may be helping us to improve our technology for precisely this reason. Although they're generally benevolent towards us, the two races are reported to hate each other. As we saw earlier, they've engaged in several battles in our skies. Presumably, they've fought many other battles elsewhere too.

- It's a form of trade. An alien race (almost certainly the Tall Whites) is understood to have signed a deal (the Grenada Treaty) with the American Government in 1954. (See Chapter 3.) The treaty allowed the aliens to establish bases on Earth and temporarily abduct people for non-lethal examination and experimentation. In exchange, the aliens agreed to give us access to some of their technology and work with our scientists and engineers to develop those technologies on Earth.

The aliens may have violated the treaty by abducting millions more people than was agreed. Or, more likely, another alien race (almost certainly the Greys) may have abducted them after we refused to sign a deal with them. We'll look at the possible reasons for this later in the chapter.

- They aren't giving us the technologies willingly. These are the technologies we've developed ourselves after studying crashed extraterrestrial spacecraft. The extraterrestrials themselves may have played no part in it, and might even have objected to it.

The versions we've developed are probably rather primitive in comparison with theirs. But if we hadn't come across them on their craft, we might never have developed them at all.

13.8 How the aliens share their technologies with us

Our engineers usually work alongside the aliens to learn about their technology. Or they study and reverse-engineer a particular technology from a crashed alien spacecraft. Once they understand it sufficiently, they pass the information on to approved universities, scientists, contractors, and commercial companies (collectively known as "the Club") that work in industrial, military, aerospace and medical fields.

Representatives from those organizations may be approached by one or more of the engineers at a conference relating to a particular technology. Or the information might be leaked to selected individuals. Once it's in the hands of the scientists, researchers, engineers or academics at a government-approved institution, the information is generally patented and then licensed to approved commercial companies. The institution retains the patent.

The recipients of the technology may be unaware that it came from an extraterrestrial source. They're generally told it was acquired from another nation.[13-27a]

Even if the recipient knows of its true origins, they might not share that knowledge with their colleagues or employer, and the knowledge might be lost when they retire, or the patent is sold, or the company is acquired by another organization.

The US Government has a formal program called the Technology Transfer Program,[13-27b] which releases patents and allows smaller companies to license them. Many big-name American corporations are involved in this program, and they go on to develop and release technologies that were acquired from extraterrestrial sources. They also commercialize technologies that were developed as part of the space program.

A similar program, which seems to be concerned mainly with extraterrestrial electronics, is Project CARMA (Commercialization of Alien Resources for Market Assimilation).[13-29b]

Not everything that the companies develop from these technologies finds its way into commercial products though. A great deal of it remains classified for decades or is restricted to military use only.

According to researchers and witnesses,[13-29] the corporations include (or have included) such household names as:

- Apple
- AT&T
- Bell Laboratories
- Boeing
- Convair
- Curtiss-Wright

- Dow Chemicals
- DuPont
- Fairchild (now ON Semiconductor)
- Fairchild-Hiller Aircraft (now split into separate companies)
- General Electric
- IBM
- Intel
- Lear
- Lockheed Martin
- Mcdonnell Douglas (now owned by Boeing)
- Monsanto
- North American Aviation (now split into separate companies)
- Northrop Grumman
- Philips
- Raytheon
- Sandia National Laboratories
- Sikorsky
- Sperry-Rand (now Unisys and Honeywell)
- Union Carbide
- United Technologies

Plus several other major corporations and hundreds of smaller companies. Government agencies such as NASA and the various branches of the US Military, and especially the Air Force, have of course benefited enormously.

13.9 What technologies have we developed?

Since our extraterrestrial visitors have shown a strong dislike for our nuclear capabilities, it seems we must have developed this technology for ourselves. The extraterrestrials have shown themselves to be vehemently anti-nuclear. And they've made it clear during their meetings with senior government and military representatives that they don't approve of us having this technology.

Their craft have been seen near just about every nuclear facility in the world, whether it's concerned with nuclear power or nuclear weapons.

> The US Air Force is believed to have used this information to its advantage. There are reports that they deliberately placed nuclear weapons at one of their bases in Germany in order to lure extraterrestrials to the area. They then monitored the airspace above the facility with the intention of ambushing the aliens when they arrived. Whether or not they succeeded is unknown.

During the Cold War, extraterrestrials apparently disarmed or disabled nuclear weapons in the US and the UK on several occasions, and almost certainly in the Soviet Union too[13-30][13-31][13-32][13-33] Some researchers believe a nuclear war on Earth would be impossible because the extraterrestrials would prevent it from happening.

13.10 The Roswell UFO crash

You probably know a great deal about this incident already. We took a brief look at it earlier, and it's easy enough to find the information online, so I won't repeat it again here. But do take a look at the book I recommended: *The Day After Roswell* by Colonel Philip J. Corso (Retired). It contains a wealth of detail, it's a fascinating read, and at least some of it is unquestionably true. It might actually be one of the most important books ever written.

Almost immediately after the Roswell incident, the USA's National Security Act of 1947[13-34] was signed. It reorganized the US Military and established the Central Intelligence Agency (CIA), the National Security Council (NSC), and (allegedly) the secret Majestic 12 (MJ-12) committee.[13-35]

> Majestic 12's existence is still officially denied to this day. Many people believe it's a hoax. In my opinion, a committee of this sort *must* exist, but under a different name. It's likely that one of its policies is to change its name at frequent intervals. You can see this process in action below, where (basically) the same classified project used three different names in five years.

Project Sign[13-36] (succeeded by Project Grudge[13-37] in 1949 and Project Blue Book[13-38] in 1952) was also established shortly after the Roswell incident. Its purpose was to "investigate" reports of UFO sightings. Project Sign remained secret until 1956 – the disclosure of its existence may have been unintentional.

These three projects concluded that virtually all sightings could be explained by other phenomena. These included:

- unusual cloud formations
- swamp gas
- ball lightning
- weather balloons
- conventional aircraft
- classified experimental aircraft
- misidentified stars and planets
- paper lanterns
- fireworks

Humans Are Not From Earth

- pranks
- fakes
- hallucinations
- optical illusions
- unreliable witnesses
- and so on

The few that couldn't be explained may have been actual extraterrestrial craft, but the investigators said there was insufficient data to determine their origin.

Project Blue Book officially ceased operations in 1970. The existence of any successor projects is denied (but they almost certainly exist).

13.11 Why do the extraterrestrials abduct people?

There are all sorts of reasons why the aliens might want to abduct us.[13-39][13-40][13-41][13-42][13-43][13-44] Some of the reasons are fairly benign while others are downright scary. If you're of a nervous disposition, you might want to skip this section.

Abductions that are carried out under the auspices of the Grenada Treaty are always benign. The aliens are simply monitoring our development, taking DNA samples, carrying out intelligence and psychological tests, and so on. These are the same sorts of tests that we would carry out ourselves if we wanted to monitor a species' progress. The tests are harmless, and the abductees are released shortly afterward. Some researchers speculate that the aliens could be looking for – and possibly testing – a genetic cure for our inherent violence.

Sometimes a tiny device is implanted under the abductee's skin.[13-45] This is usually placed in their hand, foot or lower leg. It may allow them to be monitored or tracked remotely. There's some evidence that the implants may be intricately connected to the abductee's nervous system.

It's been suggested that the implants might have a secondary purpose. One day they could all be triggered, and the abductees will be compelled to gather together in one place. The reason for this, and whether there's any truth to it, is unknown.

One of the main reasons for monitoring us might be to ensure we don't become a threat to the wider galactic community.

The extraterrestrials are probably also looking at how well (or not) we've adapted to living on a planet that doesn't entirely suit us. They'll want to see how our bodies have adapted and changed since we were first brought here. That might be because they're considering living here themselves, and they might be thinking of taking over the planet.

They might also be looking for the best candidates for breeding programs in order to create hybrids. Many people, including some renowned scientists, believe this is the main reason behind most abductions. They believe the aliens are creating a hybrid race that will eventually take over the Earth – and in particular its mineral wealth – on the aliens' behalf. The hybrids will look like us but have the aliens' mental and psychic abilities. I don't subscribe to this theory myself; it sounds like a rehash of the Anunnaki myth we looked at in Chapter 5.

Some abductees have reported having eggs or sperm removed from them. Others say they were ordered to have sexual intercourse with other humans or aliens, or they were raped. Some female abductees have claimed they had a fetus implanted into them, and they were told they were pregnant. Many of them said they were then abducted again between nine and eleven weeks later and the fetus was removed.

Apparently, once they'd reached that stage, the fetuses could continue the rest of their development in synthetic wombs.[13-46]

Many abductees said they were asked to interact with hybrid children. They were asked to play games with them and teach them, in the same way that they would interact with human children. This seems to be a vital part of the hybrids' development. Human children have reportedly also been abducted for this purpose.

Now for the scary part. If you think you might have been abducted, or if you're connected to anyone who's gone missing, please skip ahead to the next section: *Are we the aliens?*

Some researchers believe that the reason for the millions of abductions that have occurred over the last few decades is that we're being harvested for food. Some of the reptilian races apparently regard us as no more than cattle. Unlike the more benign races, they don't attempt to make deals with our governments. They simply turn up in their spacecraft and pluck us up whenever they want to restock their meat lockers. It could happen to any of us at any time.

> As I mentioned earlier, the number of abductions has declined significantly in recent years. Hopefully, that means they've now found a better food supply somewhere else, and they'll leave us alone.

This could explain the many missing people – some of them well known – who have vanished without trace.[13-47]

The world's governments will, of course, be fully aware that this is going on, but they're powerless to stop it. Rather than scare us by revealing the truth, senior police officials are instructed to give an "opinion" that the missing people have probably been murdered and their bodies buried.

Sometimes they fund investigations to try to find the missing person or their "killer." When that produces no results, they might leave the case open indefinitely. But, even though it might take decades, they usually convict *someone* of murdering the missing person, even if their body is never found.

The person they convict will almost certainly be someone who's already been convicted of killing someone else. Often, the supposed killer will be in poor mental health, near death or already dead, so it's easy to pin an extra case on them, and they're in no position to object. They might even confess to it. At the very least, the police will raise the *suspicion* that they *might* have killed more people. That's generally enough in the public's eyes. In cases where the missing person's vehicle is found abandoned, the media is instructed to spread the word that the person had been "showing signs of depression" in recent days, and has "probably committed suicide." Either way, the case is "solved."

An online search for "famous unsolved missing person cases" will bring up plenty of results. They make fascinating reading.[13-48] Try reading between the lines, looking for signs that the truth has been covered up.

Since the aliens who carry out these unauthorized abductions didn't sign a deal with us, they don't give the government a list of who they've abducted or harvested. So the government has no more idea than the rest of us what really happened to the missing people. For all they know, they *could* have been murdered or committed suicide. Only after the police and intelligence services have conducted thousands of hours of investigation and come up with no evidence are they forced to consider the abduction/harvesting explanation. But of course, they never make that public.

> Most countries have a law that says a missing person can be declared dead after a given period without contact – typically seven years.

13.12 Are we the aliens?

Well, it's possible, but I think it's unlikely. We've already considered (and pretty much rejected) the possibility that one of the alien races could be humans from the future who've traveled back to our time. It could also be the case that the aliens who brought us here were the same species as us. That would make them humans too.

But how much have our genomes been modified to help us survive here? How much of our DNA has been spliced in from other alien species or from Earth's native hominins? Can we still be considered the same species as those who brought us here? You could argue it both ways.

In Chapter 3, we saw confirmed evidence of ancient settlements in places where they shouldn't have existed until thousands of years later. Some researchers believe they weren't built by *us*, as such, but by an advance party of aliens from our home planet. As they may have been the same species as us (or at least the same *base* species), the settlements appear to be human constructions. The aliens may have been testing the environment to see if it was possible to survive here long-term.

There's evidence that many of those settlements were abandoned abruptly, and the aliens (or their descendants) may have returned to their home planet *en masse*. The reason for this is unknown, but an erupting super-volcano would be a reasonable guess.

The aliens then returned to Earth thousands (or millions) of years later, and this time they brought a much larger group of people with them – perhaps as many as 20,000. Again, these people were members of their own species, but they might also have been us.

By this point, the aliens would have learned what it took to survive here. The people they brought with them may have been genetically modified versions of their own species.

As we saw earlier, they may have brought us here as prisoners, because of our excessive level of violence. We may have been brought here as embryos which had been identified as being predisposed to violence when they grew up. Or we might have been volunteers and their family members – some of us not yet born.

Of course, there's always the possibility that the aliens who left behind those early settlements and artifacts, and footprints alongside dinosaur tracks, were simply having a bit of fun. They may have been fully aware of the confusion they'd cause in the distant future. But exactly who they were, whether members of our own species, time travelers, or another alien race, we'll never know.

14

Conclusions

Well, here we are at the end of the book. What a ride! So, what have we learned?

- Our bodies are so poorly adapted to living on Earth that it's obvious we didn't evolve here. In comparison, Earth's native creatures are well adapted.

- We have features and traits that imply a continuous trail of evolution from lower forms of life. But the fact that we're so poorly adapted, and the missing link in our timeline, suggest otherwise. And the missing link isn't where most people think it is. It's the one that separates us from the Earth's hominins, not the one that separates the hominins from the apes.

- Life, DNA and evolution work in exactly the same way on other planets. They follow a universal formula and a set of optimal patterns.

- We probably evolved from lower forms of life on a different planet – our home planet. Life forms there almost certainly belong to the same classes that we find on Earth, and we would recognize most of them, though the individual species would be different. Even so, many of them might be (just about) biologically compatible with their Earthly equivalents.

- Living things are extremely complex. The probability that they evolved naturally even once is infinitesimally small. Such an occurrence would take far longer than the age of the universe. The probability that they evolved multiple times throughout the universe seems to be impossible.

- The fact that life appeared on Earth within just 200 million years of the planet forming suggests it must have been created by some form of intelligence.

- The theory of evolution might be completely wrong. Life forms might only evolve within their own species, not into other species.

- The first invertebrates appeared fully formed during the Cambrian era. There's no evidence that there was anything much before them.

- We might not be animals, but a higher form of life.

- We didn't evolve in Africa. We can find evidence of several much older human settlements elsewhere in the world.

- Extraterrestrials seem to have made numerous attempts to introduce us to Earth. Their early experiments millions of years ago failed. Their most recent ones just about succeeded.

- Our genome bears hundreds of scars from where it's been altered – probably in an attempt to help us survive here.

- Most of our genomes contain Neanderthal or Denisovan DNA, even though we didn't descend from them and they may have been biologically incompatible with us.

- We almost became extinct several times. Our numbers may have dwindled to just 600 at one point. The extraterrestrials may have brought more of us here from our home planet to restore our population to a viable size.

- We've since multiplied at an unsustainable rate, exceeding the size of population that the planet can sustain. We're acting like an infestation.

- But there are several reasons to think that our numbers might be about to reduce quite significantly.

- Our region of space is a gigantic void, remote and isolated from other galaxies.

- Most of the other civilizations in our galaxy, if they exist, will be much closer to the galactic center, around 27,000 light years away. It's unlikely they're even aware of us.

- At least two extraterrestrial factions seem to be closely involved with the Earth. One seems to want to hold back our progress while the other seems to want to drive it forward. The two factions are reported to be at war with each other, and witnesses have reported seeing their battles in our skies.

- The US Government probably signed a deal with one of those factions in 1954, but refused to deal with the other one because they wanted us to get rid of our nuclear capabilities.

- Governments are powerless against the aliens and can only respond with diplomacy and doing what's asked of them.

- Extraterrestrial cover-ups were probably instigated by the aliens themselves.

- Mainstream scientists are indoctrinated to follow a set pathway and ignore or refute all evidence to the contrary. Deviation from that pathway can end their careers.

14.1 Three theories in harmony

Throughout the book, we've discussed three major theories: the creation of the universe, the origins of life, and how we came to be on the Earth. All three theories sit perfectly well alongside each other.

Creation

This theory says that after the big bang, matter began clumping together, eventually forming dust clouds, stars, and planets. Some of those planets were just the right distance from their stars, they had water and an atmosphere, the chemistry was right, and lightning strikes caused amino acids to form. Some of those amino acids randomly stuck together to form protein chains. Occasionally, some of those chains turned out to have exactly the right information encoded in them that they could start catalyzing enzymes. The protein chains and enzymes continued to bump around in the water, sometimes randomly linking together. A few of them formed something that would work as a primitive life form, and they were fortunate when lipid bubbles formed around them, also trapping exactly the right chemicals they needed. Some of them had exactly the right enzymes they needed to turn the lipid bubbles into cell walls. Some of them were able to reproduce themselves. They were alive and began multiplying.

Alternatively:

Some form of universal intelligence triggered the big bang. It waited while matter clumped together and cooled down. On planets where the conditions were right and amino acids formed, it guided them to link together and form protein chains. It guided the protein chains to form strands of RNA, which began catalyzing enzymes. When protective lipid bubbles formed around them, it guided the primitive cells to turn the bubbles into cell walls, and they began reproducing.

Alternatively:

God placed the first primitive cells on Earth – and perhaps other planets. The cells were already fully formed and alive.

Alternatively:

None of this happened.

Evolution

The primitive cells evolved into single-celled organisms, complete with a variety of internal organelles. Some of them clumped together to form multicellular organisms. Over millions of years, in response to changing environmental conditions, they evolved from microscopic water-dwelling organisms all the way up the chain of evolution, culminating in the hominins.

Alternatively:

God – or some other form of universal intelligence – began populating the young planet with fully formed species, starting with primitive plants and invertebrates. Over millions of years, He created more advanced species and placed them on the planet too, ensuring they had all the resources they needed. He may have done this on many different planets. The species evolved into more advanced and diverse versions of themselves, but didn't evolve into different species.

Humans

We evolved from one of the species of hominin that evolved on Earth. There's a wealth of evidence to refute this, but it's the version of events that mainstream science sticks to.

Alternatively:

We evolved from one of the species of hominin that evolved on another planet. We were then brought to Earth, presumably by extraterrestrials. We don't know why. But we've explored several potential reasons in this book.

Alternatively:

We were created by God as a higher form of life above all other creatures, and we were placed on the Earth fully formed.

Other theories

There are plenty of other theories. For example, there's the one that says we might all be computer simulations. But then we have to consider who created the computer programmers and the universe they live in. It all comes back to creation and evolution in the end. Or maybe an intelligent designer or God.

14.2 Rejection by mainstream science

Mainstream scientists have made it clear that, in their opinion, there's only one path through these theories:

- the big bang

- galaxies, stars, and planets formed

- chemicals randomly clumped together to form amino acids when lightning struck

- protein chains formed

- they catalyzed enzymes and began reproducing

- evolution took over

- eventually leading to humans

As we've seen, few scientists will even consider the alternative theories. The main reasons are that they've been indoctrinated to refute them, and they fear the loss of their reputations and funding if they don't comply. But I wonder if some of them might also be afraid of the implications if any of the other theories turn out to be true.

We heard mainstream scientists say, "We can't test evidence that isn't physical." But when we present them with an abundance of evidence that's very much physical and comes from credible sources, they won't test that either. If you let them keep it, they'll lock it away so no one will ever see it again and they won't have to worry about it.

This presents us with something of a quandary. If no one is prepared to look at the evidence or carry out peer reviews on the theories, the mainstream science publications have the perfect excuse not to publish anything about them. So it all gets covered up.

Perhaps things will change one day, but I think it'll be a long time coming. Someone brave will have to make the first move. He or she will be labeled a crackpot, of course – just as all the great scientists once were.

14.3 Acceptance by the church

Interestingly, the Vatican issued a statement in May 2008 that said there was no conflict between believing in God and believing in extraterrestrials. God could very well have created them as well.

Or maybe it was science.

14.4 Final thoughts

I admit there were some holes, and even a few errors, in the first edition of this book. My aim was to share what I knew at the time, and to gather more evidence from readers. The response was incredible.

My aim in writing this edition was to fill all the holes, correct the errors, and include as much of the credible and valid evidence as I could. I'm sure you'll let me know whether I've succeeded.

Despite the harsh things I've said about mainstream scientists, I believe we're slowly starting to make progress. The amount of indisputable evidence is reaching a critical mass. The public is opening its eyes to the fact that other theories might have some merit. There will come a time when even the most blinkered of them has to accept that some of the things they've been told are "proven beyond doubt" ... might not be.

Ellis

x

15

References

Dead links? No problem!

All of the websites listed below were accessed shortly before going to press and were confirmed to be working. If you find that a link no longer works, you should still be able to view an archived copy. Just copy the link, go to www.archive.org and paste it in there. If there's a choice of dates when the item was indexed, I recommend selecting the earliest one.

In the unlikely event that there's no archived copy, other sites will usually have the same information. Use your favorite search engine to look for the main keywords from the page's title (for example: oldest human fossil).

Credibility of the sources

Where possible, I've only included links to sources that are credible, or where the information is available nowhere else. Some of the sources might seem less than credible at first glance, but they're included because they cite links to credible sources, amalgamate or simplify complex information, and often provide images too. I excluded sources that didn't cite other credible sources or weren't themselves an original, credible source – apart from a handful of exceptions where not citing a source would have been seen as a serious omission. These are mostly to be found in chapters 3 and 11.

The accuracy of the information in this book is very much dependent on the accuracy and reliability of these sources. In cases where the information isn't available elsewhere, and couldn't be independently verified, it is taken entirely on trust and used in good faith.

Chapter 2

[2-01]   The Telegraph (2 March 2017) Sarah Knapton
Oldest fossil ever found on Earth shows organisms thrived 4.2bn years ago – and provides strongest evidence yet for similar life on Mars
bit.ly/hanfe-2-01

[2-02]   Wikipedia (accessed 10 September 2017)
Nictitating membrane
bit.ly/hanfe-2-02

[2-03]   The Baltimore Sun (4 April 2015) Ian Duncan
A wrong turn at the NSA can bring trouble
bit.ly/hanfe-2-03

[2-04]   Norwich Evening News (9 January 2013) David Bale
Pilot who stepped into propeller may have been dazzled by sun
bit.ly/hanfe-2-04

[2-05]   AAA Exchange (accessed 10 September 2017)
Dangers of Driving Into Sun
bit.ly/hanfe-2-05

[2-06]   Ski Weekends (22 February 2013) Marianne Pang
Wear ski goggles to prevent snow blindness
bit.ly/hanfe-2-06

[2-07]   New Scientist (16 January 2013) Paul Marks
Blinded by sun? Let your steering wheel guide you
bit.ly/hanfe-2-07

[2-08]   Cracked (19 January 2016) Anonymous, Evan V. Symon
Your Purebred Is Inbred: 5 Realities Of Dog Breeding
bit.ly/hanfe-2-08

[2-09]   Wikipedia (accessed 10 September 2017)
Cataract
bit.ly/hanfe-2-09

[2-10]   Social Science & Medicine 1983;17(22):1693-702.
Cataract: the leading cause of blindness and vision loss in Africa
bit.ly/hanfe-2-10

[2-11]   Science Daily (31 January 2008) University of Copenhagen
Blue-eyed humans have a single, common ancestor
bit.ly/hanfe-2-11

[2-12]   WebMD (5 October 2000) Mike Fillon
The Dark Eyes Have It -- a Higher Risk of Cataracts, That Is
bit.ly/hanfe-2-12

[2-13]   Duke Health (27 August 2013)
Myth or fact: people with light eyes more sensitive to sunlight
bit.ly/hanfe-2-13

[2-14]   Nature (22 July 2015) Ling Zhao et al
Lanosterol reverses protein aggregation in cataracts
bit.ly/hanfe-2-14

[2-15]   The Guardian (30 May 2002) David Hambling
Let the light shine in
bit.ly/hanfe-2-15

[2-16]   BBC News website (22 May 2015) James Gallagher
Quarter of skin cells 'on road to cancer'
bit.ly/hanfe-2-16

[2-17]   IFLScience (27 May 2016) Elise Andrew
What Does Your Skin Look Like Under UV Light?
bit.ly/hanfe-2-17

[2-18]   BBC News website (27 July 2006)
Dark skin 'does not block cancer'
bit.ly/hanfe-2-18

[2-19]   Skin Cancer Foundation (2009) Maritza Perez
Ask the Expert: Can dark-skinned people get skin cancer?
bit.ly/hanfe-2-19

[2-20]   Wikipedia (accessed 10 September 2017)
Ultraviolet index
bit.ly/hanfe-2-20

[2-21]   Made for Mums (10 July 2017)
Sunscreen for kids – how often, how much to use and expiry dates
bit.ly/hanfe-2-21

[2-22]   The Guardian (16 April 2015) Anita Bhagwandas
Beauty for dark skin: a guide to wearing suncream
bit.ly/hanfe-2-22

[2-23]   Science (20 February 2015) Sanjay Premi et al
**Chemiexcitation of melanin derivatives induces DNA
photoproducts long after UV exposure**
bit.ly/hanfe-2-23

[2-24]   Gizmodo (20 February 2015) Jamie Condliffe
Sun Keeps Damaging Skin Cells For Hours After Exposure
bit.ly/hanfe-2-24

[2-25]   BBC News website (28 July 2016) James Gallagher
Cancer found in ancient human ancestor's foot
bit.ly/hanfe-2-25

[2-26]   News-Medical.net (12 November 2015) Yolanda Smith
Melanoma History
bit.ly/hanfe-2-26

[2-27]   Reuters (1 May 2012) Kate Kelland
Insight: Cancer in Africa: Fighting a nameless enemy
bit.ly/hanfe-2-27

[2-28]   Smithsonian National Museum of Natural History
(accessed 10 September 2017)
Modern Human Diversity – Skin Color
bit.ly/hanfe-2-28

[2-29]   Cancer Research UK (accessed 10 September 2017)
Skin cancer incidence statistics
bit.ly/hanfe-2-29

[2-30]   WhiterSkin (5 September 2009) Hessa
Black skin, white skin, Asian skin – what's the difference?
bit.ly/hanfe-2-30

[2-31]   Nature (8 October 2015) Ewen Callaway
How elephants avoid cancer
bit.ly/hanfe-2-31

[2-32]   The Straight Dope (14 April 2009)
various comments on message board
Do any other species get sunburn?
bit.ly/hanfe-2-32

[2-33]
International Journal of Pharmaceutics 2001 Mar 14;215(1-2):51-6
Schmook, Meingassner & Billich, Novartis Research Institute
Comparison of human skin or epidermis models with human and animal skin in in-vitro percutaneous absorption
bit.ly/hanfe-2-33

[2-34]   Science (9 November 2010) Virginia Morell
Whales Get Sunburns, Too
bit.ly/hanfe-2-34

[2-35]   Daily Mail (11 November 2010) Michael Hanlon
Why whales get sunburn, but pigs and hippos don't
bit.ly/hanfe-2-35

[2-36a] Earthables (29 August 2016 – via archive.org)
The Disturbing Reason Why You Should Never Swim With Dolphins, If You Love Them
bit.ly/hanfe-2-36a

[2-37] The New York Times (14 May 2012) C. Claiborne Ray
The Sun's Unrelenting Rays: Can animals get sunburn too?
bit.ly/hanfe-2-37

[2-38] World Health Organization (26 June 2017)
Who is most at risk of getting skin cancer?
bit.ly/hanfe-2-38

[2-39] Wikipedia (accessed 10 September 2017)
Vitamin D
bit.ly/hanfe-2-39

[2-40] Mercola (16 June 2011) Joseph Mercola
Sun Can Actually Help Protect You Against Skin Cancer
bit.ly/hanfe-2-40

[2-41] Canadian Centre for Occupational Health and Safety (22 June 2016) **Skin Cancer and Sunlight** (fact sheet)
bit.ly/hanfe-2-41

[2-42] Chris Kresser (11 July 2014) Chris Kresser
Does Avoiding The Sun Shorten Your Lifespan?
bit.ly/hanfe-2-42

[2-43]   Quora (26 January 2012) various comments
Do furry animals absorb vitamin D from sunlight?
bit.ly/hanfe-2-43

[2-44]   BBC News website (27 January 2014) Rebecca Morelle
Hunter-gatherer European had blue eyes and dark skin
bit.ly/hanfe-2-44

[2-45]
Abroad in the Yard (accessed 10 September 2017) John Worthington
20 physical traits you may have inherited from a Neanderthal
bit.ly/hanfe-2-45

[2-46]   The Lancet (10 Jun 2010) Roger Bouillon
Genetic and environmental determinants of vitamin D status
bit.ly/hanfe-2-46

[2-47]   Mercola (28 May 2014) Joseph Mercola
7 Signs You May Have a Vitamin D Deficiency
bit.ly/hanfe-2-47

[2-48]   Wellness Mama (11 June 2017) Katie Wells
Why I "Eat My Sunscreen" To Protect Skin from the Inside Out
bit.ly/hanfe-2-48

[2-49]   Environmental Contamination and Toxicology
February 2016, Volume 70, Issue 2, pp 265–288. C. A. Downs et al
**Toxicopathological Effects of the Sunscreen UV Filter,
Oxybenzone (Benzophenone-3), on Coral Planulae and Cultured
Primary Cells and Its Environmental Contamination in Hawaii
and the U.S. Virgin Islands**
bit.ly/hanfe-2-49

[2-50]   Independent (17 February 2013) Steve Connor
Why humans lost their body hair: to stop their brains from overheating as we evolved
bit.ly/hanfe-2-50

[2-51]   The Guardian (7 August 2012) Emily Gibson
Pubic hair has a job to do – stop shaving and leave it alone
bit.ly/hanfe-2-51

[2-52]   Wikipedia (accessed 10 September 2017)
Quaternary glaciation
bit.ly/hanfe-2-52

[2-53]
Oxford Academic (7 September 2010) Toups, Kitchen, Light & Reed
Origin of Clothing Lice Indicates Early Clothing Use by Anatomically Modern Humans in Africa
bit.ly/hanfe-2-53

[2-54]   All About Wildlife (2 November 2009) Paul Guernsey
Endangered Species Population Numbers
bit.ly/hanfe-2-54

[2-55]   Journal of Anthropological Archaeology
Volume 44, Part B, December 2016, Pages 235-246
Collard, Tarle, Sandgathe & Allan
Faunal evidence for a difference in clothing use between Neanderthals and early modern humans in Europe
bit.ly/hanfe-2-55

[2-56]   Popular Science (9 August 2016) Meaghan Lee Callaghan
Neanderthals' Clothing Could Have Killed Them
bit.ly/hanfe-2-56

[2-57]   NASA (22 July 2004) Shelley Canright, Brian Dunbar
Seasons on Other Planets
bit.ly/hanfe-2-57

[2-58]   Universe Today (3 June 2008) Jerry Coffey
Does Mars Have Seasons?
bit.ly/hanfe-2-58

[2-59]   NHS Choices (31 March 2017)
10 Winter Illnesses
bit.ly/hanfe-2-59

[2-60]   Graphiq (20 January 2016) Sabrina Perry
9 Worst Winter Illnesses
bit.ly/hanfe-2-60

[2-61]   Scientific American (25 April 2014) Sheena Faherty
Can Humans Hibernate? Ask the Dwarf Lemur
bit.ly/hanfe-2-61

[2-62]   9 News (22 April 2014) Erin Tennant
Hawaiian plane stowaway 'fell into hibernation'
bit.ly/hanfe-2-62

[2-63]   Scientific American (23 July 2010) Katherine Harmon
How Does a Heat Wave Affect the Human Body?
bit.ly/hanfe-2-63

[2-64]   Slumberwise (10 June 2013) K. Alexander
Siesta: The Little Nap with a Big History
bit.ly/hanfe-2-64

[2-65]   BBC News website (14 May 2009) Leon Mann
What makes Usain Bolt tick?
bit.ly/hanfe-2-65

[2-66]   BBC News website (5 July 2017) Beth Rose
Hidden disabilities: Pain beneath the surface
bit.ly/hanfe-2-66

[2-66a] Daily Express (15 July 2016) Katrina Turrill
First signs of Alzheimer's disease can be spotted in children as young as three years old
bit.ly/hanfe-2-66a

[2-67]   Arthritis Care (accessed 10 September 2017)
My child has arthritis
bit.ly/hanfe-2-67

[2-67a]
Answers in Genesis (27 May 2010) Georgia Purdom & David Menton
Did People Like Adam and Noah Really Live Over 900 Years?
bit.ly/hanfe-2-67a

[2-68]   Answers in Genesis (16 July 2010) Bodie Hodge
Why Did People Start to Have Shorter Lives After the Flood?
bit.ly/hanfe-2-68

[2-69]   The Bible Study Site (accessed 10 September 2017)
Why did man live longer before the flood?
bit.ly/hanfe-2-69

[2-70]   BBC News website (8 March 2017) Helen Briggs
Neanderthals 'self-medicated' for pain
bit.ly/hanfe-2-70

[2-71]   Max Planck Society (7 June 2017) Jean-Jacques Hublin et al
**The first of our kind: Scientists discover the oldest *Homo sapiens*
fossils at Jebel Irhoud, Morocco**
bit.ly/hanfe-2-71

[2-71a] BBC News website (2 August 2017) James Gallagher
Human embryos edited to stop disease
bit.ly/hanfe-2-71a

[2-72]   BBC News website (29 January 2014) Paul Rincon
Neanderthals gave us disease genes
bit.ly/hanfe-2-72

[2-73]   Live Science (25 August 2011) Charles Q. Choi
Sex with Neanderthals Gave Humans Immunity Boost
bit.ly/hanfe-2-73

[2-74]   New Scientist (15 June 2011) Michael Marshall
Breeding with Neanderthals helped humans go global
bit.ly/hanfe-2-74

[2-75]   Independent (11 April 2016) Andrew Griffin
Neanderthals might have contracted diseases from early humans that helped make them extinct, scientists say
bit.ly/hanfe-2-75

[2-76]
Medical Hypotheses Volume 75, Issue 1, July 2010, Pages 99-105
Horst Wolff & Alex D.Greenwood
Did viral disease of humans wipe out the Neanderthals?
bit.ly/hanfe-2-76

[2-77]   The Guardian (2 June 2013) Robin McKie
Why did the Neanderthals die out?
bit.ly/hanfe-2-77

[2-78]   Celestial Healing (accessed 10 September 2017)
Akilah Mohammad El
How humans are not physically created to eat meat
bit.ly/hanfe-2-78

[2-79]   National Geographic (18 February 2005) Hillary Mayell
"Evolving to Eat Mush": How Meat Changed Our Bodies
bit.ly/hanfe-2-79

[2-80]   PETA (accessed 10 September 2017)
The Natural Human Diet
bit.ly/hanfe-2-80

[2-81]   BBC News website (6 January 2014) Jonathan Amos
Moroccan Stone Age hunters' rotten teeth
bit.ly/hanfe-2-81

[2-82]   Mail Online (16 February 2017) Stephen Matthews
If you want grandchildren, make sure you eat protein
bit.ly/hanfe-2-82

[2-83]   BBC News website (14 January 2014)
Paignton Zoo monkeys banned from eating bananas
bit.ly/hanfe-2-83

[2-84]   Popular Science (22 September 2016) Claire Maldarelli
Obesity Might Not Have Evolved To Protect Us From Starvation
bit.ly/hanfe-2-84

[2-85]   The Health Guide (24 August 2016) Simon Scott
Unhealthy Food Cravings Are a Sign of Mineral Deficiencies
bit.ly/hanfe-2-85

[2-86]   io9 (1 August 2012) Esther Inglis-Arkell
10 Foods You Crave – And Why You Crave Them
bit.ly/hanfe-2-86

[2-87]   WebMD (accessed 10 September 2017) Elaine Magee
The Facts About Food Cravings
bit.ly/hanfe-2-87

[2-88]   Wikipedia (accessed 10 September 2017)
Raw milk
bit.ly/hanfe-2-88

[2-89]   The Vegetarian Resource Group
(accessed 10 September 2017) Reed Mangels
Calcium in the Vegan Diet
bit.ly/hanfe-2-89

[2-90]   Care2 (accessed 10 September 2017) Becky Striepe
25 Vegan Sources for Calcium
bit.ly/hanfe-2-90

[2-91]
Proceedings of the Society for Experimental Biology and Medicine
1992 Jun;200(2):149-52
**Comparison of osteoporosis and calcium intake between Japan
and the United States**
bit.ly/hanfe-2-91

[2-92]   Wikipedia (accessed 10 September 2017)
Inuit Diet
bit.ly/hanfe-2-92

[2-93]   KidsHealth (October 2014) Rupal Christine Gupta
Tapeworm
bit.ly/hanfe-2-93

[2-94]   Pet Informed (accessed 10 September 2017)
Veterinary Advice Online – Taenia Tapeworm Life Cycle
bit.ly/hanfe-2-94

[2-95]   Wikipedia (accessed 10 September 2017)
Cestoda (a class of flatworms)
bit.ly/hanfe-2-95

[2-96]   Parasites in Humans (accessed 10 September 2017)
Parasites in Humans
bit.ly/hanfe-2-96

[2-97]   World Health Organization (accessed 10 September 2017)
Low back pain
bit.ly/hanfe-2-97

[2-98]   BBC News website (25 February 2014) Joe Miller
Is back, neck and muscle pain hurting the UK economy?
bit.ly/hanfe-2-98

[2-99]   Wikipedia (accessed 10 September 2017)
Australopithecus
bit.ly/hanfe-2-99

[2-100] Wikipedia (accessed 10 September 2017)
Sahelanthropus
bit.ly/hanfe-2-100

[2-101] IFLScience (6 October 2015) Josh Davis
Chimps Walk Bipedally In A Similar Way To Humans
bit.ly/hanfe-2-101

[2-102] IFLScience (6 October 2015) Elise Andrew
**Newly Discovered Human Ancestor's Feet And Hands Were
Strikingly Similar To Our Own**
bit.ly/hanfe-2-102

[2-103]
European Spine Journal 2008 Sep; 17(Suppl 2): 327–330
Jochen Weber & Carsten Matthias Pusch
The lumbar spine in Neanderthals shows natural kyphosis
bit.ly/hanfe-2-103

[2-104] Discover magazine (March 2016) Gemma Tarlach
20 Things You Didn't Know About ... Your Back
bit.ly/hanfe-2-104

[2-105] Wikipedia (accessed 10 September 2017)
Neanderthal anatomy
bit.ly/hanfe-2-105

[2-106] The Conversation (1 May 2014) Tim Hatton
Why did humans grow 4 inches in 100 years? It wasn't just diet
bit.ly/hanfe-2-106

[2-107] International Business Times (8 April 2015) Hannah Osborne
Netherlands: Tallest people on Earth getting taller due to natural selection
bit.ly/hanfe-2-107

[2-108] Wikipedia (accessed 10 September 2017)
List of tallest people
bit.ly/hanfe-2-108

[2-109] ResearchGate (October 2002)
Holmberg, Stiernström, Thelin & Svärdsudd
Musculoskeletal Symptoms among Farmers and Non-farmers: A Population-based Study
bit.ly/hanfe-2-109

[2-110]
American Journal of Industrial Medicine 2001 Dec;40(6):646-54
Risk factors for back pain among male farmers: analysis of Iowa Farm Family Health and Hazard Surveillance Study
bit.ly/hanfe-2-110

[2-111] Yahoo! Answers (accessed 10 September 2017)
various comments on message board
What are the advantages of bipedalism (walking upright)?
bit.ly/hanfe-2-111

[2-112] Neuroanthropology (26 July 2009) Greg Downey
Lose your shoes: Is barefoot better?
bit.ly/hanfe-2-112

[2-113] The Guardian (22 August 2013) Michael Crawley
Why barefoot isn't best for most runners
bit.ly/hanfe-2-113

[2-114] The Telegraph (13 February 2017) Henry Bodkin
Prescribe exercise not drugs for lower back pain, say US health chiefs
bit.ly/hanfe-2-114

[2-115] BBC One (29 September 2016)
The Doctor Who Gave Up Drugs
bit.ly/hanfe-2-115

[2-116] World Health Organization (accessed 10 September 2017)
Low back pain
bit.ly/hanfe-2-116

[2-117] NPR (8 June 2015) Michaeleen Doucleff
Lost Posture: Why Some Indigenous Cultures May Not Have Back Pain
bit.ly/hanfe-2-117

[2-118] The Telegraph (8 February 2001) Roger Highfield
Modern humans' dexterity drove out Neanderthals
bit.ly/hanfe-2-118

[2-119] Learning Mind (16 January 2012) Anna LeMind
Did humans come from another planet?
bit.ly/hanfe-2-119

[2-120] Discover magazine (March 1997) Rachel Preiser
Sleep and Snake Oil
bit.ly/hanfe-2-120

[2-121] IFLScience (10 April 2017) Alfredo Carpineti
Being A Night Owl Might Be Written In Your Genes
bit.ly/hanfe-2-121

[2-122] Quora (16 August 2013) various comments on message board
Is it a coincidence that human sleeping patterns are so tightly correlated with the length of a day?
bit.ly/hanfe-2-122

[2-123] The Atlantic (26 February 2015) Tom Chmielewski
Jet Lag Is Worse on Mars
bit.ly/hanfe-2-123

[2-124] Science Alert (13 November 2015) David Nield
Humans Can Sleep For Days When Living Alone Underground, Experiments Show
bit.ly/hanfe-2-124

[2-125] Wikipedia (accessed 10 September 2017)
Circadian rhythm
bit.ly/hanfe-2-125

[2-125a]   PubMed (accessed 27 August 2017) H. Helmuth
Body height, body mass and surface area of the Neanderthals
bit.ly/hanfe-2-125a

[2-126] Wikipedia (accessed 10 September 2017)
Night owl
bit.ly/hanfe-2-126

[2-127] The Telegraph (27 April 2007) Roger Highfield
Gene explains why people are night owls
bit.ly/hanfe-2-127

[2-128] Evolutionary Anthropology 24:225–237 (2015)
David R. Samson & Charles L. Nunn
Sleep Intensity and the Evolution of Human Cognition
bit.ly/hanfe-2-128

[2-129] How Sleep Works (accessed 10 September 2017)
Sleep Anthropology – Sleep In The Animal Kingdom
bit.ly/hanfe-2-129

[2-130] Max Planck Society (7 June 2017) Jean-Jacques Hublin et al
The first of our kind: Scientists discover the oldest *Homo sapiens* fossils at Jebel Irhoud, Morocco
bit.ly/hanfe-2-130

[2-131] Wikipedia (accessed 10 September 2017)
Ethiopia
bit.ly/hanfe-2-131

[2-132]
United Nations Development Programme (accessed 27 August 2017)
Selim Jahan et al
Human Development Report 2016
bit.ly/hanfe-2-132

[2-133] Exploding Kittens (accessed 10 September 2017)
The Kitty Convict Project (protecting indoor cats)
bit.ly/hanfe-2-133

[2-134] Animal Friends (accessed 10 September 2017)
What Happens to Stray Dogs?
bit.ly/hanfe-2-134

[2-135] Cracked (15 February 2010) Nathan Birch
6 Human Character Flaws (That Saved the Species) #2 Gossip
bit.ly/hanfe-2-135

[2-135a]   Nature Israel (accessed 27 August 2017)
Israeli animals
bit.ly/hanfe-2-135a

[2-136] BBC News website (25 July 2017) Pallab Ghosh
Sperm count drop 'could make humans extinct'
bit.ly/hanfe-2-136

[2-137] BBC News website (28 November 2016) Deborah Cohen
'No solid evidence' for IVF add-on success
bit.ly/hanfe-2-137

[2-138] The Economist (16 November 2013)
Thyme to touch: Children seem to be born with an innate distrust of plants
bit.ly/hanfe-2-138

[2-139] The Guardian (30 June 2013) Alice Roberts
Why must childbirth be such hard labour?
bit.ly/hanfe-2-139

[2-140] Harvard Gazette (23 March 2015) Peter Reuell
Hip correction: Study shows that wider does not equal less efficient locomotion
bit.ly/hanfe-2-140

[2-141] Futurity (14 April 2015) Kate Becker, Boston University
Wide hips aren't worse for getting around
bit.ly/hanfe-2-141

[2-142]
Bulletin of the World Health Organization, 1996, 74 (2): 209-216
J. T. Boerma, K. I. Weinstein, S. O. Rutstein & A. E. Sommerfelt
Data on birth weight in developing countries: can surveys help?
bit.ly/hanfe-2-142

[2-143] BBC News website (7 December 2016) Helen Briggs
Caesarean births 'affecting human evolution'
bit.ly/hanfe-2-143

[2-144] Worldpress.org (13 November 2011) Kat Russell
Childbirth in Developing Countries
bit.ly/hanfe-2-144

[2-144a]   Into the Wild (accessed 27 August 2017)
Chimpanzees
bit.ly/hanfe-2-144a

[2-144b]   Cracked (15 February 2010) Nathan Birch
6 Human Character Flaws (That Saved the Species)
bit.ly/hanfe-2-144b

[2-145] Forbes (7 June 2013) Parmy Olson
How The Human Face Might Look In 100,000 Years
bit.ly/hanfe-2-145

[2-146] Slate (27 September 2012) Forrest Wickman
**Is Giving Birth Easier for Other Animals? Dolphins have it easy,
but hyenas sure don't**
bit.ly/hanfe-2-146

[2-147] Live Science (18 May 2008) Charles Q. Choi
Causes of Morning Sickness Revealed
bit.ly/hanfe-2-147

[2-148] Wikipedia (accessed 10 September 2017)
Concealed ovulation
bit.ly/hanfe-2-148

[2-149] FSEM Human Animal (22 November 2009)
Loss of estrus: Evolution of Concealed Ovulation in Humans
bit.ly/hanfe-2-149

[2-150] Wikipedia (accessed 10 September 2017)
Gombe Chimpanzee War
bit.ly/hanfe-2-150

[2-151] The New York Times (6 July 1999) William J. Broad
Evidence Puts Dolphins In New Light, As Killers
bit.ly/hanfe-2-151

[2-152] Live Science (25 February 2009) Heather Whipps
The Evolution of Human Aggression
bit.ly/hanfe-2-152

[2-153] Gizmodo (22 October 2015) Maddie Stone
Did Our Hands Evolve to Throw Punches? One Biologist Thinks So
bit.ly/hanfe-2-153

[2-154] Military.com (1 March 2005) David L. Thomas II
Violence: Learned Behavior or Genetically Inherited?
bit.ly/hanfe-2-154

[2-155]
Journal of the Royal Society of Medicine 2003 May; 96(5): 211–214
Mariya Moosajee
Violence – a noxious cocktail of genes and the environment
bit.ly/hanfe-2-155

[2-156] IFLScience (26 February 2015) Elise Andrew
Stephen Hawking Claims Aggression Will Be Downfall of Human Race
bit.ly/hanfe-2-156

[2-157] Wikipedia (accessed 10 September 2017)
United Kingdom parliamentary expenses scandal
bit.ly/hanfe-2-157

[2-158] Scottish Beaver Trial (accessed 10 September 2017)
Do beavers cause damage to farmland and the wider countryside?
bit.ly/hanfe-2-158

[2-159] WikiAnswers (accessed 10 September 2017)
How did hunter-gatherers affect the environment in which they lived?
bit.ly/hanfe-2-159

[2-160] Swarthmore College Environmental Studies
(6 February 2003) T. Nguyen
Pre-Agricultural Human Environmental Impact
bit.ly/hanfe-2-160

[2-161] The Royal Society (8 February 2017)
Sean Tomlinson, Kingsley W. Dixon, Raphael K. Didham & S. Donald Bradshaw
Landscape context alters cost of living in honeybee metabolism and feeding
bit.ly/hanfe-2-161

[2-162] The Guardian (17 June 2015) Alison Benjamin
Why are bees important?
bit.ly/hanfe-2-162

[2-163]
Chem Volume 2, Issue 2, 9 February 2017, Pages 224-239
Svetlana A. Chechetka, Yue Yu, Masayoshi Tange & Eijiro Miyako
Materially Engineered Artificial Pollinators
bit.ly/hanfe-2-163

[2-164] The Independent (29 September 2015) Doug Bolton
Nasa discovers flowing water on Mars, but contamination fears put further investigation in doubt
bit.ly/hanfe-2-164

[2-165] European Space Agency (2 May 2016)
ExoMars Mission (2020) overview
bit.ly/hanfe-2-165

[2-166] IFLScience (28 June 2017) Kristy Hamilton
Strict Rules Around Contamination Hamper Exploration For Life Beyond Earth
bit.ly/hanfe-2-166

[2-167] Smithsonian National Museum of Natural History (accessed 10 September 2017)
Human Characteristics: Brains
bit.ly/hanfe-2-167

[2-169] Wikipedia (accessed 10 September 2017)
Orphan gene
bit.ly/hanfe-2-169

[2-170] The Atlantic (13 October 2015) Ed Yong
Searching for the Genes That Are Unique to Humans
bit.ly/hanfe-2-170

[2-171] Biology Stack Exchange (accessed 10 September 2017)
various comments on message board
**Do apes and humans share 99% of DNA or 99% of genes?
What is the difference?**
bit.ly/hanfe-2-171

[2-172]
International Business Times (14 December 2013) Philip Ross
**Oldest Human DNA Is 400,000 Years Old, But Why Do Scientists
Call Discovery 'Irritating?'**
bit.ly/hanfe-2-172

[2-173] Wikipedia (accessed 10 September 2017)
Cognitive dissonance
bit.ly/hanfe-2-173

[2-174]
The Tech Museum of Innovation (20 October 2010) Khameeka Kitt
Understanding genetics: blood types
bit.ly/hanfe-2-174

[2-175] NCT (accessed 10 September 2017)
Rhesus negative blood and pregnancy
bit.ly/hanfe-2-175

[2-176a]   Wikipedia (accessed 10 September 2017)
Aquatic ape hypothesis
bit.ly/hanfe-2-176a

[2-177] The Independent (8 May 2013) Benjamin Mee
Did humans come from the seas instead of the trees?
bit.ly/hanfe-2-177

[2-178] Breatheology (accessed 10 September 2017)
Your inner dolphin (the mammalian dive response)
bit.ly/hanfe-2-178

[2-178a]   Hack Spirit (5 August 2017)
A scientist reveals what being near the ocean actually does to your brain
bit.ly/hanfe-2-178a

[2-179] Smithsonian (16 April 2012) Erin Wayman
A New Aquatic Ape Theory
bit.ly/hanfe-2-179

[2-180]
The University of Texas at Austin (accessed 10 September 2017)
The human evolutionary timeline
(image courtesy of Pearson Education, Inc.)
Note that this image shows that *Homo erectus* became extinct before *Homo sapiens* appeared, making evolution from *H. erectus* impossible. But there are no other species we could have evolved from. Other sites dispute these dates.
bit.ly/hanfe-2-180

[2-181] Exploratorium (accessed 10 September 2017)
Tracing Fossil Finds : A Hominid Timeline
This series of photos of hominin skulls shows that humans look nothing like their supposed ancestors and relatives.
bit.ly/hanfe-2-181

[2-182] interestscientific (25 December 2015)
Simple Human Evolution Timeline
It's interesting to note that this site gives the Neanderthals the latin name *Homo sapiens neanderthalis* rather than the more usual *Homo neanderthalis*. The image of the skull – particularly the face and jaw – looks nothing like ours though.
bit.ly/hanfe-2-182

[2-183] BBC (4 February 2016) Melissa Hogenboom
Chins are a bit useless, so why do we have them?
bit.ly/hanfe-2-183

[2-184] Wikipedia (accessed 10 September 2017)
Baculum (penis bone)
bit.ly/hanfe-2-184

[2-185] IFLScience (6 April 2016) Elise Andrew
The Human Penis Is A Puzzler, No Bones About It
bit.ly/hanfe-2-185

[2-186] The Royal Society (14 December 2016)
Matilda Brindle & Christopher Opie
Postcopulatory sexual selection influences baculum evolution in primates and carnivores
bit.ly/hanfe-2-186

[2-187a]   Cracked (15 January 2017) Dibyajyoti Lahiri
5 Ways Evolution Designed Your Body To Be Awesome At Sex, #2 We Might Have Become Monogamous To Avoid STDs
bit.ly/hanfe-2-187a

[2-188] Cracked (15 January 2017) Dibyajyoti Lahiri
**5 Ways Evolution Designed Your Body To Be Awesome At Sex,
#1. We Lost Our Penis Bones In Order To Have Sex In Different
Positions**
bit.ly/hanfe-2-188

[2-189] Sex Positions Club (accessed 10 September 2017)
More than 245 different sex positions
bit.ly/hanfe-2-189

[2-190] Physics Forums (18 August 2007)
various comments on message board
**Are humans the only species that has the troublesome prostate-
urethra relation?**
bit.ly/hanfe-2-190

[2-191]
Johns Hopkins Medicine: Prostate Cancer Update (Winter 2000)
Angelo De Marzo & Don Coffey
Evolution and Prostate Cancer
bit.ly/hanfe-2-191

[2-192] BBC News website (11 April 2016)
Gender identity clinic for young people sees referrals double
bit.ly/hanfe-2-192

[2-193] BBC News website (18 September 2016)
'I'm a non-binary 10-year-old'
bit.ly/hanfe-2-193

[2-194] Sky News (23 April 2016)
Student 'Comes Out' As Non-Binary To Obama
bit.ly/hanfe-2-194

[2-195] Cracked (11 June 2016) Amanda Mannen
I'm Neither Male Nor Female: Growing Up Intersex
bit.ly/hanfe-2-195

[2-196] National Geographic (22 September 2013) Liz Langley
7 Gender-Altering Animals
bit.ly/hanfe-2-196

[2-197] Wikipedia (accessed 10 September 2017)
Pansexuality
bit.ly/hanfe-2-197

[2-198] BBC News website (13 July 2017)
Tube to change 'ladies and gentlemen' announcements
bit.ly/hanfe-2-198

[2-199] Sky News (23 May 2017) Russell Hope
Missing link may have been European, not African, ancient fossils suggest
bit.ly/hanfe-2-199

[2-201] Wikipedia (accessed 10 September 2017)
Piltdown Man
bit.ly/hanfe-2-201

[2-202] New Scientist (24 March 2010) Rowan Hooper
Animals do not commit suicide
bit.ly/hanfe-2-202

[2-203] Live Science (29 March 2012) Katharine Gammon
Can Animals Commit Suicide?
bit.ly/hanfe-2-203

[2-204] NBC News (11 June 2013) Gillian Spear & Tracy Connor
**Do Legos need anger management? Figurines grumpier than
ever, study says**
bit.ly/hanfe-2-204

[2-205] Wikipedia (accessed 10 September 2017)
Self-destructive behavior
bit.ly/hanfe-2-205

[2-206] Lonerwolf (accessed 10 September 2017) Aletheia Luna
17 Habits Of The Self-destructive Person
bit.ly/hanfe-2-206

[2-207] ResearchGate (accessed 10 September 2017) Havi Carel
**Born to be Bad: Is Freud's Death Drive the Source of Human
Evilness?**
bit.ly/hanfe-2-207

[2-208] Quora (accessed 10 September 2017)
various comments on message board
**Why do humans (as opposed to other animals) believe in god(s)
and practice religious worship?**
bit.ly/hanfe-2-208

[2-209] Ask MetaFilter (2 January 2006)
various comments on message board
Why do we worship 'higher' beings?
bit.ly/hanfe-2-209

[2-210] EurekaAlert (26 October 2015) David Orenstein
Capacity to regenerate body parts may be the primitive state for all 4-legged vertebrates
bit.ly/hanfe-2-210

[2-211] New World Encyclopedia (accessed 10 September 2017)
Bushmen
bit.ly/hanfe-2-211

[2-212] Clean Clothes (accessed 10 September 2017)
Lina Stotz & Gillian Kane
Facts on The Global Garment Industry
bit.ly/hanfe-2-212

[2-212a]   My Best Contacts (24 July 2014) Heather Creekmore
Who in the World has the Worst Vision Problems?
bit.ly/hanfe-2-212a

[2-213] Science of Aging (accessed 10 September 2017)
Mortality Increases Exponentially with Age
bit.ly/hanfe-2-213

[2-214] The Straight Dope (accessed 10 September 2017)
various comments on message board
Natural human lifespan in the wild, without modern medicine
bit.ly/hanfe-2-214

[2-215] Biology Stack Exchange (accessed 10 September 2017)
various comments on message board
Is there any evidence of increased life expectancy for animal species?
bit.ly/hanfe-2-215

[2-216] Time (29 August 2012) Maia Szalavitz
Want to Live Longer? Don't Try Caloric Restriction
bit.ly/hanfe-2-216

[2-217] Wikipedia (accessed 10 September 2017)
Menopause
bit.ly/hanfe-2-217

[2-218] Popular Science (12 January 2017) Rachel Feltman
To understand the evolution of menopause, just look at family drama – in killer whales
bit.ly/hanfe-2-218

[2-219] io9 (7 February 2014) George Dvorsky
The Most Unfortunate Design Flaws in the Human Body
bit.ly/hanfe-2-219

[2-220a]   Encyclopedia.com (accessed 10 September 2017)
Choking
bit.ly/hanfe-2-220a

[2-221a]   BBC News website (14 January 2002)
Choking
bit.ly/hanfe-2-221a

[2-222a]   Wikipedia (accessed 10 September 2017)
Indigenous Australians
bit.ly/hanfe-2-222a

[2-223a]   Wikipedia (accessed 10 September 2017)
Polynesia
bit.ly/hanfe-2-223a

[2-224a]   Wikipedia (accessed 10 September 2017)
Melanesia
bit.ly/hanfe-2-224a

[2-225a]   BBC News website (14 October 2015) Paul Rincon
Fossil teeth place humans in Asia '20,000 years early'
bit.ly/hanfe-2-225a

Chapter 3

[3-01]   Ancient Code (accessed 10 September 2017)
Iron cup discovered inside a piece of Coal that is 300 million years old
bit.ly/hanfe-3-01

[3-02]   Ancient Code (accessed 10 September 2017)
300 Million-year-old piece of ancient vehicle found in Russia
bit.ly/hanfe-3-02

[3-03]   Wikipedia (accessed 10 September 2017)
Ica stones
bit.ly/hanfe-3-03

[3-04]   Wikipedia (accessed 10 September 2017)
Hueyatlaco
bit.ly/hanfe-3-04

[3-05]   Wikipedia (accessed 10 September 2017)
Serra da Capivara National Park
bit.ly/hanfe-3-05

[3-06] The New York Times (27 March 2014) Simon Romero
Discoveries Challenge Beliefs on Humans' Arrival in Americas
bit.ly/hanfe-3-06

[3-07] Ancient Code (accessed 10 September 2017)
The Enigmalith: A 100,000 year old electrical component found embedded in stone
bit.ly/hanfe-3-07

[3-08] The Epoch Times (30 March 2009) Leonardo Vintini
The Williams Enigmalith
bit.ly/hanfe-3-08

[3-09] ABQ Techzonics (accessed 10 September 2017)
John J. Williams
Weird, Strange, Unusual, Religious, Fortean, Collectibles
(scroll down for the entry on the Williams Enigmalith, written by the man who found it)
bit.ly/hanfe-3-09

[3-10] Wikipedia (accessed 10 September 2017)
Antikythera mechanism
bit.ly/hanfe-3-10

[3-11] IFLScience (28 November 2014) Stephen Luntz
Ancient Computer Even More Ancient Than We Thought
bit.ly/hanfe-3-11

[3-12] IFLScience (13 June 2016) Tom Hale
A Decade Of Work Has Decoded This Ancient Greek Astronomy "Computer"
bit.ly/hanfe-3-12

[3-13]   Wikipedia (accessed 10 September 2017)
Voynich manuscript
bit.ly/hanfe-3-13

[3-14]   The Guardian (5 July 2017) Danuta Kean
Author of mysterious Voynich manuscript was Italian Jew, says scholar
bit.ly/hanfe-3-14

[3-15] New Scientist (3 February 2014) Lisa Grossman
Mexican plants could break code on gibberish manuscript
bit.ly/hanfe-3-15

[3-15a] IFLScience (12 September 2017) Rosie McCall
Researcher Claims To Have Deciphered The Mysterious Voynich Manuscript
bit.ly/hanfe-3-15a

[3-16]   Wikipedia (accessed 10 September 2017)
London Hammer
bit.ly/hanfe-3-16

[3-17]   Wikipedia (accessed 10 September 2017)
Coso artifact
bit.ly/hanfe-3-17

[3-18]   Ancient Code (accessed 10 September 2017 – via archive.org)
Evidence of Prehistoric Civilizations: 3 pieces of advanced ancient technology hundreds of millions of years old
bit.ly/hanfe-3-18

[3-19]   Disclose.tv (19 August 2015) Lukas Magnuson
14-million-years-old Vehicle Tracks Found In Turkey
bit.ly/hanfe-3-19

[3-20]   Ancient Code (accessed 10 September 2017) Ivan Petricevic
Geologist states: these traces were left by vehicles that belonged to an advanced ancient civilization 14 million years ago
bit.ly/hanfe-3-20

[3-21]   Ancient Code (accessed 10 September 2017)
An Ancient Map that challenges the entire 'official' history of Mankind
bit.ly/hanfe-3-21

[3-22]   Ancient Code (accessed 10 September 2017)
Six Ancient Maps that should not exist according to mainstream Scholars
bit.ly/hanfe-3-22

[3-23]   Collective Evolution (24 February 2015) Arjun Walia
500 Year Old Map Was Discovered That Shatters The "Official" History Of The Planet
bit.ly/hanfe-3-23

[3-24]   Ancient Code (accessed 10 September 2017)
The Buache Map: A Controversial ancient chart depicting Ice-Free Antarctica
bit.ly/hanfe-3-24

[3-25]   Ancient Code (accessed 10 September 2017)
9 Ancient maps that should not exist
bit.ly/hanfe-3-25

[3-26] Cartographic Images (accessed 10 September 2017)
Jim Siebold
King-Hamy world map
bit.ly/hanfe-3-26
See also: www.myoldmaps.com

[3-27] Ancient Code (accessed 10 September 2017)
The remains of a 200,000 year old advanced civilization found in Africa
bit.ly/hanfe-3-27

[3-28] Archaeology Online (29 April 2014) Tarini Carr
The Harappan Civilization
bit.ly/hanfe-3-28

[3-29] IFLScience (19 September 2016) Ben Taub
Was The Indus Valley Civilization Really A Non-Violent, Egalitarian Utopia?
bit.ly/hanfe-3-29

[3-30] Wikipedia (accessed 10 September 2017)
Tiwanaku
bit.ly/hanfe-3-30

[3-31] Ancient Code (accessed 10 September 2017)
Rewriting History: A Huge Million-Year-Old, Man-Made Underground Complex?
bit.ly/hanfe-3-31

[3-32] Ancient Wisdom (accessed 10 September 2017)
Sacsayhuaman
bit.ly/hanfe-3-32

[3-33] Ancient Code (accessed 10 September 2017) Ivan Petricevic
Ollantaytambo like you've never seen it before: 50 images
bit.ly/hanfe-3-33

[3-34] Gizmodo (24 November 2010) Brian Barrett
Watch Focused Sunlight Melt Steel, Rock, and Anything Else
bit.ly/hanfe-3-34

[3-35] Wikipedia (accessed 10 September 2017)
Gornaya Shoria megaliths
bit.ly/hanfe-3-35

[3-36] Ancient Code (accessed 10 September 2017)
Larger than Baalbek: Huge Megaliths found in Russia defy explanation
bit.ly/hanfe-3-36

[3-37] Wikipedia (accessed 10 September 2017)
Göbekli Tepe
bit.ly/hanfe-3-37

[3-38] Ancient Code (accessed 10 September 2017) Ivan Petricevic
Ancient stone carvings confirm comet impact in 11,000BC which gave rise to civilization
bit.ly/hanfe-3-38

[3-39] Geoarchaeology and Archaeomineralogy
Proceedings of the International Conference, 29-30 October 2008
Vjacheslav I. Manichev & Alexander G. Parkhomenko
Geological Aspect Of The Problem Of Dating The Great Egyptian Sphinx Construction
bit.ly/hanfe-3-39

[3-40]   Wikipedia (accessed 10 September 2017)
Orion correlation theory
bit.ly/hanfe-3-40

[3-41]   Wikipedia (accessed 10 September 2017)
Sphinx water erosion hypothesis
bit.ly/hanfe-3-41

[3-42]   Wikipedia (accessed 10 September 2017)
Destruction of cultural heritage by ISIL
bit.ly/hanfe-3-42

[3-43]   Ancient Code (accessed 10 September 2017)
5 History-changing facts mainstream scholars cannot explain
bit.ly/hanfe-3-43

[3-44]   Binary Research Institute (accessed 10 September 2017)
Walter Cruttenden et al
Various papers
bit.ly/hanfe-3-44

[3-45]   Wikipedia (accessed 10 September 2017)
Dogon people
bit.ly/hanfe-3-45

[3-46]   Philip Coppens (accessed 10 September 2017) Philip Coppens
Dogon shame
bit.ly/hanfe-3-46

[3-47]   Wikipedia (accessed 10 September 2017)
The Sirius Mystery
bit.ly/hanfe-3-47

[3-48]   Ancient Code (accessed 10 September 2017)
5 'Alien' skulls that science cannot explain
bit.ly/hanfe-3-48

[3-49]   Higher Perspective (17 January 2014 – via archive.org)
Sam Benson
The 13 Alien-Like Skulls Found in Mexico
bit.ly/hanfe-3-49

[3-50]   Sunday Express (31 December 2015) Jon Austin
Could bizarre skulls with 'non-human' DNA be proof of aliens on Earth?
bit.ly/hanfe-3-50

[3-51]   Ancient Code (accessed 10 September 2017) Ivan Petricevic
Were the Pharaohs of Ancient Egypt hybrid Aliens?
bit.ly/hanfe-3-51

[3-52]   Ancient Code (accessed 10 September 2017)
An Atomic Bomb went off on Earth 12000 years ago?
bit.ly/hanfe-3-52

[3-53]
Aramco World, September/October 1979, Volume 30, Number 5
John W. Olsen & James R. Underwood
Desert Glass – An Enigma
bit.ly/hanfe-3-53

[3-54]   Wikipedia (accessed 10 September 2017)
Libyan desert glass
bit.ly/hanfe-3-54

[3-55]   Nexus Magazine, Volume 7, Number 5 (August-September 2000 – via archive.org) David Hatcher Childress
The Evidence for Ancient Atomic Warfare
bit.ly/hanfe-3-55

[3-56]   University of the Witwatersrand Johannesburg (9 October 2013 – via archive.org)
Jan Kramers, David Block & Marco Andreoli
First ever evidence of a comet striking Earth
bit.ly/hanfe-3-56

[3-57]   Wikipedia (accessed 10 September 2017)
Sahara
bit.ly/hanfe-3-57

[3-58]   The Register (9 November 2011) Lewis Page
Lost cities found beneath sands of Sahara by satellites
bit.ly/hanfe-3-58

[3-59]   IFLScience (15 March 2017) Tom Hale
Did Ancient Humans Help Create The Sahara Desert?
bit.ly/hanfe-3-59

[3-60]   Prezi (6 June 2016) Lali Wilde
The Rhetoric of US Presidents on UFOs
bit.ly/hanfe-3-60

[3-61]   Daily Express (9 March 2016) Jon Austin
What really happened when Hillary and Bill Clinton tried to open UFO truths 21 years ago?
bit.ly/hanfe-3-61

[3-62]   Sunday Express (6 March 2017) Jon Austin
UFO Cover up: George W. Bush pressed about top-secret alien disclosure files
bit.ly/hanfe-3-62

[3-63]   American University, Washington DC (28 January 2004) Michael E. Salla
Eisenhower's 1954 Meeting With Extraterrestrials: The Fiftieth Anniversary of First Contact?
bit.ly/hanfe-3-63

[3-64]   Before It's News (24 February 2014)
President Eisenhower Had 3 Secret Meetings w/ aliens in 1954 including the Anunnaki former Pentagon consultant & Military deep insiders claim
(Not a credible site but it corroborates the other sources and gives additional information.)
bit.ly/hanfe-3-64

[3-65]   Mail Online (15 February 2012) Anthony Bond
President Eisenhower had three secret meetings with aliens, former Pentagon consultant claims
bit.ly/hanfe-3-65

[3-66] Biblioteca Pleyades (accessed 10 September 2017)
Eisenhowers's 1954 meeting with extraterrestrials
bit.ly/hanfe-3-66

[3-67]   UFO Digest (accessed 10 September 2017) Ian Brockwell
Churchill UFO cover-up supports Eisenhower's alleged meeting with Aliens
bit.ly/hanfe-3-67

[3-68]   Sunday Express (17 August 2016) Jon Austin
Is 'unidentified mystery man' in White House snap an alien stood behind JFK?
bit.ly/hanfe-3-68

[3-68a] The Epoch Times (17 May 2014) Tara MacIsaac
Did the US Government Make a Pact With Aliens to Get Technology?
bit.ly/hanfe-3-67a

[3-70]   YouTube (accessed 10 September 2017)
Medvedev talks about aliens on Earth
bit.ly/hanfe-3-70

[3-71]   Wikipedia (accessed 10 September 2017)
Paul Hellyer
bit.ly/hanfe-3-71

[3-72]   NASA (accessed 10 September 2017)
Communications Transcripts: Mercury Through Apollo
bit.ly/hanfe-3-72

[3-73]   Ronald Record (accessed 10 September 2017)
Ronald Joe Record
Ham radio transcripts from the Apollo 11 mission, 11 July 1969
(Some of these appear to be fabricated, but the same story is told by numerous radio operators.)
bit.ly/hanfe-3-73

[3-74]   About.com (23 August 2016) Billy Booth
Apollo 11 Tapes Lost
bit.ly/hanfe-3-74

[3-74a] Disclose.tv (accessed 10 September 2017)
NASA Erased 40 Rolls Of Film Of The Apollo Program
bit.ly/hanfe-3-74a

[3-75] The Object Report (18 March 2013)
Did Neil Armstrong Encounter an Alien Presence on the Moon?
bit.ly/hanfe-3-75

[3-76] YouTube (accessed 10 September 2017)
Lights in the Sky: Neil Armstrong on NASA's Parrots, and Truth's Protective Layers
bit.ly/hanfe-3-76

[3-77] Alien UFO Sightings (accessed 10 September 2017)
Buzz Aldrin: On the Moon we were ordered by aliens to move away
bit.ly/hanfe-3-77

[3-78] Wikipedia (accessed 10 September 2017)
Edgar Mitchell
bit.ly/hanfe-3-78

[3-79] Observer (25 August 2015) Robin Seemangal
Edgar Mitchell, Apollo 14 Astronaut, Speaks Out on Roswell & the Existence of Aliens
bit.ly/hanfe-3-79

[3-80] The Sun (14 October 2016) Tom Gillespie
'They Come in Peace' Former NASA astronaut 'claims the Pope knows aliens exist and want to help humans but a space war is imminent'
bit.ly/hanfe-3-80

[3-81]   Wikipedia (accessed 10 September 2017)
Gordon Cooper
bit.ly/hanfe-3-81

[3-82]   UStream (accessed 10 September 2017)
NASA: Live ISS Stream
bit.ly/hanfe-3-82

[3-83]   Wikipedia (accessed 10 September 2017)
Brian O'Leary
bit.ly/hanfe-3-83

[3-84]   Ancient Code (accessed 10 September 2017) Ivan Petricevic
A Second NASA Scientist States 'Somebody Else' Is On The Moon
bit.ly/hanfe-3-84

[3-85]   Exopolitics.org (26 December 2016 – via archive.org)
Michael Salla
Interview With Charles Hall – Motivations Of Tall White ETs and Their Exopolitical Significance
bit.ly/hanfe-3-85

[3-86]   Proof of Aliens Life (25 March 2016) Kim Jones
10 Evidences Of Tall White Aliens In Charles Hall's Books
bit.ly/hanfe-3-86

[3-87]   Exopolitics.org (11 August 2016 – via archive.org)
Michael Salla
UFO Crash Retrievals & Extraterrestrial Communications – Clifford Stone Interviews
bit.ly/hanfe-3-87

[3-88] Extraterrestrial Contact (accessed 10 September 2017)
UFO Researchers & People: Clifford Stone
bit.ly/hanfe-3-88

[3-89] Huffington Post UK (11 July 2012) Darren Perks
Solar Warden – The Secret Space Program
bit.ly/hanfe-3-89

[3-90] Ancient Code (accessed 10 September 2017)
Solar Warden: A fully operational, top-secret 'Black Budget'
Space Program
bit.ly/hanfe-3-90

[3-91] Wikipedia (accessed 10 September 2017)
Kary Mullis
bit.ly/hanfe-3-91

[3-92] London Review of Books (17 November 2011) Jenny Diski
What might they want?
bit.ly/hanfe-3-92

[3-93] Exopolitics Great Britain (12 March 2012)
Obituary: Stefano Breccia – A tribute to an Italian Professor who
revealed that extraterrestrials are among us
bit.ly/hanfe-3-93

[3-94] Before It's News (20 July 2013) Warren P. Aston
Alien propulsion details revealed
bit.ly/hanfe-3-94

[3-95]   Collective Evolution (5 July 2015) Joe Martino
**Aliens Are Real & They Will Look Like Humans – Claims
Cambridge University Scientist**
bit.ly/hanfe-3-95

[3-96]   Ancient Code (accessed 10 September 2017)
U.S. Defense Physicist Speaks about 'Alien' Structures on moon
bit.ly/hanfe-3-96

[3-97a] Collective evolution (23 June 2015) Arjun Walia
**2nd Director Of Lockheed Skunkwork's Shocking Comments
About UFO Technology**
bit.ly/hanfe-3-97a

[3-97b] Collective evolution (25 September 2014) Arjun Walia
**NASA Brings Scientists & Theologians Together To Prepare
World For Extraterrestrial Contact**
bit.ly/hanfe-3-97b

[3-97c] True Strange Library (14 September 2010 – via archive.org)
Xeno
Ben Rich Lockheed CEO Admits on Deathbed: ET UFO Are Real
bit.ly/hanfe-3-97c

[3-98]   Wikipedia (accessed 10 September 2017)
USWeb
bit.ly/hanfe-3-98

[3-99]   Timothy Good – UFO Authority
(accessed 10 September 2017)
Timothy Good – personal website
bit.ly/hanfe-3-99

[3-100] Project Camelot (accessed 10 September 2017)
Phil Schneider
bit.ly/hanfe-3-100

[3-101] UFO Digest (accessed 10 September 2017)
The Mysterious Life and Death of Philip Schneider
bit.ly/hanfe-3-101

[3-102] Those Conspiracy Guys (29 August 2015)
The Death of Phil Schneider
(caution: contains images that may cause distress or offense)
bit.ly/hanfe-3-102

Chapter 4

[4-01]   Alien Seek (accessed 10 September 2017)
List of the UFO crashes up to 1992 with recovery information
bit.ly/hanfe-4-01

[4-02]   The Museum of Unnatural Mystery (1996) Lee Krystek
UFO Crashes in the 19th Century
bit.ly/hanfe-4-02

[4-03]   Cool Interesting Stuff.com (accessed 10 September 2017)
The top 10 real UFO crash sites
bit.ly/hanfe-4-03

[4-04]   Huffington Post (20 April 2014)
That Time Subterranean Aliens Killed 60 People in New Mexico
bit.ly/hanfe-4-04

[4-05] Mail Online (25 October 2008) Rebecca Camber
U.S. fighter pilot: 'I was ordered to fire 24 rockets at UFO flying over East Anglia'
bit.ly/hanfe-4-05

[4-06] Wikipedia (accessed 10 September 2017)
Mantell UFO incident
bit.ly/hanfe-4-06

[4-07] Wikipedia (accessed 10 September 2017)
Philip J. Corso
bit.ly/hanfe-4-07

[4-08] Wikipedia (accessed 10 September 2017)
The Day After Roswell
bit.ly/hanfe-4-08

[4-09] The Guardian (15 November 2001)
Top 10 literary hoaxes, #8 The Day After Roswell
bit.ly/hanfe-4-09

[4-10] Wikipedia (accessed 10 September 2017)
Roswell UFO incident
bit.ly/hanfe-4-10

[4-11] Huffington Post (4 July 2013) Lee Speigel
Roswell UFO Crash: 66 Years Of Unanswered Questions
bit.ly/hanfe-4-11

[4-12]   Cover-up Research (accessed 10 September 2017)
Roswell, New Mexico, July 2 – 8, 1947
(includes all the photos and newspaper cuttings)
bit.ly/hanfe-4-12

[4-13]   Ancient Code (accessed 10 September 2017) Ivan Petricevic
Does this 'Top-Secret' memo finally prove a UFO did crash in Roswell?
bit.ly/hanfe-4-13

[4-14]   The New York Times (28 February 1960)
Air Force Order on 'Saucers' Cited: Pamphlet by the Inspector General Called Objects a "Serious Business"
bit.ly/hanfe-4-14

[4-15]   Wikipedia (accessed 10 September 2017)
Robertson Panel
bit.ly/hanfe-4-15

[4-16]   IFLScience (28 June 2017) Robin Andrews
EPA Officials "Bullying" Its Scientists Into Lying To The Public
bit.ly/hanfe-4-16

[4-17]   Ancient Code (accessed 10 September 2017)
Secret Space Program Whistleblower claims Humans are on Mars since 70s
bit.ly/hanfe-4-17

[4-18]   Ancient Code (accessed 10 September 2017) Ivan Petricevic
A Second NASA Scientist States 'Somebody Else' Is On The Moon
bit.ly/hanfe-4-18

[4-19]   American University, Washington DC (23 November 2003)
Michael E. Salla
The Black Budget Report: An Investigation into the CIA's "Black Budget" and the Second Manhattan Project
bit.ly/hanfe-4-19

[4-20]   Ancient Code (accessed 10 September 2017)
A top-secret, black budget Space program built with reverse-engineered alien tech
bit.ly/hanfe-4-20

[4-21]   Wikipedia (accessed 10 September 2017)
Black budget
bit.ly/hanfe-4-21

[4-22]   The Washington Post (29 August 2013)
Wilson Andrews & Todd Lindeman
Special Report: The Black Budget National Intelligence Program
bit.ly/hanfe-4-22

[4-23]   Wired (1 November 1995) Phil Patton
Exposing the Black Budget
bit.ly/hanfe-4-23

[4-24]   Wired (15 February 2012)
Robert Beckhusen & Noah Shachtman
The Pentagon's $51 Billion 'black' Budget for 2012
bit.ly/hanfe-4-24

[4-25]   Daily Beast (6 March 2014) Brandy Zadrozny
Read the Pentagon's $59 Billion 'Black Budget' for 2014
bit.ly/hanfe-4-25

[4-26]   Universe – Galaxies and Stars (accessed 10 September 2017)
Black projects are secret military stealth programs
(lists previously classified black projects)
bit.ly/hanfe-4-26

[4-27]   Wikipedia (accessed 10 September 2017)
Special access program
bit.ly/hanfe-4-27

[4-28]   Global Research (5 June 2015)
Report Reveals $8.5 Trillion Missing From Pentagon Budget
bit.ly/hanfe-4-28

[4-29]   USA Today (10 March 2013) Samuel Weigley
10 companies profiting the most from war
bit.ly/hanfe-4-29

[4-30]   Swiss Bank Claims (May 1997) William Z. Slany
U.S. and Allied Efforts To Recover and Restore Gold and Other Assets Stolen or Hidden by Germany During World War II
bit.ly/hanfe-4-30

[4-31]   Exopolitics (18 January 2012) Michael E. Salla
Trillion dollar lawsuit exposes secret Bilderberg Gold Treaty & funding of extraterrestrial projects
bit.ly/hanfe-4-31

[4-32]   Independent (25 August 2016) Ben Kentish
Nazi gold train search abandoned – but brings in £150 million for Polish town
bit.ly/hanfe-4-32

[4-33]   Humans Are Free (accessed 10 September 2017)
The Real 'Men In Black' – Complete Accounts
bit.ly/hanfe-4-33

[4-34]   Wikipedia (accessed 10 September 2017)
Shadow government (conspiracy)
bit.ly/hanfe-4-34

[4-35]   Constitution Society (1994)
The Shadow Government
bit.ly/hanfe-4-35

Chapter 5

[5-01]   IFLScience (8 April 2014) Stephen Luntz
Confirmation of Human Neanderthal Interbreeding
bit.ly/hanfe-5-01

[5-02]   Live Science (29 January 2014) Charles Q. Choi
At least 20% of Neanderthal DNA Is in Humans
bit.ly/hanfe-5-02

[5-03]   BBC News website (18 December 2013)
Mystery early human revealed by DNA data
bit.ly/hanfe-5-03

[5-04]   ABC News Australia (28 March 2016) Bianca Nogrady
Genetic map reveals impact of interbreeding with ancient Denisovans and Neanderthals
bit.ly/hanfe-5-04

[5-05]   The Telegraph (14 August 2012)
Neanderthals did not interbreed with humans, scientists find
bit.ly/hanfe-5-05

[5-06]   Live Science (13 August 2012) Megan Gannon
Did Humans Have Sex With Neanderthals?
bit.ly/hanfe-5-06

[5-07]   Nature (19 November 2013) Ewen Callaway
Mystery humans spiced up ancients' sex lives
bit.ly/hanfe-5-07

[5-08]   IFLScience (25 October 2016) Josh Davis
**Our Ancestors Were Breeding With At Least Four, But
Potentially More Species Of Other Hominins**
bit.ly/hanfe-5-08

[5-09]   IFLScience (25 November 2013) Elise Andrew
Interbreeding Among Early Hominins
bit.ly/hanfe-5-09

[5-10]   Science (7 April 2016) Ann Gibbons
**Modern human females and male Neanderthals had trouble
making babies. Here's why**
bit.ly/hanfe-5-10

[5-11]   Smithsonian (15 August 2012) Rose Eveleth
**Hot for Hominids – Did Humans Mate With Neanderthals Or
Not?**
bit.ly/hanfe-5-11

[5-12]   Past Horizons (17 February 2016)
Neanderthals mated with modern humans much earlier than previously thought
bit.ly/hanfe-5-12

[5-13]   Spiegel Online (24 December 2009) Frank Thadeusz
Alcohol's Neolithic Origins – Brewing Up a Civilization
bit.ly/hanfe-5-13

[5-16]   New Scientist (17 December 2015) Michael Slezak
New species of human may have shared our caves – and beds
bit.ly/hanfe-5-16

[5-17]   The Telegraph (2 March 2017) Sarah Knapton
Oldest fossil ever found on Earth shows organisms thrived 4.2bn years ago – and provides strongest evidence yet for similar life on Mars
bit.ly/hanfe-5-17

[5-18]   Humans Are Free (accessed 10 September 2017) Richard J. O'Neill
Are Humans Alien to Planet Earth? Analysing the Evidence
bit.ly/hanfe-5-18

[5-19]   Icarus, Volume 19, Issue 3, July 1973, Pages 341-346 Francis Crick
Directed panspermia
bit.ly/hanfe-5-19

[5-20] Popular Science (24 August 2010) Clay Dillow
Earth Bacteria Survive a 553-Day Space Exposure on the Exterior of the ISS
bit.ly/hanfe-5-20

[5-21] Wikipedia (accessed 10 September 2017)
Reports of *Streptococcus mitis* on the Moon
bit.ly/hanfe-5-21

[5-22] Wikipedia (accessed 10 September 2017)
Chandra Wickramasinghe
bit.ly/hanfe-5-22

[5-23] Your News Wire (12 August 2015) Sean Adl-Tabatabai
Scientists Say That Human DNA Comes From Another Planet
bit.ly/hanfe-5-23

[5-24] Wikipedia (accessed 10 September 2017)
Panspermia
bit.ly/hanfe-5-24

[5-25] Huffington Post (13 February 2015) Lee Speigel
UK Scientists: Aliens May Have Sent Space Seeds To Create Life On Earth
bit.ly/hanfe-5-25

[5-26] Scott Adams' Blog (1 June 2014) Scott Adams
Proof (Almost) of Intelligent Design
bit.ly/hanfe-5-26

[5-27]   Sci Tech Daily (25 July 2012)
Amino Acids in Meteorites Provide a Clue to How Life Turned Left
bit.ly/hanfe-5-27

[5-27a] The Why Files (accessed 10 September 2017)
Asteroidal Assassins: the History of Asteroid Impacts
bit.ly/hanfe-5-27a

[5-28]   Wikipedia (accessed 10 September 2017)
Toba catastrophe theory
bit.ly/hanfe-5-28

[5-29]   YouTube (accessed 10 September 2017)
Bioluminescent rat
bit.ly/hanfe-5-29

[5-30]   Veterans Today (4 August 2013) Preston James
Secret Space War VII: Joint USG/Alien Hybrid Program
bit.ly/hanfe-5-30

[5-31]   The New 49'ers (accessed 10 September 2017) John Hiller
Gold in the Ancient World
bit.ly/hanfe-5-31

[5-32]   CMI Gold & Silver (31 March 2011) Paul Carter
The World's 10 Most Prolific Gold Fields
bit.ly/hanfe-5-32

[5-33]   Ancient Code (accessed 10 September 2017)
Anunnaki structures before the flood: The 200,000-year-old ancient City in Africa
bit.ly/hanfe-5-33

[5-34]   Ancient Code (accessed 10 September 2017)
Scientists: Unexplained details in Human DNA might be Extraterrestrial in nature
bit.ly/hanfe-5-34

[5-35]   Arcturi.com (accessed 10 September 2017)
Grey Aliens Agenda: Human Hybrid Integration Program
bit.ly/hanfe-5-35

[5-36]   National UFO Center (30 November 2011) George Filer
Are Humans Part Alien?
bit.ly/hanfe-5-36

[5-37]   YouTube (12 April 2011)
Tall Caucasian Mummies of China
bit.ly/hanfe-5-37

[5-38]   NASA (16 March 2010) Adam Voiland
UV Exposure Has Increased Over the Last 30 Years, but Stabilized Since the Mid-1990s
bit.ly/hanfe-5-38

[5-39]   IFLScience (6 June 2017) Jonathan O'Callaghan
Astronomers Have Found New Evidence That We Live In A Void
bit.ly/hanfe-5-39

[5-40]   Utne Reader (January/February 2013) Wayne Roberts
Nine Meals Away from Anarchy
bit.ly/hanfe-5-40

[5-41]   International Journal of Astrobiology, Volume 10, Issue 4
October 2011, pp. 341-347. Duncan H. Forgan
Spatio-temporal constraints on the zoo hypothesis, and the breakdown of total hegemony
bit.ly/hanfe-5-41

[5-42]   Scott Adams' Blog (15 October 2012) Scott Adams
Living in a Computer Simulation
bit.ly/hanfe-5-42

[5-43]   The Guardian (2 June 2016) Alex Hern
Elon Musk: 'Chances are we're all living in a simulation'
bit.ly/hanfe-5-43

[5-44]   IFLScience (23 June 2016) Danielle Andrew
Elon Musk Says We're Probably Living In A Computer Simulation – Here's The Science
bit.ly/hanfe-5-44

[5-45]   Discover magazine (15 November 2013) Zeeya Merali
Do We Live in the Matrix?
bit.ly/hanfe-5-45

[5-46]   Nature (10 December 2013) Ron Cowen
Simulations back up theory that Universe is a hologram
bit.ly/hanfe-5-46

[5-47]   Quora (accessed 10 September 2017)
various comments on message board
If the Earth was created 6000 years ago, did God create dinosaur fossils to test man's faith in the Bible?
bit.ly/hanfe-5-47

[5-48]   Wikipedia (accessed 10 September 2017)
Fermi paradox
bit.ly/hanfe-5-48

[5-49]   Gizmodo (31 May 2017) George Dvorsky
Hibernating Aliens Could Explain the Great Silence
bit.ly/hanfe-5-49

Chapter 6

[6-01]   PBS – Nova (1 July 2004) Joe McMaster, Peter Tyson
How Did Life Begin?
bit.ly/hanfe-6-01

[6-01a] Ancient Code (accessed 10 September 2017)
Scientists claim Human DNA 'was designed by aliens'
bit.ly/hanfe-6-01a

[6-02]   Wikipedia (accessed 10 September 2017)
Miller–Urey experiment
bit.ly/hanfe-6-02

[6-03]   The Washington Post (26 April 2016) Rachel Feltman
The building blocks of life weren't that hard to put together
bit.ly/hanfe-6-03

[6-04]   Live Science (1 September 2016) Ker Than
How Did Life Arise on Earth?
bit.ly/hanfe-6-04

[6-05]   Reddit – Ask Science (accessed 10 September 2017)
various comments on message board
**I understand how evolution works but how did DNA or RNA
form in the first place or what preceded it?**
bit.ly/hanfe-6-05

[6-06]   Wikipedia (accessed 10 September 2017)
RNA
bit.ly/hanfe-6-06

[6-07]   Ancient Code (accessed 10 September 2017)
**Co-discoverer of DNA claims our genes were brought to Earth
by extraterrestrials**
bit.ly/hanfe-6-07

[6-08]   Quanta magazine (22 January 2014) Natalie Wolchover
A New Physics Theory of Life
bit.ly/hanfe-6-08

[6-09]   OZY (20 April 2015) Meghan Walsh
Jeremy England, The Man Who May One-up Darwin
bit.ly/hanfe-6-09

[6-10]   IFLScience (31 July 2017) Robin Andrews
**Life Is Inevitable Consequence Of Physics, According To New
Research**
bit.ly/hanfe-6-10

[6-11]   How Stuff Works (25 July 2001) Marshall Brain
How Evolution Works: Where Did the First Living Cell Come From?
bit.ly/hanfe-6-11

[6-12]   Wikipedia (accessed 10 September 2017)
Escherichia coli (*E. coli*)
bit.ly/hanfe-6-12

[6-13]   Wikipedia (accessed 10 September 2017)
Creationism
bit.ly/hanfe-6-13

[6-14]   Wikipedia (accessed 10 September 2017)
Progressive creationism
bit.ly/hanfe-6-14

[6-15]   Wikipedia (accessed 10 September 2017)
Intelligent design
bit.ly/hanfe-6-15

[6-16]   Ancient Code (accessed 10 September 2017)
Scientists 'prove' that the soul does not die: It returns to the universe
bit.ly/hanfe-6-16

[6-17]   Snopes (25 April 2013) David Mikkelson
Weight of the Soul: Did a physician once attempt to measure the weight of the human soul? True.
bit.ly/hanfe-6-17

[6-18] Historic Mysteries (27 January 2010)
Weighing Human Souls – The 21 Grams Theory
bit.ly/hanfe-6-18

[6-19] Bad News About Christianity (accessed 10 September 2017)
Christian Deceptions: Case Study: How Mary Stays A Virgin
bit.ly/hanfe-6-19

[6-20] Foodborne Illness (accessed 10 September 2017)
E. coli food poisoning
bit.ly/hanfe-6-20

Chapter 7

[7-01] Science and Plants for Schools (accessed 10 September 2017)
John Hewitson
Genetics, DNA, plants and humans: How much DNA do plants share with humans? Over 99%?
bit.ly/hanfe-7-01

[7-02] Wikipedia (accessed 10 September 2017)
Base pair
bit.ly/hanfe-7-02

[7-03] The Tech Museum of Innovation
(accessed 10 September 2017)
People are not as alike as scientists once thought
bit.ly/hanfe-7-03

[7-04] Wikipedia (accessed 10 September 2017)
DNA
bit.ly/hanfe-7-04

[7-05] Wikipedia (accessed 10 September 2017)
Gene
bit.ly/hanfe-7-05

[7-06] Wikipedia (accessed 10 September 2017)
Noncoding DNA
bit.ly/hanfe-7-06

[7-07] New Scientist (22 August 2012) Michael Marshall
DNA could have existed long before life itself
bit.ly/hanfe-7-07

[7-08] Learning Mind (5 October 2012) Anna LeMind
DNA seems to have telepathic abilities
bit.ly/hanfe-7-08

[7-09] Wikipedia (accessed 10 September 2017)
Spina bifida
bit.ly/hanfe-7-09

[7-10] News-Medical (28 September 2015) Yolanda Smith
Spina Bifida Epidemiology
bit.ly/hanfe-7-10

[7-11] Reproductive Science Center of New Jersey
(accessed 10 September 2017)
Genetic Causes of Infertility
bit.ly/hanfe-7-11

[7-12]   Wikipedia (accessed 10 September 2017)
CRISPR
bit.ly/hanfe-7-12

[7-13]   Nobelprize.org (accessed 10 September 2017)
The Nobel Prize in Chemistry 2015
bit.ly/hanfe-7-13

[7-14]   Wikipedia (accessed 10 September 2017)
List of potentially habitable exoplanets
bit.ly/hanfe-7-14

[7-15]   Ancient Code (accessed 10 September 2017)
Mysteriously, our genetic code stopped evolving 3 billion years ago
bit.ly/hanfe-7-15

[7-16]   Koshland Science Museum, Washington DC
(accessed 10 September 2017)
Tracing Similarities And Differences In Our DNA
bit.ly/hanfe-7-16

[7-17]   Eupedia (accessed 10 September 2017)
various comments on message board
Percentage of genetic similarity between humans and animals
bit.ly/hanfe-7-17

[7-18]   Koshland Science Museum, Washington DC
(accessed 10 September 2017)
What percent of their genes match yours?
bit.ly/hanfe-7-18

[7-19]   Gene Cuisine (4 March 2011) Michael Musso
Human DNA similarities to chimps and bananas, what does it mean?
bit.ly/hanfe-7-19

[7-20]   New Scientist (24 April 2015) Jessica Hamzelou
Police can now tell identical twins apart – just melt their DNA
bit.ly/hanfe-7-20

[7-21]   National Institutes of Health (30 September 2015)
Steven Benowitz
Scientists create world's largest catalog of human genomic variation
bit.ly/hanfe-7-21

[7-22]   ResearchGate (11 Jan 2014)
various comments on message board
Percentage DNA difference within and between species?
bit.ly/hanfe-7-22

[7-24]   Mail Online (13 March 2015) Mark Prigg
Mystery of our 145 'alien' genes: Scientists discover some DNA is not from our ancestors – and say it could change how we think about evolution
bit.ly/hanfe-7-24

[7-25]   National Geographic (10 May 2013) Carl Zimmer
The Lurker: How A Virus Hid In Our Genome For Six Million Years
bit.ly/hanfe-7-25

[7-26]   IFLScience (23 March 2016) Robin Andrews
19 Pieces Of Non-Human DNA Found In Human Genome
bit.ly/hanfe-7-26

[7-27]   IFLScience (24 November 2015) Elise Andrew
Fossil Viruses Help Human Embryos Develop, Study Finds
bit.ly/hanfe-7-27

[7-28]   Wikipedia (accessed 10 September 2017)
Genetically modified organism
bit.ly/hanfe-7-28

[7-29]   Wikipedia (accessed 10 September 2017)
Paris japonica
bit.ly/hanfe-7-29

[7-30]   Wikipedia (accessed 10 September 2017)
Polychaos dubium
bit.ly/hanfe-7-30

[7-31]   Wikipedia (accessed 10 September 2017)
Chimpanzee genome project
bit.ly/hanfe-7-31

[7-32]   BBC News website (12 October 2015) Michelle Roberts
GM could make pig organs for humans
bit.ly/hanfe-7-32

[7-33]   Reddit: Ask Science (accessed 10 September 2017)
various comments on message board
How much DNA do we have in our bodies by weight?
bit.ly/hanfe-7-33

[7-34]   The New York Times (18 July 2015) Rachel Nuwer
Counting All the DNA on Earth
bit.ly/hanfe-7-34

Chapter 8

[8-01]   Slate.com (28 July 2014) Phil Plait
Poisoned Planet: the great oxygenation event – the Earth's first mass extinction
bit.ly/hanfe-8-01

[8-02]   Wikipedia (accessed 10 September 2017)
Oxygen toxicity
bit.ly/hanfe-8-02

[8-02a] Elite Diving Agency (5 October 2013) Sandro Lonardi
What Scuba Tank Gas Mixture do Divers use?
bit.ly/hanfe-8-02a

[8-03]   io9 (11 September 2015) George Dvorsky
8 Scientific Discoveries That Prove Evolution is Real
bit.ly/hanfe-8-03

[8-04]   Mail Online (30 June 2011)
**Out of Africa? New theory throws doubt on assumption all
humans evolved from the continent**
bit.ly/hanfe-8-04

[8-05]
Nature Education Knowledge 3(10):13 (2012) Katerina Harvati
What Happened to the Neanderthals?
bit.ly/hanfe-8-05

[8-06]   Wikipedia (accessed 10 September 2017)
Neanderthal extinction
bit.ly/hanfe-8-06

[8-07]   The Guardian (2 June 2013) Robin McKie
Why did the Neanderthals die out?
bit.ly/hanfe-8-07

[8-08]   Popular Science (16 April 2014) Veronique Greenwood
**You're Not Highly Evolved – Here's where our bodies still mess
up**
bit.ly/hanfe-8-08

[8-09]   Talk Origins (1992-93) Chris Colby, Loren Petrich et al
Evidence for Jury-Rigged Design in Nature
bit.ly/hanfe-8-09

[8-10]
US Department of Health and Human Services, Centers for Disease
Control and Prevention (accessed 10 September 2017)
Get the Stats on Traumatic Brain Injury in the United States
bit.ly/hanfe-8-10

[8-11]   UK Acquired Brain Injury Forum
(accessed 10 September 2017)
About brain injury
bit.ly/hanfe-8-11

[8-12]   Biology Stack Exchange (accessed 10 September 2017)
various comments on message board
Why have whales and dolphins not evolved to have gills?
bit.ly/hanfe-8-12

[8-13]   News-Medical (8 October 2007)
What does the appendix do? finally an answer!
bit.ly/hanfe-8-13

[8-14]   Wikipedia (accessed 10 September 2017)
Coccyx
bit.ly/hanfe-8-14

[8-15]   Wikipedia (accessed 10 September 2017)
Hiccup
bit.ly/hanfe-8-15

[8-16]   Wikipedia (accessed 10 September 2017)
Noncoding DNA
bit.ly/hanfe-8-16

[8-17]   Cracked (8 September 2010) Colin Murdock
**The 5 Strangest Things Evolution Left In Your Body,
#4. Flinching When You Hear High-Pitched Sounds**
bit.ly/hanfe-8-17

[8-18] Wikipedia (accessed 10 September 2017)
Darwin's tubercle
bit.ly/hanfe-8-18

[8-19] Wikipedia (accessed 10 September 2017)
Human vestigiality
bit.ly/hanfe-8-19

[8-20] Wikipedia (accessed 10 September 2017)
Goose bumps
bit.ly/hanfe-8-20

[8-21] Wikipedia (accessed 10 September 2017)
Infant swimming
bit.ly/hanfe-8-21

[8-22] Wikipedia (accessed 10 September 2017)
***Levator claviculae* muscle**
bit.ly/hanfe-8-22

[8-23] Wikipedia (accessed 10 September 2017)
Nipple
bit.ly/hanfe-8-23

[8-24] io9 (15 August 2011) Robbie Gonzalez
10 Vestigial Traits You Didn't Know You Had, #3 Male Nipples
bit.ly/hanfe-8-24

[8-25] Wikipedia (accessed 10 September 2017)
Plantaris muscle
bit.ly/hanfe-8-25

[8-26]   IFLScience (1 July 2015) Elise Andrew
Polarised Light and the Super Sense You Didn't Know you had
bit.ly/hanfe-8-26

[8-27]   International Year of Light 2015 (15 July 2015)
S. Ananthanarayanan
Polarised light in the animal kingdom
bit.ly/hanfe-8-27

[8-28]   Komar.org (accessed 10 September 2017) Alek Komarnitsky
Ultra Violet Color Glow after Cataract Surgery with Crystalens
bit.ly/hanfe-8-28

[8-29]   Wikipedia (accessed 10 September 2017)
Claude Monet
bit.ly/hanfe-8-29

[8-30]   PetaPixel (17 April 2012) Michael Zhang
The Human Eye Can See in UV When the Lens is Removed
bit.ly/hanfe-8-30

[8-31]   Reference.com (accessed 10 September 2017)
What animal can see ultraviolet color?
bit.ly/hanfe-8-31

[8-32]   The Guardian (30 May 2002) David Hambling
Let the light shine in
bit.ly/hanfe-8-32

[8-33]   Live Science (18 February 2014) Tanya Lewis
Cats and Dogs May See in Ultraviolet
bit.ly/hanfe-8-33

[8-34]   io9 (13 March 2014) George Dvorsky
Most animals can see the flashing and glowing of power lines
bit.ly/hanfe-8-34

[8-35]   Wikipedia (accessed 10 September 2017)
Vomeronasal organ
bit.ly/hanfe-8-35

[8-36]   Mental Floss (26 October 2015) Jessica Hullinger
5 Signs Humans Are Still Evolving
bit.ly/hanfe-8-36

[8-37]   Popular Science (16 April 2014) Veronique Greenwood
You're Not Highly Evolved
bit.ly/hanfe-8-37

[8-38]   Popular Science (14 September 2011) Dan Nosowitz
Ten Astounding Cases of Modern Evolution and Adaptation
bit.ly/hanfe-8-38

[8-39]   Independent (5 February 2015) Steve Connor
Humans are still evolving despite massive recent lifestyle changes, study finds
bit.ly/hanfe-8-39

[8-40]   BBC News website (1 March 2011) Olly Bootle
Are humans still evolving by Darwin's natural selection?
bit.ly/hanfe-8-40

[8-41]   Popular Science (26 August 2011) Rebecca Boyle
**Doctors Who Work With X-Rays May Be Adapting at the
Cellular Level to Withstand Radiation**
bit.ly/hanfe-8-41

[8-42]   Wikipedia (accessed 10 September 2017)
Albert Einstein's brain
bit.ly/hanfe-8-42

[8-43]   Ancient Code (accessed 10 September 2017)
**Have Humans devolved through history? Ancient Technology,
the ultimate piece of evidence**
bit.ly/hanfe-8-43

[8-44]   Forbes (7 June 2013 – via archive.org) Parmy Olson
How The Human Face Might Look In 100,000 Years
bit.ly/hanfe-8-44

[8-45]   Wikipedia (accessed 10 September 2017)
Alcohol and sex
bit.ly/hanfe-8-45

[8-46]   Huffington Post (11 December 2013) Dominique Mosbergen
**Human Intelligence Isn't Superior To That Of Other Animals,
Researchers Say**
bit.ly/hanfe-8-46

[8-47]   Mother Nature Network (15 July 2016) Katherine Butler
10 of the smartest animals on Earth
bit.ly/hanfe-8-47

[8-48] Wikipedia (accessed 10 September 2017)
Cetacean intelligence
bit.ly/hanfe-8-48

[8-49] BrainJet (accessed 10 September 2017)
10 Animals Who Are Almost as Smart as Humans
bit.ly/hanfe-8-49

[8-50] Scientific American (18 July 2012) Ferris Jabr
Does Thinking Really Hard Burn More Calories?
bit.ly/hanfe-8-50

[8-51] Fact Retriever (24 February 2017) Karin Lehnardt
66 Interesting Facts about Evolution
bit.ly/hanfe-8-51

[8-52] Wikipedia (accessed 10 September 2017)
Control of fire by early humans
bit.ly/hanfe-8-52

[8-53] Ancient Code (accessed 10 September – via archive.org)
Ivan Petricevic
290 million year old human footprint has researchers scratching their heads
bit.ly/hanfe-8-53

[8-54] Natural History Museum (accessed 10 September 2017)
When did dinosaurs live?
bit.ly/hanfe-8-54

[8-55]   The New York Times (17 June 17 1986) John Noble Wilford
Fossils Of 'Man Tracks' Shown To Be Dinosaurian
bit.ly/hanfe-8-55

[8-56]   Wikipedia (accessed 10 September 2017)
Giant of Castelnau
bit.ly/hanfe-8-56

[8-57]   World News Daily Report (accessed 10 September 2017)
**Smithsonian Admits To Destruction Of Thousands Of Giant
Human Skeletons In Early 1900's**
bit.ly/hanfe-8-57

[8-58]   Daily Star (20 March 2015) Tom Rawle
**Skeleton of giant human dubbed 'Goliath' found in ancient
fortress**
bit.ly/hanfe-8-58

[8-59]   Snopes.com (21 June 2004) David Mikkelson
**They Might Be Giants: Gas exploration in Saudi Arabia
reportedly uncovered human remains of gigantic proportions.
False**
bit.ly/hanfe-8-59

[8-60]   IFLScience (8 July 2016) Stephen Luntz
Evolution Once Operated 4,000 Times Faster Than Today
bit.ly/hanfe-8-60

[8-61]   PBS - Evolution (accessed 10 September 2017)
Daniel Simberloff
Are we in the midst of a mass extinction?
bit.ly/hanfe-8-61

[8-62]   MSN (5 July 2017)
Raziye Akkoc & Luana Sarmini-Buonaccorsi
Outcry as Turkey moves evolution from curriculum
bit.ly/hanfe-8-62

[8-63]   Answers in Genesis (accessed 10 September 2017)
Evolution? Impossible!
bit.ly/hanfe-8-63

[8-64]   Wikipedia (accessed 10 September 2017)
Transitional fossil
bit.ly/hanfe-8-64

[8-65]   Fossil Museum (accessed 10 September 2017)
Precambrian Fossils
bit.ly/hanfe-8-65

[8-66]   Wikipedia (accessed 10 September 2017)
Precambrian
bit.ly/hanfe-8-66

[8-67]   Wikipedia (accessed 10 September 2017)
Cambrian
bit.ly/hanfe-8-67

[8-68]   Amazing Facts (accessed 10 September 2017) Joe Crews
How Evolution Flunked The Science Test
bit.ly/hanfe-8-68

Chapter 9

[9-01] BBC World Service (accessed 10 September 2017)
Homo sapiens: **Out of Africa**
bit.ly/hanfe-9-01

[9-02] Scientific American (8 August 2007) Nikhil Swaminathan
Is the Out of Africa Theory Out?
bit.ly/hanfe-9-02

[9-03] IFLScience (22 August 2016) Ben Taub
World's Oldest Human Bone Reportedly Found In Saudi Arabia
bit.ly/hanfe-9-03

[9-04] Independent (11 April 2016) Andrew Griffin
Neanderthals might have contracted diseases from early humans that helped make them extinct, scientists say
bit.ly/hanfe-9-04

[9-05] New Scientist (3 February 2014) Catherine Brahic
Humanity's forgotten return to Africa revealed in DNA
bit.ly/hanfe-9-05

Chapter 10

[10-01] University of Wisconsin-Madison Department of Astronomy (accessed 10 September 2017) Chris Dolan
The Nearest Stars, as Seen from the Earth
bit.ly/hanfe-10-01

[10-02] Wikipedia (accessed 10 September 2017)
List of nearest exoplanets
bit.ly/hanfe-10-02

[10-03] Star-Fleet.com (4 June 2013) M. Bret Godfrey
Warp Speed Defined
bit.ly/hanfe-10-03

[10-04] IFLScience (25 March 2015) Elise Andrew
Newly Discovered Planet Has Four Parent Stars
bit.ly/hanfe-10-04

[10-05] IFLScience (31 March 2015) Stephen Luntz
New Paper Suggests Tatooine-type Planets Could Be Common
bit.ly/hanfe-10-05

[10-06] Wikipedia (accessed 10 September 2017)
Alpha Centauri
bit.ly/hanfe-10-06

[10-07] New Scientist (31 January 2014) Jeff Hecht
Star next door may host a 'superhabitable' world
bit.ly/hanfe-10-07

[10-08] Arxiv.org (1 October 2015)
Rory Barnes, Victoria S. Meadows & Nicole Evans
University of Washington Astronomy Department
Comparative Habitability Of Transiting Exoplanets
bit.ly/hanfe-10-08

バ

[10-09] BBC News website (24 August 2016) Jonathan Amos
Neighbouring star Proxima Centauri has Earth-sized planet
bit.ly/hanfe-10-09

[10-10] IFLScience (16 May 2017) Jonathan O'Callaghan
Proxima b, The Closest Exoplanet To Earth, Could Be Habitable
bit.ly/hanfe-10-10

[10-11] Gizmodo (8 February 2017) Rae Paoletta
We're Sorry About This Seriously Bummer Proxima B News
bit.ly/hanfe-10-11

[10-12] Sky and Telescope (22 July 2014) Maria Temming
How Far is the Closest Star?
bit.ly/hanfe-10-12

[10-13] BBC News website (22 February 2017) Paul Rincon
Star's seven Earth-sized worlds set record
bit.ly/hanfe-10-13

[10-14] Gizmodo (6 April 2017) Rae Paoletta
TRAPPIST-1's Fatal Flaw Could Ruin Our Hopes of Finding Life There
bit.ly/hanfe-10-14

[10-15] Wikipedia (accessed 10 September 2017)
LHS 1140
bit.ly/hanfe-10-15

[10-16] Sky News (20 April 2017) Russell Hope
'Super-Earth': New planet is 'best candidate' to support life beyond solar system
bit.ly/hanfe-10-16

[10-17] Ancient Code (accessed 10 September 2017)
Scientists find a second earth – and it could be home to alien life
bit.ly/hanfe-10-17

[10-18] Gizmodo (1 December 2015) Maddie Stone
The Fascinating Reason Multi-Planet Star Systems Might Harbor Life
bit.ly/hanfe-10-18

[10-19] Arxiv.org (1 December 2015) Jason H. Steffen & Gongjie Li
Dynamical Considerations For Life In Multihabitable Planetary Systems
bit.ly/hanfe-10-19

[10-20] Wikipedia (accessed 10 September 2017)
Sirius
bit.ly/hanfe-10-20

[10-21] Ancient Origins (1 February 2014) April Holloway
The ancient wonder and veneration of the dog star Sirius
bit.ly/hanfe-10-21

[10-22] University of Cambridge (2017)
Map of Life – Convergent Evolution Online
bit.ly/hanfe-10-22

[10-23] Wikipedia (accessed 10 September 2017)
Convergent evolution
bit.ly/hanfe-10-23

[10-24] Blood Pressure UK (2008)
Why salt is bad
bit.ly/hanfe-10-24

[10-25] New Scientist (20 January 2014) Catherine Brahic
Water found in stardust suggests life is universal
bit.ly/hanfe-10-25

Chapter 11

[11-01] BBC News website (1 December 2013) James Gallagher
'Memories' pass between generations
bit.ly/hanfe-11-01

[11-02] HubPages (25 March 2017) Juliette Kando
Second Brain Found in Heart Neurons – Trust your Gut Feelings
bit.ly/hanfe-11-02

[11-03] The Telegraph (1 December 2013) Richard Gray
Phobias may be memories passed down in genes from ancestors
bit.ly/hanfe-11-03

[11-04] Wikipedia (accessed 10 September 2017)
Die Glocke
bit.ly/hanfe-11-04

[11-04a]   Scribd (2005) Richard Boylan
**Classified Advanced Antigravity Aerospace Craft Utilizing Back-
engineered Extraterrestrial Technology**
bit.ly/hanfe-11-04a

[11-04b]   Dr Richard Boylan (accessed 10 September 2017)
Personal website
bit.ly/hanfe-11-04b

[11-05] Wikipedia (accessed 10 September 2017)
TR-3 Black Manta
bit.ly/hanfe-11-05

[11-06] Conspiracy Nation (19 May 2017 via archive.org) AKG
**Secret Space Program Update: TR-3B Patent Now In Public
Domain**
bit.ly/hanfe-11-06

[11-07] Google Patents (accessed 10 September 2017)
Triangular spacecraft
bit.ly/hanfe-11-07
See also below.

[11-07a]   According to the above patent, the inventor is "John St.
Clair." It's worth looking at the other inventions he's credited with.
They include electromagnetic propulsion systems for spacecraft, and
a hyperspace torque generator.
bit.ly/hanfe-11-07a

[11-08] Military.com (23 November 2013)
TR-3B Anti-Gravity Spacecrafts
(includes video of TR-3Bs in flight)
bit.ly/hanfe-11-08

[11-09] Gizmodo (23 July 2012) Jesus Diaz
These Guys Got Inside the Fuel Tank Labyrinth of a 747 Jumbo Plane
bit.ly/hanfe-11-09

[11-10] Worldbuilding Stack Exchange (accessed 10 September 2017)
various comments on message board
How much antimatter would we need in order to wipe out all humans, eradicate all animals and blow up the Earth?
bit.ly/hanfe-11-10

[11-11] Wikipedia (accessed 10 September 2017)
Tsar Bomba
bit.ly/hanfe-11-11

[11-12] Physics Forums (12 January 2011)
various comments on message board
Can radar detect flying animal?
bit.ly/hanfe-11-12

[11-13] Wikipedia (accessed 10 September 2017)
Warp drive
bit.ly/hanfe-11-13

[11-14] Wikipedia (accessed 10 September 2017)
Alcubierre drive
bit.ly/hanfe-11-14

[11-15] Wikipedia (accessed 10 September 2017)
Negative mass
bit.ly/hanfe-11-15

[11-16] BBC News website (19 April 2017)
Physicists observe 'negative mass'
bit.ly/hanfe-11-16

[11-17] Gizmodo (21 April 2017) Ryan F. Mandelbaum
No, Scientists Didn't Just Create Negative Mass or Defy the Laws of Physics
bit.ly/hanfe-11-17

[11-18] Wikipedia (accessed 10 September 2017)
Wormhole
bit.ly/hanfe-11-18

[11-19] Space.com (13 April 2015) Nola Taylor Redd
What is a Wormhole?
bit.ly/hanfe-11-19

[11-20] The Telegraph (21 January 2015) Sarah Knapton
Wormhole to another galaxy may exist in Milky Way
bit.ly/hanfe-11-20

[11-21] Sploid (28 May 2014) Jesus Diaz
Scientists think there may be a wormhole in the center of our galaxy
bit.ly/hanfe-11-21

[11-22] Wikipedia (accessed 10 September 2017)
Teleportation
bit.ly/hanfe-11-22

[11-23] Time (12 July 2017) Melissa Chan
Scientists Just Teleported an Object Into Space for the First Time
bit.ly/hanfe-11-23

[11-24] Gizmodo UK (12 July 2017) Ryan F. Mandelbaum
Scientists 'Teleport' a Particle Hundreds of Miles--But What Does That Mean?
bit.ly/hanfe-11-24

Chapter 12

[12-01] The Telegraph (2 March 2017) Sarah Knapton
Oldest fossil ever found on Earth shows organisms thrived 4.2bn years ago – and provides strongest evidence yet for similar life on Mars
bit.ly/hanfe-12-01

[12-02] IFLScience (6 November 2015) Elise Andrew
How Did Mars Lose Its Habitable Climate? The Answer Is Blowing In The Solar Wind
bit.ly/hanfe-12-02

[12-02a]   Wikipedia (accessed 10 September 2017)
Great Oxygenation Event
bit.ly/hanfe-12-02a

[12-03] IFLScience (14 March 2017) Robin Andrews
A Continental-Sized Volcanic Eruption Caused Snowball Earth
bit.ly/hanfe-12-03

[12-03a]   MSN/The Independent (17 August 2017) Ian Johnston
Mystery of how first animals appeared on Earth 'solved' by scientists
bit.ly/hanfe-12-03a

[12-03b]   BBC News website (17 August 2017) Roland Pease
The algae that terraformed Earth
bit.ly/hanfe-12-03b

[12-04] IFLScience (20 February 2017) Robin Andrews
Something Very Unexpected Happened After The "Great Dying" Mass Extinction Event
bit.ly/hanfe-12-04

[12-04a]   IFLScience (24 March 2017) Robin Andrews
Australia Suffered From A Mass Extinction Event 35 Million Years Ago
bit.ly/hanfe-12-04a

[12-05] Wikipedia (accessed 10 September 2017)
Antarctica
bit.ly/hanfe-12-05

[12-06] Sky News (23 May 2017) Russell Hope
Missing link may have been European, not African, ancient fossils suggest
bit.ly/hanfe-12-06

[12-07] IFLScience (6 October 2015) Elise Andrew
Newly Discovered Human Ancestor's Feet And Hands Were Strikingly Similar To Our Own
bit.ly/hanfe-12-07

[12-08] Quora (accessed 10 September 2017)
various comments on message board
Is there DNA evidence that *Homo erectus* was a different species from *Homo sapiens*?
bit.ly/hanfe-12-08

[12-09] SpinFold (accessed 10 September 2017)
Evolution of Man
bit.ly/hanfe-12-09

[12-10] Scientific American (8 August 2007) Nikhil Swaminathan
Is the Out of Africa Theory Out?
bit.ly/hanfe-12-10

[12-11] io9 (16 September 2015) Esther Inglis-Arkell
Close Calls: Three Times When Humanity Barely Escaped Extinction
bit.ly/hanfe-12-11

[12-12] IFLScience (24 December 2014) Janet Fang
Turkey's Oldest Stone Tool Pinpoints Human Migration to Europe
bit.ly/hanfe-12-12

[12-13] National Geographic (8 February 2014) Jane J. Lee
Oldest Human Footprints Found Outside of Africa
bit.ly/hanfe-12-13

[12-14] Wikipedia (accessed 10 September 2017)
Homo heidelbergensis
bit.ly/hanfe-12-14

[12-15] IFLScience (15 March 2016 via archive.org) Josh L Davis
Oldest Human DNA Ever Sequenced Could Rewrite Human Evolutionary Tree
bit.ly/hanfe-12-15

[12-16] Nature (14 March 2016) Ewen Callaway
Oldest ancient-human DNA details dawn of Neanderthals
bit.ly/hanfe-12-16

[12-17] International Business Times (4 December 2013) Philip Ross
Oldest Human DNA Is 400,000 Years Old, But Why Do Scientists Call Discovery 'Irritating?'
bit.ly/hanfe-12-17

[12-18] The Telegraph (28 December 2010) Peter Hutchison
Did the first humans come out of Middle East?
bit.ly/hanfe-12-18

[12-18a]   Wikipedia (accessed 10 September 2017)
Homo rhodesiensis
bit.ly/hanfe-12-18a

[12-18b]   Max Planck Society (7 June 2017)
Jean-Jacques Hublin et al
The first of our kind: Scientists discover the oldest *Homo sapiens* fossils at Jebel Irhoud, Morocco
bit.ly/hanfe-12-18b

[12-19] BBC News website (25 April 2017) Paul Rincon
Primitive human 'lived much more recently' (*Homo naledi*)
bit.ly/hanfe-12-19

[12-20] IFLScience (4 July 2017) Kristy Hamilton
**This Thigh Bone Could Force Us To Completely Rewrite The
History Of Our Species**
bit.ly/hanfe-12-20

[12-21] Nature (4 July 2017) Cosimo Posth et al
**Deeply divergent archaic mitochondrial genome provides lower
time boundary for African gene flow into Neanderthals**
bit.ly/hanfe-12-21

[12-22] Wikipedia (accessed 10 September 2017)
Neanderthal
bit.ly/hanfe-12-22

[12-23] Living Anthropologically (2012) Jason Antrosio
Archaics as Human Races: Denisovans and Neandertals
bit.ly/hanfe-12-23

[12-24] Wikipedia (accessed 10 September 2017)
Denisovan
bit.ly/hanfe-12-24

[12-25] Mail Online (30 June 2011)
**Out of Africa? New theory throws doubt on assumption all
humans evolved from the continent**
bit.ly/hanfe-12-25

[12-26] Gizmodo (26 April 2017) George Dvorsky
Controversial Study Makes a Staggering Claim About When the First Humans Settled North America
bit.ly/hanfe-12-26

[12-27] BBC News website (26 April 2017) Paul Rincon
First Americans claim sparks controversy
bit.ly/hanfe-12-27

[12-28] BBC News website (14 October 2015) Paul Rincon
Fossil teeth place humans in Asia '20,000 years early'
bit.ly/hanfe-12-28

[12-29] New Scientist (6 August 2014) Catherine Brahic
Human exodus may have reached China 100,000 years ago
bit.ly/hanfe-12-29

[12-30] Time (14 October 2015) Jeffrey Kluger
Here's Proof That the First Modern Humans Were Chinese
bit.ly/hanfe-12-30

[12-31] BBC News website (20 July 2017)
Australia human history 'rewritten by rock find'
bit.ly/hanfe-12-31

[12-32] Mail Online (22 October 2014) Sarah Griffiths
Oldest complete human genome sequenced: DNA of 45,000-year-old man who roamed Siberia unravelled – and it sheds light on when we stopped interbreeding with Neanderthals
bit.ly/hanfe-12-32

[12-32a]   Wikipedia (accessed 10 September 2017)
Anatomically modern human
bit.ly/hanfe-12-32a

[12-33] Wikipedia (accessed 10 September 2017)
Cro-Magnon
bit.ly/hanfe-12-33

[12-34] The Guardian (2 June 2013) Robin McKie
Why did the Neanderthals die out?
bit.ly/hanfe-12-34

[12-35] IFLScience (17 January 2017) Katy Evans
Humans Arrived In North America 10,000 Years Earlier Than We Thought
bit.ly/hanfe-12-35

[12-36] New Scientist (17 December 2015) Michael Slezak
New species of human may have shared our caves – and beds
bit.ly/hanfe-12-36

[12-37] Wikipedia (accessed 10 September 2017)
Younger Dryas impact hypothesis
bit.ly/hanfe-12-37

[12-38] IFLScience (16 March 2017) Robin Andrews
Did A Mysterious Asteroid Impact Wipe Out Prehistoric Native Americans?
bit.ly/hanfe-12-38

[12-39] Ancient Code (accessed 10 September 2017) Ivan Petricevic
Ancient stone carvings confirm comet impact in 11,000BC which gave rise to civilization
bit.ly/hanfe-12-39

[12-40] Reference.com (accessed 10 September 2017)
When was beer invented?
bit.ly/hanfe-12-40

[12-41] Wikipedia (accessed 10 September 2017)
Wheel
bit.ly/hanfe-12-41

[12-42] IFLScience (6 April 2015) Stephen Luntz
Why Do Europeans Have White Skin?
bit.ly/hanfe-12-42

[12-43] New Scientist (7 April 2016) Vijay Shankar
Missing Y chromosome kept us apart from Neanderthals
bit.ly/hanfe-12-43

[12-44] Unknown source (accessed 10 September 2017)
Image of the hominid timeline
bit.ly/hanfe-12-44

[12-45] Futurism.com (accessed 10 September 2017)
Timeline of hominid evolution
bit.ly/hanfe-12-45

[12-46] Smithsonian Museum of Natural History
(accessed 10 September 2017)
Human evolution timeline – interactive
bit.ly/hanfe-12-46

[12-47] New Scientist (4 September 2006) John Pickrell
Timeline: Human Evolution
bit.ly/hanfe-12-47

[12-48] New Scientist (20 April 2009)
Becoming human: A timeline of human evolution
bit.ly/hanfe-12-48

[12-49] BBC Earth (accessed 10 September 2017)
The 15 Tweaks That Made Us Human
bit.ly/hanfe-12-49

[12-50] National Geographic (4 December 2013) Carl Zimmer
An Ancient, Mysterious Scrap of Human DNA
bit.ly/hanfe-12-50

Chapter 13

[13-01] Deviant Art (accessed 10 September 2017) Humon
Artwork: alien races deeply involved with humans
(Just for fun!)
bit.ly/hanfe-13-01

[13-02] Wikipedia (accessed 10 September 2017)
Grey alien
bit.ly/hanfe-13-02

[13-03] Think About It (accessed 10 September 2017)
Roswell humanoid
bit.ly/hanfe-13-03

[13-04] Wikipedia (accessed 10 September 2017)
Barney and Betty Hill (claimed to be alien abductees)
bit.ly/hanfe-13-04

[13-05] Wikipedia (accessed 10 September 2017)
Reptilians
bit.ly/hanfe-13-05

[13-06] Wikipedia (accessed 10 September 2017)
Quetzalcoatl
bit.ly/hanfe-13-06

[13-07] Ancient Code (accessed 10 September 2017)
Experts claim there are 3 hostile alien species visiting Earth
bit.ly/hanfe-13-07

[13-08] Wikipedia (accessed 10 September 2017)
Nordic aliens
bit.ly/hanfe-13-08

[13-09] Wikipedia (accessed 10 September 2017)
Pleiades
bit.ly/hanfe-13-09

[13-10] Wikipedia (accessed 10 September 2017)
List of alleged extraterrestrial beings
bit.ly/hanfe-13-10

[13-11] Mail Online (8 January 2014) David McCormack
Aliens already walk among us and are refusing to share their technology until we change our warring and polluting ways, claims former Canadian defense minister
bit.ly/hanfe-13-11

[13-12] Think About It (accessed 10 September 2017)
Alien types
bit.ly/hanfe-13-12

[13-13] Think About It (accessed 10 September 2017)
Seventy civilizations from other planets on Earth
bit.ly/hanfe-13-13

[13-14] Ancient Code (accessed 10 September 2017) Ivan Petricevic
82 known Alien species are in contact with Earth claim experts
(video)
bit.ly/hanfe-13-14

[13-15] The Guardian (20 July 2015) Martin Rees
Let's listen out for alien life – and remember we might not understand it
bit.ly/hanfe-13-15

[13-16] Gizmodo (11 September 2015) Maddie Stone
Where In Our Galaxy Are All The Aliens?
bit.ly/hanfe-13-16

[13-17] Wikipedia (accessed 10 September 2017)
Sloan Digital Sky Survey
bit.ly/hanfe-13-17

[13-18] IFLScience (25 October 2016) Alfredo Carpineti
Scientists Claim To Have Found 234 Alien Civilizations
bit.ly/hanfe-13-18

[13-19] Educating Humanity (11 October 2010)
UFO and Alien Technologies We Have Benefited From
bit.ly/hanfe-13-19

[13-20] Educating Humanity (17 September 2011)
Did some of our Best Technologies have Alien Origins?
bit.ly/hanfe-13-20

[13-21a]   True Strange Library
(14 September 2010 – via archive.org) Xeno
Ben Rich Lockheed CEO Admits on Deathbed: ET UFO Are Real
bit.ly/hanfe-13-21a

[13-22] The Cold War Museum (accessed 10 September 2017)
Kevin Crowley
The Strategic Defense Initiative (SDI): Star Wars
bit.ly/hanfe-13-22

[13-23] Ancient Code (accessed 10 September 2017)
Shocking similarities between Ancient Civilizations: A hidden pattern that explains it all
bit.ly/hanfe-13-23

[13-24] Gawker (4 July 2011) Rich Bard
The 18 Most Suppressed Inventions Ever
bit.ly/hanfe-13-24

[13-25] True Disclosure (accessed 10 September 2017)
Suppressed Technology
bit.ly/hanfe-13-25

[13-26] The Mind Unleashed (10 September 2014) Nick Bernabe
3 Suppressed Technologies that Could Revolutionize Daily Life
bit.ly/hanfe-13-26

[13-27] Activist Post (13 September 2015) Paul A. Philips
7 Suppressed Inventions That Would Have Changed The World
bit.ly/hanfe-13-27

[13-27a]   UFO Encounters (15 October 2014) Paul Geraghty
Philip J. Corso and the Use of Alien Technology
bit.ly/hanfe-13-27a

[13-27b]   NASA (accessed 10 September 2017)
Technology Transfer Program
bit.ly/hanfe-13-27b

[13-28] The Disclosure Project (2002) Theodore C. Loder, III
"Outside The Box" Space And Terrestrial Transportation And Energy Technologies For The 21st Century
bit.ly/hanfe-13-28

[13-28a]   REALfarmacy.com (accessed 10 September 2017)
Arjun Walia
Florida Makes Off-Grid Living Illegal – Mandates All Homes Must Be Connected To An Electricity Grid
bit.ly/hanfe-13-28a

[13-29] Seeking Alpha (7 December 2012) Joseph P. Porter
The Companies Of Area 51
bit.ly/hanfe-13-29

[13-29a]   WikiVisually (accessed 10 September 2017)
United States gravity control propulsion research
bit.ly/hanfe-13-29a

[13-29b]   News Punch (14 March 2016) Sean Adl-Tabatabai
Apple Insider Claims Steve Jobs Used Alien Technology
bit.ly/hanfe-13-29b

[13-30] The Telegraph (27 September 2010) Andy Bloxham
Aliens have deactivated British and US nuclear missiles, say US military pilots
bit.ly/hanfe-13-30

[13-31] Live Science (30 September 2010) Benjamin Radford
Did UFOs Disarm Nuclear Weapons? And If So, Why?
bit.ly/hanfe-13-31

[13-32] Fox News (15 August 2015)
Apollo 14 astronaut claims peace-loving aliens prevented 'nuclear war' on Earth
bit.ly/hanfe-13-32

[13-33] Mail Online (12 August 2015) Ellie Zolfagharifard
'Aliens tried to save America from nuclear war': UFOs shot at missiles in White Sands to protect Earth, claims former astronaut
bit.ly/hanfe-13-33

[13-34] Wikipedia (accessed 10 September 2017)
National Security Act of 1947
bit.ly/hanfe-13-34

[13-35] Wikipedia (accessed 10 September 2017)
Majestic 12
bit.ly/hanfe-13-35

[13-36] Wikipedia (accessed 10 September 2017)
Project Sign
bit.ly/hanfe-13-36

[13-37] Wikipedia (accessed 10 September 2017)
Project Grudge
bit.ly/hanfe-13-37

[13-38] Wikipedia (accessed 10 September 2017)
Project Blue Book
bit.ly/hanfe-13-38

[13-39] Wikipedia (accessed 10 September 2017)
Alien abduction
bit.ly/hanfe-13-39

[13-40] Collective Evolution (4 November 2013) James Branson
**The Shocking Truth About Alien Abductions (They're More Real
Than You May Think)**
bit.ly/hanfe-13-40

[13-41] Alien Abduction Experience and Research
(accessed 10 September 2017)
Why do aliens abduct people?
bit.ly/hanfe-13-41

[13-42] Biblioteca Pleyades (accessed 10 September 2017)
Abduction questions
bit.ly/hanfe-13-42

[13-43] Humans Are Free (accessed 10 September 2017)
72 Possible Signs of Alien Abduction Detailed by Abductees
bit.ly/hanfe-13-43

[13-44] International Center for Abduction Research
(accessed 10 September 2017)
A Typical Abduction Event
bit.ly/hanfe-13-44

[13-45] MUFON (3 April 1998)
Alien Implant Removals: Before And After Effects
bit.ly/hanfe-13-45

[13-46] Aliens And Children (accessed 10 September 2017)
Michael Menkin
Alien Abduction Explained
bit.ly/hanfe-13-46

[13-47] Wikipedia (accessed 10 September 2017)
List of people who disappeared mysteriously
bit.ly/hanfe-13-47

[13-48] First To Know (30 December 2015) Elysia McMahan
Vanished Forever: 10 Oldest, Unsolved Missing Persons Cases in America
bit.ly/hanfe-13-48

16
Bibliography

Ancient Aliens In Australia: Pleiadian Origins of Humanity
Steven Strong and Bruce Fenton with Evan Strong and Daniella
Fenton
(CreateSpace Independent Publishing Platform, 2013)

*Blue Mind: The Surprising Science That Shows How Being Near,
In, On, or Under Water Can Make You Happier, Healthier, More
Connected, and Better at What You Do*
Wallace J. Nichols
(Little, Brown and Company, 2014)

*Children Who Remember Previous Lives: A Question of
Reincarnation*
Ian Stevenson, MD
(McFarland & Company, Inc., Revised Edition, 2001)

Everything You Know Is Wrong – Book One: Human Origins
Lloyd Pye
(Adamu, 1998)

Forbidden Archeology: The Hidden History of the Human Race
Michael A. Cremo and Richard L. Thompson
(Bhaktivedanta Book Trust, Second Revised Edition, 1993)

Journey of Souls: Case Studies of Life Between Lives
Michael Newton
(Llewellyn Publications, 1994)

Destiny of Souls: New Case Studies of Life Between Lives
Michael Newton
(Llewellyn Publications, 2000)

Life on a Young Planet: The First Three Billion Years of Evolution on Earth
Andrew H. Knoll
(Princeton Science Library, Updated Edition, 2015)

Return to Earth
Buzz Aldrin with Wayne Warga
(Random House, 1973)

Solomon Islands Mysteries: Accounts of Giants and UFOs in the Solomon Islands
Marius Boirayon
(Marius Boirayon, 2009)

Species with Amnesia: Our Forgotten History
Robert Sepehr
(Atlantean Gardens, 2015)

Textbook Folly: Bias and Indoctrination in College Textbooks
Mark Hodges
(Mark Hodges, 2012)

Textbook Propaganda: Education or Indoctrination?
Mark Hodges
(Mark Hodges, 2013)

The Day After Roswell
Colonel Philip J. Corso with William J. Birnes
(Pocket Books, 1997)

The Dynamic Human
Maciej Henneberg and Arthur Saniotis
(Bentham Science Publishers, Ltd., 2016)

*The Evidence of God in an Expanding Universe: Forty American
Scientists Declare their Affirmative Views on Religion*
Edited by John Clover Monsma
(Putnam, 1958)

*The Real Men In Black: Evidence, Famous Cases, and True
Stories of These Mysterious Men and their Connection to the
UFO Phenomena*
Nick Redfern
(New Page Books, 2011)

The Roswell Incident
Charles Berlitz and William Moore
(Grosset & Dunlap, 1980; Berkley Publishing Group, 1988; MJF
Books, 1997)

50 Years of Amicizia (Friendship)
Stefano Breccia
(CreateSpace Independent Publishing Platform, 2013)

17
About the Author

Dr. Ellis Silver is an American ecologist and environmentalist.

He now spends the majority of his time in Europe, the Middle East, and northeast Africa – mostly on boats.

He is happy to answer sensible questions by email on the rare occasions when he has a decent internet connection.

Contact address: silver.ellis@gmail.com

18

Acknowledgements

Thank you so much for taking the time to read this book. I hope it made you think, opened your mind a little, and made you question some of the illogical and disproven theories the mainstream keeps perpetuating. At least we now know why they do it.

Once again, I'd like to give my special thanks to Dave Haslett of ideas4writers. His brainstorming, mind-mapping, and editing skills are nothing short of astounding. This book would not exist without his massive contribution. He somehow managed to turn more than 900 pages of notes, 20+ hours of interviews and dictation, a mind-map diagram the size of a wall, and a hard drive full of photographs, web pages, reviews and readers' comments into the book you're reading now. I think it hangs together pretty well.

Our timeline is constantly changing, with significant new discoveries being made every week. So, despite our best endeavors, some parts of this book are undoubtedly out of date already. I'll continue monitoring the news and collecting evidence, and perhaps there will be a third edition of this book one day.

I'd like to correct some of the misinformation that has appeared in the media. I'm not a professor, and nor have I ever been. I'm not affiliated to any universities. And I'm not Australian.

I've said it throughout the book, but it's worth repeating one more time: I'm not a Creationist or a Scientologist. Nor do I belong to any organized religion, cult, fraternal organization or street gang.
Do I believe in God? Well, maybe not as such. But I do believe that those strands of primitive RNA couldn't have formed by themselves, or developed into a living form by themselves. At the very least, some kind of intelligence must have been guiding it. But I have no idea who or what it was, or whether we should be worshipping it.

I'd be happy to hear from you if you'd like to get in touch, but I can't promise to respond to every message.

19

Index

Printed in Great Britain
by Amazon

41500055R00366